Paper Sovereigns

Paper Sovereigns

Anglo-Native Treaties and the
Law of Nations, 1604–1664

Jeffrey Glover

PENN

UNIVERSITY OF PENNSYLVANIA PRESS

Philadelphia

Copyright © 2014 University of Pennsylvania Press

Published by
University of Pennsylvania Press
Philadelphia, Pennsylvania 19104-4112
www.upenn.edu/pennpress

Printed in the United States of America on acid-free paper
10 9 8 7 6 5 4 3 2 1

Library of Congress Cataloging-in-Publication Data

Glover, Jeffrey.
Paper sovereigns : Anglo–Native treaties and the law of nation, 1604–1664 / Jeffrey Glover—1st ed.
p. cm.
Includes bibliographical references and index.
ISBN 978-0-8122-4596-7 (hardcover : alk. paper)
1. Indians of North America—Government relations—To 1789. 2. Indians of North America—Legal status, laws, etc.—History—17th century. 3. Indians of North America—Treaties—History—17th century. 4. United States—Politics and government—To 1774. 5. United States—Ethnic relations—Political aspects—History—17th century. 6. Great Britain—Foreign relations—1603–1688—Treaties. I. Title.
E91.G55   2014
323.1197—dc23   2013046741

What will it availe you to take that by force you may quickly have by love?

—Powhatan, chief of the Powhatans, as quoted in John Smith, *The Generall Historie of Virginia, New-England, and the Summer Isles* (1624)

—٨٨—

Contents

—ↈↈↈ—

A Note on Naming and Spelling
—ᴡᴡ—

The question of how to refer to the pre-Columbian inhabitants of North America has been politically charged for many centuries. It is further complicated by the inaccurate descriptions of European settlers and by the many migrations and displacements that occurred after European arrival. Where possible, I use contemporary names for specific tribes. In cases where a tribe did not survive the colonial period, I use the most widely accepted transcription of its name. I also use the most widely accepted names for individual Native Americans, with the acknowledgment that these are usually European renderings of names that did not take alphabetic form. I use "Native" as the default descriptor for pre-Columbian North Americans, but I also use "Indian," especially when paraphrasing European points of view or referring to European concepts of American people. European spelling presents problems as well. In general, I have preserved the punctuation and spelling of early modern sources. However, I have corrected "u" to "v," "i" to "j," "VV" to "w." I have also silently modernized all shorthand or unusual typographical practices, changing "ye" to "the," "Yf" to "if," and "consultacòn," to "consultation." I have deleted the spaces that early modern printers sometimes left before colons and semicolons. Finally, I have emended in brackets all obvious compositors' errors. I have retained the capitalization of the titles of printed works, with the exception of words that are entirely capitalized, which are capitalized only in their first letter here (articles and most prepositions excepted).

Introduction: A Great Shout

—ᴍ—

The Indian guide was trying to get the sailors' attention before it was too late. They were docked by a waterfall, waiting for the Indian king to arrive. The sailors were confident. They had feasted with the king the day before, and their captain, Christopher Newport, had "kyndly imbraced" him, confirming "a leauge of fryndship."[1] This next meeting would go well, they were sure. But the Indian guide was worried. The night before, the sailors had departed without offering the formal goodbye required by Powhatan diplomacy. They could be excused that once—they were new, after all. But the guide had to show them how to behave this time around, or risk offense to the king.

Raising his voice over the steady roar of the falls, the guide made a quick demonstration of proper protocol. It was simple. When the king arrived, they were to shout in unison. When he left, they were to shout again, bringing things to a close. The shout, a simple rhythmic cadence, was easy to learn. It felt familiar to the sailors, who did the same thing for important people in England. When the king finally appeared, they followed the guide's example, shouting a happy welcome. And later, when he turned to go home, they did it again, "two severall times," and the Indians "answer[ed] [their] shout with gladnes in a friendly fashion."[2] In some ways, the day had not gone well. The king had politely rebuffed their request to travel farther upriver, and the sailors were no longer so confident. But the shouting seemed to leave things on good terms. As they sailed home to the newly built fort at Jamestown, they were sure the king was their friend.

At some point in the days following the meeting at the falls, Gabriel Archer, the secretary of the settlement venture, sat down to compose an account of the trip. This letter was crucial to their fortunes. Investors in London were eager to know how they had gotten along with nearby Indians, and it was Archer's job to inform them. Archer was equally aware that other people might read his letter, too—rival English adventurers, for example, who were ready to stake their own claims, or, more frightening, Spanish spies, who might intercept a copy in London, and were eager to see England's colonies destroyed. To stave off these threats, it was important that he describe the journey upriver in a way that clearly established English rights to the land.

Curiously, though, Archer's letter did not resemble what most Europeans would have recognized as a legal document of any kind—much less a land claim. There were no references to the New World as a waste space, void, or empty territory waiting to be taken by the first Christians who found it. Instead, there was a detailed account of the many "kynges" who ruled the area.[3] And there were scant descriptions of forts, houses, or fences (the way Europeans usually showed ownership). Such details were pushed aside in favor of an almost theatrical account of diplomacy among the Indians, with feasting, dancing, and other ceremonies taking center stage. Perhaps most surprising was the way Archer documented Indian treaties, like the league with the king. There were none of the Latin formulas so familiar in European treaties, no lists of witnesses, no signatures—not even the x-marks found in treaties between the English crown and illiterate Irish clansmen. In a startling departure from European conventions, Archer offered an account of treaty making on Indian terms, pointing to the exchange of shouts and other indigenous rituals as proof of friendship between Newport and the king.

English colonists in the first decades of the seventeenth century spent a surprising amount of energy documenting the political life of the people whose territory they invaded. They described Native leaders as *kings*, and referred to tribal polities as *nations* and *empires*.[4] They detailed Native ceremonies, set down the speeches of Native leaders, and reported on the proceedings of tribal councils. Most of all, when it came to recounting treaties, they often chose to describe Native ways of making and marking agreement, preferring stories of feasts, shouting, and tribute to the somber signing rituals of European diplomacy.

This book tries to explain why Archer and so many other English colonists were interested in coastal treaties, and why they so often focused on Native rituals in their writings home. That colonists cared about Native politics at all may seem like a surprising thing to assert, given what we know about how things turned out. An important body of scholarship has shown that colonists imposed their own political and legal systems on Native people.[5] In what follows, there will be much to confirm this story. In early North America, as in other places of encounter, the law and its rituals were undoubtedly instruments of conquest. But as Archer's document so vividly shows, English colonists were far from dismissive of coastal treaty practices. One reason for their interest was the simple desire to survive. Newport and his group were outnumbered, as were most English colonists in the first years after arrival, and settling on anything other than Native terms was out of the question. But this does not explain why writers like Archer described coastal rituals in such detail in letters home, at times even choosing Indian protocols over their own. Understanding that, I will argue in this book, requires looking beyond the riverbank to the palaces, halls, and council rooms where European crowns negotiated rights to American territory.

Though Archer focuses on the politics of the coast, his report also reflected dramatic shifts in European legal systems in the decades before English settlement. The English set sail for the New World at a time of great uncertainty about international law, or what they called the law of nations. While European princes had for many centuries viewed themselves as members of a *res publica Christiana*, an order of Christian crowns answering to the pope, over the course of the sixteenth century many declared their autonomy from papal authority and asserted their sovereignty, or absolute power, over territory, peoples, and foreign affairs. These challenges to papal authority extended to the New World, as northern crowns contested the pope's donation of America to Spain and Portugal and formulated their own protocols for conquering land across the seas. In this book, I argue that treaties with Native Americans were one way the English crown and its colonists sought to demonstrate possession of foreign territory. In ancient legal traditions, there were many precedents for conquering land with treaties. According to early modern glosses of ancient Roman texts, a sovereign power could lay claim to territory through a treaty with its inhabitants. These treaties, which had to represent *consensus ad idem*, a "meeting of the minds" or voluntary agreement between parties, served as proof that a claim was pacified, or under control. I will argue here that English colonists publicized treaties with Native Americans precisely in order to advertise this kind of possession. They used treaties to show other Europeans that the English crown had brought American territory under control. And while this was no doubt an imperialistic strategy, having as its goal the conquest of land, I will argue that it led to a profound irony, one that powerfully shaped English colonial writing. When the English pointed to treaties with Native peoples as evidence of possession, Native words, gestures, and other ways of marking agreement suddenly became highly charged evidence in international legal disputes, even as Natives themselves lost their land and power.

Today's global powers rarely dispute the form of treaties. International accords are embodied in written texts. News coverage of treaties often depicts heads of state bent over official documents, poised to ratify them with the sweep of their pens. Such rituals date to the early modern period, when princes or their representatives concluded leagues and pacts by signing embossed documents.[6] The Treaty of London (1604), which brought an end to the Anglo-Spanish War (1585–1604) and opened the way for English colonization, was signed first by James I (who also swore an oath to abide by its articles) and then ratified by Philip III in a separate ceremony. The treaty was widely publicized in paintings and publications, which many of the Virginia colonists probably encountered.[7] Set beside such grand acts of state, the treaty with the river Indian king hardly seems to merit comparison. However, while the early seventeenth century was a time of great agreements between princely powers, it was also a time of great uncertainty about the nature of sovereignty and the proper mode of its expression, especially when it came to the New World. Though European princes had well-established protocols for making treaties with each other, the application of the law of nations to supposedly heathen peoples—who were believed to be incapable of taking oaths or signing their names—led to widespread controversy over how to ratify treaties. While many authorities believed that pagans were not subjects of the law of nations, and that their political rituals had no capacity to register consent to a binding agreement, others, including Spanish friars and Protestant jurists, debated the possibility that all the peoples of the world were governed by natural law, and could make treaties according to their own customs, however strange or savage those might seem.[8]

Existing scholarship on treaties has tended to focus on the eighteenth century, when colonists had more power, and frontier treaties looked like their European counterparts, with articles and signatures.[9] In the early period, however, there was little uniformity in treaty making.[10] English and Native people ratified treaties with chants, shouts, gestures, and feasts; they exchanged gifts, trade goods, animals, weapons, and hostages (including women and children); they marked the landscape with footpaths, inscriptions, and monuments; and they engaged in many other kinds of shared practices that combined elements from

Native and European traditions. English treaty records reflected the diversity of coastal politics. Until the middle of the seventeenth century, colonists rarely set down Indian treaties in signed documents (it was true, after all, that Indians could not sign their names or take oaths, at least as Europeans understood such things). They put them instead in genres better suited to portraying the politics of the coast. Like Archer, they recorded treaties in diplomatic relations, writing of feasts and solemn orations. Other times, they described them in land deeds, receipts of purchase, or other commercial genres, and the boundaries between trade, treaty, and purchase were (often intentionally) blurred. Still other treaties were printed in histories or evangelical exhortations, and became a medium for arguing about politics or religion at home. Nor was the English idea of a treaty limited to formal acts of ratification, like shouting or feasting. Colonists also wrote about the informal behaviors of their Native partners, their facial expressions, their postures, their negotiating strategies, their emotions, and anything else that might bear upon the question of consent. All these forms of expression, formal and informal, could be called on to prove Native acceptance of the English presence, and therefore English control of territory.

Early Anglo-Native treaty documents were never simply rote accounts of political transactions, set down according to some preexisting formula. They were rhetorical documents, crafted to meet the needs of particular constituencies (English and Native), and bundled with claims about land, sovereignty, and trade. Europeans used treaties for a variety of conflicting ends. In the early years of Virginia settlement, the joint-stock companies that financed colonial ventures cited treaties to show the crown and potential rivals that they had the Chesapeake Bay under control, and had reached a settlement with Powhatan, the paramount chief who commanded most of the nearby tribes. However, Spanish diplomats and spies eagerly disputed Virginia colonists' reports of peace on the frontier, and rival English adventurers put forward counter-narratives of treaty negotiations that challenged the truth of reports like Archer's. After the 1620s, the Spanish no longer posed a serious threat to England's North American settlements, but English colonists were acutely aware of their Dutch and French rivals, and they continued to dispute land rights with each other, submitting treaty documents in petitions to the king. In the middle of the seventeenth century, Native treaties factored into contests between colonists, traders, and religious dissenters, all of whom pointed to treaty agreements to support various kinds of appeals to the crown. This transatlantic traffic in treaties was enormously consequential. A convincing treaty document could persuade the crown (and international onlookers) of the integrity of a claim. A broken treaty could cost colonists the king's support, and invite threats from belligerent rivals at home and abroad. Indeed, as I will show at the end of this book, the Massachusetts Bay Colony's failure to respect Indian treaties was one reason the English crown reviewed its charter and asserted direct control over its government after the Restoration.

Even though most of them could not write, Native people used treaties just as adeptly as the newcomers. Indeed, I will argue here that Anglo-Native treaties only make sense if we view them as part of a broader world of political communication that included oral and gestural politics as well as the written word. Scholarship has sometimes portrayed settlers and Natives as standing on opposite sides of a communication divide. The settlers were creatures of writing, while the Natives lived in an oral culture, and thus became the victims of written treaties they could not understand. The victim part of this story is certainly true. Many Native groups were destroyed, and others nearly so, through airborne pathogens to which they had no immunity, military assaults that left them divided and overwhelmed, and the slower genocide of territorial dispossession. But Natives were not helpless or ignorant. Especially in the first decades of settlement, they eagerly sought alliances with colonial governments to gain an advantage over rival tribes and chiefdoms. Many prospered for decades from such relationships before falling prey to hardening colonial policies or the encroachments of squatters.[11] In extending these alliances, Native people often worked through transatlantic diplomatic channels.[12] While few acquired alphabetic literacy in the seventeenth century, it was not always necessary to read or write in order to influence transatlantic politics. Native people learned early on that settlers were transmitting news to distant places where powerful kings resided. They sought to discern which colonists were in favor with these faraway powers and to shape the flow of information and authority to their benefit. They told stories to English secretaries and scriveners and gave objects to English travelers for delivery to the king as tokens of alliance. They also traveled, addressing English leaders in person. Of course, Native Americans could not communicate or travel across the Atlantic without intermediaries, and Europeans publicized the Native point of view only when it was useful to them. But this does not mean that Natives never worked through transatlantic channels to advance their own agendas. They did, often to powerful effect.

The Law of Nations and Native America

When the English crown and its advisors first began to justify their possession of overseas territories, their primary concern was defending themselves against the Spanish, who claimed the Americas on the basis of papal grants dating to the time of Columbus's voyages.[13] Spanish explorers also claimed rights of conquest over the people who inhabited the Indies, holding that Christians could lawfully make war against infidels who resisted evangelism. The most striking formulation of these rights came in the *Requerimiento*, a declaration read aloud to Indians shortly after Spanish arrival on American shores. The *Requerimiento* justified the seizure of land, peoples, and property on the basis of resistance to evangelism: "if you do not [accept evangelism], and maliciously make delay in it," it read, "we shall powerfully enter into your country, and shall make war against you in all ways and manners that we can, and shall subject you to the yoke and obedience of the Church and of their Highnesses."[14] On this basis, Spanish conquistadors took any (real or imagined) Native refusal of evangelism as the basis for a war of conquest.[15]

While other European crowns were reluctant to recognize these rights, a succession of Spanish monarchs clung to them for over a hundred years. Conquistadors read the *Requerimiento* to Native peoples until the 1550s, and, well into the seventeenth century, the Spanish crown insisted that the presence of other European settlements in the Americas was a violation of its claims.[16] In the early sixteenth century, this embargo was of little concern to English diplomats. English activities in the Atlantic were limited to fishing and trading in northern waters (where there was less danger of Spanish attack), and carrying out piracy on Spanish trading routes (an activity of questionable legality at best).[17] However, when the English crown turned its attention to permanent settlement in the sixteenth century, the threat of Spanish confrontation made it imperative to establish claims in ways that would compel international recognition.[18] In using treaties for this task, the English were primarily guided by Roman law, which offered crowns a way of justifying their sovereignty and dominion at home and abroad.[19]

Revived in the eleventh century, Roman law was widely disseminated and studied throughout early modern Europe. The Catholic Church derived many aspects of its canon law from Roman law, and by the thirteenth century Roman-influenced canon law had come to shape legal systems in Spain, France, and Holland.[20] While jurists at Oxford had begun to teach canonical writings in the twelfth century, Roman law was not as influential in England, where common law traditions were well established.[21] However, as Ken MacMillan has recently shown, English princes and jurists embraced Roman legal codes when attempting to explain the crown's independence from the pope and assert its absolute prerogative over international affairs.[22] The Roman law of nations, in particular, answered the need for a normative legal system to govern interstate relations in the absence of papal authority. An outgrowth of natural law, the *jus gentium*, or law of nations or peoples, held that nations were bound by unwritten laws common to all mankind and rooted in human nature.[23] As written in Justinian's *Institutes*, a widely glossed sixth-century compilation of Roman law, "the law which natural reason has established among all mankind and which is equally observed among all peoples, is called the Law of Nations, as being that which all nations make use of."[24] The law of nations held that certain practices were shared by all peoples, that these practices were rational and natural, and that they offered a customary or normalized way of dealing with foreigners and strangers, even those who were pagans or heretics.[25] Throughout the sixteenth century, the law of nations saw wide adoption as European princes sought to define their *imperium*, or rule, and *dominium*, or territorial possessions, in relation to other sovereigns. In the late sixteenth century, many European jurists claimed acceptance of the law of nations as an international legal system. The English crown, in particular, encouraged the study of Roman law as a way to legitimate its power at home and abroad.[26]

Particularly salient for the English crown were Roman criteria for defining legal possession of *terra incognita*, or undiscovered territory, a topic about which the common law offered no guidance.[27] As codified by Justinian, Roman law specified that land must be brought under control for possession to hold. Valid title demanded more than *animus*, or future plans to settle. As Justinian's *Digest* put it, "we cannot acquire possession solely by intention."[28] Legitimate title also required *corpus*, or physical possession. This criterion gave the English a powerful rhetorical lever in negotiations with Spanish crowns. While the Spanish had claimed the American landmass since the fifteenth century, they had settled only as far north as present-day Florida, leaving northern latitudes theoretically open for the taking. Throughout the late sixteenth and early seventeenth centuries, English colonists frequently made claims to the North American coast, asserting that unoccupied land was the property of the first Christian prince to settle it.[29] Just as often, however, English claims included territories that, far from being empty, were heavily populated and defended by Native polities.

To claim control of such territories demanded justifications that described the conquest of occupied territory.[30] Many scholars of colonial law have associated conquest almost exclusively with New Spain and the infamous *Requerimiento*. They have argued that the English established New World claims by building fences and fortifications rather than by conquering people.[31] This is true, if one defines conquest in military terms. English colonists almost never sought to incorporate Native people into their societies after defeating them in wars.[32] However, the term *conquest* possessed a range of meanings in early modern England, many of which had little to do with military subjugation.[33] While the English sometimes waged holy wars of the kind justified by the *Requerimiento*, they preferred to advertise New World conquest as a benevolent pursuit, involving the peaceful subjugation of land and peoples.

In this book, I will argue that treaties were part of the English strategy for carrying out a supposedly peaceful conquest. This may seem like a paradoxical claim. Today, we think of a treaty as an agreement between equal states, not a conquest of one party by another. Yet this is largely a modern view. Early modern princes frequently made treaties with inferiors, including vassals, feudal lords, and even rebellious subjects.[34] These *foedera vel inaequalia*, or treaties between unequal parties, could involve many different matters, such as land rights, political loyalties, trade agreements, and even religious commitments. Unequal treaties were of particular interest to monarchs during the early period of colonial settlement, when the question of competing claims to overseas territory was increasingly becoming part of European treaty negotiations.[35] Indeed, long before the English set their sights on New World settlement, Spanish monks had debated the legality of the *Requerimiento*, suggesting that Spain's claims to the Indies violated the natural rights of the inhabitants. In a series of lectures printed throughout Europe, the Dominican friar Bartolomé de Las Casas argued that Indian treaties offered a means of conquering territory that was consistent with natural law.[36] "Is it customary and right, in reason and natural law," he asked in 1526, "to ask [the Indians] to swear obedience to a foreign king without establishing a treaty or contract or covenant with them regarding the good and just way in which the king would rule them?"[37] Beginning around 1530, Francisco de Vitoria, a Dominican who taught at the School of Salamanca from 1527 until 1540, likewise argued that treaties offered a way to claim American lands.[38] In a series of lectures later published by his students, Vitoria refuted the idea that the Spanish monarchy had power over the Indians in "temporal and civil matters," such as the possession of territory.[39] Vitoria argued instead that the world was governed by natural law, which held sway over all people, Christians and unbelievers alike. Postulating that "Any commonwealth can elect its own master," he argued that the Spanish could claim dominion if "the barbarians recognized the wisdom and humanity of the Spaniards' administration, and one and all, both masters and subjects, spontaneously decided to accept the king of Spain as their prince."[40] Vitoria viewed indigenous consent to Spanish rule as a theoretical source of title, as long as the treaty was made in the absence of "fear and ignorance" and therefore satisfied the criteria of *consensus ad idem*.[41]

The arguments of Las Casas, Vitoria, and other critics of the *Requerimiento* were never widely embraced by Spanish monarchs.[42] However, starting in the late sixteenth century, many Protestant jurists adapted such ideas to the project of colonial justification. During the first decades of English colonization, Alberico Gentili, a professor of civil law at Oxford, published widely about the law of nations. His writings and frequent public lectures strongly influenced English colonial promoters and the royal councilors who lent financial and legal support to colonial endeavors.[43] In 1589, he published *De Jure Belli Libri Tres*, an authoritative application of Roman texts to legal problems arising from war and colonization. In particular, Gentili addressed the problem of how refugees, exiles, or settlers from populous countries could lawfully acquire sparsely occupied land that was nevertheless claimed by another sovereign. Gentili argued that "because of that law of nature which abhors a vacuum, [such lands] will fall to the lot of those who take them." However, he specified that the original sovereign would "retain jurisdiction over them." In describing how such an arrangement might work, Gentili approvingly quoted Aeneas's vow to Latinus during the Trojan invasion of Italy. "'I do not ask for dominion. Let both nations [Italians and Trojans] unconquered form a union on equal terms and live under equal laws.'"[44] The idea of a union between Christians and pagans was also put forward by Hugo Grotius, a Dutch jurist who published several widely read treatises on the law of nations. The work of Grotius did not circulate widely in England until settlement was well under way, but many colonial writers turned to his texts for support. Like Vitoria, Grotius addressed the question whether Christian powers could make agreements with unbelievers. "A question frequently raised concerning treaties," he wrote, "is whether they are lawfully entered into with those who are strangers to the true religion." Grotius held that "According to the law of nature" there is "in no degree a matter of doubt" about the lawfulness of such treaties. Grotius pointed to the contract between the

Jews and the Egyptians as a biblical precedent for the lawfulness of treaties between believers and idolaters.[45]

At the same time that jurists were making arguments about Indian treaties, English sailors and travelers were putting such ideas into practice, largely as an anti-Spanish strategy. In 1572–1573, English privateers formed ad hoc military alliances with the *cimarrónes*, groups of freed slaves and Native people who had fled the Spanish.[46] Sir Francis Drake and John Oxenham described the raids in letters that were widely read by English colonial promoters, such as Richard Hakluyt, who advised that colonists "have firme amitie" with neighboring indigenous peoples so as to become "strong in force" and better able to resist Indian or European enemies.[47] Native treaties were also a way of giving an appearance of legality to overseas activities that the Spanish crown viewed as piracy. During a voyage to California in 1579, Drake reportedly sat down to feast with a king who gave him a crown and scepter while his people sang a song "with one consent, and with great reverence."[48] Drake completed this act of possession by planting a monument inscribed with the queen's name (and his own under it).[49] In a printed account of his exploration of Guiana, Sir Walter Raleigh likewise described delegating his men "to treate with the borderers, and to drawe them to his partie and love."[50] Adventurers such as Drake and Raleigh needed to be on good terms with nearby people to ensure the safety and food supply of their ventures, but publicizing such relationships in writing was a way of showing the Spanish that the English had begun to establish land claims.

While both jurists and travelers embraced the notion that Native peoples could form treaties—and that such treaties could support land claims—the English crown and its diplomats were at first cautious in their handling of such arguments, largely because the Spanish rejected the notion that Indians could make treaties. At first, the crown focused on the meaning of treaties for trading rights. In negotiations over the African coast in 1562, for example, Queen Elizabeth and her councilors asserted the right to trade with coastal peoples in Guinea regardless of Portugal's claims to Africa.[51] This argument relied upon the commonly held notion that independent nations possessed a natural right to trade with one another that no sovereign power could abridge.[52] Arguments about natural law and Native peoples also found their way into the statements of English ambassadors during negotiations with the Spanish over the Treaty of London (1604). During that conference, the crown's delegates argued that the English had every right to "trade with divers great kings of those countryes [in America] but as forrayners and strangers." They claimed that "it is not in

[Philip III's] power to barre ourselves by accord" from trading with foreign peoples.[53] In the end, the Treaty of London remained silent on the question of the Indians, leaving the matter for future negotiations.

These kinds of arguments were suitable for defending trading ventures, which involved no meaningful occupation of territory, but as soon as the English created permanent colonies, it became necessary to clarify relations with neighboring peoples, who might also conceivably possess a claim to the territory, or the means to challenge English control. The labor of publicizing treaties fell primarily to colonists, who were required to complete the king's claims by taking and holding territory. Colonists demonstrated possession in many ways, such as building forts or subjecting land to husbandry. But it was also crucial that they reach some kind of settlement with coastal polities to show that all questions of title were resolved. One way to do so was simply to purchase land from its indigenous owners. These purchases were good under common law, and were also recognized under the law of nations.[54] However, simple purchase was rarely enough to establish firm possession. People other than the sellers might come forward and claim the land was theirs, or neighboring tribes might be unhappy with the presence of the newcomers and attack them anyway. Even if the English viewed such challenges as illegitimate, they still troubled English claims, since possession required physical control. Treaties solved (or appeared to solve) such problems. They showed that nearby Indians were friends and not likely to challenge English holdings. In the early period, when the power balance favored the Indians, the English made treaties of nonaggression or military support with neighboring tribes. Later, after the newcomers had more power, they made treaties in which the Indians recognized the majesty of the English crown, or subjected themselves to English authority, ceding power to the newcomers in exchange for protection (these kinds of treaties were especially useful, because they showed other Europeans that the English were exercising sovereignty, even if the English had little desire to rule Indians in practice). Treaties often involved other issues as well, such as trade, hospitality, weapons, and rights of passage and extradition. Whatever the specifics, however, the English always had one goal—to defuse any Indian threat, and thereby secure claims under the law of nations.

The kind of security represented by treaties was even more important in places where colonists and Native Americans were at war. When the English first attempted to establish permanent settlements, many had predicted that the Indians would immediately recognize English superiority and gladly cede power to the newcomers. Events in the early settlement period, such as the violent end to the attempted settlement at Roanoke, soon cast doubt on this assumption.[55] Despite promoters' and jurists' statements about amity between peoples, war quickly became a norm of Anglo-Native relations. This forced promoters and colonists to change their legal strategy. Robert A. Williams, Jr., has argued that the English crown "Protestantized" the Spanish discourse of conquest, placing the English sovereign in the position of the pope as lord of the world, and depicting its own colonists as conquerors of pagan peoples.[56] Spanish writings were undoubtedly useful to the English crown and its jurists as they sought to redefine conquest for their own ends. While Vitoria did not believe in conquest as a means of evangelism, he argued that Indian refusal of Spanish rights of trade and travel could indeed serve as a pretext for a just war. "[O]nce the Spaniards have demonstrated diligently both in word and deed that for their own part they have every intention of letting the barbarians carry on in peaceful and undisturbed enjoyment of their property," Vitoria wrote, "if the barbarians nevertheless persist in their wickedness and strive to destroy the Spaniards, they may then treat them no longer as innocent enemies, but as treacherous foes against whom all rights of war can be exercised, including plunder, enslavement, deposition of their former masters, and the institution of new ones."[57] The English most commonly employed these justifications during highly publicized wars with Natives, such as the Powhatan Uprising (1622), the Pequot War (1636–1638), and King Philip's War (1675–1678). Yet I will argue that conquest by just war was not always opposed to the strategy of possession by treaty. In the early decades of colonization, the English did not usually have the manpower or political will to carry out the kind of total conquest described by Vitoria. Colonists viewed treaties and war as complementary measures, to be pursued together, depending upon the circumstances. As William Strachey, a Virginia colonist, had written, "Planting . . . may well be divided into two sorts, when Christians, by the good liking and willing assent of the salvadges, are admitted by them to quiett possession; and when Christians, being inhumanely repulsed, doe seeke to attayne and mayntayne the right for which they come."[58] Colonists often depicted themselves using war, or the threat of it, to secure "willing assent" to their presence. This may seem like a contradiction. The presence of any coercion was inimical to *consensus ad idem* in Roman law, just as violence is inimical to consent today.[59] As Vitoria had written, a treaty made in "fear and ignorance" was no treaty at all. When it came to explaining treaties that had been made during or after wars, colonists therefore faced a pointed dilemma. English writers had for decades criticized Spanish warfare against Native peoples while assuming that their own benevolence would lead to peaceful subjection. When this failed to happen—indeed, when Natives stalwartly defended themselves against English invaders—colonists tried to frame military settlements as voluntary treaties. This required publicizing new kinds of diplomatic approaches that combined friendship with deception, threats, and violence. To this end, the English implemented what I will call a divide-and-ally strategy. Divide-and-ally was pioneered in Virginia during the First Anglo-Powhatan War (1610–1614), when Jamestown governors sought to defeat Powhatan, the leader of the Powhatans, by making treaties with subjects at the periphery of his control while waging a so-called just war against Powhatan himself.[60] The governors of the Plymouth Colony and the Massachusetts Bay Colony also employed this strategy during their wars with the Algonquian-speaking peoples of southern New England. Divide-and-ally enabled colonists to reconcile war and peace, conquering enemies while making treaties with friends. Indeed, in their writings about violent conflicts with Natives, the English often depict war against enemies as bringing them closer to their friends.

Whether they described peaceful agreements, or Native consent obtained amid violence and strife, treaties were never ironclad proof of English possession. Claims about Native acquiescence were riddled with contradictions and tensions, just as visible then as they are now. Why, for example, would a powerful Native king voluntarily submit to a foreign power, as Hakluyt had predicted? European kings did not do such things; why would their Native counterparts? The attempt to argue that violence could coexist with voluntary consent raised even more questions. Could a treaty signed immediately after or even during a war truly represent a meeting of the minds, an agreement without coercion? Were threats enough to compel an entire nation to submit to English rule, and if they were, could such submission ever be construed as voluntary? As I will show in the chapters that follow, such questions frequently animated correspondence between the English crown, its colonial proprietors, and their European rivals.

The crown's application of Roman law to Native peoples led to many local adaptations and controversies, as English colonial negotiators and secretaries published documents and narratives of coastal politics in an attempt to show they had things under control.[61] Yet treaty relations were never merely applications of ancient texts to new territories. While the English viewed themselves as the superiors of Native Americans in almost every way, their legal strategy turned Native consent into evidence of English possession, leaving them iron-ically reliant upon the words and deeds of the people they sought to conquer.

Making Treaties

Scholarly accounts of international law have tended to conceive of Native polities as local or regional actors, operating on the periphery of the world of European crowns.[62] This narrow view of early modern geopolitics ignores the expansionist designs and territorial reach of many coastal groups, as well as their participation in European debates about territorial possession. In the early period of settlement, the English entreated, befriended, and fought with a wide variety of polities.[63] These included the Powhatans, an expansion-minded chiefdom led by a hereditary sachem. They included the Susquehannocks, a commercially driven tribe that had largely remade its economy around markets in European furs. They also included the Patuxets, a group depopulated by ep-idemic, who pursued treaties with the English in an attempt to reclaim their own land. These groups had widely different politics and goals, but they shared some beliefs about law and diplomacy.

Just as many Europeans believed that laws ultimately came from the Chris-tian God, so did many Algonquians view political and legal power as flowing from a creator.[64] In the Chesapeake and Potomac, this figure was called Ahone. In New England, he was Manitowoc. His power was called *manitou*. Other gods, people, animals, and objects were viewed as embodiments of *manitou*. Algonquians believed that everything in the world contained *manitou* to some degree. People, animals, objects, even words, utterances, and movements—all possessed *manitou*. Roger Williams captured the pervasiveness of *manitou* in his phrasebook of the Narragansett dialect of Algonquian, *A Key into the Language of America* (1643). "[T]here is a generall Custome amongst them," he wrote, "at the apprehension of any Excellency in Men, Women, Birds Beasts, Fish, &c. to cry out *Manittóo*, that is, it is a God."[65]

This notion of *manitou* in all things was at the center of coastal practices for marking agreement and building political order. For many Algonquian groups, the creator was something of a distant figure. He existed as a force in the uni-verse, seldom communicating with humans directly. This distance necessitated mediators known as *quiyoughcosughs*, a category of lesser powers that included human leaders such as chiefs, or *werowances*. Algonquians viewed their leaders both as embodiments of gods and as figures who kept the world of humans in balance with the world of spirits. Relations with foreigners were important to the power of *werowances*. Goods from distant places were understood as special objects from the spirit world that endowed their holders (and givers) with power. Chiefs created and maintained authority by acquiring prestige goods, demanding them as tribute when others acquired them, and dispensing them as gifts. While these rituals of distribution and alliance were linked to religion (in the same way, perhaps, as Christian teachings informed natural law), they also served more pragmatic purposes. Gifts, the historian Anne Keary writes, "were understood to be as much diplomatic exchanges as exchanges of wealth. They were formalized in oral rituals conducted at large interband gatherings, where marriages were also arranged, religious ceremonies performed, and gifts traded and tribute offered as a sign and seal of an interband alliance."[66] The relationship between *werowances* and tributary groups little resembled that of princes and subjects in Europe. It had little of the absolutism characteristic of European crowns' demands of total subjection. Lesser peoples gave *werowances* goods or access to resources; in turn, *werowances* promised military assistance or support at times of shortage or crisis. Unlike European subjection, this kind of submission was flexible. Greater or more frequent tribute strengthened relations; a lessening of amount or frequency introduced distance and independence. Smaller groups frequently acted on their own accord, or periodically dropped their affiliation with a chiefly power. Like all political systems the world over, those of coastal peoples were fraught with uncertainty and conflict. Some *werowances* exercised little power, while others violently compelled tribute. Nor were tributary systems historically static. The introduction of European trade goods in the fifteenth century altered the economies of tribute along the coast. The appearance of European pathogens also profoundly disrupted longstanding political routines, leading to massive reorganizations that offered openings for newcomers.[67]

When the first English colonists sent home accounts of treaties with Native Americans, they were usually describing exchanges that Natives understood in terms of tribute.[68] However, the concept of tribute formed the basis of a wide variety of political practices that varied markedly across tribes and regions. Coastal leaders made oral agreements; they exchanged gifts, trade goods, animals, and hostages; and they marked the landscape with inscriptions and monuments. Though not dependent on alphabetic writing, these ways of performing and documenting agreements were binding expressions of consent, much like signatures in Western cultures.[69]

When colonists first arrived in the Chesapeake Bay, they documented their participation in such practices in an effort to show that their neighbors were tolerating their presence. A treaty made in coastal fashion, they hoped, was a sure sign the Indians would not attack them, or otherwise challenge their control. However, while colonists and crowns viewed treaties as evidence for their own claims, such rituals only gained meaning in Europe through the written word. It was not enough to cite Roman legal texts or relevant contemporary authorities. Settlers also had to publicize their treaties in a way that would command legal recognition. This meant putting pen to paper, and finding ways to explain the significance of treaty practices many Europeans viewed as strange or barbaric.

Writing Treaties

When drafting treaties with Native peoples, colonists always had government audiences in mind.[70] On the first returning supply ship, they usually sent home letters attesting to the sincerity and friendliness of their neighbors. There were few agreed-upon conventions for documenting treaties in America. Vitoria, Gentili, and others had argued that treaties with Indians were good and valid, but colonists had scant precedents to guide them when it came to recording such treaties, especially when they had been ratified in Native fashion. At first, they documented treaties primarily for the councils of the joint-stock companies that funded colonization. These councils wanted to show the crown that they were seizing territory and holding it against potential foreign threats, and treaties supported this aim. Colonists usually reported such treaties in diplomatic relations, or letters to royal authority.[71] As a genre that recounted words and behaviors, the diplomatic relation offered a way to describe modes of treaty ratification that lacked any clear analogue in the annals of European practice. Relations captured both official acts of ratification and the many behaviors and negotiations that surrounded them, all of which were understood as potential evidence of consent. Colonists who were out of favor with the crown, or not important enough to merit its attention, turned to other genres and venues. Sometimes, they printed Native treaties in reports or histories, seeking to leverage the publicity of the press to their benefit. After John Smith was ousted from the leadership of the Virginia Colony, he published a dissenting account of Powhatan treaty negotiations on the press at Oxford, hoping to inspire the colony's stakeholders to throw their support behind him. Religious dissenters such as Roger Williams or Samuel Gorton pursued a similar tactic during the

English Revolution, packaging accounts of Native treaties with reformist exhortations in the hopes of influencing Parliament on their behalf.

While colonists usually addressed treaties to royal authorities, they were also aware that others would read what they wrote. European diplomats were one such audience. Foreign agents collected and perused colonial relations and digested them for home governments. Alongside this officially recognized traffic in diplomatic papers, there was also an illicit circulation of narratives and stories about treaties. The Anglo-Spanish War saw the withdrawal of many official diplomatic embassies and an increase in spying and surreptitious written correspondence.[72] While England, Spain, and France maintained diplomatic embassies throughout the early colonial era, diplomats often doubled as spies, intercepting documents and cultivating sources among discontented courtiers or religious dissenters. As well as addressing English authorities, colonists wrote for a shadow coterie of rivals. This coterie acted as a surveillance force, spying upon English settlements and intercepting their written communications. Colonists were extremely fearful of such spying. The establishment of the first English settlements coincided with rampant hysteria about Catholic conspiracy, stoked by the Gunpowder Plot as well as by James I's deeply unpopular attempts to establish a marriage alliance with a Hapsburg princess. While this fear-mongering exaggerated the reality of Spanish power, Spanish ambassadors, Catholic loyalists, and English renegades frequently intercepted accounts of Native alliances and scrutinized them for evidence that Native leaders were less than fully agreeable to English designs. For example, Pedro de Zúñiga, the Spanish ambassador in London during the early years of Virginia settlement, intercepted letters and narratives from returning colonists and collected information from Irish Catholic spies at Jamestown. He used this information to characterize Jamestown as a piratical venture and attempted to compel James I to distance himself from the settlement. He also tried to persuade Philip III to attack the Chesapeake Bay. Rivalry with France likewise inspired fear about the interception of treaty documents. In 1624, the French captured the English agent Robert Cushman as he was returning from Plymouth Colony on a supply ship bound for London and held him and the rest of the crew at an island. The governor of the island, Marquis de Cera, "opened and kept what he pleased" of the colonists' papers, including a narrative of Indian treaties by William Bradford, the governor of Plymouth.[73] To be sure, spies and raiders did not intercept all correspondence from the colonies. However, the English were always cognizant that they might, and this fear shaped the way they recorded alliances. As a

London Council circular had put it in 1610, "The eyes of all Europe are looking upon our endeavors."[74]

International contests over treaty documents were particularly intense during the first decades of permanent English settlement, when Spain still cherished claims north of Florida. However, even after English settlements gained strength in the 1620s and Spain largely dropped its protests, conflicts over treaties continued between the English and their Dutch and French rivals, and became particularly intense among English colonists themselves. Indeed, much of my narrative will concern figures at the margins of the colonial world, such as disgruntled officials, religious dissenters, and fur traders, who sought to acquire power by penning their own stories of treaty making. Dutch shippers, for example, appealed to the English crown for trading rights on the basis of agreements with Native peoples, employing the natural law arguments the English crown had itself used against Spain. English squatters also pointed to land purchases from Native leaders as part of appeals to the English Parliament for charters for their settlements. In the course of such controversies, the English crown often found itself resisting the very arguments it had made to Spain just a few decades earlier.

This culture of quasi-official treaty making was a central part of English colonial politics. Many important issues, such as the proper boundaries of colonies, the lawfulness of English fur trading, and the legitimacy of religious dissent, were adjudicated on the basis of evidence in Native treaties. However, the use of Anglo-Native treaties for strategic purposes was not limited to Europeans. After all, treaties were only meaningful because they carried some sign of consent from an important Native person—a transcript of a speech, for example, or a tale of a ceremony or ritual. Coastal political leaders also used treaties—and transatlantic communication—to gain an upper hand over Europeans and rival tribes alike.

Native Americans and Early Colonial Treaties

In many accounts of Native American history, treaties are synonymous with tragedy. From the beginnings of settlement on, Europeans made and broke many treaties, often with devastating results for Native peoples. From this fact, many have concluded that Native Americans had little agency in treaty making, or little knowledge of what treaties meant. Their lack of alphabetic literacy has reinforced the notion that they were at an inherent disadvantage when it came to the settlers, who wrote everything down, and could thus keep separate accounts, promising one thing while doing another. In a powerful account of the Treaty of Waitangi, an 1840 agreement between Maori chiefs and the government of New Zealand, D. F. McKenzie has shown how New Zealand officials exploited Maori leaders' lack of written English literacy to induce them to transfer sovereignty to the English crown.[75] Undoubtedly, the lack of alphabetic literacy was a disadvantage in many cases. Natives, for example, did not have written duplicates of treaties, which was a liability if some clause later came into dispute. But this does not mean that Native negotiators failed to understand the newcomers or their means of communication, or had little knowledge of what treaties meant. Lack of written literacy did not prevent Native leaders from manipulating political negotiations to their own ends, especially in the early period, when many treaties took Native form. Of course, even in situations where Natives had most of the power, discerning their intentions today is always a great deal harder than figuring out those of Europeans.[76] The English went to great lengths to document their plans, leaving few of their intentions to conjecture. Native people, by contrast, appear through second-hand accounts of speeches or ritual actions, or, in later decades (after documentary treaties became more common), x-marks and pictographic signatures. To make matters more complicated, the English always framed or altered these expressions for their own ends. These many layers of mediation seem to make it difficult to recover how Native people used treaties, or what they thought of them.[77] In recent decades, however, many literary scholars have begun to consider European writing as a potential medium of Native agendas, intentions, and meanings. A tradition of scholarship on the settlement cultures of Latin America has pointed the way toward understanding Native uses of writing and print. This work has examined how Natives appropriated a number of literary and visual genres to their own ends.[78] Scholars in North American colonial studies have made parallel contributions to this field, showing how Northeastern Native people participated in English modes of communication, such as preaching, printing, and scribal publication.[79] This work has focused on how Native people used English technologies for reasons other than those its originators intended.[80]

Understanding the Native perspective is crucial to interpreting treaty documents. Europeans only cared about treaties because they captured Native intentions. Treaties therefore cannot be understood without an inquiry into how and why Native people participated in their making. Native people left their figurative and literal marks on treaties in a variety of ways. When Virginia colonists arrived in the Chesapeake Bay region, for example, they confronted the Powhatans, a tribal chiefdom whose leader welcomed them as potential subjects and sources of trade goods. They also made contact with groups at the periphery of Powhatan control, who saw the newcomers as an opportunity for escaping subjection to the Powhatans. The complexity of Powhatan interband alliances, and the contentious nature of English transatlantic governance, meant that many different parties in the Chesapeake Bay wrote down accounts of treaties, producing a vast and verbally detailed archive of narratives of diplomacy and records of political accord, much of which made its way back to England. In such situations, it is often possible to compare multiple documents, and reconstruct what Native people thought about treaties and what they hoped to gain from them. North of the Virginia grant, things were different. Merchants and Catholic settlers in Maryland encountered Native groups already heavily invested in the fur trade, such as the Susquehannocks. These commercial interactions produced a much sparser written archive of Native words and deeds, as Virginia-based adventurers and their rivals in Maryland recorded interactions with the Susquehannocks and other groups in written receipts of land purchase and trade. In some cases, though, absences can speak volumes, as when the Susquehannocks refused to make trade agreements with Maryland because they were angry at how its governors had treated their Virginia trading partners. The situation in southern New England was different still. There, a plague introduced by European traders had decimated many tribal groups, upturning political balances that had evolved in response to the fur trade. When Plymouth and Massachusetts Bay colonists arrived in the 1620s, they assumed a powerful hand in their negotiations with weakened tribes, seeking to buy their land or to subject them to English power. At the same time, many religious dissenters and figures at the margins of Plymouth Colony and the Massachusetts Bay Colony tried to make treaties with Native peoples in order to acquire power and land. Many Native groups were interested in cooperating, creating a detailed archive of treaties signed by pictographs, which southern New England Natives had learned to use so they could participate in the fur and land market and in political settlements after wars. The development of pictographic signatures enabled the Narragansetts to communicate directly with Parliament, greatly strengthening their position against the Massachusetts Bay Colony. While these and other negotiations were often carried out in the name of larger groups, such as crowns or chiefdoms, it is also important to remember that they were shaped by individual agendas as well. Different tribes had different visions for the future, but many Natives, like many Europeans, were often only looking out for themselves. Their political actions were not always determined by tribal identity, tradition, or religion. Sometimes their speeches, gestures, x-marks, and pictographs represented individual rather than collective agendas.

Each chapter of this book focuses on a particular treaty or group of treaties. It starts with an account of what happened during the treaty negotiations, and then branches out to offer interpretations of the many uses Europeans and Indians made of treaty records. Chapter 1 considers the crowning of Powhatan sachems in early colonial Virginia. When the English crown and its councilors granted the territory around Chesapeake Bay to the Virginia Company, they were aware that the area was occupied by populous groups. During the first years of settlement, colonial governors sought to bring the Powhatans under control by crowning them as vassals of the English king. These crowning ceremonies, written up for transatlantic audiences by colonial secretaries, publicized the Powhatans' consent to treaties and the crown's corresponding possession of American land. Powhatans interpreted them differently, as marking English submission to them. These differing interpretations led to a series of stand-offs, eventually culminating in a violent conflict known to historians as the First Anglo-Powhatan War. As the colony's relations with the Powhatans deteriorated, a number of English writers, most notably John Smith, wrote home to criticize the colony's approach to tribal diplomacy. Arguing that the colony's "stately kinde of soliciting" had emboldened Powhatan leaders, Smith lobbied for a diplomatic approach based around Spanish models.[81] As I will show, the stakes of this debate were quite high. The Spanish spied on Jamestown and circulated counter-narratives of Anglo-Native treaties designed to cast doubt on Powhatan alliances and inspire Philip III to raze the settlement, an action that at this time was still well within his power. While Europeans debated the meaning of the crowning ceremonies, Powhatan, the chief of the Powhatans, used the ceremonial objects he had acquired in such rituals to increase his own authority over Chesapeake Bay Native peoples.

Chapter 2 considers the international public relations war over the kidnapping and marriage of Pocahontas, the daughter of Powhatan. In 1613, Samuel Argall, an English navigator, abducted Pocahontas in order to ransom her for English captives and goods he claimed the Powhatans had stolen. After the kidnapping failed to resolve the conflict, Pocahontas married John Rolfe, an Englishman. The Virginia Company tried to advertise the marriage as a dynastic union between Jamestown and the Powhatans, claiming that the first male offspring would govern Chesapeake Bay as a cross-cultural leader. This strategy was useful in the wake of the First Anglo-Powhatan War. It enabled colonists to articulate a vision of peaceful order under English sovereignty. After securing funding, the Virginia Company brought Pocahontas to London to advertise their success at converting her to Anglicanism and turning her into a cross-cultural ambassador. While in London, Pocahontas became a pawn in negotiations between the English, Spanish, and French crowns over the composition of Catholic-Protestant alliances after the end of the Anglo-Spanish War. Hopes for an Anglo-Powhatan government perished when Pocahontas died shortly before her return voyage, leaving her son in England. Still, as I will show, colonists continued to debate the meaning of her marriage (and death) for Anglo-Powhatan alliances for years.

Chapter 3 shifts north to Plymouth Colony, describing the diplomatic activities of the Leyden Separatists, known in American history as the Pilgrims. While the Virginia settlement had been troubled by the threat of Spanish invasion, by the 1620s the Spanish had begun to accept England's rights. And while the French and Dutch cherished competing claims to the land north of Virginia, they did not have the military strength to destroy the English outright. However, the increasing power of the English crown in North America did not mean that colonists abandoned natural law as a vocabulary for framing treaties. Instead, figures with uncertain legal standing, such as the Pilgrims, turned to the law of nations as a way of explaining their own legitimacy to the English crown and nearby European traders. Publishing Native treaties gave dissenters a way of proving their own standing to an English government that ignored them or was hostile to their plans. In Chapter 3, I describe how the Pilgrims used treaties with Native leaders to display their own power and legitimacy to transatlantic readers. The Pilgrims' relations with neighbors were characterized by tension and sporadic violence. In their published works, the Pilgrims focus on their friendly relations with the Pokanokets, and draw upon the laws of war to defend their violence against enemy tribes, such as the Massachusetts and the Narragansetts.

After the consolidation of its possessions in Virginia and New England, the English crown increasingly encountered protests from Dutch and French rivals, as well as from English travelers involved in disputes with the chartered colonies. Chapters 4 and 5 consider the publication of Native treaties by figures operating beyond the bounds of chartered settlements. Many of the Europeans who traveled to the North Atlantic coast in the early seventeenth century went as traders. These commercial concerns had little interest in land rights. However, they did pursue various kinds of legal authorization that were articulated in the language of the law of nations. In Chapter 4, I examine how fur traders used Native treaties to assert rights to trade in North Atlantic waters. The question of who owned the seas was sharply contested in the early decades of English colonization. Before permanent English settlements were established, the English crown frequently asserted *mare liberum*, or the right to universal free trade, as a way of making inroads against Spanish claims. By 1630, the crown had begun to assert *mare clausum*, or exclusive rights to waters off the North American coast. This shift in legal strategy, I will show, drove fur traders under various flags to pursue Native alliances as a way of protecting their own rights against the English crown. I consider the documentary correspondence of two financial concerns, the Dutch ship the *Eendracht* and the trading post of the English adventurer William Claiborne. Both of these concerns were threatened by the crown's assertion of *mare clausum*, and both tried to assert rights by arguing that Native people had given them permission to occupy parts of the coast and the waters adjacent to it. Both appeals were unsuccessful, but their efforts show how figures at the margins of the English colonial system used a variety of treaty documents to assert their own rights, as well as how those rights became entangled with those of Native peoples. The Susquehannocks used the written correspondence between traders and the English crown for profit and to protect themselves from Iroquois enemies.

My final chapter considers the writings of religious dissenters in Narragansett Bay. After being exiled by the governors of the Massachusetts Bay Colony, many religious dissenters purchased land from Narragansett sachems and began to settle the bay without royal permission. I examine the writings of two such dissenters, Roger Williams and Samuel Gorton. Both used transatlantic accounts of purchasing land from Narragansett sachems in order to appeal to Parliament for royal protection. Unlike the fur traders I discuss in the fourth chapter, Williams and Gorton were successful, securing royal charters that placed them on the same legal footing as the Massachusetts Bay Colony. These legal contests over the meaning of Native purchase occurred at the same time as the English colonies were pursuing the military conquest of the Algonquin-speaking peoples of southern New England. I close the chapter by considering how Narragansett sachems used Williams and Gorton to make their own appeal for protection to the recently seated English Parliament, which had assumed authority over colonial affairs during the English Revolution. This appeal was spectacularly successful and changed the political relationships between the crown, its colonies, and coastal tribes, initiating a shift to direct royal control of New England that ended the transatlantic traffic in treaties.

The story I tell in this book spans several decades. It begins with the settlement of Virginia in the wake of the Treaty of London (1604), and concludes with the English crown's direct assertion of authority over New England Indians in 1664, an event that led most English colonists to abandon the transatlantic publication of Native treaties. In the window of time between these two events, settlers frequently publicized treaties with Native peoples to show their possession of territory (and sometimes waters). Many scholarly accounts have viewed these treaties as documents of barbarism—not the kind of barbarism the English projected onto Native Americans, but the kind we now associate with those who violate human rights. This much is true. But this way of looking at things can conceal the many agendas that converged on treaties or later found expression in them. Native treaties were part of a centuries-long attempted genocide, but neither Europeans nor Native people knew what the future would hold. It is this uncertainty—about what treaties meant, about whether they would be broken, and about who would triumph if they were—that I take as my starting point.

Chapter 1

—⚬⚬⚬—

Heavy Heads: Crowning Kings in Early Virginia

On a placid morning in October 1608, Christopher Newport pushed off from the shore of the York River and pointed his boat toward Werowocomoco, the seat of the Powhatan chiefdom. It had been more than a year since his first journey inland, the one that had culminated in the great shout and the treaty with the river king. Since that time, much had happened. The English had traded with some Indians, fought with others, and established diplomatic relations with Powhatan, the paramount chief of the bay. Yet as Newport landed on the opposite shore of the river and his men began to unpack their barges, it immediately became clear that this was not a routine visit. Treading carefully so as not to lose their footing in the mud, they carried ashore a washbasin painted with the royal insignia of James I, a scarlet cloak made of wool, a decorative pitcher, an English bedstead, and finally a copper crown, burnished to a rosy shine.

A letter from London explained the purpose of this unusual cargo. On the king's authority, it commanded Newport to recruit Powhatan into an alliance with the English crown. The plan included an elaborate protocol modeled on the ceremonies through which European lords created vassals, or feudal land-holders.[1] Newport was to stage a ritual coronation of Powhatan, deputizing him as a local authority while confirming his subjection to James I. The wash-basin, bedstead, and cloak signified English goodwill. The crown, bestowed on the Indian king in a ceremony, would confirm his agreement in the matter.[2]

On paper, the mission seemed simple enough: awe the chief with gifts and induce him to kneel and receive the crown. But what happened next became the subject of a debate that extended far beyond the Chesapeake Bay. According to a written account published by the Virginia Company, the joint-stock venture that financed settlement, the ceremony was a success.[3] Powhatan, the "Emperour" of the Powhatans, stooped and "received voluntarilie a crowne and a scepter," a gesture that "licensed" the English "to negotiate among them, and to possesse their countrie with them."[4] But other observers came forward to challenge this version of events. Soldiers and secretaries scribbled their own accounts of the crowning on notepaper. These, too, made their way to London, and were eventually published in a compilation of reports entitled *The Proceedings of the English Colonie in Virginia* (1612). This book described the coronation as a botched affair. Powhatan had refused to recognize the subject status conferred by the crown, instead interpreting the ceremony as English recognition of his power. The all-important stoop had been coerced; the English had resorted to leaning on his shoulders to place the crown on his head. Worse yet, a cannon fusillade meant to commemorate the peace had frightened the Indians, scattering Powhatan's entourage and leading to shouted accusations of an ambush. The ceremony had been a catastrophe.

Still other accounts circulated through international channels. Frances Magnel, an Irish laborer living in Jamestown, also witnessed or heard about the coronation. He traveled to Madrid, where he gave a deposition to an Irish Catholic archbishop, who translated it into Castilian and secretly conveyed it to the Spanish crown.[5] If the Virginia Company cited the bow to confirm English rights to rule New World territory, the uncertain outcome of the ceremony called into question the very legality of the settlement. Pedro de Zúñiga, a Spanish ambassador, was "amused" that the English were treating Indians like princes. He fiercely disputed the claim that they could establish rightful possession through such ceremonies. The colonists, he wrote in a letter to Philip III, were merely using negotiations with Indians to give an appearance of legality to attempts to "carry on piracy" against Spanish ships.[6] As reports spread, Powhatan's response took on increasing significance for international agreements with Spain.

In Powhatan's stoop to receive the crown, Christopher Newport found confirmation of English power in the New World. In the chief's scowls and angry words, Newport's rivals at home and abroad saw an exposure of English weakness, even a challenge to the legal basis of English settlement. Newport's attempted crowning of Powhatan was one of many treaty ceremonies conducted between colonists and Powhatans during the early years of Virginia colonization. And like other such ceremonies, it had consequences well beyond the coast. The crowning inspired clashing reports, stories, and rumors that spread throughout the bay, the colonial Atlantic, and the channels of diplomatic communication that connected European crowns.[7] The transmission of these stories across space and time reflected complex alliances and agendas. English, Spanish, Irish, and Native people all retold the story in different ways in order to advance competing visions of political order. As Powhatan and Newport faced off over the crown, they were acutely aware that it was only the first engagement in a longer struggle over the meaning of the ceremony, one waged through stories as well as rituals.

This chapter considers political negotiations between English and Powhatan peoples in early Virginia. It examines how treaty ceremonies involving Native leaders influenced European debates about territorial possession. Existing scholarly accounts have examined how English colonists used written treaties to give an appearance of legality to the theft of Native land. These accounts have argued that the English disregarded indigenous political systems and sought to impose written forms of political documentation on Native peoples. This chapter sets out to revise that picture. The English crown financed colonial ventures in order to acquire control of territory. This meant claiming Indian lands. But as I will show here, this did not mean rejecting Natives' right to speak for themselves. Indeed, according to many early modern understandings of the law of nations, Christian princes could acquire control over territory through the creation of treaty agreements with pagans. In order to establish claims in this way, the English needed to capture the voluntary consent of Native people according to *consensus ad idem*, a legal criterion deriving from Roman law. *Consensus ad idem* required that treaties should represent a "meeting of the minds," or voluntary agreement between parties. To this end, the English crown instructed colonists to "entreate" Native people and send home written accounts of Native alliances.[8] On some occasions, these treaties were formatted like European-style articles of agreement, but more often they came in the form of narratives and letters describing ritual performances, such as orations, exchanges of gifts, or crowning ceremonies. By setting down these acts in writing, the English sought to show that Native people had given newcomers permission to settle on or near their land, or had transferred sovereignty to them altogether, making them masters of the coast.

This chapter describes how different ways of making treaties came to support conflicting assertions of ownership and power in the Chesapeake Bay. Most of the bay was controlled by Powhatan, a hereditary sachem. Born with the name Wahunsunacawh, Powhatan had inherited power over several tribes and conquered several others. At some point during his conquests, he had assumed the name Powhatan as a title recognizing his supreme authority. By using this title as his name, the English showed their respect for his power, yet there was also strategy behind their choice. In calling him Powhatan, the English conflated the chief with his people, known as the Powhatans, and authorized him to make treaties on their behalf. In reality, Powhatan's territory, known as Tsenacomoco to the people who lived there, was a turbulent and divided world. Powhatan was closely allied with the tribes nearest to his seat at Werowocomoco, but was frequently at odds with those on the periphery of his holdings. These friendships and conflicts were mediated by complex and evolving practices for marking alliance and affiliation. Powhatans formed political agreements through exchanges of gifts, elaborate speeches, and ceremonial feasts. These bonds were often described as symbolic kinship alliances between fathers, brothers, and sons. Yet even as kinship metaphors suggested intimate links between peoples, they masked a violent reality. Powhatan frequently used force to compel tribute or labor from subjects, even destroying entire families or kin groups when it suited his purposes.[9]

When settlers first arrived in the Chesapeake Bay, they were usually compelled to negotiate on Powhatan terms. They listened to orations, feasted and danced with Powhatans, offered gifts of tribute, including English goods and animals, and even exchanged captives, giving Powhatan an English boy, Thomas Savage, in exchange for a Powhatan boy named Namontack.[10] In this chapter, I will describe how such exchanges led to conflicting accounts of Native consent to treaties. I begin by reprising my discussion of Gabriel Archer's "A relatyon of the Discovery of our River, from James Forte into the Maine" (1607). In the "Relatyon," Archer, the official "Recorder" or secretary of the Virginia Colony, documents Jamestown's first diplomatic negotiations with the Powhatans. Archer depicts the New World as a political order of monarchies, much like Europe, and in many ways his relation resembles European diplomatic writings. Archer describes how the English make treaties with the peoples they encounter, entering into alliances with sovereign kings. Yet there is one key difference. Archer reports that Native people make treaties through acts of tribute rather than signatures or vows. While language barriers separate the English and the Powhatans, he claims that coastal practices such as exchanging gifts or standing in the presence of authorities can express consent to treaty arrangements. By describing such protocols, Archer tries to show that the Indians have granted legitimacy to the English presence. The embassy culminates in Powhatan authorities crowning Newport, an act Archer interprets as Powhatan recognition of English power.

Archer's account reflected many of the assumptions about pliant Indians that were common during the Elizabethan era. However, his narrative arrived in London with stories of mismanagement, starvation, and war. In response to these developments, the colony's governing council in London installed new leadership and commanded the colonists to take a new approach to coastal diplomacy. Now, the colonists would bring war against Powhatan, while seeking to form alliances with tribes at the outskirts of his control. This shift in policy required a new set of legal justifications, as well as new models of diplomacy that could secure treaties at the edges of Tsenacomoco while the colonists waged war against Powhatan and his allies. Among the most prominent colonists to respond to these new imperatives was Captain John Smith, a former president of the colony. In two books published together, *A Map of Virginia* and *The Proceedings of the English Colonie in Virginia* (1612), Smith attacks the diplomatic approach to Indian treaties publicized by Archer and puts forward his own model of treaty making. While Archer depicts the Powhatans peacefully consenting to the English presence with welcoming gestures and gifts, Smith's books argue that the Indians' outward shows of welcome have only given cover to acts of pillage and ambush. Adopting a skeptical attitude toward diplomacy, Smith argues that the Powhatans' ceremonial gestures offer little access to their true intentions. Assembling his book from reports by soldiers, Smith argues for a political order based on violent threats and forced subjection rather than mutual recognition. Paradoxically, Smith portrays threats as a way of achieving the forms of voluntary agreement that straightforward diplomacy cannot.

Anglo-Powhatan alliances were not just a subject of controversy in English colonial government. A number of England's rivals spied on Jamestown and its negotiations with surrounding groups. Among the most vocal was Pedro de Zúñiga, Spanish ambassador to James I during the early years of the Jamestown settlement. In his letters, Zúñiga attacks the legality of English settlement by exposing what he believes is the fraudulent nature of Powhatan treaty ceremonies. In secret correspondence with the Spanish crown, he points to intercepted reports of Powhatan resistance as evidence that Jamestown is an illegal settlement and should be destroyed.

Parties with many different agendas told stories about Powhatan diplomacy. Standing behind all of them, however, were the words and gestures of the Powhatans themselves. While Europeans framed Native ceremonies for their own ends, Powhatan likewise told stories about his interactions with the English, which were occasionally recorded by English observers. In the concluding section of the chapter, I will consider what colonial records can tell us about Powhatan's intentions.

Alliance and Discovery: Archer's "Relatyon"

"[Pawatah] (very well understanding by the wordes and signes we made; the significatyon of our meaning) moved of his owne accord a leauge of fryndship with us."[11] Gabriel Archer's "Relatyon" culminates with "the greate kyng Powatah" (Archer's spelling of Powhatan) spontaneously offering a treaty alliance to Jamestown leaders.[12] The moment dramatizes the great king's consent to the English presence. But Archer also seems worried that his version of events might not be believed on the other side of the Atlantic. Archer's narrative is interspersed with parenthetical asides that translate the Indian's words into English and assure the reader that he means what he says. The scene concludes with a final act of tribute that provides added proof of his sincerity: "for concluding therof, [Pawatah] gave [Newport] his gowne, put it on his back himselfe, and laying his hand on his breast saying Wingapoh Chemuze (the most kynde wordes of salutatyon that may be) he satt downe."[13] If doubts about the "understanding" between Newport and the king remain, the gift of the gown, complete with dramatic embrace, surely removes them. Hand on his heart, the king makes plain his love for the English in his own language, helpfully translated by Archer. Who could be skeptical, even thousands of miles away?

The moment is a surprising conclusion for a document identified, in a neat secretary hand at the top of its first page, as the story of a "discovery." Narratives of discovery were a common product of state-sponsored explorations of uncharted territory in the New World, Africa, and the Far East. Spanish and Portuguese settlers published discoveries to make claims to land unexplored by other Europeans. English travelers in the Elizabethan and Stuart eras imitated this literary tradition, circulating their own accounts of the discovery of the North Atlantic coast.[14] But Archer departs from the conventions of the genre in a significant way. While the James River is not controlled by any Christian prince, it is far from empty. Indeed, Virginia is under the jurisdiction of a figure identified, familiarly enough, as a king. And while Archer describes river peoples as "Salvages," he finds their king sitting in state and conducting diplomacy in much the same manner as the Christian princes of Europe.[15] Archer's

"Relatyon" reveals a land that is both awaiting discovery and lively with the politics of its inhabitants.

Dispatched to London on a supply ship returning from Jamestown in 1607, Archer's "Relatyon" was the first account of the Virginia Colony's diplomatic interactions with the Powhatan peoples. The handwritten narrative tells the story of the settlers' exploration of the James River and Christopher Newport's early diplomatic triumphs among the chiefs of Tsenacomoco. Like many colonial dispatches, the "Relatyon" was composed with an international audience in mind. In many ways, it resembles prior Spanish narratives of the possession of Hispaniola and Florida. Archer tells how Newport discovers new lands and claims them by planting a cross in the name of James I, a ritual borrowed from accounts of earlier explorers. Yet in staking a claim to Virginia, the "Relatyon" does more than merely imitate earlier accounts. Most of the text is devoted to chronicling the diplomatic interactions between the English and the indigenous kings that rule the rivers. Far from denying the jurisdiction of these figures, Archer depicts them as legitimate leaders, holding territory and exercising sovereignty over loyal subjects. Their most important acts, however, involve their acceptance of the foreigners. The riverbank kings extend a formal welcome to the English, granting them recognition as a political power in the bay.

Virginia colonists sailed to the New World with a great deal of anxiety about their legal status. While James I had asserted the right of the crown to annex New World territory, and had given the Virginia Company a grant to the Chesapeake Bay, both the crown and its colonial proprietors were fearfully conscious of Spain's continuing claims to land north of Florida.[16] They could look to the massacre at Fort Caroline, a French Huguenot outpost destroyed by Spanish raiders, for evidence of the fate that might await Jamestown colonists if Philip III decided to assert Spanish claims.[17] The English had many ways of defending colonies from the Spanish, such as building forts or hiding settlements from view. Yet writing was also an important mode of defense. The crown viewed written reports as a central part of the public defense of New World rights. It was up to colonists to complete the crown's claims by taking possession of land and sending home "relations" or reports of their activities. English colonists used many kinds of writing to document their possession of New World territory. They described the construction of fortifications, the tilling of fields, and the extension of fences, hedgerows, and other ways of marking English property.[18] However, much of the territory in the Chesapeake claim was densely populated by indigenous people. Claiming this land demanded a different legal strategy—the assertion of treaty rights. The company's instructions to the colonists made clear how this transatlantic relay of treaty documents would work. The colonists would "entreate those salvages in those parts," bringing them to "God" and "Obedience," and would likewise "Send a perfect relation by Captain Newport of all that is Done" on the first returning supply ship.[19]

The company's appointment of Gabriel Archer as secretary was one part of the plan for carrying out this directive. Archer possessed considerable expertise in writing and law, having studied at Cambridge and Gray's Inn. Before arriving in Virginia, Archer tested his education widely, accompanying Bartholomew Gosnold on a transatlantic voyage in 1602 and penning a report on the results of the expedition.[20] Archer sailed to Virginia on the first fleet of ships under the command of Newport. After the party's arrival in the Chesapeake Bay, he recorded many of the colony's official proceedings, but devoted the majority of his writing to settlers' interactions with coastal Native groups. While the company had known Indians would be nearby, "entreat[ing]" surrounding leaders turned out to be a far more complicated venture than the colony's meager instructions had anticipated. Hostile groups immediately approached the first landing party, and on May 21, 1607, Christopher Newport led a discovery and diplomatic outreach up the James River with the hopes of establishing a peaceful rapport. Over the course of the exploration, the party encountered several smaller *werowances*, or leaders, affiliated with Powhatan. They exchanged goods and friendly words with those who came forward to greet them, giving them penny knives, scissors, bells, beads, and toys. Despite the English provenance of the gifts, the exchanges were largely conducted on Native terms. The Powhatans viewed these items as desirable not because they were easily dazzled by shiny things, as some observers would later conclude, but because foreign objects had value in the tributary networks that tied together the chiefdom.[21] The embassy culminated in the meeting with the great Indian king. Afterward, Newport planted a cross inscribed with the name of James I, much to the confusion of his Indian guide.[22]

From the English point of view, Newport's discovery accomplished a number of things. It signified the peaceful intentions of the English (at least in the short term), offering some measure of protection against the numerically superior Powhatans. It opened trading routes, which would be crucial to the colony's survival. Yet the discovery was also an act of possession. By describing the journey in writing, the colony's governors intended to announce the crown's rights to the area, and to show that the Indians were not going to interfere.

As the colony's chief recorder, Archer accompanied Newport on the discovery. Archer's "Relatyon," sent to London with Newport, was one of the first official reports on the colony's progress. Based on Archer's records, it is clear he took notes as the party went along. The "Relatyon" is organized by date, and includes information on weather and the distance the party traveled each day.[23] Archer describes how Newport claims the river for the English crown by planting a cross and performing other acts of possession. However, Archer also combines the genre of the discovery with the story of the peaceful conclusion of a treaty with the king who rules the river. Archer's text details the words, gestures, and gifts exchanged between sovereign parties and enumerates the binding agreements that result. Like the planting of the cross, these agreements support English possession by suggesting that Newport's claims will not be troubled by Native challenges.

The "Relatyon" moves chronologically, charting the party's progress up the James River. Along the way, they treaty with indigenous leaders of increasingly impressive rank. After departing from Jamestown, Newport and his party arrive at the first great Indian "kyngdome," which Archer calls "Wynauk." The people respond to the English arrival with "rejoycing."[24] The next day, a canoe approaches. Its passengers happily greet the English, and one of them, quickly taking to Archer's pen and paper, offers to draw a map of the river and its kingdoms. The people bring mulberries, acorns, wheat, and beans to sustain the party on their travels. These preliminary acts of diplomacy lead to the narrative's first encounter with a political leader. Journeying past several poor cottages, Newport and his men find a figure clothed in savage garb but also immediately recognizable as a king in state. "We found here a Wiroans (for so they call their kynges)," Archer writes, "who satt upon a matt of Reedes, with his people about him." "[H]is name is Arahatec," Archer goes on, "the Country Arahatecoh."[25] The image is exotic, hearkening to sixteenth-century texts of Near Eastern exploration, which depicted sultans sitting in lavish surrounds.[26] But Archer's description of Arahatec's body also fixes the moment in a framework familiar to European readers. In audiences with diplomats, kings frequently retained a sitting or relaxed posture while subjects stood arrayed at attention. This was especially the case in diplomatic proceedings. While the mat is an exotic touch, Arahatec's posture makes him the equivalent of a European king receiving visitors. Archer's description authorizes the king to offer a treaty to the English.

Greeting the newcomers to his kingdom, Arahatec "cause[s] [a mat] to be layd for Captain Newport" and immediately bestows upon Newport "his Crowne which was of Deares hayre dyed re[d]."[27] While the English used copper crowns to deputize lesser authorities, Archer emphasizes that Arahatec gives Newport his own crown, thereby placing the English captain in the position of a superior.

Though implausibly free of any friction, Archer's narrative corresponds in some particulars to what contemporary anthropologists have reconstructed of coastal diplomacy. As Helen C. Rountree has shown in her account of Powhatan foreign policy, the Powhatans used mats, crowns, and smoking as diplomatic implements.[28] Smoking and sitting was a way of "breaking the ice," or defusing tension before important negotiations. Given how numerically weak the English were, Arahatec likely understood the exchange as confirming Powhatan authority.

The treaty offer from Arahatec is only a prelude to an encounter with a more powerful king, whom Archer calls "Pawatah." The "Pawatah" the party encountered was not, in fact, the paramount chief Powhatan. It was instead his son, Parahunt, whom Newport and Archer misidentified as Powhatan.[29] As Newport and his party banquet and smoke with Arahatec, they are interrupted by "Newes . . . that the greate kyng Powatah was come." As in his description of Arahatec's riverside court, Archer carefully choreographs the king's appearance. When the great chief appears, Archer writes, "[the Indians] all rose of their mattes (save the kyng Arahatec); separated themselves aparte in fashion of a Guard, and with a long shout they saluted him." Arahatec's subjects recognize his authority, standing on his arrival and shouting, while Arahatec remains seated, preserving his status as a king. For their part, the newcomers follow this protocol. The English, Archer writes, "saluted [the great king] with silence sitting still on our mattes, our Captaine in the myddest."[30] Like Arahatec, Newport sits in the middle of his subjects, marking him as a sovereign in the presence of other princely powers. But crucially missing in the English response is the spontaneous standing that had accompanied the chief's welcome by Arahatec's subjects. The English remain seated, identifying them as superiors to the Indians. Through an intricate rendering of gesture and posture during treaty negotiations, Archer divides Natives into subjects and kings, while the English, seated confidently on their mats, collectively embody the crown and its power.

Soliciting a treaty agreement from the more powerful sachem proves tricky. While Arahatec gives Newport his crown, no such act of welcome is forthcoming from the paramount Indian. Indeed, far from accepting English power, the king issues a mandate, commanding the English to travel no farther. Intimidated, Newport backs down. That Archer would portray an Indian leader giving commands to Newport—and Newport obeying them—is somewhat surprising, given his concern with establishing the legal rights of the English crown. Indeed, the moment is difficult to explain if one assumes that English colonial writers always selectively edited Native treaties to suit their agenda. Archer's intended audience was thousands of miles away, and he could have omitted the incident altogether. That he did not do so sheds light on the role that Native diplomacy played in transatlantic correspondence. As I will detail later in this chapter, the first Jamestown government was composed of figures with many different agendas. Even before the discovery of the river, the colony's government had seen considerable controversy. Newport had detained John Smith on the charge of attempting to usurp the company's authority, releasing him a short while later. Archer was well aware that Smith or others might challenge his account. It was therefore imperative to compose treaty narratives that could withstand the scrutiny of hostile readers. This meant acknowledging diplomatic setbacks while putting them in the best possible light. Archer deals with the embarrassment of Newport's defeat by portraying it as an act of reasonable diplomacy rather than a concession to Native power. After the English are commanded to halt their explorations, Archer writes, "our Captayne out of his Discretyon (though we would faine have seene further, yea and himselfe as Desirous also) Checkt his intentyon and retorned to his boate; as holding it much better to please the kyng (with whome and all of his Comaund he had made so faire Way) then to prosecute his owne fancye."[31] Newport backs down because he wants to preserve his diplomatic progress. He concedes the demand, not out of obedience to the king, Archer is clear, but rather to preserve the "faire Way" he has made with the king and the lesser sachems who have been impressed by English courtesy. In this way, Archer tries to turn the setback into a success.

Still, the moment leaves Archer in a difficult position. Far from welcoming the English, the king pushes them around. At this moment in the text, Archer alters his strategy. Instead of describing a diplomatic parley between political principals, as he does in the case of Arahatec's meeting with Newport, Archer asserts English sovereignty by describing how Newport plants a cross at the falls of the river, claiming the territory for the crown. Given that Newport performed this ceremony at least twice, and that the cross was engraved with the name of the king, it seems likely that the colonists brought these crosses with them from England. Planting crosses on islands or at other inland portals was a common way in which Europeans advertised claims to other Christians[32] (see Figure 1). In planting the cross, Newport recoups some of the face he lost when he conceded to the king's wishes to travel no farther. The moment is a dramatic expression of English power, made even bolder by its disregard for Parahunt's previous order to the party. Yet Archer does not depict the cross as a unilateral assertion of English power. Instead, it is a means for getting Parahunt's consent to the English presence, and, from the English point of view, establishing possession under the law of nations. Archer writes, "upon one of the little Ilettes at the mouth of the falls [Newport] sett up a Crosse with this inscriptyon Jacobus Rex. 1607 . and his owne name belowe: At the erecting hereof we prayed for our kyng and our owne prosperous succes in this his Actyon, and proclaymed him kyng, with a greate showte."[33] While the act is in some sense a riposte to the Indian king, and an assertion of English power in the face of diplomatic defeat, Archer is also careful to frame it, at least to the Indians, as a confirmation of their voluntary alliance with the English. "The kyng Pawatah was now gone," he writes, "and all the Salvages likewise save Navirans [an Indian guide], who seeing us set up a Crosse with such a shoute, began to admire; but our Captayne told him that the two Armes of the Crosse signifyed kyng Powatah and himselfe [Newport], the fastening of it in the myddest was their united Leaug, and the shoute the reverence he dyd to Pawatah. which cheered Navirans not a litle."[34] While the English shout their own subjection to the cross, Navirans can only "admire." Archer uses the word "admire" in the early modern sense of the word, meaning to display shock or surprise in the face of a visual spectacle or sensory experience.[35] Navirans's spellbound stare is interrupted by Newport, who translates the meaning of the cross into the terms of the earlier alliance. This explanation is a shrewd legal sleight of hand. The Indian king recognizes no subordination. He views any friendship as implying English subjection to him, or at the very least an unsteady equality. But by telling Navirans that the cross represents a league, Archer symbolically subordinates the coastal alliance to the power of the English king. Newport and the Powhatan chief are united in alliance, but this league of friendship is quite literally framed by the overarching sovereignty of the crown. Newport never directly explains this treaty to the king, relying instead on Navirans to relay it to him and secure his consent to it: "sending Navirans up to [the king], he came downe to the water syde, where he went a shore single unto him, presented him with a hatchet, and staying but till Navirans had tolde (as we trewly perceived) the meaning of our setting

Figure 1. Theodor de Bry's engraving of Columbus claiming the island of Guanahani, from Theodor de Bry, *Americae Pars Quarta* (1594). The image portrays explorers raising a cross while Columbus accepts gifts from the island's indigenous inhabitants. English explorers imitated such rituals by combining Christian acts of possession with Native treaties. Courtesy of The Newberry Library.

up the Crosse, which we found Dyd exceedingly rejoyce him."[36] Here, then, is the big prize: the acquiescence of the great king to the power of the crown, as demonstrated by his rejoicing response to the cross. The king affirms the alliance, welcoming the English as neighbors and providing proof of their safe possession of the territory under the law of nations.

The moment satisfies the legal requirement for *consensus ad idem*; the king understands the meaning of the cross and agrees to the alliance represented by it. However, Archer's account of the moment seems slightly troubled. He emphasizes the faithfulness of English witnesses to the scene. The English "trewly perceived" that Navirans had accurately explained it. Archer's insistence on the truth of English perceptions seems a tad defensive, as if he anticipates that others might challenge this account, and he wants to assert his own credibility and the integrity of the treaty. Archer had good reason for this wariness. After Newport's party returned home, Jamestown was attacked. Archer's "Relatyon" closes with another appearance by an Indian guide, who blames the attack on some enemy Indians and helpfully reaffirms the alliance described in the preceding pages.[37] But Archer was right to suspect that his glowing account of alliances would not be enough to quiet criticism. There were other people in Jamestown with pen and paper, and they would have other stories to tell about the great kings of the river.

Kidnapping Your Brothers: Ambush and Alliance in John Smith's *Proceedings*

"For we had his favour much better, onlie for a poore peece of Copper, till this stately kinde of soliciting made him so much overvalue himselfe, that he respected us as much as nothing at all."[38] This is how John Smith describes the results of Christopher Newport's diplomacy in *The Proceedings of the English Colonie in Virginia*, an account of the colony's first years. While Archer describes Newport's diplomatic achievements as the key to peace on the coast, Smith claims that this decorous approach to Powhatan has led to a different outcome: the chief loses all respect for the English, viewing them as subjects to his power. Though they might have placated him for the moment, Newport's gifts, courtesy, and deference have only diminished the English. According to Smith, this loss of diplomatic standing has had dire consequences. While Powhatan and his many lieutenants nod and accept English gifts, they also plan ambushes and violent assaults on Jamestown. "[A]ll the woods were laid with Ambuscadoes to the number of 3 or 400 Salvages," Smith continues, "commaunded to betray us, by *Powhatans* direction."[39] Far from sticking to the diplomatic script like Archer's "Powatah," Smith's Powhatan embraces political tactics akin to those of Machiavelli's *Prince*: cloying in official ceremonies, he is not hesitant to betray allies when it suits him.[40]

Like Archer before him, Smith writes about treaties in order to make an argument about New World possessions. He seeks to show how different models of diplomacy produce different kinds of political outcomes. But Smith's portrayal of New World negotiation diverges sharply from Archer's. Official ceremonies and staged meetings do little to create treaties or secure consent. The real struggles unfold outside the venues of official diplomacy, where promises are broken and peace betrayed. Inviting the English to parley, Powhatan plans in secret to murder them. However, in spite of Powhatan's violent intentions, Smith and the other authors of the *Proceedings* do not abandon the legal strategy of asserting English rights through voluntary agreement. Instead, they describe a different way of accomplishing that end. Throughout the book, Smith launches ambushes of his own, "curb[ing]" the Indians' "insolencies" and eventually bringing them back to the bargaining table where a stronger peace, one based on mutually assured destruction, takes hold.[41] If the English are to wield authority in the New World, Smith suggests, they must set aside the "stately kinde of soliciting" for white-knuckle tactics that mirror the Indians' own.[42] An answering threat of force, rather than diplomatic politesse, wins the day.

Printed at Oxford, *The Proceedings* was pieced together from Smith's own writings and from those of soldiers and secretaries who had accompanied him on trading voyages. The book was admittedly rough. Its editor, Thomas Abbay, apologized for the "false orthography or broken English" of its soldier authors.[43] Yet the book also deviated from previous accounts of American diplomacy in another way. It depicted not civility, but threats; not friends, but enemies; not easy subjection, but rather the violent suppression of Indian revolt. Why did the book's authors and editors, many of whom had a financial stake in the colony's success, make public a story that departed so profoundly from the Jamestown leaders' carefully cultivated image as benevolent ambassadors to Virginia Indians?

The answer to this question lies in a series of events that transpired after the events documented in Archer's "Relatyon." After the arrival of Archer's letter, the Virginia Council of London received many reports that seemed to contradict his politic account of Indian diplomacy, and to suggest that Virginia was headed the way of Roanoke. The colony's first presidents were deposed under a cloud of controversy, and its food stores proved inadequate, leading to mass starvation and reports of cannibalism.[44] The ill-advised attempt to crown Powhatan did nothing to help diplomatic relations, and was followed by a bloody war between camps, known to historians as the First Anglo-Powhatan War.[45] In response to such news, James I issued a second charter, giving more control to the colony's investors in London. The colony's governing council immediately appointed a new governor, Thomas West (3rd Baron De La Warr), and new deputies, George Percy, Sir Thomas Dale, and Sir Thomas Gates (the last of whom arrived in the colony after being shipwrecked on Bermuda).[46] The council also instituted stricter laws in the hopes of restoring order and making the colony profitable. Finally, they implemented a new approach to diplomacy; rather than entreating Powhatan, the colonists would attack him, explaining themselves with the doctrine of just war, which held that it was lawful to make war against a sovereign who impeded natural commerce or committed acts of aggression against well-intentioned visitors. Claiming that "there is no trust to the fidelitie of humane beasts, except a man will make a league, with Lions, Beares, and Crocodiles," a 1610 company publication stated that Powhatans had "violated the lawe of nations, and used our Ambassadors as *Ammon* did the servants of *David*," making the Indian king a lawful target of war.[47] However, despite this drastic change of plan, the Virginia Company did not abandon voluntary alliances as a way of possessing territory. Instead of offering treaties to Powhatan, they shifted their diplomatic efforts to the periphery of Tsenacomoco, hoping to turn Powhatan's more restless subjects against him. "If you make freindeship with any of these nations, as you must doe," their 1609 "Instructions" to Gates commanded, "Choose to doe it with those that are farthest from you and enemies unto [the Powhatans] amonge whom you dwell."[48] Armed with these justifications, and a new plan for making treaties beyond Powhatan's territory, the colonists attacked and defeated their Paspahegh neighbors, Powhatan's allies, and embarked upon diplomatic missions to the Patawomecks and other groups living on the periphery of Tsenacomoco.

The downturn in the colony's fortunes was accompanied by hurried transatlantic correspondence, as various parties scrambled to show their cooperation with the new policy. While company leaders had initially wanted to keep the issue of Indian rights out of their direct correspondence with the Spanish, believing they would be no match for Spanish jurists schooled in the law of nations, the outbreak of war with the Powhatans brought the question of the colony's legitimacy out into the open.[49] John Smith was among the first to capitalize on the controversy over the colony's legal standing. A disgraced former president of the colony, Smith had attended many of the early diplomatic conferences with Powhatan. Smith had also been in charge of trade relations with tribal polities. From 1607 until his departure from the colony in 1609, Smith conducted three food raids that were notable for their brutality.[50] One observer compared Smith's aggressive attempts to extort food from Indians to the violence that Spanish conquistadors had brought to the search for El Dorado a century earlier. "The Spanyard never more greedily desired gold then [Smith] victuall," he wrote (partly inspired by Spanish narratives, Smith approvingly printed the statement in the *Proceedings*).[51] Many Powhatan-affiliated groups responded to Smith in more than kind; on one voyage, Smith was kidnapped and held for several weeks before his release, a mercy he would later credit to the smitten pleading of Powhatan's daughter Pocahontas.[52] Smith also claimed that Powhatan had adopted him as a symbolic son in treaty negotiations that occurred while Smith was in captivity.[53] But while later the stuff of print romance, these incidents alarmed many in Jamestown, who feared not only for their lives but also for the precarious diplomatic arrangements on which their claims to possession depended. While the colony increasingly came to rely on the foodstuffs Smith acquired on his raids, some in colonial government accused him of being a "peace-breaker" whose violent tactics would undo Newport's careful diplomacy and expose the colony to assault from Indians or Spanish fleets.[54] Smith countered that the colony's government was foolish to believe Powhatan's commitment to peace. Smith's embrace of warfare indirectly led to his departure. In late summer or early fall 1609, he was severely burned while experimenting with gunpowder aboard a barge, and his enemies in colonial government seized on his momentary incapacitation to ship him back to England.[55]

The dispute over Smith's diplomatic tactics might have died in Virginia. However, the transatlantic controversy over the colony's policies gave him a way of intervening from London. As a discredited and physically crippled leader of a venture that had failed to produce any return for its investors, Smith possessed little credibility among metropolitan councilors. But he did have one asset: his Indian papers and those of the soldiers who had accompanied him on trading missions. Like Smith's negotiating tactics themselves, these documents skirted the edges of legality; the company charter included statutes forbidding the shipment of unauthorized writing across the Atlantic.[56] As the colony's fortunes took a turn for the worse, however, letters, reports, and narratives by various pens began to find their way to London. This flow of ink and information presented the colony with a public relations problem. Few of the letters reflected the kinds of glowing descriptions that Archer and others had sent home during the colony's first years. One way the company responded was by censoring or editing damaging reports. Indeed, a critical letter by Smith himself was heavily redacted and published anonymously under the title *A True Relation of such occurrences and accidents of noate as hath hapned in Virginia* (1608).[57] The company also printed a series of reports, tracts, and sermons that reassured investors of its eventual prosperity.[58]

While the company saw increased transatlantic correspondence as a threat, Smith saw it as an opportunity for rejoining the debate about Virginia's future, only this time from a position much closer to the center of power. In 1612, Smith brought into print *A Map of Virginia* and *The Proceedings of the English Colonie in Virginia* on the press at Oxford. Smith's choice of print as a medium reflected his marginal position in colonial politics. Councilors were occupied with the new government, and were not particularly interested in Smith's perspective. Yet by printing his work, Smith ensured that a wide variety of people, from potential investors to European diplomats, would read it. The books defend Smith's reputation, and blame his opponents for the colony's collapse. However, in making his case, both volumes largely sidestep colonial squabbles. Smith directs his attention instead to the colony's diplomatic relations with the Powhatans. The books document how Powhatan takes advantage of Newport's diplomatic gullibility in order to drive up corn prices, ambush the colony's traders, and subject Jamestown to Powhatan authority. The only solution to the problems in Virginia, Smith suggests, is to wage war against the Powhatan chiefdom. Crucially, however, Smith avoids depicting actual violence. He suggests instead that ambushes, threats, and bullying will persuade the Indians to acquiesce, leading to a peace that Newport's "stately kinde of soliciting" has failed to achieve.

The story of how Smith's two books found their way to the press at Oxford offers a vivid illustration of how cross-cultural negotiations in America could create political opportunities in London.[59] While the company had no interest in publishing his work, Smith found a sympathetic ear in Sir Edward Seymour, the earl of Hertford and an investor in the colony. With Seymour's financial support, Smith began to assemble maps, notes, and other materials that would support his account of the colony's first years. Crucial to Smith's efforts was the arrival from Jamestown of Richard Pots, the clerk of the Virginia colony's governing council during Smith's presidency. Pots brought with him a host of letters, narratives, and sketches from Smith's supporters. With the help of William Symonds, an Oxford graduate and Anglican preacher, Smith arranged the materials into separate volumes, *A Map of Virginia*, containing an engraved map of Tsenacomoco by the artist William Hole, along with a "a description of the countrey" by Smith himself, and *The Proceedings of the English Colonie in Virginia*, a report on the colony's Indian diplomacy "written out of the writings" of "diligent observers."[60] Both books trace the problems in the colony's government to its leaders' overly ceremonious approach to Indian diplomacy. The two volumes might be read as working together, with Smith's *Map* and description laying out the political landscape of Tsenacomoco, and the *Proceedings* showing just how badly Newport, Archer, and the colony's first governors have misjudged the Indians' intentions. Yet for all of its condemnation of the Powhatans and their tactics, the books suggest a surprising solution to the colony's diplomatic dilemma. While the Indians are depicted as violent peace breakers, Smith claims that it is only by abandoning diplomacy themselves that the colony's governors can restore calm.

Like Archer's "Relatyon," Smith's *Map* conceives of Virginia Indians as an autonomous kingdom. The book is divided into several parts, including a list of phrases in English and Algonquian, a map of Tsenacomoco, and Smith's descriptions of the Virginia landscape and the government and religion of the Indians. The centerpiece of the book, and the section that has received the most attention from scholars, is the map, which is bound into the book as a foldout page (see Figure 2). In many ways, the map dominates the volume, in terms of both its massive size and its level of detail. It is bewilderingly complete, containing hundreds of place-names in transliterated Algonquian. Many of these are identified by a key in the upper right-hand corner as "Kings howses," or seats of government. Indeed, the map presents the New World as virtually swarming with Native power, with around two dozen separate locations marked as seats of indigenous kings. Taken in at a glance, the map suggests Native dominance of American geography.

The map leaves no uncertainty about who commands this kingdom. Powhatan is depicted sitting in "state" in an inset in the upper left-hand corner, with the word "Powhatans" snaking downward across the rivers and their many polities. In the opposite corner stands a figure identified as one of the "Sasquesahanugh," a group of neighboring Indians to the north. The corner detail of Powhatan in state was adapted from Theodor de Bry's *The Tombe of their Werowans or Cheiff Lordes* (1588).[61] The appropriation of an image of a tomb to depict Powhatan hints at some of the arguments that will appear later in the book. While Powhatan clearly reigns supreme, he is also boxed in, surrounded by plumes of smoke and crowded by underlings. His figure stands in stark contrast to that of the Susquehannock, who stands astride the landscape itself and is described on the map as representing "a Gyant like people."[62] The suggestion, conveyed in visual form, is that Powhatan operates behind closed doors. While he controls the landscape, he does so from a covert position, not through the kind of open or transparent diplomacy that would inspire trust.

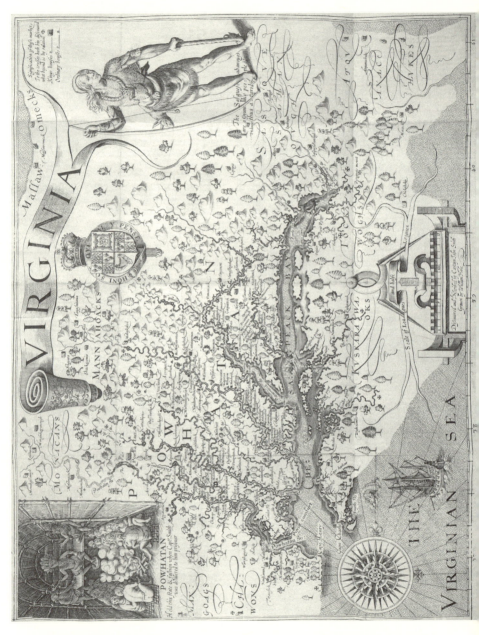

Figure 2. Foldout map from John Smith's *A Map of Virginia* (1612). Smith's map depicts a New World dominated by Powhatan power. Courtesy of The Newberry Library.

Smith's "Description," which follows the foldout, delves into the smoke-shadowed workings of Powhatan's government. Smith begins conventionally enough, sketching out the landscape and discoursing on the natural commodities that make Virginia a profitable site for settlement. But this promotional language soon shifts into a discourse on the Indians and their "manner of . . . governement." Smith uses the language of political economy when describing the Indians. "The forme of their Common wealth is a monarchicall governement," he states, "one as Emperour ruleth over many kings or governours." And though barbaric, Powhatan is similar to an expansion-minded European prince. "Their chiefe ruler is called *Powhatan*, and taketh his name of the principall place of dwelling called *Powhatan*," Smith writes. Like his European counterparts, Powhatan has several claims to power. "Some countries he hath which have been his ancestors, and came unto him by inheritance." Others, however, "have beene his severall conquests." Smith depicts all of these holdings, inherited or conquered, as a peaceful realm, subject to the sovereignty of Powhatan. "Although the countrie people be very barbarous, yet have they amongst them such governement, as that their Magistrats for good commanding, and their people for du subjection, and obeying, excell many places that would be counted very civill."[63] While the people may be unusual in appearance, in their government they more resemble Europeans than savages.

While Powhatan's kingdom appears orderly, however, there is a darker reality just below the surface. What holds this commonwealth together, Smith reports, is fear of Powhatan's tyranny. Here, the Powhatan of the smoky room makes his appearance. "It is strange to see with what great feare and adoration all these people doe obay this *Powhatan*," Smith writes. "What he commandeth they dare not disobey in the least thing."[64] Powhatan is depicted imposing severe penalties on disloyal subjects, executing them or expelling them from his lands. Smith does not describe these exercises of power because he is concerned for Powhatan's victims. Rather, he is interested in their implications for English conquest. While Powhatan's terrifying command creates domestic order, it leads to a volatile political situation abroad. Smith's description of Powhatan's foreign affairs includes a catalogue of the "many enimies" that encircle his empire.[65] This observation aligns Smith's own views with the strategy recently expressed in the "Instructions" to Gates. The suggestion, subtly conveyed, is that the English can undermine Powhatan by making treaties with tribes that oppose him.

While war is the order of the day among the Powhatans, the reality of New World combat differs radically from what European readers might expect. War is not separate from diplomacy, but is itself a diplomatic tactic, a way of pressuring other parties for favorable terms. When engaging with foreign leaders, Smith continues, the Powhatans do not hesitate to employ "Stratagems, trecheries, or surprisals."[66] Most prominent is a military tactic Smith calls "Ambuscado." *Ambuscado*, or ambush, was not a Powhatan word or concept. In early modern military theory, the term described the use of surprise or deception to gain a military advantage. Smith likely encountered the concept during his military training in the Netherlands, where he had served before traveling to Virginia. In *The Theorike and Practike of Moderne Warres* (1598), Robert Barrett defined "Ambuscado" as "a Spanish word" that "signifieth any troupe or company of soldiers either foot or horse, lodged secretly in some covert, as in woods, hollow wayes, behind bankes, or such like." It could also mean "to entrappe the enemy secretly attending his comming."[67] Many authorities depicted *ambuscado* as a violation of natural law.[68] The term was frequently associated with the military tactics of Turks and Ottomans.[69] It was also associated with the Irish, who were viewed by Elizabethan military commanders as unfair fighters.[70] In his *Map*, Smith employs the concept in a similar way. Powhatan's acts of ambush stand in violation of the laws of war and expose the Native king to lawful conquest by invaders. But Smith also adapts the concept of *ambuscado* to his own purposes. Powhatan's lawless acts encourage his subjects to make alliances with the colonists, and give the English legal clearance to launch ambushes of their own.

According to Smith, ambush is universal in Virginia. Americans are virtually built for surprise attack. "They are very strong, of an able body and full of agilitie," he writes, "able to endure to lie in the woods under a tree by the fire, in the worst of winter, or in the weedes and grasse, in *Ambuscado* in the Sommer."[71] Ambushing is not only part of war, however. It is also a tactic Powhatan uses to surprise ostensible allies at treaty negotiations. Smith relates a cautionary tale of Powhatan's willingness to launch surprise attacks against friends: "In the yeare 1608, [Powhatan] surprised the people of *Payankatank* his neare neighbours and subjects. The occasion was to us unknowne, but the manner was thus. First he sent diverse of his men as to lodge amongst them that night, then the *Ambuscadoes* invironed al their houses, & at the houre appointed, they all fell to the spoile, 24 men they slewe." These are not the kindly Indians described by Archer. They visit Payankatank on a diplomatic errand, yet when night falls, Powhatan takes advantage of his hosts' hospitality to slay them and take their land. At his next parley with the English, Powhatan brandishes his grisly spoils to gain an advantage at the bargaining table. "The lockes of haire with their skinnes he hanged on a line unto two trees," Smith writes. "And thus he made

ostentation of as great a triumph at *Werowocomoco*, shewing them to the E[n]
glish men that then came unto him at his appointment, they expecting provision, he to betray them, supposed to halfe counquer them by this spectacle."[72]
Collecting scalps at one meeting, Powhatan brandishes them at the next, using
his conquest of one neighbor to try and cow another into submission.

Throughout *A Map*, Smith laments the "terrible crueltie" of such acts.[73]
However, Smith also sees the violent nature of Virginia diplomacy as offering an
opportunity for the English conquerors, if only the colonial government will abandon any pretense of recognizing Powhatan and instead seek out alliances with his
enemies. Of the effect of Powhatan's reign of diplomatic terror, Smith writes, "The
Sasquesahanocks, the *Tockwoughes* are continually tormented by [the Powhatans]:
of whose crueltie, they generally complained, and very importunate they were
with Captaine *Smith* and his company to free them from these tormentors." The
Indians flee into the arms of the English, "offer[ing] food, conduct, assistance, &
continuall subjection." However, the colony's official policy stands in Smith's way.
Clinging to an older model of diplomacy, the Jamestown governors "would not
thinke it fit to spare [Smith] 40 men," Smith complains.[74] Nevertheless, Smith
soldiers on, enjoying a partial triumph. "I lost but 7 or 8 men," Smith writes at the
close of *A Map*, "yet subjected the Savages to our desired obedience, and receaved
contribution from 35 of their kings, to protect and assist the[m] against any that
should assalt them, in which order they continued true & faithful, and as subjects
to his Majestie, so long after as I did govern there, untill I left the Country."[75] Powhatan's tactics, though awful to behold, give the English an unlikely diplomatic
opening. While he intimidates the newcomers, he also alienates his own subjects,
pushing them into the arms of the newcomers. With only a small number of men,
Smith forms the lasting league that has so eluded Newport, making the Indians
"true & faithful" friends of the English, at least until Smith's untimely departure.

In the *Proceedings*, Smith offers a more detailed account of his treaty-making
strategy. The book picks up where its companion volume leaves off, describing
"how [the Indians] have revolted, the Countrie lost, and againe replanted, and
the businesses hath succeeded from time to time."[76] The *Proceedings* might be
described as offering a narrative accompaniment to the *Map*'s ethnographic portrayal of Powhatan's warlike ways. Powhatan is again a villain. However, as sinister as he is, he is not the book's true target. The book is instead an indictment
of the colony's government during its first years. It blames the colony's problems
on Newport's diplomatic approach to Powhatan, arguing that Newport's overly
solicitous diplomacy has led to the colony's collapse and the subjection of its lead-

ers to an emboldened Powhatan. In place of this failed policy, Smith presents a model of treaty making based around retaliatory ambushes and kidnappings, which he claims will induce the Powhatans to treaty in good faith.

In choosing to title the book the *Proceedings*, Smith and the editors identified their volume with a familiar generic tradition. The English crown printed proceedings of Parliament and other bodies in order to legitimize its own actions and publicize the business of English government to international readers.[77] Aristocratic houses, joint-stock companies, and churches also published accounts of their proceedings in order to raise funds or inspire supporters or adherents.[78] Proceedings were often a compilation of different genres, such as speeches, accounts of battles, official documents, and other scribal forms. Often, published proceedings offered an apology for apparent mismanagement of government affairs. Thomas Digges's *A Breife and true report of the Proceedings of the Earle of Leycester* (1590), for example, described the battle for the town of Sluce in the Eighty Years' War (1568–1648), in an attempt to show that Sir Robert Dudley "was not in anie fault for the losse of that towne."[79] While military leaders or other interest groups often explained their conduct to the king in relations or letters, printed proceedings offered a means of publicizing political business for readers at home and abroad.

Like Digges's book, *The Proceedings of the English Colonie in Virginia* is concerned with apologizing for overseas failure. As the preface announces, "Long hath the world longed, but to be truely satisfied what Virginia is, with the truth of those proceedings, from whence hath flowne so manie reports of worth, & yet few good effects of the charge, which hath caused suspition in many well willers."[80] The book includes dramatic renderings of a number of government rituals, such as speeches, meetings, coronations, and depositions. It also includes "the Salvages discourses, orations and relations of the Bordering neighbors, and how they became subject to the English." However, these political performances are not cast into the stately forms of Archer's "Relatyon." The volume presents, not official documentation of treaty negotiations, but rather accounts by "diligent observers, that were residents in Virginia."[81] The book might be described as an exposé of colonial government. While Archer views Anglo-Powhatan diplomatic rituals as producing political amity in a transparent and verifiable way, the *Proceedings* seeks to expose the failure of official diplomacy. Rather than taking Indian words and gestures at face value, Smith suggests that coastal politics demands a shrewder understanding of Native communication and a willingness to use violence.

From the beginning, the *Proceedings* draws a connection between Smith's colonial feuds and his fight to subdue the frontier. On the voyage over, Smith is "restrained as a prisoner" when Newport accuses him of intending to "usurpe the governement."[82] From his position as a captive, Smith observes the suspiciously "kindly" visitations of the "Salvages," and advises Newport to prepare for an attack. While Newport ignores him and instead pursues diplomatic outreach, Smith is soon proved right. When the discovery party begins to explore the area around the Jamestown fort, they find themselves "kindly intreated" by the Indians, just as Archer had reported in his "Relatyon."[83] Yet on their return, Smith writes, they find "17 men hurt, and a boy slaine by the Salvages." In his report, Archer had attempted to dismiss this attack as an aberration, but the *Proceedings* hints instead at a causal connection between Newport's diplomatic errand and the Indians' sudden aggression. Embracing friendly diplomacy, Newport leaves the colony exposed. After this incident, Newport can no longer deny the Indians' belligerence, and finally heeds Smith's advice. "Hereupon," Smith gloats, "the President was contented the Fort should be pallisadoed ... for many were the assaults, and Ambuscadoes of the Salvages."[84]

In the midst of these troubling events, Smith appears as the only figure who can subdue the Indians. After the intervention of the colony's minister, Robert Hunt, Smith is unchained and "reconciled" with Newport. The Indians, violent before, immediately seek out a treaty agreement: "the good doctrine and exhortation of our preacher Mr. *Hunt* ... caused Captaine *Smith* to be admitted of the Councell; the next day all received the Communion, the day following the Salvages voluntarily desired peace, and Captaine *Newport* returned for England with newes."[85] This narrative implies a causal link between Smith's promotion to the council and the Indians' willingness to make a treaty with the English. Smith's hard-nosed approach, not Newport's diplomacy, is the reason for the successful conclusion of any treaties.

While there is some overlap between the *Proceedings* and the events recounted in Archer's "Relatyon," the bulk of Smith's books details what happens after Archer's letter ends. The *Proceedings* charts, in troubling detail, the breakdown of Anglo-Powhatan diplomacy and the disintegration of peace, and it seeks to pin the blame on Newport and his negotiating strategies. While Smith criticizes many aspects of Virginia's government, he attributes its woeful state of affairs primarily to the fact that Newport and his group have made too many concessions to Powhatan's demands. "[T]hose at the fort so glutted the Salvages with their commodities," the book complains, "as they [the colonists] became not regarded."[86] Smith did not invent this explanation for the colony's trouble. The notion that the colonists lost political standing by paying tribute to the Powhatans was widely repeated, even appearing in the 1609 "Instructions" to Gates, which (without naming Newport) partly blamed trading policy for the high corn prices that had imperiled the food supply.[87] The accusation probably had some truth to it. While gifts played a largely ceremonial role in European diplomatic negotiations, for the Powhatans, trade was crucial to determining political hierarchy. When the English arrived in the Chesapeake Bay, the Powhatans demanded gifts in exchange for corn and permission to settle. Jamestown leaders complied with these demands, and in writing described the Indians' acceptance of goods as an acknowledgment of English power. This made the English look powerful under the law of nations, but according to Smith, it lowered them in Powhatan's regard. In a description of Powhatan's trading with Jamestown leaders, Smith illustrates the pitfalls of Newport's approach: "being kindly received ashore" for a trading summit, "*Powhatan* strained himselfe to the uttermost of his greatnes to entertain us, with great shouts of Joy, orations of protestations, and the most plenty of victuall hee could provide to feast us."[88] After "3. or 4. daies" of "feasting dancing and trading," Powhatan initiates official trade relations between Werowocomoco and Jamestown, beginning with a formal oration that suggests that coastal rather than English customs should govern negotiations. "Captain *Newport*," he says, "it is not agreeable with my greatnis in this pedling manner to trade for trifles, and I esteeme you a great *werowans*, Therefore lay me down all your commodities togither, what I like I will take, and in recompence give you that I thinke fitting their value."[89] Powhatan dismisses English models of exchange as a "pedling" way to proceed. Instead, he flatteringly suggests that a great leader like Newport should trust the great chief to do the valuing himself. Powhatan's words evoke what the anthropologist Marcel Mauss has described as a gift economy, in which extravagant exchange symbolizes power and recognition.[90] Smith, however, does not believe that Powhatan's gesture is reflective of any traditional Indian ways. He sees Powhatan's oration as a ploy to raise prices and conquer the English. Smith warns Newport of the stratagem, whispering in his ear that the hidden intention behind Powhatan's grandiose gesture is "but to cheat us." To Smith's horror, Newport falls for it anyway, caught up in the imperative to flatter Powhatan with gifts: "captaine *Newport* thinking to out brave this Salvage in ostentation of greatnes, & so to bewitch him with his bounty . . . [offered] to have what [Powhatan] listed."[91]

At this moment, according to Smith, the colony teeters on the brink of disaster, standing to lose both financially and politically if the trading goes forward. As he did after the raid on Jamestown, however, Smith comes to the rescue, bringing to bear another approach to diplomacy, one more attuned to the subtlety of Powhatan's maneuvers. "*Smith* . . . smothering his distast (to avoide the Salvages suspicion) glaunced in the eies of *Powhatan* many Trifles who fixed his humour upon a few blew beads; A long time he importunatly desired them, but *Smith* seemed so much the more to affect them, so that ere we departed, for a pound or two of blew beads he brought over my king for 2 or 300 bushels of corne, yet parted good friends."[92] Here, then, is a radically different negotiating tactic. Rather than taking Powhatan's words at face value, Smith reads Powhatan's eyes to discover the true desire behind the façade—the shiny blue beads imported from English glassworks for use as currency. With the colonists' blue beads glinting in Powhatan's eyes, Smith moves to "affect them" himself, driving up their value despite their practical worthlessness to the English. Taken in by this ploy, Powhatan happily agrees to give up corn for beads, securing for the English a triumph of both trade and diplomacy.

While Archer construes Native actions as a transparent expression of political intentions, for Smith, words and gestures hide as much as they reveal. Smith's account of glinting eyes and feinting gestures evoked broader debates in early modern England about the relationship between outward expression and inner intentions. While some scholastic authorities believed that gestures and facial expressions unwittingly revealed the truth of the heart, others saw them as possessing a capacity for artifice and deceit.[93] In contrast to Archer's model of diplomacy, which simply assumes the Indians are sincere, Smith points to a split between outward show and secret purpose.

Smith's diplomacy of suspicion prevails during trade negotiations, preserving the peace and a precarious equality between parties. Yet by his own account, Smith's approach also has limits, especially considering the ulterior goals behind Powhatan's attempts to cheat the English. According to Smith, Powhatan is not only attempting to swindle the colonists at the bargaining table. He is also attempting to subjugate them, and this threat demands a different response. After the botched coronation, which repeats the lesson of the corn-trading episode, Powhatan secretly institutes an embargo against the English, forbidding other people from trading with them. His aim, as Smith later finds out, is to lure the colonists into an ambush disguised as a trading summit. Extending an invitation to trade, Powhatan offers to "loade [Smith's] shippe with corne" in exchange for commodities and the help of Jamestown laborers in building an English-style house.[94] As Smith travels to Werowocomoco, a "kind Salvage" named Weraskoyack tips off the already suspicious Smith about the chief's true plans: "Captaine *Smith*," he warns, "you shall finde *Powhatan* to use you kindly, but trust him not, and bee sure hee have no opportunitie to seaze on your armes, for hee hath sent for you only to cut your throats."[95] As Weraskoyack makes clear, Powhatan aims to treat the English like the people of Payankatank; his diplomatic overtures conceal intentions to kill or enslave them.

In response to this bit of frightening intelligence, Smith suggests that the English ambush the chief themselves before he can put his plans into motion. Over the protests of others, Smith assembles a company of English soldiers disguised as laborers and travels to Pamaunke, the proposed site of the house. What follows in the *Proceedings* is an intricate account of an openly hostile series of negotiations that constantly threaten to dissolve into outright violence. Smith again uses gestural interpretation and facial reading to divine Powhatan's true intentions. However, he also openly embraces violence as a negotiating tactic that will restore order and bring about treaty agreement. Powhatan begins the entertainment with the same invitation to open giving he had extended to Newport. Addressing Smith from inside his old house, he declares, "Captaine *Newport* gave me swords, copper, cloths, a bed, tooles, or what I desired, ever taking what I offered him, and would send awaie his gunnes when I intreated him." At this moment, Powhatan's real desires are exposed to all who know how to read him. The gift he truly wants is not found in any precious object—it is, menacingly, the disarmament of the colonists. Rather than allowing himself to be led to his death by this bit of deception, Smith responds to Powhatan's offer with an ambush of his own: "*Smith* seeing this Salvage but trifled the time to cut his throat . . . gave order for his men to come ashore, to have surprised the king, with whom also [Smith] but trifled the time till his men landed."[96] Smith sees through Powhatan's friendly overtures, and, maintaining decorum, signals to his men to make ready for attack. Yet English victory is not yet in hand. When Powhatan discovers Smith's countermove, he keeps up the façade, sending his wives to make small talk with Smith and slipping out the back while his men encircle the house. This leaves Smith in a bind; while each party has been planning murder behind smiles, Powhatan's men get to the house first.

Smith's response to this predicament dramatizes his central solution to the problem of forming treaties during wartime—a solution he enacts again and again in the latter part of the *Proceedings*. When Smith realizes that Powhatan's plan has been sprung into motion before his own, he recovers the initiative by storming out of the house "with his Pistol, Sword & Target" while the Indian men flee in every direction. This abrupt move has an immediately pacifying effect. After Smith's wild display, the Indians immediately "dissemble" their treacherous intentions and send Smith "a great bracelet, and a chaine of pearle," valuable diplomatic gifts recognizing Smith's power.[97] More important from Smith's point of view, they satisfy his demands for corn, offering him as much as he can carry back to Jamestown. This violent rapprochement is not a perfect solution. After conceding to Smith's demands, the Indians suggest again that the soldiers put their guns down to carry the baskets to the barges. However, the English threateningly cock their weapons, frightening the Indians back into submission. "[T]he verie sight of cocking our matches against them," Smith writes," caused them to leave their bowes & arrows to our gard, and beare downe our corne on their own backes."[98] While Powhatan had planned to trick the English into putting their weapons down so he could cut their throats, Smith's violent bluffing compels the Indians to load their corn on English barges. The flow of tributary goods is reversed, and with it, the relation of authority.

Smith is well aware that this strategy poses a legal problem. The colony's international legitimacy hinged in part upon voluntary treaties. Smith's actions more resemble those of the Spanish conquistadors of the Black Legend—the very image many metropolitan supporters of colonization wanted to avoid. Later in the narrative, Smith seeks to distinguish his own brand of violence from that of the Spanish and to show that his actions are consistent with the legal strategy of proving possession through treaties. After sacking Werowocomoco, Smith heads upriver toward the kingdom of the sachem Opechancanough, Powhatan's brother. The king greets them with the "strained cheerefulnes" Smith believes is typical of Powhatan diplomacy, and Smith finds himself in the familiar position of a target of ambush, with "6. Or 700. of well appointed Indians [having] invironed the house and beset the fields."[99] This time, however, Smith's thoughts concern not his immediate danger but rather the question of how an international audience will react when news of his violent entanglements finds its way across the Atlantic. Smith delivers a "speech to his company" on the international legal predicament in which they have found themselves. "Worthy countrymen," he says, "were the mischiefes of my seeming friends [the colony's governing council], no more then the danger of these enemies, I little cared, were they as many more, if you dare do, but as I. But this is my torment, that if I escape them, our malicious councell with their open mouthed minions, will make mee such a peace-breaker (in their opinions) in England, as wil break my neck"[100] Even before violence is joined, Smith is acutely conscious that the moment will be recounted in transatlantic correspondence. Indeed, his "greater torment" is not the sting of Indian arrows but rather the knowledge that he will be drowned out in transatlantic space by the "open mouthed minions" who dominate the colony's correspondence with the London Council. If Smith takes Opechancanough's friendly overtures at face value, as Newport did, the party will be massacred, clinging to their stately diplomatic protocols while the Indians fall upon them. Yet if Smith fights his way out, he will be construed as a "peace-breaker" and hanged for treason.

As in the earlier escape from ambush, Smith's solution is found in an abrupt and violent violation of diplomatic courtesy—this time, the kidnapping of Opechancanough. Smith "snatche[s] the king by his vambrace [or armor] in the midst of his men, with his pistoll ready bent against his brest: thus he [leads] the trembling king, (neare dead with feare) amongst all his people, who delivering the Captaine his bow and arrowes, all his men were easily intreated to cast downe their armes."[101] Like the previous outburst among Powhatan's men, this sudden and unpredictable gesture leads to an improbably swift resolution of the colony's diplomatic problems. After Smith releases Opechancanough into the custody of the terrified Powhatan retinue, "The rest of the day [is] spent with much kindnesse. . . . And what soever we gave them, they seemed well contented with it."[102] Though the kidnapping is a violation of the terms of the old peace, it intimidates the Indians into embracing a new one, based on their willing acceptance of English demands. And though Smith breaks the peace by laying hands on Opechancanough, his actions create peaceful subjection without spilling any blood.

Smith was right to believe that the moment would find an audience in London and beyond. After *The Proceedings* was published, the kidnapping acquired some degree of folk prominence among readers in Europe. It was engraved by Robert Vaughan, and Smith later printed the engraving in his heavily embellished *The Generall Historie of Virginia, New-England, and the Summer Isles* (1624) (see Figure 3). The image hearkened back to stories of Spanish conquistadors kidnapping Indian kings.[103] However, in the *Proceedings*, Smith carefully severs it from any association with lethal force. He is a conquistador without the killing. Indeed, Smith invites readers to compare his own narrative to those of Spanish conquest, emphasizing his ability to do without bloodshed what Spanish conquerors had carried out with great violence. "[P]eruse the Spanish Decades, the relations of *M. Hacklut,*" he directs readers "and tell mee how many ever with such smal meanes, as a barge of 2 Tunnes; sometimes with 7. 8. 9, or but at most 15 men did ever discover so many faire and navigable rivers; subject so many severall kings, people, and nations, to obedience, & contribution with so little bloud shed."[104] Smith's conquests are comparable in scope to those of the Spanish, yet they involve none of the actual bloodletting that (according to English propagandists) had made Spanish conquest unlawful.

C. Smith taketh the King of Pamavnkee prisoner 1608

Figure 3. Robert Vaughan's engraving of John Smith kidnapping Opechancanough, from John Smith, *The Generall Historie of Virginia, New-England, and the Summer Isles* (1624). Courtesy of The Newberry Library.

When words fail to guarantee peaceful intentions, the threat of violence paradoxically creates the calm political order that diplomacy cannot. In the wake of the disasters brought on by Newport's stately overtures to Powhatan, Smith's confrontational tactics pacify the Indians. But if Archer is worried about the credibility of Native words and gestures for international readers, Smith faces a problem of his own. If violence, or the threat of violence, inspires agreement, how are readers to know that such agreement is any more sincere than the false promises that led to violence in the first place? Smith's model of treaty making seems to lead to an infinite regress, with broken promises begetting only more violence. Smith addresses this problem in a culminating chapter entitled "How the Salvages became subject to the English." The chapter describes how Smith unravels a Dutch conspiracy against Jamestown while simultaneously bringing Indians to treaty through threats. The ultimate effect of violence, in Smith's account, is not simply to produce fearful acquiescence, but rather to inspire the kind of credible promises necessary for *consensus ad idem*. After discovering the betrayal of the English by the Dutch and their Indian co-conspirators, Smith explodes into action with typical decisiveness. He "burn[s] their houses, [takes] their boats . . . and . . . resolve[s] not to cease till he had revenged himselfe upon al that had injured him." As in previous encounters, the Indians "thr[ow] downe their armes and desir[e] peace" in the face of Smith's hectic peace-breaking.[105] This time, however, the concession leads to a treaty that satisfies the criteria of *consensus ad idem*. An Indian orator named Ocanindge steps forward to deliver what the narrative calls a "worthie discourse." Ocanindge notes Smith's destructive intentions. "[W]e perceive & well knowe you intend to destroy us," he says. But Ocanindge also turns the tables, reminding Smith that the Indians can destroy the English as well: "we can plant any where . . . and we know you cannot live if you want our harvest." This threat leads to an offer of truce backed up not by ceremonial gestures, such as the exchange of gifts, but rather by a recognition of the mutually assured destruction the two camps can visit upon one another: "if you promise us peace we will beleeve you, if you proceed in reveng, we will abandon the Countrie," Ocanindge declares. Smith is impressed by this geopolitical reasoning, and the English and Indians come to an agreement: "Upon these tearmes the President promised them peace, till they did us injurie, upon condition they should bring in provision, so all departed good friends."[106] Smith will agree not to destroy the Indians (and, by implication, himself) if the Indians will continue to bring the English provisions. A treaty at last.

In practice, the compelled promise that ends the *Proceedings* seems little different from the acts of extortion Smith carried out earlier. But here extortion is formalized by a verbal agreement that has real force. The two parties promise each other, and this time, because of the threat that lurks behind their words, the promise is real. As well as compelling submission, violence ironically produces the truth in speech necessary for treaties. Smith and Ocanindge can trust each other because they are not bound by superficial norms of engagement that would provide a ceremonial cover for deception. The excessive (and deceptive) courtesy that fills Archer's pages is replaced by mutually assured destruction and the paradoxically honest agreements that follow from it. Smith's book concludes with a triumphant image: Powhatan and his underlings, cowed into submission, and ready to consent to the newcomers' conditions. In place of diplomacy, Smith offers peace by other means.

Though it described the events of the colony's early years, Smith's bellicose volume answered to the needs of the colony's governing council during a period of doubt about Jamestown's survival. In publishing the book, Smith was not simply attempting to settle old scores. He was joining a debate about the colony's future, and using Indian treaties to position himself as the most capable adventurer to return and lead Virginia. In this, he failed. The colony's London directors were not anxious to entrust its fate to a figure associated with so much controversy, and Smith soon threw in his lot with New England explorers. However, his book was successful in another way. Smith's attempt to reconcile warlike tactics with treaty justifications proved influential within the company, which had need of a way of making war look like peace. The company's directors knew the English were not alone in Jamestown. Travelers and spies from other nations were also there, or possessed illicit access to the colony's transatlantic correspondence, and they too had stories to tell about Native diplomacy.

Shows of Sovereignty: Zúñiga's Correspondence

"I have been amused by the way they honour him," Spanish ambassador Pedro de Zúñiga sardonically reported to Philip III in 1608. Zúñiga was describing the arrival in London of one of Powhatan's sons, "a lad," who had traveled there with Newport to confirm the crown's friendship with Virginia Indians.[107] Of the many signs of alliance exchanged between the Powhatans and English colonists, the boy was the most compelling in the eyes of European onlookers. Named Namontack, he was part of a diplomatic exchange that also included an English boy named Thomas Savage, who was sent to live with the

Powhatans. The exchange had involved disingenuous statements on both sides. Powhatan had told Jamestown governors that Namontack was royalty, and they had told him the same thing about Savage.[108] Both sides were comfortable with such fictions, however. Powhatan stood to gain from the presence of an English boy. He could learn the newcomers' language and pry into their plans. And the Virginia Company was likewise eager to embrace Namontack. By introducing him in London as a foreign prince, they could show diplomats at court that Tsenacomoco was a sovereign nation and that its leaders could offer legal consent to English colonists. To this end, the company outfitted Namontack in copper jewelry and presented him to important stakeholders in English colonial endeavors. Yet as with the Jamestown governors' diplomacy in the Chesapeake Bay, these diplomatic performances inspired controversy.[109] For his part, Zúñiga believed none of it. In a letter, he characterizes the entire display as artifice, an act, and bristles at the pretension. "I hold it for surer that he must be a very ordinary person," not a prince at all, Zúñiga concludes.[110]

The presentation of Namontack to London society restaged for a metropolitan audience the same kind of cross-cultural diplomatic rituals that were common in Virginia. It involved a familiar legal strategy: recognize the Indians as royalty so they can bestow legitimacy on the English. Usually, this legal strategy was publicized in writing. This time, however, it was embodied by a Powhatan ambassador, who would perform before James I what Powhatan and others had supposedly enacted before Newport. There were strategic advantages to such direct lobbying. If carried out successfully, Namontack's presentation to the king could demonstrate the colony's powerful coastal alliances for international onlookers at court. When Namontack arrived in London, for example, the ambassador from Venice, Zorzi Giustinian, noted it as a significant political visit, writing that "one of the chief inhabitants" of the New World had arrived "to treat with the King for some agreement about that navigation."[111] Yet Namontack's appearance also involved considerable risk. By bringing the boy to London, the Virginia Company exposed him to the critical eyes of foreign ambassadors. Enemies watched, and they were skeptical of what they saw.

Native treaties were a precarious form of legal evidence; when they held, they could make the English appear powerful, but their potential collapse could call into question the legal standing of settlement ventures. I now seek to examine how Spanish diplomats scrutinized English treaties for evidence that might invalidate English claims. Spain, like other monarchies with New World interests, maintained surreptitious networks of correspondence through various overseas agents who spied on foreign governments and their colonial holdings. These networks included priests, exiles, disaffected English Catholics, and other travelers with an interest in New World projects. After the Anglo-Spanish War, the ranks of such "intelligencers," as the English called them, increasingly came to include diplomats such as Zúñiga, who served officially as overseas representatives but unofficially as clearinghouses of rumors and reports. Zúñiga's letters give some evidence of the kinds of information that came his way from Virginia. He cites depositions from English Catholics, intercepted copies of letters from the English traveler Francis Perkins, and Virginia Company ledgers, as well as his own first-hand observations of the behavior of Powhatan guests at diplomatic receptions in London. At one point, Zúñiga even claims to have a spy on the London Council itself.[112] Here I will consider Zúñiga's letters as a strategic account of Anglo-Powhatan treaties. Like the English authors whose texts he intercepted, Zúñiga had a vested interest in circulating a particular image of Anglo-Powhatan relations. His account of an Indian boy playing prince makes an argument about the conduct of New World diplomacy and about who rightfully owns Virginia. If the English stake possession on the recognition of Native kings, Zúñiga tries to rebuff English claims by denying the royalty of Powhatan's ambassadors. Through this counter-narrative of Anglo-Indian ceremonies, Zúñiga asserts Spanish rights over the New World and the right of Philip III to destroy English outposts. Yet Zúñiga does not simply dismiss the legal strategy of the Virginia Company. He argues instead that the company's various documents and legal rituals, including its treaties with Native people, are bits of theatrical artifice, designed only to disguise the colony's true purpose as a staging ground for piracy against Spanish fleets. Zúñiga accepts the theoretical validity of Native treaties, but attempts to prove, through his own accounts of Anglo-Powhatan negotiations, that Jamestown has not resolved the question of Native consent.

The print publications of Smith and his allies were intended to be as public as possible. Indeed, Smith's future involvement in English colonial ventures largely depended upon reaching potential supporters indirectly through the medium of print. Zúñiga's correspondence, by contrast, was a covert affair. While Zúñiga sent regular dispatches to Philip III, he also composed secret letters. This secret correspondence with Philip III lasted from 1607 until Zúñiga's final return in 1612. The letters touch on a number of issues of state, such as the readiness of the English navy and English intentions in the East Indies. They also touch on trivial matters such as gossip and scandals at court.

Yet the question of the legality of the Virginia Colony is never far from Zúñiga's concerns. From the beginning of his correspondence about the New World, Zúñiga depicts colonization itself as a kind of diplomatic intrigue, a show intended to conceal the English crown's piratical intentions.

In the first letter to deal with Virginia at any length, written in January 1607 shortly after the departure of Newport's first fleet, Zúñiga relays sinister intelligence about the colony, depicting settlement as part of an international conspiracy against Spanish claims. "After I informed your Majesty that the English were equipping some ships to send to Virginia," Zúñiga writes, "the matter was held up a great deal, and now I learn that they have made an agreement, in great secrecy, for two ships to go there every month.... [and] they have agreed with the Rebels [the Dutch] to send what people they can."[113] In citing a conspiracy with "the Rebels," Zúñiga is referring to the English alliance with the Dutch in the Eighty Years' War against the Spanish. Throughout the war, the English crown financially supported the armies of Dutch states and sent English conscripts to help them in the fight against Spain. A number of figures in Virginia had been involved in these efforts, including John Smith.[114] However, while the Anglo-Dutch alliance had been officially ratified in the Treaty of Nonsuch (1585), Zúñiga views it as a conspiracy, and portrays colonization as an extension of a broader, global plot against the Spanish. "The justification they advance is that this King [James I] has given them licence and letters patent for planting their religion there, provided they do not plunder anyone, under pain of losing his protection if they do not obey," Zúñiga writes.[115] While James has widely publicized his rights and dominion in Virginia, Zúñiga views the crown's legal justifications as mere propaganda intended to conceal sinister motives.

Zúñiga's fear that the New World could be a site of conspiratorial alliance is reflective of the kind of paranoia that characterized correspondence from both English and Spanish spies. As Garrett Mattingly has shown in his account of early modern diplomacy, Protestant and Catholic diplomats depicted themselves as soldiers in a global war for religious and national supremacy.[116] Zúñiga reads the colony's accounts of Powhatan negotiations with the same kind of conspiratorial eye, viewing Indian treaties as a maneuver in a worldwide struggle. In a letter dated March 15, 1609, he describes intercepting the colony's correspondence about Indian affairs and collecting information as to its real meaning. "I have also seen a letter written by a gentleman who is there in Virginia to a friend of his who is an acquaintance of mine, and he showed it to me," Zúñiga reports. "It says that he will find out from Captain Newport, the bearer, just what is going on there. . . . He says also that they have deceived the King of that region [Powhatan] with an English boy whom they gave him, saying that he is the son of this King [James I], and he [Powhatan] makes much of him."[117] The letter was most likely a report that detailed the first meeting between Newport and Powhatan. The "English boy" was undoubtedly Thomas Savage.[118] Zúñiga characterizes the whole exchange as a kind of geopolitical charade, a deceptive performance designed to make the Virginia Colony appear legitimate. Like the colony's patents and legal documents, the exchange of boys gives an appearance of legality to a conspiracy against Spanish interests.

Zúñiga likewise portrays Namontack's appearance in court as an act staged for international benefit. In a letter dated June 26, 1608, he describes Namontack's debut in London society. "This Newport brought a lad who they say is the son of an emperor of those lands and they have coached him that when he sees the King he is not to take off his hat, and other things of this sort."[119] The English, Zúñiga concludes, are pretending that Namontack is a prince so they can cite treaties as evidence of their own possession. But Zúñiga also reveals what he believes to be the artifice behind such a strategy—the colonists have coached Namontack to decline to doff his hat before the king. In describing this gesture, Zúñiga was referencing hat honor, an important diplomatic protocol in early modern courts. Like bowing before the king, doffing one's hat was a way of showing submission. Loyal subjects were expected to take off their hats in the presence of kings, or even before an empty throne.[120] However, princes sometimes made a distinction between domestic subjects and visitors. Throughout his reign, James I insisted that foreign dignitaries keep their hats on as a way of recognizing their status as representatives of foreign powers. In 1614, the Russian secretary Alexis Ziuzin reported to Tsar Mikhail I that James had refused to allow Russian ambassadors to take off their hats in his presence. "King James said to the ambassadors that they should put on their hats, and he reminded them about it twice and three times, and by his royal word he strongly insisted on it."[121] In coaching Namontack to keep his hat on in the presence of the king, the company presents him as a visiting ambassador from a foreign power. Namontack's hat, safe on his head, elevates him to the same status as European ambassadors. There is certainly a tragic irony here. By coaching Namontack to keep his hat on, the company seeks to give him the authority to welcome the English to his land.[122] They give him rights so he can give them up. But this is not Zúñiga's criticism. He does not attack the company out of respect for

Namontack or Powhatan sovereignty. Instead, he claims that the wearing of the hat is a mere show intended to deceive onlookers into believing Jamestown has formed alliances with Powhatan leaders. In couching his criticism in this way, Zúñiga stops short of denying Native sovereignty or dominion outright. He does not comment on whether real Indian kings should keep their hats on. He claims instead that Namontack himself is something less than a prince and therefore not qualified to make a treaty.

Zúñiga's silence on the true nature of Native sovereignty had a certain advantage. While the Spanish crown denied the rights of Native kings on the basis of their supposed heresy or lack of intellectual faculties, the Spanish also gained occasional diplomatic advantage from recognizing Native rights and employing arguments like those advanced by the English crown. In a letter of March 15, 1609, Zúñiga takes a page from the English book, voicing his concern for Powhatan welfare: "I understand that once they have fortified themselves well, they will manage to destroy that King [Powhatan] and the savages, so as to take possession of everything."[123] While the English frequently criticized what they believed to be the lawless violence of Spanish conquest, here, Zúñiga ironically applies the same criticism to the English, portraying them as violent conquerors bent on seizing land. Zúñiga's remark illustrates the provisional nature of colonial arguments over Native rights. While the English frequently borrowed from Spanish texts in order to construct hybrid legal arguments, this traffic could occasionally run in the other direction, with Spanish diplomats adopting English frameworks. As the balance of power shifted, so did legal positions about Native rights.

According to Zúñiga, the farcical nature of the crowning of Powhatan boys undercuts the legal rationale of the English crown. Amusing though they may be, such performances provide a cover for mayhem, with the English plotting the murder of their Indian neighbors just as they plan assaults on Spain. With the same letter that describes the English conspiracy against Powhatan, Zúñiga encloses a map that shows English settlements and fortifications.[124] Though the English crown has offered legal rationales for this expansion, Zúñiga warns that the English conquerors are threatening to engulf New Spain after they finish with the Indians. He offers the official recommendation that the colony should meet the same fate as the French Huguenot settlement at Fort Caroline, which had been destroyed by Spanish agents: "Your Majesty should command that this be summarily stopped," Zúñiga urges darkly.[125]

Though Zúñiga pleads for Philip III to act, his letters implicitly concede the

English colonists' position on treaties. Unlike the Spanish ambassadors who negotiated the Treaty of London, Zúñiga does not deny the Powhatans' standing. Rather, he seeks to prove that the English have staged treaty agreements and coached Native people into supplying words and gestures that establish English possession. The English are pacifying coastal people with offers of treaty only to spring violence on them later. By pulling back the curtain on Anglo-Powhatan treaty negotiations, Zúñiga seeks to furnish the Spanish crown with legal arguments for razing Jamestown. Philip III did not act on Zúñiga's recommendations. Zúñiga was replaced by Alonso Velasco in 1610, but returned in 1612 in a failed attempt to arrange a royal marriage. Given Zúñiga's interest in the protocol of hat honor and its meaning for diplomacy, his departure from London was accompanied by an irony. While Zúñiga was crossing Holborn Bridge, he doffed his hat to an approaching cavalier, who snatched it away and galloped off, much to the amusement of onlookers.[126] While the colony struggled during its early years, they no longer had Zúñiga to worry about.

Powhatan's bow, Ocanindge's speech, Namontack's refusal to remove his hat: colonists and diplomats recounted such words and acts in writing in order to support claims to territory. Debates about who had rights to the coast involved competing representations of Powhatan consent. None of the Europeans I have written about so far cared about recognizing the Powhatans in a way consistent with modern understandings of international law. Their letters and reports were entirely strategic, part of a violent struggle over land. The English and their rivals needed the bow, the chiefly oration, and the donning of the hat as support for their claims. But what of Powhatan himself? Somewhere, behind all the letters and printed pages, were the words and gestures that formed the basis for so many conflicting stories. Why did the Powhatan leader agree to make treaties with the English? Europeans made so much of their treaties with him, but what did he do with the objects he received from the newcomers? Can the writings of the colonizers provide an answer to that question?

Crowns and *Manitou*: Treaty Objects in Powhatan Politics

Powhatans and English people made treaties in many ways, offering promises, exchanging gifts, and even resorting to violence to compel agreement. While some of these practices were unfamiliar to Europeans, it was easy for them to imagine analogies between Powhatan acts of tribute and their own rituals. The English shouted their respect for sovereigns, and bowed in the presence of princes, just as the Powhatans seemed to do. However, coastal diplomacy was different from its European counterpart in at least one significant way. While European politics involved many kinds of performances (not to mention a heated traffic in rumors), Europeans nevertheless viewed writing as the most powerful and permanent way of expressing political agreement. To many historians, this fact has seemed to leave Native people at a disadvantage when it comes to treaty negotiations. And there is much truth to this claim. While the speeches of Powhatan and other Indians fill the pages of Smith's books, Powhatan could not read those books or respond to them. But as I will suggest now, this does not mean that he was a passive participant in the debates about territory and sovereignty that occupied Europeans. Nor does it mean that he was necessarily a victim of English treaties.

As I have argued so far, the English did not just establish possession by citing European legal authorities. They also looked to Native acts of consent, which could come in many forms. The English solicited some sign of agreement and then framed it in a way that supported their claims. For them, treaties were primarily about words, gestures, or other acts that showed agreement. As Smith's *Proceedings* shows, however, for the Powhatans, treaties were primarily about acquiring trade goods, such as beads, metal tools, textiles, and decorative items. While the English recorded treaties in writing, the Powhatans symbolized them in objects.

To modern-day readers, these treaty objects have lost much of their legibility. Colonists like Archer cared about Powhatan expressions only to the extent that they confirmed particular visions of English power. They generally omitted any description of what treaties meant to Native people. Smith, for example, portrayed Powhatan as desiring blue beads purely out of a mindless fascination with decorative objects and a treacherous desire to conquer the English. But there are many accounts of treaties from travelers who did not have the interest in law or diplomacy that animated Archer, Smith, or Zúñiga. Ironically, these observers may tell us something about Powhatan precisely because they saw no need to frame his words according to legal imperatives.

One such observer is Henry Spelman, an English interpreter who lived at Tsenacomoco from 1609 to 1611. On his return to England, Spelman drafted a narrative of his time among the Powhatans. An unimportant person from the perspective of the Virginia Colony's government, Spelman was not present at the coronation in October 1608. However, when he arrived home he produced a written report that describes Powhatan's incorporation of an English crown into tribal ceremonies. Spelman's narrative certainly has its own kinds of bias. For example, he goes to great lengths to show that he has retained his Englishness while living among the Indians, whom he depicts as savage. However, though Spelman renders the Powhatans exotic in order to emphasize his difference from them, his account sheds light on the way they may have viewed the English crown and other objects they acquired during the course of treaty negotiations.

There are two mentions of a crown in Spelman's narrative. Early on, in a section entitled "Of ther servis to their gods," Spelman describes the brandishing of an English crown and bedstead in a religious display. "As with the great Pawetan," Spelman writes, "he hath an Image called Cakeres which most comonly standeth at Yaughtawnoone [in one of the Kinges houses] or at Oropikes in a house for that purpose and with him are sett all the Kings goods and presents that are sent him, as the Cornne. But the beades or Crowne or Bedd which the Kinge of England sent him are in the gods house at Oropikes, and in their houses are all the Kinge ancesters and kindred commonly buried."[127] Spelman identifies the "Crowne" and "Bedd" as diplomatic presents from "the Kinge of England." Powhatan keeps the items in a structure at Oropikes that is used to house an image or representation of a god and as a grave for his ancestors. In a section entitled "The manor of settinge ther corne with the gatheringe and Dressing," Spelman describes the ceremonial use of these items during the planting of corn:

> let me not altogither forgett the setting of the Kings corne for which a day is apoynted wherin great part of the cuntry people meete who with such diligence worketh as for the most part all the Kinges corne is sett on a daye After which setting the Kinge takes the croune which the Kinge of England sent him beinge brought him by tow men, and setts it on his heade which dunn the people goeth about the corne in maner backwardes for they going before, and the king followinge ther faces are always toward the Kinge exspectinge when he should flinge sum beades among them which his custum is at that time to doe makinge thos which had wrought to scramble for them But to sume he favors he bids thos that carry his Beades to call such and such unto him unto whome he giveth beads into ther hande and this is the greatest curtesey he doth his people, when his corne is ripe the cuntry people cums to him againe

and gathers drys and rubbes out all his corne for him, which is layd
in howses apoynted for that purpose.[128]

Unlike Archer or Smith, Spelman is not interested in the implications of the
crown for treaties, or questions of consent. He notes its status as a gift from
James I, but he describes its use in a corn-planting ritual that involves only
Powhatan and his subjects. The description corroborates his view that the Powhatans are strange and barbaric savages who practice occult pagan ceremonies.
But his focus is different from that of more powerful correspondents, and a
different picture of Powhatan emerges. Spelman takes us beyond the spaces of
cross-cultural diplomacy, and finds Powhatan using European objects to confirm his power over his own people.

In an account of power struggles in Tsenocomoco during the early years
of colonization, James D. Rice has described Powhatan motives for collecting
European objects. According to Rice, the foreign origins of chiefs were central
to religious cosmology and political order, and collecting and deploying objects
from different places was one way *werowances* consolidated and displayed power.
As Rice puts it, "Chiefly lineages emphasized their foreign origins in order to
demonstrate that they were part of a universal spiritual order rather than local
parvenus."[129] If what Spelman writes is true, Powhatan and his subjects did not
understand the concept of a foreign nation in the same way as Europeans. The
crown does not simply represent the recognition of an external power, the way
a diplomatic gift in Europe might. Rather, it is a key source of Powhatan's own
authority to demand the planting of corn from his subjects and to reward his
favorites with gifts of beads. He incorporates the crown into his own story of
coming to power. His might and command of resources flows from the object
and the spiritual trajectory it represents.

Spelman's story suggests that for Powhatan the crowning ceremony was
only partly about reaching a settlement with the newcomers. Because of the
importance of a distant lineage to his own power, he looked to the newcomers
and their trade goods as a way of maintaining authority over his own subjects.
Though this authority was spiritual in nature, it had political uses. While the
exact nature of the ceremony and its meaning to Powhatan and his subjects
may never be known, it should be remembered that, among the Powhatans as
among the English, the significance of a ritual was never entirely predetermined
by religion or custom. There is sometimes a tendency to view Natives as traditional, while thinking of colonists as modern. But like the English, who used

natural law texts to stake land claims, Powhatan manipulated *manitou* and its embodiment in English goods to control his own subjects. That he used English material goods in these ceremonies may have suggested to his subjects that he had the crisis of English arrival under control, and that channels for distributing food and goods would continue to function reliably as long as he was in power.[130] He may have been suggesting that the arrival of the newcomers had made him more, not less, powerful, and that a new kind of political order was emerging from his triumph over them.

Though many Europeans were keenly interested in Powhatan's foreign policy, Spelman is one of the few to mention these ceremonies. One reason for their absence in other records may be that Powhatan did not want any of the more powerful newcomers to see them. One of the first things Powhatan did when he met the newcomers was to try and figure out who was in charge. Then he acted accordingly, receiving them according to their rank. But the corn ceremony was intended to confirm Powhatan's own power, not to recognize that of others. And as a person without any real standing, Spelman was ironically in a position to observe and report things that major power players could not. Another reason Europeans may not have recorded such rituals was that they troubled claims of English possession. The incorporation of a crown into Powhatan ceremonies suggests continued Powhatan independence and sovereignty. It may also suggest control over the newcomers.[131] Spelman, however, was not particularly concerned with questions of international law or possession. This left him in a position to record things higher-ranking English people either did not understand or did not want to publicize.

Powhatan's use of the crown in a corn-planting ceremony was certainly alien to English understandings of politics. However, it is a mistake to understand Powhatan's political behaviors as belonging to an oral or ritual political sphere separate from written treaties. The English relied on the meaning Powhatan attached to the crown for the success of their own strategy, framing his gestures according to their own (conflicting) understandings of the law of nations. In many ways, he relied on them for the same thing. If they appropriated his words and gestures, he appropriated their objects. Though the English and the Powhatans were at odds, they needed each other's political symbols.

The First Anglo-Powhatan War dramatically altered Powhatan's relationship with English governors. The contested flow of tribute among colonists and *werowances* stopped. English and Powhatan people waged war, stole goods, and held one another for ransom. John Smith's *Proceedings* was an attempt to make this warfare consistent with the imperative to pacify the region according to the norms of the law of nations. But if the Powhatans were ever afraid of Smith, they were not intimidated by the Virginia presidents who replaced him. War continued, despite Smith's claim that violence would end violence. Yet even as narratives of war made their way among reading audiences in London, Jamestown leaders were formulating a new plan, one authorized in the company's 1609 "Instructions" to Gates. They would kidnap and ransom a high-profile Indian, Pocahontas, the charismatic daughter of Powhatan. As the English well knew, kidnapping by itself would not demonstrate possession under the law of nations. It was necessary to justify the act as a means of obtaining peace. In this endeavor, Jamestown governors were aided by a bit of luck. After Pocahontas was kidnapped in 1613, John Rolfe, a Virginia colonist, fell in love with her and married her in 1616. According to European customs, marriage was a sound basis for treaty alliance, and the colony immediately went to work publicizing Pocahontas's nuptials. Yet even amid the celebration of marriage rites, it still remained to explain the kidnapping itself. If the crowning of Powhatan had been controversial, the kidnapping of an Indian princess—and her subsequent marriage to an Englishman—would demand an even more intricate justification under the law of nations.

Chapter 2

—ɯɯ—

The Ransom of Pocahontas: Kidnapping and Dynastic Marriage in Jamestown and London

"[M]uch a doe there was to perswade her to be patient, which with extraordinary curteous usage, by little and little was wrought in her, and so to *James* towne she was brought."[1] This is how Ralph Hamor describes the kidnapping of Pocahontas in his pamphlet, *A True Discourse of the Present Estate of Virginia* (1615). Hamor's emphasis on "extraordinary curteous usage" seems out of place in a story of deception and abduction. Hamor relates how Samuel Argall, an English sailor, persuades some Patawomeck Indians to lure Pocahontas onto a boat so Argall can ransom her for the return of captives held by her father, Powhatan. But Hamor depicts the kidnapping as much more than an act of war. Pocahontas is eventually won over by English ways, converts to English religion, and, with her father's blessing, marries John Rolfe, a pious Englishman. By the end of the book, the kidnapping has become the basis for a "peace concluded with the Indians."[2]

In the first chapter, I described how Gabriel Archer documented treaties with Powhatan leaders in order to demonstrate the Virginia Colony's control of the Chesapeake Bay. Archer pointed to such alliances as evidence that the colonists had legal possession of territory. Yet this strategy sparked controversies that stretched from Tsenacomoco to Spain. Led by an expansion-minded chief, the Powhatans were unwilling to play their part in treaty ceremonies scripted by the London Council. On the contrary, they viewed Jamestown colonists as invaders, and sought to exploit them for trade goods, leading to a series of running battles over food, weapons, and captives. As diplomacy degenerated into violence, critics circulated counter-narratives of Anglo-Powhatan alliances, offering their own models for how to capture Indian consent.

This chapter examines the attempts of Virginia Colony leaders to publicize a renewed peace with the Powhatans after the conclusion of the First Anglo-Powhatan war. While John Smith was the first to formulate a detailed model of diplomacy that acknowledged the violent reality of the Chesapeake Bay, the colony's new leaders were not far behind him. They understood, as had the colony's first government, that their good relationship with the crown depended upon their ability to publicize treaties. Yet this work of transatlantic publicity was vastly more complicated in 1613 than it had been only years earlier. Powhatan was now openly hostile to the English, refusing diplomatic parley and engaging the colonists in violent skirmishes. Many reports of war, starvation, and disorder had appeared in London, and damaging rumors traveled across the Atlantic on returning supply ships.[3] The colony also faced threats from England's imperial rivals. In 1612, Argall had destroyed French outposts north of Virginia, sparking protests.[4] Only a few months later, near Jamestown itself, several Spanish spies had been captured and imprisoned at Jamestown fort. One of them, Diego de Molina, had secretly dispatched letters describing the colony's military readiness and relations with Indians.[5] These threats made it all the more urgent for the colony to demonstrate its possession of territory, even as wars with Indians made it more difficult to do so.

In this chapter, I will describe how Jamestown leaders publicized Pocahontas's marriage as a treaty. I will show how colonial governors and their agents circulated accounts of the kidnapping and marriage in order to assert control over a region that, in the eyes of many onlookers, seemed in danger of slipping from English hands. For centuries, marriage had been a way of making alliances.[6] Monarchs and their ambassadors arranged marriages between royal families in order to unite dynastic lines and create or maintain political friendships. In the decades after the Treaty of London, for example, the English crown considered matches with both Spanish and French princesses.[7] In depicting Pocahontas's marriage to Rolfe as a way of making peace, Hamor sought to associate Pocahontas's marriage with this ancient custom. Yet Hamor and the colony's leaders also faced a rhetorical problem in publicizing Pocahontas's union with Rolfe. Pocahontas was not just a bride. She was also a captive, and had been seized, against her will, as an act of retribution against her father for his supposed crimes against the English.[8] As colonial leaders well knew, depicting Pocahontas's marriage as a treaty demanded more than the usual publication of nuptial rites. It required, in addition, a careful handling of the question of Powhatan's consent to the arrangement. As a woman, Pocahontas was not understood by either side to have much of a say in the matter, but her father's blessing was crucial. Without it, the kidnapping would be just another act of war.

In this chapter, I focus on debates about the meaning of Pocahontas's kidnapping and marriage for English possession. As many studies have shown, captivity was common in the colonial world. Europeans abducted Natives in order to acquire information about gold and natural resources, learn indigenous languages, and impose their will on Native polities.[9] While scholars have documented the experiences of colonial captives, however, they have paid less attention to the legal justifications offered for kidnapping in intertribal and international diplomacy. While kidnapping was often brutal, it was not necessarily a lawless act in the eyes of Europeans or Natives. Like other interactions between princely powers and foreign polities, kidnapping was understood within the context of many kinds of legal frameworks and historical precedents. Ancient texts such as Justinian's *Code* and canonical works such as the writings of St. Thomas Aquinas offered detailed rules for justifying ransom and captivity.[10] Jurists such as Vitoria and Gentili described the exchange of hostages as a diplomatic tool and a normalized protocol of treaty making.[11] Native peoples, too, had for millennia used kidnapping as a way of incorporating vanquished allies into victorious polities and securing peace at the end of wars.[12] Captivity was subject to multiple (and often conflicting) systems of norms that comprehended the seizure of bodies as a routine diplomatic practice.

In this chapter, I consider letters, printed works, and diaries that portray the abduction and marriage of Pocahontas and the negotiations that surrounded it. The colony's governors were quite aware that the kidnapping was an act of war, and they knew they needed Indian consent for peace. Their narratives of the kidnapping consequently focus on official treaty rituals, such as the marriage itself, and on other kinds of informal behaviors, such as Pocahontas's response to the kidnapping, her father's reactions to news about her, and her comportment in London during an official visit to meet with the crown and its councilors. I start with Samuel Argall's letter to Nicholas Hawes (1613), which is the only existing first-hand account of the kidnapping. While Argall had been closely involved in the abduction—conceiving of the plan himself and orchestrating its execution through Patawomeck allies—he was not the natural person to describe it for transatlantic readers. Argall was a soldier, not a secretary, and had scant expertise in diplomatic correspondence. However, he did possess detailed knowledge of the many kinds of unwritten codes that regulated trade relations on the coast. In his letter to Hawes, Argall describes the abduction in terms of the coastal practice of pledging, or the exchange of hostages as a form of surety on a treaty. Widely recognized by fur traders and tribes alike, pledging was frequently employed by English mariners who sailed up the coast from Jamestown and interacted with groups at the periphery of Tsenacomoco. As Argall tells it, the whole episode is less a story about Pocahontas than an instance of the colony's success in manipulating the rules of hostaging to its benefit. Much like John Smith, who adapted Powhatan practices of ambush to English purposes, Argall uses pledging to show that the English are controlling the coast through forms of negotiation and treaty making that Indians recognize.

Though lacking the diplomatic polish of Archer's "Relatyon," Argall's narrative had serious implications for the colony's standing under international legal systems. It advertised the colony's success at negotiating the coastal political systems that were central to the maintenance of trading alliances, a key concern as French traders inched closer to Chesapeake Bay waters. In its depiction of Anglo-Patawomeck alliances, Argall's letter also showed that the colony was capable of playing Powhatan's tributary subjects against him, as the 1609 "Instructions" had commanded. Yet while Argall's account served many purposes, it was incomplete as a statement of possession. The kidnapping was a blow to Powhatan's power, but he was not conquered by any stretch of the imagination. While the abduction of Pocahontas might suggest that the English had the upper hand, by itself, it did not demonstrate English control under the law of nations. Ralph Hamor's *True Discourse*, the colony's official, printed account of Pocahontas's kidnapping, goes beyond Argall's letter to portray the kidnapping as the basis of a marriage alliance that has Powhatan's agreement, and therefore satisfies the criterion of *consensus ad idem*. While Hamor affirms the credibility of Argall's narrative, and even incorporates some of Argall's language into his account, he also attempts to show that the tactics employed by Argall have been superseded by a new approach—a voluntary embrace of marriage alliances by both parties. Hamor's book ends with the story of an English treaty with the Chickahominies, who decide to submit to the crown after hearing of Pocahontas's marriage. In portraying the marriage as the primary inspiration for the submission, Hamor attempts to show that the union between Pocahontas and Rolfe will inspire Anglo-Native alliances throughout the bay.

Hamor's *True Discourse* was intended to advertise Jamestown's pacification of the coast after the end of the war. It was offered to London readers as ostensible proof that Virginia was finally under control after years of uncertainty. In pointing to Pocahontas's nuptials as the basis of a treaty, Hamor combines concepts from Roman law with the civilizing narrative heralded many decades earlier by Elizabethan promoters, who had claimed that the superiority of English culture would inspire the Indians to submit to the newcomers. While this narrative had quickly proved useless as a predictor of the Powhatans' behavior, Pocahontas's marriage led the English to revive it as a strategy for motivating treaties. After Pocahontas gave birth to a son, Thomas, the colony's leaders saw an opportunity to publicize the alliance in a more powerful way, and decided to take Pocahontas herself to London as part of a company campaign.[13] Colonial governors presented her to courtly society as an example of their progress in converting Native people to Christianity and making treaties with their leaders. Like Namontack's visit a few years earlier, Pocahontas's journey was an extension of a colonial treaty. It was an attempt to embody agreement in person and prove English power to French and Spanish onlookers, who at this time were fighting for influence over James I's overseas policy. Yet, as I will show, Pocahontas's embassy was an important opportunity for the Powhatans as well. Numerous Natives accompanied her, including a priest, Uttamatomakkin, who conducted reconnaissance on the English population. During her visit to England, Pocahontas also encountered John Smith, and criticized him for his violent diplomacy. While the record of their conversation is filtered through Smith's perspective, it provides a dramatic counterpoint to the narrative of acculturation and peace publicized by Hamor and other colonists.

Pocahontas is an elusive figure in the archive of Virginia Company correspondence, yet she is far more famous today than any other figure associated with Virginia. The notion that Smith and other writers fabricated much of what they wrote about her has for centuries shadowed her legend, and has found some confirmation in recent scholarship on Chesapeake Bay groups.[14] Yet I will argue that it is possible to find traces of Pocahontas's voice in the English colonial archive, despite the fact that Smith and others who wrote about her had little regard for modern-day standards of factual accuracy. Her marriage to John Rolfe was indeed voluntary, though not in the way the English claimed. Instead, it represented her own plan for cross-cultural coexistence on Powhatan terms, a plan that survived her death and was later co-opted by the English as they tried to assume power after the death of Powhatan. Any hope for a diplomatic solution to the conflict between Tsenacomoco and Jamestown died in the Powhatan Uprising of 1622, which saw Opechancanough, one of Powhatan's brothers, lead Chesapeake Bay groups in a surprise attack against the English.[15] Nevertheless, I will argue that Pocahontas's political ambitions are still visible in English texts, despite the great distance that separates us from them today. Virginia Company propaganda gave Pocahontas a forum of her own, one she used to indict the English for failing to live up to their treaties with her father.

Ransom Notes: Samuel Argall's Letter to Nicholas Hawes

News of Pocahontas's kidnapping first escaped Virginia in the form of a letter. In June of 1613, Samuel Argall wrote to Nicholas Hawes, a merchant and investor in the Virginia Company, to tell how he had come "to possesse" the "Great *Powhatans* Daughter *Pokahuntis,*" and how he had used his prized captive to compel her father's acquiescence to English demands.[16] Company officials were not surprised to hear from Argall. He had only recently departed from London with supplies for the colony, and they were anxious to know if he had made it. But they did not expect a report of the kidnapping of a princess, or the end of the fighting that had plagued their venture from the start.

Unlike many who wrote from the colonies, Argall was not trained in law or diplomacy. A veteran of the Eighty Years' War, Argall found himself in the position of transatlantic correspondent because of his role as the company's maritime navigator. Argall first traveled to Virginia as the captain of the ship that delivered Lord De La Warr, Sir Thomas Dale, and other members of the new government to Virginia in 1610. Soon after their arrival, De La Warr retained Argall as an explorer and trader, and selected him to captain a naval militia that attacked Powhatan villages throughout 1610 and 1611.[17] This campaign was in keeping with the colony's new policy of belligerence toward the Powhatans. As part of this military assignment, Argall was also charged with forming alliances with groups outside of the Powhatan chiefdom. The colony's government hoped these groups could be peeled away from the Powhatans and persuaded to form alliances with the English. To this end, and for the equally crucial purpose of acquiring food, Argall pursued trade with the Patawomecks, a multitribal chiefdom that controlled the Potomac River. Argall lived among the Patawomecks from 1612 to 1613, supplying them with English goods in exchange for maize. During this time, he made a trading alliance with a minor *werowance,* Iopassus, who wanted English help against the Powhatans.[18]

The alliance with the Patawomecks was crucial to the kidnapping of Pocahontas. Indeed, according to Argall's letter, Pocahontas's capture was less a triumph of English culture, as Hamor would later claim, than a crafty implementation of the divide-and-ally strategy of turning Powhatan's satellite subjects against him. While trading along the Potomac River, Argall heard from his connections among the Patawomecks that Pocahontas was staying there. Argall persuaded Iopassus to lead her onto his boat, where, in the face of her angry protests, the English detained her. After giving her English clothing (and presumably privacy in which to put it on, if reports of Argall's "curteous usage" are to be believed), Argall sailed to Jamestown, where Pocahontas was imprisoned. Befitting her station as the daughter of an influential leader, Pocahontas was afforded some aristocratic comforts. English servants likely waited on her, for example, making sure her needs were met.[19] This treatment stood in stark contrast to that afforded other Powhatan captives, who were sometimes put to death.[20] While colonists negotiated the terms of her release, she received compulsory instruction in the English language, and listened to sermons from Robert Hunt, the colony's minister.[21]

After the kidnapping, Argall traveled north, where he attacked and destroyed French trading posts. Argall's letter to Hawes, drafted shortly after this mission, traveled to London on a returning supply ship. Like the illicit writings that made up Smith's *Proceedings*, Argall's letter is not an official communication. In formatting and style, it more resembles a captain's log than a diplomatic relation. In rough phrasing, Argall conveys requisite information about coastal geography, his acquisition of food, and his dealings with the Indians. Yet Argall is careful to describe the kidnapping in terms of the divide-and-ally strategy articulated in Gates's "Instructions." He writes, most of all, to explain the meaning of the kidnapping for coastal treaties. He is concerned less with Powhatan, whom he views as a legitimate target of just war, than with the Patawomecks, who join the plot to capture the princess. Argall portrays himself as forging alliances and carrying out the kidnapping through his deft manipulation of cross-cultural rules for pledging hostages.

Though today it is a violation of international law, pledging hostages was widely accepted by Argall's readers.[22] In early modern wars, military leaders frequently exchanged prisoners or captives in order to bind parties to various kinds of treaties. Sometimes, these exchanges were between parties of relatively equal standing. Often, however, conquerors demanded opposing leaders or their children as hostages in order to ensure the continued submission of the defeated. In Ireland, for example, the English frequently seized the children of rebels to guarantee the compliance of Irish lords.[23] While the Irish had fiercely

resisted the practice, American peoples received it differently. While some re-
taliated against kidnappers even years later, many others, including Powhatan-
affiliated peoples, recognized the pledging of hostages as resembling their own
practices of alliance and adoption.[24] When forming agreements, Algonquian-
speaking groups frequently exchanged children as signs of friendship. Such exchanges displayed the trust, goodwill, and commitment to future cooperation
that they believed were necessary for ongoing diplomatic relations. Pledging
hostages was particularly important to fur trading. An exchange of captives was
one way to ensure that parties would meet in the same place the next season
in order to recommence trade. Natives and newcomers also swapped hostages
in order to open lines of communication and keep an eye on one another. The
exchange of Thomas Savage for Namontack was one such example, and many
others followed it. By 1612, a number of English and Indian men in Virginia
had effectively been trained as cross-cultural diplomats under this system of
reciprocal pledging.[25]

When the English decided to create alliances beyond Tsenacomoco in 1609,
pledging offered one way of making new friendships. In his letter to Hawes,
Argall describes the importance of pledging to the formation of northern alliances, recounting for his readers how he has exchanged captives with Indians
as a form of surety on agreement. While earlier "trading with the *Indians*," for
example, Argall encounters Iopassus, "the King of *Pastancie*," who is hunting
along the Pembroke River. The king is "very glad" of Argall's return, and tells
him that the Indians are his "very great friends" and have a "good store of Corne
for [him]."[26] The trading that ensues includes the mutual exchange of people as
well as corn. "I carried my ship presently before his Towne," Argall writes, "and
there built me a stout shallop, to get the Corne aboard withall, which being
done, and having concluded a peace with divers other *Indian* Lords, and likewise given and taken Hostages: I hasted to *James* Towne."[27] Argall's description
of the hostages as "given and taken" emphasizes the reciprocity of the practice,
in his view. He takes some Indians to guarantee that they will trade with him
next time, and leaves some Englishmen to show his intention to return.

In reporting such exchanges, Argall showed company readers that he was
successfully carrying out their policy. Stories of peaceful and seasonal trading
were consistent with the colony's overall strategy of pursuing friendship with
groups around the periphery of Tsenacomoco and turning them against Powhatan. However, pledging also serves another purpose in Argall's narrative. It
provides a means of orchestrating—and justifying—the kidnapping of Poca-

hontas. As I showed in Chapter 1, treaties were a powerful way of asserting control, yet they also invited questions about Native intentions. Many Elizabethan writers had assumed that Indians would spontaneously flock to English leaders out of fear of Spanish conquistadors or cannibalistic neighbors, yet such sanguine accounts often inspired skepticism in Europe. Archer, and John Smith after him, did not simply report Indian words of consent. They went to great lengths to describe the negotiations that had preceded such consent. An account of informal communications, such as gestures or facial expressions, proved more definitively that Indians meant what they said. In his letter, Argall uses pledging as a way to explain the negotiations that have led up to the treaty with the Patawomecks. Above all, pledging offers Argall a way of communicating to London readers why the Patawomecks would consent to an alliance that leaves them in the dangerous position of opposing Powhatan.

Argall begins the story by describing how intelligence of the princess's whereabouts first reaches him. While foraging along the shore of the Potomac for minerals, Argall is "told by certaine *Indians*, [his] friends, that the Great *Powhatans* Daughter *Pokahuntis* was with the great King *Patowomeck*." The idea of kidnapping Pocahontas immediately presents itself. Snatching the princess will give the English a decided advantage over Powhatan, Argall concludes, and enable him to extort "some quantitie of Corne, for the Colonies reliefe." However, Argall does not have the political authorization to take the princess by force. Given that the Patawomecks have hardly done anything to provoke him, and have traded freely with the English, taking Pocahontas from their midst would be an obvious violation of their sovereignty. Faced with this legal obstacle, Argall tries to persuade the Patawomecks to agree to a treaty against Powhatan, which will oblige them to kidnap Pocahontas and deliver her to the English. The terms seem shockingly one-sided; the Patawomecks appear to lose much by abandoning friendship with Tsenacomoco for an alliance with the seemingly weak and starving newcomers. But by situating the negotiations in terms of the logic of reciprocity inherent to pledging, Argall provides a rationale for why the Patawomecks agree to his demands. "So soone as I came to an anchor before the towne," he writes, "I manned my Boate and sent on shoare, for the King of *Pastancy* and *Ensigne Swift* (whom I had left as a pledge of our love and truce, the Voyage before) who presently came and brought my pledge with him: whom after I had received, I brake the matter to this King, and told him, that if he did not betray *Pokohuntis* into my hands; wee would be no longer brothers nor friends."[28] Launching his plan into action, Argall anchors at the town and demands that Iopassus appear, along with James Swift, a hostage Argall had earlier left as a sign of "love and truce." Argall then commands the Indian king to abduct Pocahontas, not because Argall is his superior, but because the chief owes Argall a service under the terms of the treaty represented by the pledge of Swift. While the exchange of hostages normally implies reciprocity between the two peoples, in this case, the presence of a pledge among the Patawomecks leaves them in debt to the English.

Argall's blunt offer—with its dark hint that the Patawomecks may be targeted for attack if they refuse—seems to leave the Indians little choice. In this, it appears to violate *consensus ad idem*, or the principle that treaties must be voluntary. As I have argued so far, the English largely preferred agreement to violent conquest, not because they inherently respected Native sovereignty, but because agreement was the easiest way to prove control. Recognizing that his approach leaves little room for such voluntarism, Argall becomes suddenly more diplomatic after issuing the ultimatum, emphasizing the fact that the Patawomecks do indeed have a free choice, even if they lack appealing options. Iopassus initially begins to refuse Argall's request, worrying that "*Powhatan* would make warres upon him and his people" in retaliation for their snatching a favorite daughter. Yet in addition to hinting that the English will attack the Patawomecks if Iopassus does not go along, Argall also "promise[s]" that the English will "joyne with [Iopassus] against [Powhatan]," protecting the tribe if the evil chief retaliates. After mulling over this sweetened offer, Iopassus informs his brother "the great King of *Patowomeck*, who being made acquainted with the matter," Argall reports, "called his Counsell together: and after some few houres deliberation, concluded rather to deliver her into my hands, then lose my friendship: so presently, he betrayed her into my Boat, wherein I carried her aboord my ship."[29] Compared to the discussion among the Patawomecks, the kidnapping itself seems almost an afterthought. Argall is more interested in the Patawomecks' political process than he is in narrating the precise means by which they take the princess. And indeed, he had good reason for this point of emphasis: the "few houres deliberation" are convincing evidence of the satisfaction of *consensus ad idem* in the Anglo-Patawomeck alliance. This was important to Argall and his readers, because collective assent was stronger than a simple word of agreement from a sachem.[30] The deliberative nature of the decision is evidence that Iopassus and the other Native leaders have the support of their people and are not merely promising an alliance that their followers will later abandon. It also prevents Iopassus or his brother from blaming any future raids against the

English on uncontrollable followers, as Powhatan had often done. The Indians meet and conclude of their own accord to kidnap the princess and deliver her to Argall. Her body, secure in Argall's hands, is proof of English control of the Patawomecks as much as it is a sign of triumph over Powhatan.

Of course, from Argall's perspective, the fact that the Patawomecks carried out the kidnapping has the added benefit of leaving English hands mostly clean in the matter. The violation, if there is any, is on Patawomeck heads; according to Argall's legalistic wording, they, not the English, "betra[y]" Pocahontas. However, Argall is still concerned about justifying the kidnapping. For while the agreement with the Patawomecks meets the criteria for a treaty under the law of nations, the kidnapping of Pocahontas is most certainly an act of war. Like John Smith, who worried that he might be hanged as a "peace breaker" for kidnapping Opechancanough, Argall is keen to explain what he knows might be viewed as a possible breach of the law of nations. On this count, the unwritten codes that govern the pledging of hostages again come into play. In addition to offering a way Argall can prove the Patawomecks are true allies, pledging also establishes a legal norm that Argall will invoke to depict Powhatan as a rogue prince who is beyond the law and its protections.

If the English and the Patawomecks exchange captives and goods through a regular diplomatic process, the kidnapping of Pocahontas is justified precisely because Powhatan has refused to follow the norms that govern this process, leaving him in violation of the law. In making this argument, Argall conceives of pledging as a natural legal system, like the law of nations, with rules and norms that are assumed to hold among all peoples. This understanding of pledging was consistent with European practice. As Susan B. Iwanisziw has shown, while there was no widely adopted code governing the pledging of hostages in early modern Europe, the system gave little quarter to bad actors. Pledging was governed by "a pan-European system of military honor" that stigmatized those who broke the rules.[31] Argall likewise conceives of the pledging system as a set of universally binding norms that Powhatan has violated in his treatment of the English. The abduction of the princess, Argall explains, is legally justified "for the ransoming of so many *Englishmen* as were prisoners with *Powhatan*: as also to get such armes and tooles, as hee, and other *Indians* had got by murther and stealing from others of our Nation."[32] Powhatan's seizure of English people and goods—a crime against a "Nation," rather than against a person—is deliberately contrasted with the peaceful exchange of captives between Argall and Iopassus. Instead of bartering for goods, Powhatan acquires them through "murther and stealing." While the English and their Indian allies exchange hostages, Powhatan keeps them in "slavery." And while the English "use . . . well" Pocahontas, Powhatan leaves English captives in "feare of cruell murther."[33] In violating norms for treating hostages, Powhatan makes himself a legitimate target of just war, and according to Argall, the kidnapping of Pocahontas is a warranted act of retaliation against a cruel tyrant.

This rhetorical isolation of Powhatan corresponded to the London Council's strategy of recruiting allies from the fringes of his chiefdom. While Archer had built Powhatan up, Argall tears him down, depicting the formerly great king as little more than a petty despot who rejects the legal norms that govern traffic between nations. Argall leaves his readers with an image of the king as a defeated tyrant, ready to cooperate with his conquerors. When Powhatan hears of his daughter's kidnapping, he is "much grieved," Argall reports, and immediately moves to comply with English demands, turning over the stolen weapons, corn, and English captives.[34] While Powhatan has not consented to anything, he has conceded to English demands, leaving the colonists in control.

Argall's version of events excited the Virginia Company. Councilors circulated his letter among the English diplomatic corps as a promising sign of growing English power in Virginia, and news of Argall's victory spread across Europe in diplomatic correspondence.[35] But unbeknownst to these metropolitan readers, negotiations over Pocahontas did not end that summer with Powhatan's initial release of prisoners and goods. After Argall turned Pocahontas over to Sir Thomas Dale, Jamestown leaders saw weakness in Powhatan's apparent willingness to cooperate, and pressed him for more concessions. Powhatan, not nearly as cowed as Argall had reported, was suddenly not so willing to bargain. The tense standoff that ensued would come to an end only with the timely appearance of a love letter.

Mixing Threats with Love: Ralph Hamor's *True Discourse*

Argall's knowledge of coastal politics was indispensable to the Virginia Colony. They needed soldiers and sailors to carry out the commands of the governing council. But Argall also posed a problem. While his letter offered a powerful justification of the divide-and-ally strategy, it also left the political balance unsettled. The kidnapping was a sign of agreement with the Patawomecks—and proof of the strength of the English hand in negotiations with Powhatan—but it did not represent control of Powhatan's territory. Indeed, it seemed to leave Anglo-Powhatan relations in a state of continued strife, with Powhatan only temporarily defeated. For the colony to assert control, it was necessary for the standoff over Pocahontas to find resolution in a peace treaty that demonstrated Indian consent and English possession.

As the English puzzled over what to do with their prize captive, an answer presented itself in the form of a letter. At some point during the time between Pocahontas's kidnapping and Powhatan's rejection of English terms, John Rolfe, an English minister, wrote to Ralph Hamor, the colony's secretary, and requested permission to marry Pocahontas. Rolfe had come to know Pocahontas during her imprisonment at Jamestown. His request may have raised some eyebrows; in another letter, Rolfe expressed worry that he would be perceived as lusting after a forbidden body, and he provided assurance that he was proposing to Pocahontas for purely evangelical reasons.[36] Such concerns seemed petty to Dale, however. From his perspective, the marriage offered a way of resolving the increasingly tense standoff over Pocahontas's release. Dale knew that the Powhatans used marriage as a means of creating alliances, and he thought Powhatan might agree to the match as a way of ending a war that both sides hated. Moreover, it was easier to justify marrying a princess than kidnapping one. It did not matter to Dale that Rolfe was not English royalty. Jamestown leaders had often lied to Powhatan about their status at home, and Dale was not interested in any actual marriage treaty of the kind Europeans made. He saw the union as a way of making it appear that the English were finally in control after the long war. There were more ambitious plans in the back of his mind, too; a marriage between Rolfe and an Indian princess might produce an heir, giving the English a nominal claim to Tsenacomoco at some future date. But the colony had more immediate problems, and the marriage was a solution. Pocahontas, christened Lady Rebecca, was married to Rolfe in April 1614. Soon after the ceremony, the colony went to work pressing the union to their advantage in transatlantic correspondence. Their first effort to this end was Hamor's *True Discourse*.

In many ways, *A True Discourse* was intended to give the colony a fresh start in the eyes of investors. Hamor had arrived in Virginia on the salvage ships that had carried Gates and Newport from Bermuda to Virginia after the wreck of the *Sea Venture*. Soon after his arrival, Hamor was appointed to the Virginia Council as a secretary, and was tasked with keeping minutes of its business and sending regular dispatches to Sir Thomas Smith, the company treasurer. Like Archer before him, Hamor was active in the colony's negotiations with the Powhatans. In May 1614, Dale chose him to negotiate with Powhatan over the potential betrothal of one of Pocahontas's sisters to Dale. After that mission failed, Hamor traveled to London to oversee the printing of *A True Discourse*.

Hamor's book circulated throughout Europe. It was later engraved by Johann Theodor de Bry. Like John Smith's volume, it is an intervention into a controversy over the future of Virginia. It targets the "malevolent detracting multitude" whose "blame" has called into question the colonial government's control of affairs.[37] However, Hamor's text also has another aim: justifying the taking of hostages as a way of creating valid alliances. When Hamor arrived in London to find the colony facing criticism from many sides, his nearest obstacle was not a member of any "malevolent detracting multitude." It was a friend, Samuel Argall, whose account of the kidnapping had arrived in London before the colony could publicize the event to more calculated advantage. Argall's letter presented Hamor with a problem. As his role in the Anglo-Powhatan war shows, Argall's military knowledge was essential to the colony's plans to control the Chesapeake Bay. However, while Argall's military accomplishments were crucial to the colony's survival, they presented a difficulty in European correspondence. It was not that the colony's government shied away from war; on the contrary, the governing council gave the colonists explicit permission to attack Powhatan. But establishing possession through acts of war required an absolute military conquest of the kind that the numerically weak and impoverished colony simply could not manage. Marriage offered a far easier way to publicize control. Before Hamor could explain the peace brought about by the marriage, he had to address Argall's warlike account of the kidnapping and argue for the renewed relevance of treaties now that the war had ended.

Unlike Argall, who defends the kidnapping by citing the norms of the pledging system, Hamor employs the vocabulary of the law of nations. Drawing on a combination of canonical and Roman traditions, he argues that the Indians have undergone a transformation that has rendered war and its justifications no longer necessary. Previously, Hamor writes, the Powhatans were "poore and innocent seduced *Savages.*" This was a familiar description to English readers of Spanish colonial texts. Some Catholic authorities held that Indians were heretics or barbarians and therefore unable to make sworn agreements.[38] Yet unlike advocates of violent conquest, who viewed the Indians as permanent targets of war on the basis of their heresy, Hamor claims that Christ has now forgiven the Indians and brought them under the protection of the law of nations: "it hath vouchsafed [Christ] now to be sufficiently revenged for their forefathers Ingratitude and treasons, *and now in his appointed time to descend in mercie, to lighten them that sit in darknes, and in the shaddow of death, and to direct their feete in the waies of peace.*"[39] While the Indians have been recalcitrant in their rejection of God's word, Christ has begun to bring them to the light, in the process making them subjects of natural law. Suddenly narrowing the scope of his argument from the theological to the political, Hamor portrays the conclusion of the First Anglo-Powhatan war as the precise moment when this new legal order arrived. "[A]fter five yeeres intestine warre with the revengefull implacable Indians," he announces, "a firme peace (not againe easily to be broken) hath bin lately concluded." While it may appear from previous reports that the Indians are inherently belligerent, Hamor is anxious to assure readers that they have changed. Indeed, this "firme peace" holds "not onely with the nighbour, and bordering In[di]ans . . . but even with that subtill old revengefull *Powhatan* and all the people under his subjection"[40] Once "implacable" and beyond the law of nations, the Indians are now rehabilitated and willing to make treaties. While violent conquest of the kind described by Argall was once justified, a new state of things has come to pass.

Realizing that such claims might inspire skepticism, Hamor acknowledges that the reader might want to know "by what meanes this peace hath bin thus happily . . . concluded." In a revisionary move, Hamor credits the peace to the "ever-worthy gentleman Capt. *Argall.*" Argall, Hamor writes, "partly by gentle usage & partly by the composition & mixture of threats hath ever kept faire & friendly quarter with our neighbours."[41] Such a description is surprising when placed in the context of Argall's own writings, which often describe kidnapping and other tactics of conquest. At this moment, Hamor performs a calculated reining in of the colony's most important soldier. While the colony has benefited from Argall's ability to carry out kidnapping and other acts of war, Hamor tries to reframe Argall's threatening behavior as only one part of a strategy for conquest that includes violence and diplomacy in equal measure.

It is this "composition & mixture" of threats and love that eventually inspires the Indians to abandon their warlike attitude toward the newcomers. According to Hamor, Argall brings about peace through a simple diplomatic tactic: making good on his promises. Whether trading with the Indians or threatening to destroy them, Argall always stays true to his word. According to Hamor, Argall's scrupulous consistency has the effect of rehabilitating the Indians from heretical savages into good subjects of the law of nations. Describing Argall's relationship with the Indians, Hamor writes, "they assuredly trust upon what he promiseth, and are as carefull in performing their mutuall promises, as though they contended to make that *Maxim*, that there is no faith to be held with Infidels, a meere and absurd *Paradox*."[42] While the Indians may once have been benighted creatures beyond the domain of treaty agreement, Argall's own behavior has so impressed them with the importance of keeping one's word that they acquire reason through exposure to his example. Hamor's claim is not that far off from those of colonial promoters who predicted that English civilization would simply rub off on the Indians. But Hamor combines this familiar civilizing narrative with concepts from treaty law. Through his example, Argall endows the Indians with the ability to become "honest performers" of their obligations.[43]

Of course, though presented as a boon to the Indians, this transformation also benefits the Virginia Colony. Having learned to make treaties, the Indians can now bless English ventures with legitimacy. As in Argall's narrative, the kidnapping of Pocahontas is framed both as proof of a treaty with the Patawomecks and as evidence of Powhatan's defeat. However, while Argall proudly describes the kidnapping as a calculated act of extortion that makes sense according to the unwritten code of the pledging system, Hamor portrays it as an act of courteous diplomacy carried out by a colonial government that clings to the law of nations in dealings with foreigners.

Hamor's account of the kidnapping involves a delicate rearrangement of Argall's narrative. Rather than depicting the abduction as a plot on the part of the English, Hamor describes it instead as a chance occurrence. Argall virtually stumbles into it while embarked upon legitimate diplomatic business. "It chaunced *Powhatans* delight and darling, his daughter *Pocahuntas* . . . to be among her friends at *Pataomecke*," Hamor writes, while "it fortuned upon occasion either of promise or profit, Captaine *Argall* to arrive there."[44] Hamor's description of Argall's business as "promise or profit" reveals his anxiety about how the kidnapping will be perceived by readers. Argall is not there to kidnap anyone, according to Hamor. He is embarked upon treaty or trade, legitimate reasons for travel according to the law of nations.[45] In his account of the kidnapping itself, Hamor follows Argall's lead, emphasizing the negotiations with the Patawomecks rather than the deception of Pocahontas. As Hamor tells it, Argall enlists "an old friend, and adopted brother," Iopassus, in his plot to take the princess. However, Hamor also departs from Argall's narrative in a significant way. While Argall depicts himself negotiating with Iopassus over the question of what is owed the English under treaty pledges, Hamor removes pledging from the equation altogether and frames the Anglo-Patawomeck

Figure 4. Johann Theodor de Bry's engraving of the abduction of Pocahontas, from Johann Theodor de Bry, *Americae Pars Decima* (1619). The image in the foreground depicts the Patawomecks persuading Pocahontas to board an English vessel. The middle image portrays her going aboard, while the background portrays the English attacking a Powhatan settlement. Courtesy of The Newberry Library.

treaty in terms of friendship. Argall tells Iopassus "how and by what meanes he [Iopassus] might procure hir captive, assuring him, that now or never, was the time to pleasure him, if he [Iopassus] entended indeede that love which he had made profession of."[46] While Argall depicts the kidnapping as the outcome of a longstanding trade alliance, Hamor portrays the Patawomecks as bound to the English by "love." While this "love" is not embodied in any written treaty, it nevertheless inspires the Patawomecks to do English bidding in the matter of Pocahontas.[47]

When it comes time to take the princess, it is again the Patawomecks, and not the English, who do the dirty work. Consistent with the company's need to justify the kidnapping before international onlookers, Hamor supplies a much more detailed account of the abduction than does Argall. Hamor heard the details second hand, possibly from Argall himself, so there is likely an element of truth in his story. However, Hamor is concerned with justifications rather than facts, and he frames Argall's actions (and Pocahontas's responses) as evidence of English power. The ruse, as Hamor describes it, is a complicated one, and involves a series of delegated responsibilities. When Argall hears that Pocahontas is among the Patawomecks, he commands Iopassus's wife to "faine" to Pocahontas "a great and longing desire to goe aboorde, and see [Argall's] shippe," in the hopes that Pocahontas will be seduced into going aboard herself.[48] When the wife carries out this ploy, Iopassus, following Argall's instructions, fakes anger, and tells her she cannot see the ship unless Pocahontas goes with her. Pocahontas goes along with Iopassus's wife, though only after "the greatest labour to win her."[49] Wearing a disguise, Pocahontas spends the night on the ship, but after she rises early to depart, Argall suddenly intervenes. As reported by Hamor, Argall's words at the moment of capture are dense with legal rationalizations, and revealing of English anxieties about how the abduction might be perceived around the world. Argall tells Iopassus, "that for divers considerations, as for that [Iopassus's symbolic] father [Powhatan] had then eigh[t] of our English men, many swords, peeces, and other tooles, which he had at severall times by treachero[u]s murdering our men, taken from them, which though of no use to him, he [Argall] would not redeliver, he would reserve *Pocahuntas*."[50] The kidnapping itself is not described. Hamor only recounts Argall's refusal to let Pocahontas go. The use of the words "redeliver" and "reserve" are telling. This language, adapted from the vocabulary of the pledging system, makes it appear that Pocahontas is simply being held as a pledge for English hostages. Indeed, Argall's choice of words implies that Pocahontas was forfeit the moment her father began to violate diplomatic protocol. Argall does not take her—he just refuses to give back what is rightfully his.

In her account of the seizure, the anthropologist Helen C. Rountree has lamented that the English did not record more of Pocahontas's words at this moment.[51] Their lack of interest in her rights is clear in Hamor's narrative. When Argall speaks to justify his actions, he offers his remarks to Iopassus, not Pocahontas. Of course, Iopassus is in on the scheme, as is every other Patawomeck and Englishman on the boat. The justification is in reality a kind of geopolitical apostrophe, addressed to readers and not to anyone on the scene. Yet, as I have argued throughout this book, such justifications were almost always found alongside dramatic renditions of Native words and actions. While the English did not acknowledge Indian sovereignty in any meaningful sense, they needed Indians to recognize English rule in some voluntary way. Without such recognition, they could lose favor with their king or expose themselves to diplomatic challenge. To this end, Hamor has much to say about Pocahontas's reaction, even if he does not report her words. His account of her response starts with her appearance on the boat. Describing her decision to board the ship, Hamor writes, "*Pocahuntas*, desirous to renue hir familiaritie with the English, and delighting to see them, as unknowne, fearefull perhaps to be surprised, would gladly visit."[52] This account of Pocahontas's motives is puzzling, even contradictory. Pocahontas comes to see the English because she is drawn to their superior culture, "delighting to see them," yet she also goes in disguise, "as unknowne," because she is afraid the English will kidnap her if they find out who she is. While Hamor elsewhere wants to depict coastal politics as undergoing a transition from barbarism to reason, at this moment, the trope of the conniving savage converges improbably with that of the willing Indian. Pocahontas is both eager to emulate English ways and anxious that they will kidnap her. When Pocahontas first boards the boat, she has a similarly mixed response. She is troubled, not because she worries that the English mean her any ill, but because she thinks she is "guilty perhaps of her fathers wrongs."[53] Here Hamor employs a somewhat unusual rhetorical tactic. While the English often inferred consent from Native behaviors, Hamor offers direct access to Pocahontas's thoughts, citing her feelings of familial culpability as evidence that her father is guilty of crimes against the English.

Upon being detained, Pocahontas is at first "exceeding pensive, and discontented." However, her resistance does not last long. If Powhatan is a vengeful enemy, Pocahontas is the model Indian of colonial propaganda, happily coming over to the English side after exposure to the settlers' culture. Her conversion starts that morning on the boat. Calming down after "courteous usage" from Argall, Pocahontas goes to Jamestown without further incident.[54] The English immediately press this to their advantage in negotiations with Powhatan. At first, colony and tribe remain locked in a vicious cycle. Dale takes Pocahontas upriver to exchange her for goods and prisoners. The Indians delay, claiming that they cannot negotiate because Powhatan is not there. Then, suddenly, they attack, raining arrows on the delegation, which includes their own princess. Fitting this act of belligerence, Argall and his men respond according to the laws of war. "Being thus justly provoked," Hamor writes, "we presently manned our boates, went ashoare, and burned in that verie place some forty houses, and of the things we found therein, made freeboote and pillage, and . . . hurt and killed five or sixe of their men, with this revenge satisfying our selves, for that their presumption in shooting at us."[55] Here the English employ the rationale for war found in Vitoria and others. They attack the Powhatans, not because they are heretics, but because they respond belligerently to a reasonable request to treaty. As the dust settles, Argall informs the Indians that the English will be less restrained should the Indians continue to refuse reasonable terms: "if finall agreement [is] not made betwixt us before [harvest], we would thither returne againe and destroy and take away all their corne, burne all the houses upon that river, leave not afishing *Weere* standing, nor a *Canoa* in any creeke thereabout, and destroy and kill as many of them as we could."[56] If the Indians will not concede to fair and lawful terms, the colonists will pursue another mode of conquest, securing their territory by force.

At this point, Hamor's *True Discourse* has taken the reader as far as Argall's letter. The kidnapping is justified on the basis of Powhatan's prior actions and the refusal of his people to treaty according to widespread norms. But Hamor now faces the problem of taking the story further and showing how the kidnapping leads to lasting peace. Hamor performs this reversal, not through a legal argument, but rather through a narrative device—the dramatic arrival of the letter from Rolfe professing love for Pocahontas. As Argall's bellicose declaration hangs in the air, Hamor rushes up to Dale with the letter. Even in the midst of the speech making and saber rattling, Dale understands that a marriage will enable the colony to accomplish a conquest by treaty, rendering Argall's strident justifications obsolete. "Long before this time," Hamor reports, "a gentleman of approved behaviour and honest cariage, maister John *Rolfe* had bin in love with *Pocahuntas* and she with him, which thing at the instant that we were in parlee with them, my selfe made known to Sir Thomas *Dale* by a letter from him, whereby he intreated his advise and furtherance in his love, if so it seemed fit to him for the good of the Plantation, and *Pocahuntas* her selfe, acquainted her brethren therewith: which resolution Sir Thomas *Dale* wel approving, was the onely cause: hee was so milde amongst them, who otherwise would not have departed their river without other conditions."[57] This moment almost certainly represents dramatic license on Hamor's part; it is unlikely he waited to disclose the letter in the middle of a battle. In the narrative, however, it is an important turning point. Like Argall's willingness to make and keep promises among the Patawomecks, Rolfe's declaration of love transforms the Indians. Once incorrigible savages beyond legal norms, they are now rational agents ready to treaty and negotiate under the law of nations. "The bruite of this pretended marriage came soone to *Powhatans* knowledge, a thing acceptable to him, as appeared by his sudden consent thereunto," Hamor reports, "and ever since we have had friendly commerce and trade, not onely with *Powhatan* himselfe, but also with his subjects round about us; so as now I see no reason why the Collonie should not thrive a pace."[58] The news of the marriage seems to calm the Indians almost by itself. As the "bruite," or news, reaches Powhatan, he puts down his arms and concedes English terms. While Argall's warlike approach to the Indians is legally justified, it can only be accomplished by a military conquest that potentially involves the colony in protracted war. The marriage alliance, on the other hand, produces the willing "consent" that defines a peace treaty.

According to Hamor, the marriage has a salutary effect on the entire region. Its most immediate effects are felt on the periphery of Tsenacomoco, where Powhatan's unhappy subjects dwell. After "hearing of [the] concluded peace," Hamor writes, the Chickahominies, a people "free from *Powhatans* subjection," come to Jamestown and offer their submission to Dale. The narrative that follows, which for a moment leaves Pocahontas herself behind, is perhaps the most detailed account of Anglo-Native treaty negotiations in English colonial writing. In it, Hamor attempts to show how the matrimonial alliance between Rolfe and Pocahontas is working in the service of the divide-and-ally strategy articulated in the 1609 "Instructions." Negotiations are opened when the Chickahominies send "two fat Bucks" to Dale, whom they view as a "king" of the English (a misconception the English make no move to correct). Along with the gift of venison, they "offe[r] themselves and service unto him, alleadging that albeit in former times they had bin our enemies, and we theirs, yet they would now if we pleased become not onely our trustie friends, but even King JAMES his subjects and tributaries." The Chickahominies' offer reads more like a laundry list of English demands than a voluntary proposal. The Chickahominies offer to "relinquish their old name" and "take upon them, as they call Us the name of *Tossantessas*."[59] They "intreate Sir Thomas *Dale* as King JAMES his deputie to be their supreme head, King and governor." Finally, they pledge to be "ready at all times to aide him" against other enemies. In exchange for this voluntary yielding, they ask "onely . . . to injoy their owne lawes and liberties."[60] This, of course, was ideal from the English point of view. Such a *laissez-faire* treaty submission nominally extended English claims into Chickahominy territory without requiring the English to exert much effort governing the Chickahominies or converting them to English religion. It may seem hard to believe the Chickahominies would agree to such terms, and there could very well be considerable fiction in the English account. However, as the historian Jenny Hale Pulsipher has argued, subjection was not always a last resort of the defeated. Many tribes sought to subject themselves to the English crown to gain what protection they could from a distant ally which they rightly believed was unlikely to try to rule them directly.[61] There were good reasons for the Chickahominies to submit to the English, beyond the ones Hamor recorded. Powhatan's power at this time appeared to be weakening, and the kidnapping of Pocahontas had not helped his image. In submitting to Dale, the Chickahominies may have been hedging their bets against his collapse.[62]

Whatever the Chickahominies intended to accomplish by the offer, Hamor depicts it as an unprecedented opportunity for the English. In response, Dale and an English delegation, including Argall and Hamor, travel to Chickahominy territory to negotiate the voluntary submission of the tribe. In contrast to the earlier meetings between Newport and Powhatan, which involved Native implements such as mats and pipes, this negotiation unfolds almost exclusively on English terms. The English decline the extended hospitality characteristic of Chesapeake Bay diplomacy, instead demanding that the Chickahominies quickly "sen[d] for their principle men" who "hast[en]" to the scene.[63] Absent as well are any extended orations in Native style. In their stead, Argall delivers a "long discourse" in which he reminds them of their "former proceedings" against the English while the Chickahominies remain cooperatively silent.[64] The treaty takes European form as well; the negotiation culminates in Argall's proposal of six "Articles" listed in the manner of written treaties between Christian princes.[65] The articles are clearly one-sided; the Chickahominies disarm, for example, while the English keep their weapons, and Chickahominy warriors pledge to bring annual tribute to King James. Perhaps most importantly, the concessions include the tribe's agreement to a change of name, signifying their peaceful subjection to the English crown. The Chickahominies agree "that they should take upon them, as they promised, the name of *Tassantasses* or English men, and be King JAMES his subjects, and be forever honest, faithfull and trustie unto his deputie in their countrie."[66] Given Hamor's insistence earlier in the narrative that Indians are benighted savages, this seems a strange kind of conversion indeed. While Pocahontas submits by leaving behind Native ways and coming over to English culture, changing her name to Lady Rebecca, the Chickahominies become instead *tassantasses*—the Algonquian word for English. In one sense, this appears to be a moment of cultural inclusiveness in *A True Discourse*. Hamor depicts English empire as a multinational order that can accomodate linguistic difference; whether the Chickahominies are "English" or "Tassantasses" matters little. Yet this apparent cosmopolitanism brings with it a key strategic benefit, one Hamor leaves only implied. The kidnapping of Pocahontas had been a complicated business, involving many risks and demanding tortured legal justifications, and the cash-strapped colony had already expended much on her upkeep. In describing the treaty with the Chickahominies in terms of the incorporation of difference into English order, Hamor is keen to show that conquering Indians will not always involve complicated plots or expensive labors of conversion. The Chickahominies keep their language and traditional ways even as they change their allegiance; one can subdue the Indians and extend authority over their land without converting them or ruling them directly, Hamor implies. The terms of the Chickahominies' subjection are a reminder of the strategic place of the civilizing mission in the plans of the Virginia Company. For colonists, civilizing Native people went hand in hand with establishing control over territory. When the civilizing project became costly or difficult, as it had in the case of Pocahontas's kidnapping and marriage, the English were eager to embrace other models of political friendship. For Hamor, the treaty with the Chickahominies suggests that Pocahontas's conversion will trigger a series of treaty submissions, which will bring territory under English control without endless negotiations or protracted evangelical missions.

Like others who wrote for transatlantic audiences, Hamor must assure his readers that they can believe his account of what the Indians have done and said. In the aftermath of the First Anglo-Powhatan War, company publicists faced a particular challenge to their credibility. Treaties like the one in Archer's "Relatyon" were confirmed by the words and gestures of Native *werowances*. In these documents, Native forms of expression, though unwritten, served the same purpose as signatures on European treaties. They embodied *consensus ad idem* and proved the validity of an agreement. However, the publication of John Smith's *Proceedings* and other critical narratives called into question this way of representing consent. As Smith recorded in violent detail, Powhatan's promises did not always mean peace. His subject tribes ambushed English trading routes and supply lines while Powhatan himself denied involvement. It was not

Figure 5. Johann Theodor de Bry's engraving of the Chickahominies ratification of a treaty with the English, from Johann Theodor de Bry, *Americae Pars Decima* (1619). The Chickahominy leader turns to the members of his tribe, who offer unanimous consent to the treaty. Courtesy of The Newberry Library.

enough to report a king's acquiescence. The English needed more convincing ways of representing consent.

In his account, Hamor addresses this problem by depicting the Chickahominies making collective decisions. "After these Articles were thus proposed," Hamor writes, "the whole assembly assenting thereunto, answered with a great shout, and noise, that they would readily and willingly perform them all."[67] While negotiations with the Powhatans might be complicated by the "revengefull" attitude of their chief, the English negotiate with the Chickahominies as a group.[68] From Hamor's perspective this is a more secure form of treaty than any between crown and Indian king. There will be no ambushes by uncontrollable subjects and no plausible deniability on the part of Chickahominy leaders. The collective shout guarantees the tribe's performance of the articles—and, by extension, the unopposed control of the English.

Despite this evidence of unanimous consent, Hamor does not attempt to deceive his readers as to the real reason behind the Chickahominies' submission. While the obedient Chickahominies may conform in some respects to the propagandistic image of the pliant Indian, Hamor knew that his audience was unlikely to believe such a shallow explanation of their motives. In an attempt to appear more credible, he lays out what he claims is the true impetus behind the Chickahominies' sudden and surprising offer. The reason for the "unexpected friendship," he writes, is not the superiority of English religion, or the allure of English culture, but rather the Chickahominies' own "sodaine feare of *Powhatans* displeasure."[69] Though the Chickahominies are strong enough to resist Powhatan, they realize they cannot withstand the Anglo-Powhatan alliance represented by Pocahontas's marriage to Rolfe. They therefore "chose rather to subject themselves to us, then being enemies to both, to expose & lay themselves open to *Powhatans* tiranny, & oppression." The Chickahominies' rebellion against Powhatan entirely suits Hamor's purposes. It has the benefit of corroborating English attempts to paint Powhatan as the villain of American politics, much as Smith had done in his *Proceedings*. Yet while Smith and Argall demonize Powhatan outright, describing him as a tyrannical murderer, Hamor puts the condemnation of the Powhatan leader in the mouths of the Chickahominies. "[T]hey ... insist ... that he was an ill *Weroaules*," Hamor writes, "full of cruelty and inj[u]stice, covetous of those things they had, and implacable if they denied him whatsoever he demaunded."[70] These lines have implications for the English understanding of the war. It was the result of Powhatan's evil disposition, Hamor suggests, not any inherent Native hostility. With the evil chief's power waning, colonization can proceed apace. Moreover, the Chickahominies' words give validity to the alliances that formerly Powhatan-affiliated groups have sought out with the English. They make peace with the English out of fear of Powhatan. While this is not exactly a free and voluntary agreement, the coercion is applied by Powhatan and not the English, leaving the integrity of the Anglo-Chickahominy treaty beyond question, at least in Hamor's view.

Though the marriage alliance inspires surrounding groups to submit and walk "in the waies of peace," it still leaves one political goal unaccomplished: the subjection of Powhatan himself. While Powhatan agrees to the alliance, he does not return all of the captives or stolen goods, and disavows any involvement in whatever depredations his less obedient subjects might have committed against the English. Hamor addresses this unfinished business by concluding his book with an account of a visit to what he calls Powhatan's "Court."[71] The real reason for this visit was an attempt by Dale to consolidate the Anglo-Powhatan alliance by marrying one of Powhatan's daughters himself. Powhatan bluntly refused the offer, claiming the daughter in question had already been married to a man from another tribe. While this response was a setback, Hamor describes the visit as a diplomatic success in spite of Powhatan's refusal. Hamor travels to Powhatan accompanied by Thomas Savage and some Indian guides. Upon their arrival, Powhatan sharply questions Hamor about the fact that he is not wearing a chain of pearls that, according to prior agreement, would authorize lesser Englishmen like Hamor to visit important Powhatans: "his first salutation, without any words at all, was about my necke, and with his hand he feeled round about it, so as I might have imagined he would have cut my throate . . . he asked me where the chaine of pearle was"[72] (see Figure 6). In the face of this interrogation, Hamor stutters his way to a response, claiming he believed the presence of the guides had made the necklace unnecessary. The answer seems to satisfy Powhatan, and negotiations proceed with small talk and the smoking of tobacco. In a typically indirect Powhatan style, the conversation slowly works its way around to Pocahontas. After Powhatan inquires after his daughter, Hamor tells the chief the princess "would not change her life to returne and live with him." Powhatan's response breaks the tension that surrounds the topic—"he laugh[s] heartily" at the news of his precocious daughter's easy adaptation to English ways.[73] This reported laughter may have reflected Powhatan's true feelings. Many sources indicate that he had a playful rapport with Pocahontas—indeed, the name "Pocahontas" itself, which meant "playful one," was a nickname he had given her (her real name was Matoaka). Yet Hamor is not particularly interested in their relationship. He cares only about the political implications of the chief's laughter, and reports it to show that Powhatan accepts the marriage as inevitable. The hearty chuckle, echoing across the meeting site, further illustrates the great chief's consent to the union.

After establishing this friendly footing, Hamor broaches the possibility of a second marriage between Dale and a younger daughter of Powhatan. Suddenly, Powhatan is quiet. While he appears to consent to Pocahontas's marriage, he refuses to entertain another offer. The moment seems like a defeat. Perhaps the alliance is not as strong as the English believe? Yet Hamor parleys the refusal into a success. It signifies, he explains, not Powhatan's rejection of the English, but rather his belief that one marriage is sufficient to tie the peoples. Powhatan

Figure 6. Powhatan inspects Hamor for the necklace that would authorize him to negotiate, from Johann Theodor de Bry, *Americae Pars Decima* (1619). Courtesy of The Newberry Library.

delivers an oration in characteristically high style. "I desire no firmer assurance of [the English king's] friendship," he says, "then [Dale's] promise which he hath already made unto mee; from me, he hath a pledge, one of my daughters, which so long as she lives shall be sufficient."[74] That Powhatan is opposed to the second offer is therefore of little importance, as Hamor tells it. The alliance stands as long as Pocahontas herself lives. If not entirely under English control, Powhatan is at least pacified.

The Powhatan of *A True Discourse* is a far more agreeable figure than the villain of Argall's letter. He is not in any way a pliant Indian; his physical man-handling of Hamor and his irked rejection of the second marriage offer show his independence. But he is more accommodating, or, at the very least, aware that the English have the upper hand. As an instance of Powhatan's newfound willingness to negotiate, Hamor describes a brief dispute over whether Powhatan escorts will deliver Hamor and his party back to Jamestown. While they

are readying to depart, Hamor and his men discover one of the English captives, who Powhatan had previously claimed was dead, "growen so like both in
complexion and habite to the *Indians*" that Hamor "onely [knows] him by his
tongue to be an Englishman."[75] A squabble quickly ensues. Powhatan agrees
to relinquish the captive, but refuses to send guides to take the party home.
Hamor tells him that if anything happens to the English on their way back,
all treaties will be null and void and they will attack him. Powhatan stomps
away with a scowl, but later returns and delivers a long speech in which he
agrees to the English request for escorts as long as they will pay him in prestige
goods. The moment illustrates, Hamor writes, "how charie *Powhatan* is, of the
conservation of peace . . . as may appeare by his answeres to my requests, and
also by my safe passage thither, & homwards, without the lest shew of injury
offred unto us, though divers times by the way, many stragli[n]g Indians met
us, which in former times, would gladly have taken so faire occasion to worke
their mischiefe and bloody designes upon us."[76] The passage heralds the end
of the war by *ambuscado* described in such detail in Smith's *Proceedings*. While
Powhatan had previously allowed his underlings to wreak havoc upon the English while denying involvement, now he has reined in the "stragli[n]g Indians."
Even if the evil chief has not formally submitted, the party's peaceful procession
home shows that his territory is safe ground. Proof enough of possession, from
Hamor's point of view.

Hamor's book was an attempt to frame Pocahontas's kidnapping as the
basis of a marriage alliance. This project involved a careful reconciliation of
existing narratives and colonial legal strategies. It also involved a meticulous
negotiation between voluntary treaty and just war as protocols of conquest. The
fact that the Virginia Company paid to have Hamor's book printed suggests
the advantages of publicizing the story. By emphasizing marriage instead of
war, they showed readers that the coast was pacified. However, in the climate
of skepticism that surrounded English colonial ventures, printed narratives
could only accomplish so much. To many in Virginia, Pocahontas's apparent
embrace of English ways suggested a far more intriguing possibility. As Hamor
was in London publishing his book, Dale was advocating for a strategy that, if
successful, could dramatically alter the colony's relationship with the English
government. He wanted to bring Pocahontas herself to London.

Pocahontas in the Metropolis

As I discussed in the first chapter, transatlantic visits were a central part of the Virginia Company's strategy for publicizing treaties with Native peoples. Much could be gained from advertising the colony's alliances in letters and print, but Indian visitors meant even more. They could testify in person to the integrity of treaties. They could bow to the king (or not, as in the case of Namontack). And they could profess their loyalty to the English crown. Yet bringing Indians to London was also risky. If the visitors voiced a contrary understanding of Anglo-Native alliances, the colony could find itself in an embarrassing position. If they possessed less than regal bearing, questions might arise as to the truth of the colony's claims about them. This was what had happened during Namontack's visit to James I in 1609. After that, war had swept across the Chesapeake Bay, and a transatlantic diplomatic campaign had been far from everyone's mind.

The colony revived this strategy with Pocahontas's visit to London in 1616. The visit offered a fascinating sight to onlookers in the court of James I, and scholars have written about it for hundreds of years. Nineteenth-century historians pointed to Pocahontas's conversion to English ways as a triumph of Anglo-American religion, even as they doubted the story that she had saved Smith from certain death.[77] In the latter part of the twentieth century, scholars approached the visit from a Powhatan perspective, emphasizing Pocahontas's agency, her acquisition of literacy, and her role in the sexual politics of colonization.[78] My discussion will emphasize a narrower set of topics—her role as a pawn in diplomatic negotiations between the English crown and Spanish and French ambassadors, and her involvement in publicizing and contesting the meaning of Anglo-Powhatan treaties in conversations with colonists. Pocahontas did not officially travel to London as a diplomat. Legal authorities and diplomatic manuals were silent about whether a Christian Indian could serve as an ambassador to a European prince, but as a woman Pocahontas could not serve as a diplomatic representative of her father. She was instead presented by the Virginia Company as foreign royalty. This does not mean that her visit did not have diplomatic significance, however. As I will discuss below, Pocahontas's words, dress, and comportment all had significance for how James I and the Europeans at his court understood Anglo-Powhatan treaty alliances.

Dale began to plan a trip across the Atlantic almost immediately after Pocahontas's marriage to Rolfe. Even though there were many precedents for such an embassy, Dale encountered a number of obstacles. One was financial. The company was badly in arrears and had little money to spend on what seemed to some a questionable extravagance. Councilors resisted Dale's requests for financial support. The violence of the war was too fresh in their minds, and it would undermine the colony's claims about peace if Pocahontas appeared hostile, or drew criticism from international observers.[79] Powhatan diplomacy also came into play. Powhatan agreed to the visit, but he wanted to exert control over the colony's plans. Since he had blessed the marriage, he no longer considered Pocahontas an English captive. On the contrary, he considered Rolfe a symbolic son. Rolfe and Pocahontas had even made regular visits to him throughout 1614, which Powhatan may have viewed as a measure of Rolfe's integration into the political life of Tsenacomoco.[80] Powhatan therefore insisted on retaining a degree of influence over where his daughter traveled, especially when it came to political embassies. He was willing to let her go to London if his priest, Uttamatomakkin, could go as well, along with a retinue of other Powhatans. This condition made Dale particularly uneasy. Presenting Pocahontas to high society was a complex enough endeavor, but Uttamatomakkin possessed an unshakable dedication to Native religion and power and was unlikely to play the part of pious convert.[81] If the colony wanted the political advantages that could come from a Powhatan visit to London, they had to face the risks as well.

After protracted negotiations over finances, the company finally agreed to bring Pocahontas, her family, and other Powhatans to London. One encouraging development, from the company's point of view, was Pocahontas's embrace of English religion. Colonial leaders had written home about Pocahontas's acculturation to English ways. As John Smith wrote, summarizing these reports, "Lady *Rebecca*, alias *Pocahontas*, daughter to *Powhatan*, by the diligent care of Master *John Rolfe* her husband and his friends, was taught to speake such *English* as might well bee understood, well instructed in Christianitie, and was become very formall and civill after our *English* manner."[82] However, while the colonists framed Pocahontas's conversion as a rejection of Indian culture, it was more likely a diplomatic choice. Powhatan women frequently negotiated multiple political and sexual identities. For decades, many of Pocahontas's sisters had played their part in marriage alliances designed to expand the Powhatan chiefdom.[83] It was expected that they would learn the language or dialect of their adoptive tribe and serve as liaisons between their old and new homes. From an early age, Pocahontas had probably anticipated such a marriage. Indeed, before she married Rolfe, she had been married to a Powhatan man named Kocoum, a fact Hamor conveniently omitted from *A True Discourse*.[84] Of course, English codes governing dress, sexuality, and female mobility differed radically from those of the Powhatans in ways too numerous to list. Yet, as I will now argue, Pocahontas understood English demands not as impositions, but rather as challenges befitting the importance of her office as a married envoy. While Europeans did not understand visiting female royalty as capable of engaging in formal diplomatic activities, Pocahontas behaved like an ambassador throughout her visit.

Pocahontas arrived in England in late June 1616. Her entourage was large, and must have seemed exotic even to those Londoners who had seen Native people before. It included John Rolfe and Pocahontas's son Thomas, as well as Dale and Argall, who were there to represent the colony. It also included numerous Powhatans, such as Uttamatomakkin, Matachanna, one of Pocahontas's half-sisters, and three women and four men whose names were not recorded.[85] The size of the entourage is evidence of Powhatan's hand in shaping the embassy. The company was financially strapped, yet agreed to provide for the travel of a large number of Powhatan visitors despite the costs and risks. They would not have done so unless they were under considerable pressure from Powhatan, who wanted his own interests represented.

While the procession attracted the attention of onlookers, the company did not intend for Pocahontas and her countrymen to be a public spectacle. They hoped instead to gain her introduction into elite circles where they might advertise their evangelical progress and use of treaties to control territory. Company leaders prepared the way for the visit by writing letters of introduction. News also spread through word of mouth. Unfortunately, few of these promotional materials are extant, but records of the visit in letters and diaries give some sense of how the Virginia Company publicized Pocahontas. John Chamberlain, a court attendant who recorded the details of her trip in a series of letters to Sir Dudley Carleton, ambassador to the Netherlands, described her arrival as a visit from foreign royalty. "Sir Thomas Dale is arrived from Virginia," he wrote, "and brought with him some ten or twelve old and younge of that countrie, among whom the most remarkable person is Poca-huntas (daughter of Powatan a kinge or cacique of that countrie) married to one Rolfe an English man."[86] Though brief, Chamberlain's remarks are revealing in two ways. First, he finds the matter worth mentioning to an ambassador. This is not surprising, given that early Powhatan envoys had met with Sir Robert Cecil, who at that time was Secretary of State.[87] Still, the fact that Chamberlain mentions

Figure 7. Compton Holland's engraving of Simon de Passe's 1617 portrait of Pocahontas, from John Smith, *The Generall Historie of Virginia, New-England, and the Summer Isles* (1624). Courtesy of The Newberry Library.

the matter to Carleton shows that the visit was viewed as a diplomatic affair, and not just a mere curiosity. Furthermore, news of Pocahontas's arrival apparently came to Chamberlain bundled with information about her royal lineage. This suggests the importance of her political status to the Virginia Company. Pocahontas's visit would have geopolitical significance only if she herself was an important figure, and company promoters emphasized her high birth in order to heighten her dignity. It is worth noting that Chamberlain describes Powhatan as a *cacique*. Spanish writers used this Arawakan word to refer to Indian vassals, and it had been introduced to English readers in Richard Eden's translation of Peter Martyr's *The Decades of the newe worlde* (1555), a compilation of Spanish narratives of exploration and conquest. By using the term, Chamberlain portrays Powhatan as a local leader answering to the English crown. The analogy may have been Chamberlain's own, but it also fits with the Virginia Company's changing relationship with the Powhatans. In 1607, they had coached Namontack to leave his hat on in order to show James I that he was a powerful person in America. By 1617, they had shifted to portraying Powhatan himself as a willing vassal of the crown.

Consistent with their claims about her royal status, the company outfitted Pocahontas as an aristocratic lady. In an engraving made by Simon de Passe near the end of her visit (the only contemporary image of her), Pocahontas appears outfitted in the clothing of a noblewoman with a quill pen in her right hand (see Figure 7). This clothing had a crucial purpose. If Pocahontas was going to gain entrance to English society as part of a foreign delegation, it was necessary that she be outfitted as a lady. The inclusion of the quill visually reiterated claims about her literacy. The fact that de Passe produced the engraving is also revealing. He later produced engravings for James I, his family members, and his allies among the nobility. That de Passe engraved Pocahontas's portrait suggests the considerable international significance of the visit.[88]

Pocahontas also paid respects to important English luminaries. While the Virginia Company promoted Pocahontas as a visiting princess, no truly important dignitaries were likely to visit her in the modest lodgings it could afford. It was up to Dale and others to seek the audience of powerful people. Widespread curiosity about Pocahontas made this task easier. The bishop of London, John King, invited Pocahontas to Lambeth Palace, where, according to Samuel Purchas, he "entertained her with festivall state and pompe, beyond what [Purchas had] seene in his great hospitalitie afforded to other Ladies."[89] Of course, respect for Pocahontas's royal lineage was probably not the only reason the Bishop staged such a lavish reception. He could add to his own reputation by publicizing his role in evangelizing Indians.[90] He may also have wanted to investigate the extent of her conversion. While no exchange between Pocahontas and Anglican authorities is recorded at Lambeth Palace, Purchas debated Uttamatomakkin in a private meeting, concluding that the Powhatan priest was a "blasphemer."[91] Though perhaps ironic in tone, Purchas's reference to "state and pomp" suggests that the Bishop extended to Pocahontas the same courtesies allowed other princesses—evidence that the company's attempts to portray her as a visiting dignitary had persuaded him of her standing.

Gaining an audience with such an important figure was a major accomplishment for the Virginia Company. A convincing performance of cultural conversion—which Pocahontas apparently delivered—had the potential to move the Bishop to invest money in the colony. More importantly, a lavish reception heightened the appearance that Pocahontas was a visiting foreign lady—a crucial concern if the marriage treaty was to appear valid. Yet Pocahontas's visit to Lambeth Palace was quickly followed by an even more important appearance. James I invited Pocahontas and Uttamatomakkin to a performance of Ben Jonson's Twelfth Night masque, *The Vision of Delight*, at Whitehall Palace. Royal masques were always sites of international intrigue.[92] Quite frequently, the seating arrangements led to squabbling among European ambassadors, who saw placement at royal spectacles as a sign of favor, and jockeyed to receive better accommodations than their rivals. Pocahontas arrived in London at a time of particularly intense lobbying over seating arrangements. Standing behind these seemingly petty struggles was a broader conflict over international alliances in the years after the Anglo-Spanish War. While Spain had resumed diplomatic relationships with the English after the signing of the Treaty of London in 1604, French and Dutch ambassadors continued to occupy preferred places at ceremonies, feasts, and masques. Diego Sarmiento de Acuña, the first count of Gondomar, a Spanish diplomat who had arrived in London in 1613 and considerably endeared himself to James I, had declared early in his tenure that he would not appear in public with the Dutch ambassador, leading to the weakening of the Dutch embassy as Gondomar's prestige grew.[93] A few weeks before the first performance of *The Vision of Delight*, Gondomar pressed his advantage, arranging to have the French ambassador excluded from the banquet celebrating Charles's crowning as the Prince of Wales.[94] This was more than minor harassment. Behind the scenes, Gondomar was lobbying for a match between Charles and the Spanish *infanta*.[95] His aim in protesting the seating arrangements was to introduce discord into the relationship between James I and the French delegation, in the hopes of troubling any possible Anglo-French alliance.[96] While Gondomar was little concerned with Pocahontas, his plans had an unintended effect on her. As the ambassadors complained bitterly about their invitations, James made the dramatic choice to seat Pocahontas and Uttamatomakkin on the royal dais at the king's left, a spot typically reserved for visiting monarchs or their ambassadors.[97] This was a diplomatic strategy akin to Newport's crowning of Powhatan. It conveyed symbolic recognition on Pocahontas and Uttamatomakkin, visually elevating them to the position of royal representatives of a foreign principality. As powerful as the image must have appeared to the gathered dignitaries, however, it is important not to confuse James's gesture with the kind of recognition he would have granted Europeans in the same seat. Neither James nor his European visitors believed that Native American chiefs or princesses were the equal of Christian monarchs (or even their diplomats), and James did not intend to signal his respect for the political autonomy or territorial boundaries of Tsenacomoco. He was using the display of recognition in the same way the colony itself had—to publicize Native treaties as a form of possession. It is possible that there was a good deal of ironic satisfaction in the gesture. While the reign of Elizabeth had been marked by war with Spain, the Spanish and French ambassadors now found themselves in competition for James's favor. Seating Pocahontas on the royal dais was a way of capriciously displaying England's rising power. James would seat whom he wanted at his left—even an Indian princess.

The masque itself was among the most expensive of James's reign. The king paid for it himself, and it was staged by Inigo Jones.[98] According to contemporary accounts, it included a number of elaborate props and devices, such as painted scenery designed to give the illusion of depth and suspended actors and chariots that seemed to levitate above the audience. A number of scholarly accounts have assumed that Pocahontas was astonished by these illusions. Philip L. Barbour imagines that "the theatrical realism and pyrotechnics of such an extravaganza must have seemed the product of inconceivable sorcery."[99] However, Pocahontas came from a political culture in which costuming and performance were central. Powhatan politics included many kinds of spectacles, and Pocahontas had helped stage them on numerous occasions.[100] It is unlikely she was overcome with awe in the face of the show. By now she knew what it meant to behave like an English lady. She probably conducted herself with the same decorum as that noted by Purchas in the procession at Lambeth Palace.

At the conclusion of the masque, the actors invited royal viewers on the dais to join them in two concluding dances, the *galliard* and the *corranto*.[101] Typically, masquers only extended such invitations to those who knew the dances or had rehearsed them beforehand. It is not known if Pocahontas was among those called down. However, it is not out of the realm of possibility. Pocahontas was an experienced diplomatic performer in Tsenacomoco, where political negotiations typically included dancing, and it is plausible that the company might have wanted to display her in this way.[102] Some of the wives and daughters of company leaders had attended masques before and may have taught her the steps of these particular dances.[103] And there was some precedent for colonial participation in courtly dances. Jonson's *The Irish Masque at Court* (1613) had portrayed Irishmen joining dances to display their acceptance of English culture and authority.[104] A mastery of such dances would have shown Pocahontas's acclimation to European ways and boosted the company's claims to have brought the coast under control. A misstep might have called into question her civility and cast doubt on the colony's propaganda.

The appearance of an Indian princess in such a highly visible position must have occasioned comment from many observers. One voice that is seemingly absent from the historical record is that of Pocahontas herself. A number of historians have remarked on her silence in company archives. Much was made of her visit, but no one in the company believed it was worth recording her opinions about the unfamiliar world in which she found herself. Many explanations have been offered for this silence in the record. Most suggest that the English ignored her because she was an Indian, a woman, or both.[105] This view is certainly justifiable; the English who interacted with Pocahontas were undoubtedly manipulating her for their own purposes, as colonists almost always did when it came to Native people. At the masque, Pocahontas was a pawn in European negotiations that had little obvious relevance to her. Yet as I argued in my discussion of Powhatan and the English crown, treaty writings were part of a broader world of political communication that included oral performances, rituals, and objects. English and Native people appropriated these symbols freely, and while most English writings come from figures with an investment in a specific understanding of the law of nations and its application to Native peoples, others had different agendas, and offer perspectives on Native political cultures that shed light on Powhatan's interpretations of events. I will now turn to a description of Pocahontas's embassy to London from an author who was an outsider to important negotiations over Pocahontas. In this case, however,

I consider not the writings of a laborer like Henry Spelman but rather those of the company's extremely articulate critic—Captain John Smith. By the time Pocahontas arrived in London, Smith was no longer important to Virginia. Pocahontas's handlers had no reason to seek out an audience with him, and as I will show below, they had many reasons not to do so. Yet Smith contacted Pocahontas shortly before she was planning to return to Jamestown, and published a brief account of their conversation several years later in his *Generall Historie of Virginia, New-England, and the Summer Isles* (1624). The book is an argument for Smith's own usefulness as a colonial guide, yet it also purports to record some of Pocahontas's views, raising the possibility that Smith's account, like Spelman's, provides a window into what the Powhatans wanted with English treaties.

Fathers, Sons, and Daughters: Pocahontas and Smith in London

The silence of Pocahontas in contemporary records was not the result of a lack of English interest in her views. On the contrary, it showed the importance of Native voices to English legal strategies. Native words and gestures could be politically explosive, and English people sought to control their circulation. Pocahontas's behavior in London was too important for the company to allow her to socialize outside controlled circumstances. The relative absence of critical comments about Pocahontas suggests that she performed adeptly in her staged interactions with important English people. Indeed, it is unlikely that James would have invited her to Whitehall had he or his ministers received reports of her behaving or speaking clumsily, or voicing opinions contrary to what the English wanted to hear. However, many people had their own reasons for wanting to see her. A number of prominent figures visited her at the Bell Savage Inn, where she and her party resided. One was Ben Jonson, who later dramatized the encounter in *The Staple of Newes* (1625). Conspicuously absent among her visitors was Smith. Smith later claimed that he was too busy to visit her. This is an unlikely explanation, given that he later went to great lengths to see her after she made a successful appearance in society. It is possible that Smith sought out an audience with her but was refused. The Virginia party had a good reason not to receive him. Smith had played a role in brokering Powhatan's first alliances with Newport and other Jamestown governors, and Powhatan continued to understand these relationships in terms of kinship ties. He viewed Newport as a symbolic brother and Smith as a symbolic son.[106] In order to escape obligations under these alliances, Jamestown leaders had told Powhatan that Smith and Newport were dead, which, according to Powhatan custom, would have voided the earlier treaties.[107] Virginia Colony leaders may not have wanted Pocahontas or Uttamatomakkin to know that Smith was still alive. If he came knocking in London, they may have ignored his requests, hoping he would go away.

They had no such luck. Smith sought out an interview with Pocahontas after her successful reception in society. Smith's desire to see her had a lot to do with his wish to return to America. Pocahontas's appearance at Whitehall, a major diplomatic venue, made any association with her even more important. His failure to see Pocahontas in London did not stop Smith from writing himself into the story of her visit. In his *Generall Historie*, Smith reprints a letter he claims to have sent to Queen Anne in 1616 to "[make Pocahontas's] qualities knowne to the Queenes most excellent Majestie and her Court" and to plead with the queen to formally receive Pocahontas.[108] As with Smith's account of his kidnapping and rescue at her hands many years earlier, there are several reasons to doubt that the letter and dialogue are authentic. No other copy of it has been found, and no other sources corroborate what it describes.[109] In printing what he claims is a 1616 letter in 1624, Smith was trying to heighten his own reputation as a cross-cultural negotiator. The letter repeats the story of Smith's rescue at her hands, and adds that she saved the starving colony by giving them corn. Smith also describes how she delivered the colony from a Powhatan conspiracy by warning them of a surprise attack. "[N]ext under God," he claims, Pocahontas "was still the instrument to preserve this Colonie from death, famine and utter confusion." Receiving her in England is important, not simply because her service should be recognized, but because it will be the key to bringing the Indians' country under control. "[I]f she should not be well received," Smith pleads, "seeing this Kingdome [England] may rightly have a Kingdome by her meanes; her present love to us and Christianitie, might turne to such scorne and furie, as to divert all this good to the worst of evill."[110] From the hindsight of 1624, Smith clearly intends this warning as a foreshadowing of the Powhatan Uprising of 1622, a costly war that claimed many English lives. Smith implies that a cross-cultural rapport of the kind he developed with Pocahontas is essential to controlling the frontier and preventing the outbreak of future wars. The letter is less a plea to Queen Anne on behalf of Pocahontas than a plea for Smith himself to be sent to New England in 1624, where he believes his facility as a diplomat will be of use in preventing future uprisings.

Though Smith's account of introducing Pocahontas to Queen Anne is probably a fabrication, Smith himself did gain an audience with Pocahontas at Branford in January 1617, shortly before she was to depart for Virginia. Dale, Argall, and other Virginia Colony leaders are not mentioned in Smith's account of the meeting, suggesting that Smith may have approached the party when he knew they would be away. And while Smith later depicted the meeting as a social visit, he had to travel a long way to see her, also suggesting considerable design on his part. Yet despite the fact that the exchange is entirely filtered through Smith's perspective, his own voice is not the only one to appear. Smith presents a conversation between himself and Pocahontas, quoting her words directly. While Smith usually frames his interactions with Native people according to English understandings of possession, this conversation finds Pocahontas giving voice to a contrary understanding of Anglo-Powhatan treaties, one that may have reflected her views at the time.

The episode opens with Pocahontas giving Smith the cold shoulder. "Being about this time preparing to set saile for *New-England*," he writes, "I could not stay to doe her that service I desired, and she well deserved; but hearing shee was at *Branford* with divers of my friends, I went to see her: After a modest salutation, without any word, she turned about, obscured her face, as not seeming well contented; and in that humour her husband, with divers others, we all left her two or three houres, repenting my selfe to have writ she could speake *English*." After maintaining this uncomfortable silence for some time, Pocahontas wheels suddenly around and issues a stern rebuke to Smith, sharply contradicting any notion that the colonists are faithful treaty partners. "But not long after, she began to talke," Smith goes on, "and remembred mee well what courtesies shee had done: saying, You did promise *Powhatan* what was yours should bee his, and he the like to you; you called him father being in his land a stranger, and by the same reason so must I doe you."[111] By angrily addressing Smith as her father, Pocahontas invokes the original 1608 agreement between Newport and Powhatan, which had made Smith a symbolic son of Powhatan. Her language is somewhat difficult to interpret, however. According to Powhatan views of kinship alliance, Powhatan and Newport were brothers. As Newport's delegate, Smith had become an adoptive son of Powhatan when the agreement was formalized. On this count, the fact that Pocahontas calls Smith "father" is puzzling. If anything, the agreement between Powhatan and Newport would seem to make Pocahontas and Smith siblings, not father and child. It could be that Pocahontas's insistence on calling Smith "father" is an ironic commentary on the English practice of making alliances for convenience. While the English break treaties when it suits them, Pocahontas insists that agreements are still binding, however far from Tsenacomoco they might be.

While it is easy to find the editorial hand of English people in the accounts of Pocahontas's kidnapping and marriage, Smith's conversation with Pocahontas is more complicated. She is concerned solely with Powhatan notions of kinship alliance, and says nothing about the law of nations. This fact raises the intriguing possibility that the lines are an accurate representation of something Pocahontas herself might have said.[112] Our knowledge of Smith's own practice as a writer suggests some reasons why Pocahontas's words may have appeared in his book in relatively unfiltered form. Like many colonial promoters, Smith compiled his books from other sources.[113] These included the narratives of other colonial travelers as well as letters and memoranda. It is possible that Smith copied Pocahontas's words from a 1616 record of the conversation. Jotting down summaries of conversations was a common practice in the courtly culture that Smith so desperately wanted to join.[114] He may have written down her words (or a rough summary of them) in 1616 and, when preparing the *Generall Historie* for the printer, inserted them into his manuscript without editing them, possibly because the Powhatan Uprising had since rendered moot Pocahontas's understanding of alliance and there was no longer any need to filter or edit her words.[115] Such an interpretation would be consistent with Smith's practice in the rest of the book, which includes many orations, letters, debates, and other kinds of directly reported communications.

However, while Pocahontas's biting words do not reference European legal systems or support English claims in any obvious way, they are not entirely inconsistent with Smith's goals in the book. As the conversation proceeds, Pocahontas continues to reproach Smith, but in a way that suggests his importance to English colonial ventures. In response to her insistence on calling him "father," Smith feigns anxiety at the fact that she has exposed his claims to royalty in Virginia, telling her that, as a commoner, he cannot accept such respect from a princess. "I durst not allow of that title [father], because she was a Kings daughter," he replies.[116] But Pocahontas sees these words as a ruse, and reminds the suddenly proper Smith that he had been bold in violating other social and political boundaries in Tsenacomoco. "Were you not afraid to come into my fathers Countrie," she asks, "and caused feare in him and all his people (but mee) and feare you here I should call you father; I tell you then I will, and you shall call mee childe, and so I will bee for ever and ever your Countrieman. They did tell us alwaies you were dead, and I knew no other till I came to *Plim-*

oth; yet *Powhatan* did command *Uttamatomakkin* to seeke you, and know the truth, because your Countriemen will lie much."[117]

In the face of English claims that the old alliance is dead, Pocahontas points out that the colonists have lied about Smith's demise, and angrily insists that she and Smith will always be allies as long as they live. She also criticizes Smith for his terrorizing diplomacy. Yet even though her words make Smith look bad, they do not necessarily harm his cause. The marriage had ushered in a new political order and rendered the treaties brokered by Smith largely irrelevant. And the Powhatan Uprising had destroyed any hope of peace. But by printing Pocahontas's accusations, Smith suggests that the early negotiations in which he played an important part were meaningful to the Powhatans for years afterward. The Indians have long memories, he implies, and his presence in the New World would still be useful.

This angry conversation was one of Pocahontas's last interactions of consequence in London. Her diplomatic itinerary was costly to the company. They had spent roughly four pounds a week to clothe and transport her in the style required of visiting royalty, and they were eager to leave before anything happened that might spoil the good impression she had made on so many important people.[118] In early March 1617, straining under the cost of the visit, the company made arrangements for the Rolfes to leave London. Pocahontas apparently objected to the decision.[119] After the whirlwind tour, she may have been less than enthusiastic about returning to her relatively cloistered existence as Rolfe's wife. Diplomacy was what she knew, and judging by her enthusiastic reception among high society in London, she moved almost as adeptly among the powerful in England as she did in Tsenacomoco. But the colony had other plans for her. The visit was an attempt to leverage power in two directions. The company wanted to increase their standing among metropolitan leaders, but they also wanted to bring Pocahontas back to Virginia and use her (and her child Thomas) to lay claim to the Chesapeake Bay.

These hopes received a blow when Pocahontas fell violently ill at Gravesend shortly after her departure from London and died around the middle of March. The cause was likely an air-borne contagion to which she had no immunity. The English people she had met in London took notice of her death. Mortality was never surprising, but the death of a foreign princess on English soil was a politically significant event.[120] Yet while Pocahontas's death inspired comment in London, it bred anxiety in Jamestown. In the months since Pocahontas's departure, Anglo-Powhatan relations had come under great strain. The adoption of the tobacco crop, and the appropriation of Indian lands for its cultivation, had renewed older hostilities and strained the new alliance. More than ever, the colonists needed someone who could negotiate between Jamestown and the new leaders, Itoyatin and Opechancanough, Powhatan's brothers, who had begun to assume control of the colony as the aging Powhatan released his grip on power.[121] The absence of any mediator turned out to be more costly than either side could have imagined. Five years and one day after Pocahontas's funeral, the Powhatans, along with many allies, attacked English settlements. The ensuing war resulted in devastating casualties on both sides and put peace forever beyond reach. Pocahontas was not there to see the diplomatic pathways she knew so well overrun by Powhatan warriors and English soldiers. It is impossible to know what difference she might have made. Yet her name and the treaty associated with her marriage were frequently invoked on both sides in the events leading up to the war. Like her kidnapping, wedding, and visit to London, Pocahontas's death was a diplomatic event, and had profound implications for peace and possession.

Mourning Pocahontas and Waging War

The Virginia Company had put considerable hopes in Pocahontas's journey to London. They believed that a good showing on her part would convince supporters of the colony's peaceful relations with the Powhatans. But the visit had meaning in Virginia as well. As Powhatan aged, Itoyatin and Opechancanough were taking control. During this transitional time, many English believed that Pocahontas and her child gave them a way of staking their own claim over the region. Her sudden death threw these plans into disarray, depriving them of an advocate for English authority. Moreover, the colony had expected Pocahontas herself to raise Thomas Rolfe as an English leader with a claim to the sachemship of Tsenacomoco. Without her, it would be much more difficult to make such a claim, especially as power shifted from Powhatan to his brothers.

As company leaders contemplated the situation at Gravesend, they decided to leave Thomas Rolfe in England, believing that the mere fact of his survival might be enough to preserve the marriage alliance. But this strategy raised a new set of publicity problems, which in turn required a new round of treaty justifications. Powhatan adherence to the marriage alliance would depend upon convincing the sachems that Thomas Rolfe would eventually return. As we have already seen in Pocahontas's confrontation of John Smith, the Powhatans knew that the English could be dishonest about matters of life and death in order to manipulate treaties. If Pocahontas had lived, she might have mediated between colony and tribe, but without her, it would not be easy for the English to convince the Powhatans that Thomas was alive, or that the English believed in any alliance. Moreover, members of the London Council were keen to know how Powhatan would view Pocahontas's death. If he accepted the idea that Thomas's survival preserved the alliance, it would represent a political victory for Jamestown. If not, or if Itoyatin and Opechancanough gained control, the colony's prospects would again be uncertain.

It is not known how Jamestown leaders communicated news of Pocahontas's death to Powhatan. Usually, they relayed sensitive diplomatic information through a messenger. This was easier on both parties—it allowed them to communicate without the performance of the elaborate diplomatic protocols demanded by a meeting between high-ranking leaders. However, there is some evidence that Rolfe personally told Powhatan about her death. There are two extant written records of Powhatan's response to the news, one a letter from Rolfe to Sir Edwin Sandys, the company's treasurer, and the other a digest of a letter from Argall to the Virginia Company. Both focus on Powhatan's emotions, gestures, and words to suggest that the marriage alliance will hold, even in the event of Pocahontas's passing.

Rolfe wrote back first in June of 1617, probably soon after landing. In his letter, he moves quickly to minimize the effect of Pocahontas's death on the colony's plans. On return, he writes, "Wee found the Colony (God be thanked) in good estate and injoying a firmer Peace." Rolfe assures readers that the news of Pocahontas's death has not diminished the Powhatans' willingness to give their children over to English households. "The Indyans [are] very loving, and willing to parte with their children," he claims. Powhatan's response to the news of Pocahontas's death is one of sadness, combined with a desire for the alliance to continue. "My wives death is much lamented," Rolfe reports, "my childe much desyred, when it is of better strength to endure so hard a passage, whose life greately extinguisheth the sorrow of her loss, saying all must die, but tis enough that her child liveth."[122] According to Rolfe, Powhatan accepts the fact that Pocahontas is dead and does not believe that the English are lying to him. He agrees with the decision to leave Thomas in London. Most importantly, he is committed to the notion that Thomas will one day return and assume power. By reporting Powhatan's words and emotions, Rolfe performs a kind of damage control. He attempts to show that Pocahontas's marriage will continue to have a pacifying effect on Virginia Indians, even after her death.

Around the same time, Samuel Argall also wrote to London to present his version of events. His letter does not survive, but a secretary in London made a digest of it. Argall's letter is more realistic about the colony's state. Virginia is in a "ruinous condition," he reports, contradicting Rolfe.[123] The Powhatans are "so poor [they] can't pay their Debts and Tribute." But like Rolfe, Argall is unwilling to abandon the marriage alliance. The friendship between peoples holds, he emphasizes, even in the face of mutually deteriorating fortunes. "Powhatan goes from place to place visiting his Country taking his pleasure in good friendship with us," the letter reports. In phrasing similar to Rolfe's, the letter relays that Powhatan "laments his Daughter's Death but [is] glad her Child is living." Both Powhatan and Opechancanough "want to see [Thomas] but desir[e] that he may be stronger before he returns."[124] Like Rolfe, Argall similarly emphasizes the prospects of an alliance based around Thomas. He cannily adds that Opechancanough has an equal investment in the child, suggesting that even if Powhatan dies or relinquishes power, Powhatan's brother will still recognize Thomas as a legitimate heir.

These letters masked what was in reality an increasingly dire situation for all sides. While Rolfe and Argall had downplayed the effect of Pocahontas's death, Opechancanough had little interest in permanently resuming the former peace. There was also concern over other intelligence that had come back from England. On his return, for example, Uttamatomakkin had sought to persuade Opechancanough of the fundamental dishonesty of the English. Argall had caught wind of these negative reports, and, hoping to minimize any damage they might do to the colony's reputation, reported to London that the Powhatans were not listening to the priest's stories. "Tomakin [Uttamatomakkin] rails against . . . English people," Argall wrote, "and particularly his best friend Tho: Dale[.] all his reports are disproved before opachanko [Opechancanough] & his Great men whereupon (to the great satisfaccion of the Great men) Tomakin is disgraced."[125] Argall's account of the Powhatans' internal deliberations is certainly reassuring from the English point of view. The "Great men" of the Powhatans shout down any skepticism about English plans and the unhappy priest is "disgraced." However, Opechancanough was far more receptive to Uttamatomakkin than Argall reports in his letter. Uttamatomakkin had been sent to collect reconnaissance, and his news was troubling. One bit of information he brought home may have concerned English numbers, long a subject of debate in Tsenacomoco. According to an account by Purchas, Uttamatomakkin had taken a mnemonic stick with him to England and had attempted to count the people he saw by making cuts along its length.[126] Its units were suitable to populations that could be counted in the hundreds, but he had run out of room long before reaching London. The English had derided him for his naïveté, yet the sheer size of the English population was cause for alarm in Werowoco-moco.[127] More importantly for the question of alliances, Uttamatomakkin had also told Opechancanough about the reception he had met with in London. He had not been not treated like an ally, he said. They had not given him gifts worthy of his stature or of the people he represented. Moreover, he had discovered that John Smith was still alive, enforcing Powhatan beliefs that the English were liars and that the 1608 treaty should retain validity. All of these pieces of information suggested that the English were not serious about the alliance. They were playing games, just as they had with John Smith. They were a greater threat than even Powhatan had imagined.[128]

In the immediate aftermath of Pocahontas's death, Anglo-Powhatan relations were peaceful. After Powhatan's death in April of 1618, Opechancanough made a treaty of military assistance with the English.[129] Argall even claimed that he gave the "Country to mr Rolfe Child and that they will reserve it from all others till he comes of yeares."[130] The Virginia Company felt confident enough that one of its ministers preached of "a happie league of Peace and Amitie soundly concluded, and faithfully kept, betweene the *English* and the *Natives*, that the feare of killing each other is now vanished away."[131] However, Opechancanough was not serious about peace, even if he publicly accepted Thomas Rolfe's legitimacy as heir to the chiefdom. He was exploiting the English willingness to make treaties in order to conceal his plans to drive them from the coast. There were many reasons that Opechancanough decided to attack the English in 1622.[132] However, Uttamatomakkin's report about treaty negotiations and the treatment of allies was likely a factor. It suggested that the English could be neither controlled nor trusted. It is impossible to know how Pocahontas might have shaped the reception of this information. Perhaps she might have brought back a different story, one that softened Uttamatomakkin's warnings and persuaded Opechancanough to act differently. Her embrace of the role of an English lady suggests that she imagined a future in which English and Powhatan people would live together and rule jointly. However, her conversation with John Smith suggests that she, too, was disenchanted by the Virginia government and had lost faith in the promises of colonial leaders. Whatever the case, when war commenced, it marked the final, violent end of stately soliciting in Chesapeake Bay.

Pocahontas's kidnapping, marriage, and death were events of geopolitical consequence. The Virginia Colony government sought to depict them as evidence of their possession of the country in the name of the crown. The Powhatan Uprising destroyed these plans, bringing an end to marriage alliance as a strategy for controlling territory in the Chesapeake Bay. After the war, the colony reverted to the justifications of conquest that Argall had so righteously articulated in his denunciation of the Powhatans in Hamor's *True Discourse*. In a book printed in 1622, Edward Waterhouse, a colonial planner, described the laws that would henceforth be applied to the Powhatans. Echoing Argall's language (which in turn echoed that of Vitoria), Waterhouse wrote, "because our hands which before were tied with gentlenesse and faire usage, are now set at liberty by the treacherous violence of the Savages, not untying the Knot, but cutting it: So that we, who hitherto have had possession of no more ground then their waste, and our purchase at a valuable consideration to their owne contentment, gained; may now by right of Warre, and law of Nations, invade the Country, and destroy them who sought to destroy us: whereby wee shall enjoy their cultivated places, turning the laborious Mattocke into the victorious Sword (wherein there is more both ease, benefit, and glory) and possessing the fruits of others labours."[133] Ironically, Waterhouse's words reverse the familiar argument that vacant or wasted land could be possessed by Christian princes. Here the Indians are not vagrants or itinerants who make no investment in the land. They are instead sedentary farmers who raise crops, which the English can now seize. In one stroke, the war solves the problems of both legal legitimacy and food shortages.

Waterhouse's words reflected official company policy after the Powhatan Uprising. After the war, the Powhatans would exist only as a conquered people and tillers of the earth, not as voluntary subjects of the crown.[134] The implementation of this policy spelled the end of Anglo-Powhatan treaties as a strategy for proving international claims. Having brought peace by the sword, the colonists no longer needed to prove it with their pens. However, this does not mean that treaties disappeared in English transatlantic correspondence. As the Virginia Colony gained a military advantage over the Powhatans and abandoned voluntary treaties for violent conquest, a numerically small group of religious dissenters many latitudes north embraced the strategy of staking claims through alliances. Unlike the Virginia colonists, these settlers were not immediately threatened by the Spanish, who, after the securing of Virginia, largely stopped protesting English movements. However, the territory north of

Virginia was traveled by French and Dutch traders and privateers, and like the Chesapeake Bay, it was controlled by Native leaders who were determined to defend it, even as they reached out to Europeans for alliances and trade. While the Virginia colonists had not known what to expect, the settlers to the north had the benefit of hindsight. They had read the books about Virginia. They had observed the Powhatan Uprising from afar. They knew that when it came to conquering the New World, guns and treaties went hand in hand.

Chapter 3

—ɱ—

Gunpowder Diplomacy: Arms and Alliance in Plymouth and Patuxet

The English governors and their Native allies gathered around the strange-looking thing that had appeared in Plymouth town. A messenger from the Narragansetts had delivered it that morning to Squanto, a Patuxet interpreter living there with the English. It was easy enough to describe what it was: "arrowes lapped in a rattle Snakes skin," as Edward Winslow, the colony's diplomat, later put it.[1] But what did it mean? It wasn't a friendly sign—they didn't need Squanto to tell them that. Arrows were a universal symbol of hostility among Europeans and Natives alike, and these were sharpened at the end, like arrows freshly prepared for war and hunting.[2] The snakeskin, too, was an obvious insult. It seemed a threatening mockery of the trade in fur skins that formed the basis of so many cross-cultural friendships in the region. But what kind of threat, exactly? Was it a declaration of war, or merely a show of disdain? After a nervous conference with Squanto, the colony decided on a catchall response. William Bradford, governor of Plymouth Colony, "stuffed the skin with powder and shot, and sent it backe."[3] This message was clear enough: whatever your intentions toward us, our weapons are better than yours.

The move was pure bluster on Bradford's part. In reality, the snakeskin bundle set off a panic in Plymouth, just as the Narragansetts hoped it would. For the next few weeks, the colony mobilized, building walls and gates and organizing a militia. That such a cryptic gesture could compel such a drastic response was a measure of their vulnerability. Their numbers depleted by hunger and sickness, the colonists knew they could not withstand an attack from the powerful Narragansetts. They felt relief, then, when the snakeskin bundle made its way back to Plymouth after the Narragansetts refused it, seemingly declining the challenge. With no attack in sight, the matter appeared settled, at least for the time being.

Just a few years later, however, the Pilgrims had occasion to repackage the snakeskin yet again, this time in the medium of the written word. In 1624, Edward Winslow traveled to London to report on the colony's first years. He published a book called *Good Newes from New-England* (1624). It opened, not with an account of the colony's religious or economic progress, but with the story of the snakeskin bundle. To Winslow, the incident, though troubling, seemed a compelling illustration of the settlers' adherence to international norms in their dealings with Indians. They had responded to the Narragansetts in a way consistent with the law of nations, "manifesting . . . desire of peace" while showing "fearelesse resolution" to defend themselves. In their treatment of the messenger, the colony's governors had observed "the Law of Armes," which prevailed "amongst [the Indians] as us in *Europe*."[4] And while causing "no small terrour" in Canonicus, the "savage King" of the Narragansetts, the snakeskin bundle had produced another political outcome.[5] It had strengthened the colonies' "continued peace" with the Pokanokets, and their sachem Massasoit, who supported English endeavors against a common Narragansett enemy.[6] The whole episode demonstrated that the colony and its backers were agents for "the inlarging of his Majesties Dominions," or the conquest of territory for the English crown.[7]

Winslow's insistence on law and diplomacy is striking, given the hostility and violence that pervade his book. Gunpowder and snakeskin were not the usual instruments of statecraft. Yet as Winslow portrays it, the return of the bundle was not an act of desperation. The fear inspired by English munitions is central to the Pilgrims' ability to control the Indians and secure the land. While English numbers are small, the colonists command the Indians by displaying their firepower. And while menacing, Bradford's response is not actually violent; he subdues the Narragansetts without spilling a drop of blood. Relaying the bundle to London through the medium of print, Winslow describes a quiet and lawful colony living in good subjection to the crown.

In this chapter, I consider the diplomatic performances and treaty documents of Plymouth Colony during the early 1620s. I examine how Plymouth colonists, like their counterparts in Virginia, used treaties with Native people to show they were controlling territory. However, in moving from the Chesapeake Bay to the sparsely populated latitudes of early New England, I also shift my focus to a new diplomatic tactic—the use of guns as a means of securing voluntary alliances. It may seem paradoxical to claim, as Winslow does, that firearms could serve as an implement of diplomacy. It may seem more paradoxical still to argue that political arrangements made at gunpoint could embody *consensus ad idem*, or voluntary agreement, a claim the Pilgrims would make many times in their writings. However, as I will detail in this chapter, the display of arms, like the pledging of hostages, was a recognized tactic of diplomacy among both Europeans and Native people.[8] As well as possessing the power to maim or kill, weapons carried many kinds of symbolic value. Brandishing guns, knives, or arrows was a way of showing strength or a willingness to use violence. Likewise, putting weapons down, or keeping them out of sight, was a sign of friendship and trust. Weapons were sought-after trade goods as well. Guns, in particular, signified economic might and connections to inland and transatlantic trading routes, and European governments tried strenuously to control their trade.[9] Weapons and munitions also carried significance in political and legal systems. Under many understandings of the laws of war, Christian princes who felt threatened by pagans' weapons were authorized to launch preemptive strikes.[10] Combat among Native peoples likewise included displays of weaponry that communicated intentions and justifications as a prologue to fighting.[11] Yet whether openly violent or slyly threatening, the brandishing of weapons was rarely just an improvised tactic. It was, I argue, a mode of diplomatic performance, a regime of expressive behaviors that possessed significance for both Native and English understandings of the power and legitimacy of political agreements.

The Pilgrims have long been associated with guns. Beginning with William Bradford, chroniclers of the colony's history have depicted them using firearms to defend themselves from hostile Indians. Nineteenth-century historians domesticated the Pilgrims' guns, depicting settlers as peacemakers and hunters, an association captured in the image of Pilgrims shooting turkeys with wide-flared blunderbusses in anticipation of a Thanksgiving feast.[12] In the latter half of the twentieth century, a number of historians have presented a radically different view of the Pilgrims and their guns, pointing to Plymouth colonists' aggressive wars against Native groups and their attempts to establish a monopoly on the regional gun trade.[13] This scholarship has done much to erase the image of the Pilgrims as judicious in their exercise of violence. Yet while the Pilgrims were undeniably aggressive toward their neighbors, I will argue that they were likewise concerned with the lawfulness of their behavior and sought to depict their gunpowder diplomacy as a means of fashioning voluntary treaties that extended the king's dominions into the highly contested territory north of Virginia.[14] While the exercise of violence was governed by the laws of war, the Pilgrims always depicted their aggression as a means of creating peace treaties—if not with the targets of their violence, then with observers, who seek friendship with the Pilgrims after seeing their weaponry.

The Pilgrims' embrace of guns as a tool of diplomacy was, in part, a response to events in Virginia. As I showed in the first two chapters, the English came to the New World with the intention of making treaties. Outnumbered, they hoped that by adopting a peaceful carriage, spreading religion, and giving tribute they could compel submissive tribes to agree to English terms. This stately soliciting quickly broke down and inspired fierce criticisms both from dissident Virginia planters and from foreign diplomats. In the wake of war with the Powhatans, figures such as John Smith and Ralph Hamor drew upon the laws of war to justify English aggression, while also emphasizing that just war with Native combatants would inspire alliances. In this chapter, I show how the Pilgrims used guns as a means of intimidating adversaries and making treaties with friends. Unlike Virginia colonists, the Plymouth settlers did not face an active Spanish threat. While Spanish ambassadors had challenged the legitimacy of the Virginia Colony, and the integrity of its treaties with Indians, by the 1620s the Spanish no longer had the military capability to challenge the English in North America. However, this does not mean that the Pilgrims had an easy time resolving the question of possession, or that they abandoned the law of nations as a framework for explaining their claims. Their nearest European rivals were the Dutch, who had negotiated rights from the English crown to trade between the fortieth and forty-fifth parallels, and had constructed forts along the Hudson River.[15] Of more concern were the French, who, though farther away, had sparred diplomatically with the English over the Virginia Colony charter and the destruction of French settlements by Argall a few years earlier.[16] The Pilgrims also had a problem closer to home—that of their own legitimacy as English subjects occupying territory in the name of the crown. For two decades prior to their emigration to North America, the Pilgrims had been in open conflict with English authorities over questions of religious orthodoxy and, on the journey over, had settled many miles north of their land grant, placing them beyond the protection of the Virginia Colony. Moreover, they had built their colony on land formerly held by the Patuxets, an Algonquian-speaking Native group decimated by a virgin soil epidemic. Many Native groups had their sights set on Patuxet, and viewed the Pilgrims as unwanted intruders.

I argue here that the diplomatic possibilities of weapons—as objects of trade, as tools of fear, and as signs of alliance—gave the Pilgrims a means of crafting treaties with Native peoples and publicizing their possession of territory. Though the Pilgrims are identified in Thanksgiving lore with the blunderbuss, they did not use these guns in reality. Their chief weapon was the matchlock, a handheld gun fired by pulling a trigger on a lock mechanism that lowered a match into a flash pan.[17] The Pilgrims carried matchlocks to almost all of their diplomatic meetings. They had many enemies, and even their alliance with the Pokanokets, which lasted for decades, was strained by misunderstanding and mistrust. But the reason the Pilgrims emphasized these weapons in letters home is that guns, powder, and knives could be used to negotiate alliances. The Pilgrims were a small and poorly defended group living on a part of the coast that had been subject to sporadic but intense conflict. They could not claim with any degree of plausibility that Indians were fleeing into their arms from a Spanish threat. Nor could they claim to have conquered Indians militarily, as the Virginia Colony had done after the Powhatan Uprising. But while the Pilgrims (and their readers in London) knew the Indians were not likely to view colonists as superiors, they believed that coastal people were impressed by guns.[18] Writing about guns and other weapons offered a way of explaining how the Pilgrims had been able to subdue their enemies and inspire their friends to stay loyal.

This strategy was not a simple one. Like John Smith's kidnapping of Opechancanough, or Argall's seizure of Pocahontas, the Pilgrims' gunpowder diplomacy demanded that they account for their actions using the laws of war as well as the law of nations, applying one legal code to their enemies and another to their friends. But like the taking of hostages, gunpowder diplomacy represented a potential for violence that did not need to be realized in order to be effective. To be sure, sometimes the Pilgrims portrayed themselves as threatening Native peoples (this was how they had intimidated the Narragansetts with the snakeskin bundle). More often, they depicted themselves as inspiring fear and compliance by carrying matchlocks at their sides during diplomatic conferences. Early modern military manuals, such as Jacob de Gheyn's *The Exercise of Armes for Calivres, Muskettes, and Pikes* (1608), printed in The Hague while the Pilgrims were residents in Leiden, offered engraved illustrations of the many ways guns could be carried, held, and used (see Figures 8 and 9).[19] Under the laws of war, the way one's adversary brandished weapons could be construed as a provocation demanding a violent response. The Pilgrims justified

Figure 8. From Jacob de Gheyn, *The Exercise of Armes* (1608). A musketeer holds a matchlock during a break in fighting. The Pilgrims depicted themselves carrying guns in order to issue a subtle threat to Native neighbors while preserving diplomatic appearances. Courtesy of The Huntington Library.

Figure 9. From Jacob de Gheyn, *The Exercise of Armes* (1608). A musketeer loads a matchlock. Courtesy of the The Huntington Library.

violent actions, such as the assassination of the Massachusett sachems in 1624, by citing the Indians' threatening carriage of weapons. However, firing guns at enemies was also a way to inspire one's friends, strengthen existing alliances, and motivate neighboring groups to form treaties. Guns enabled the Pilgrims to appear both powerful and friendly at the same time.

In what follows, I consider several narratives that portray weapons in diplomatic negotiations. First, I look at *A Relation or Journall of the beginning and proceedings of the English plantation setled at Plimoth in New England* (1622), a compilation of letters from Winslow and Bradford edited and published by the colony's London agent, Robert Cushman. The book, often referred to as *Mourt's Relation* after the name of its publisher, describes colonists' first negotiations with the Pokanokets and their sachem Massasoit. Alongside their account of the public ceremonies and friendly exchanges that result in a treaty of peace in 1621, the authors describe Massasoit's nervous response to European guns. I argue that the casual display of guns during peaceful negotiations was central to the Pilgrims' cultivation of a powerful image in transatlantic correspondence. By portraying themselves as carrying unused firearms at their sides, and even putting those firearms away at the Indians' request, the Pilgrims disavow any responsibility for the fear they may have inspired, enabling them to preserve *consensus ad idem* in their treaties while still intimidating their neighbors.

As documented in *Mourt's Relation*, the 1621 treaty with the Pokanokets publicized the colonists' alliances and their control of territory. However, the Pilgrims' friendship with the Pokanokets also led to violent complications that in turn required further justification abroad—this time by the laws of war. Though the Pilgrims presented a largely untroubled account of Anglo-Native treaty making in *Mourt's Relation*, the alliance with the Pokanokets was not a force for peace. The Narragansetts, an expansion-minded group, viewed the Pokanokets as their subjects and resented the intrusion. The exchange of the snakeskin bundle was one of many mutually threatening gestures that passed between their sachem, Canonicus, and his English counterparts. At the same time as these conflicts were unfolding, the Pilgrims were also becoming increasingly belligerent toward their weaker neighbors, culminating in the assassination of Massachusett sachems by Plymouth governors and soldiers in 1623. The attack, which was based on misinterpreted intelligence of a Massachusett conspiracy, destabilized the region and inspired transatlantic controversy among both supporters and critics of the Pilgrims.[20] The Pilgrims went into print again, sending Edward Winslow to London to describe their running war with the Narragansetts and their attack on the Massachusetts. The result, the curiously titled *Good Newes from New-England*, reprises the Pilgrims' earlier treatment of weapons as key legal and diplomatic symbols. Yet in describing the colonists' actions, Winslow focuses on a different legal framework for understanding weapons—that of preemptive war. While *Mourt's Relation* details the Pilgrims' use of guns to compel a treaty while preserving consent, *Good Newes* documents the Massachusetts' traffic in weapons in order to unravel a conspiracy against Plymouth Colony and justify the colony's preemptive assassination of Massachusett leaders. Like the Virginia colonists, who portrayed war with the Powhatans as part of a broader strategy that included treaties with Native friends, Winslow depicts the assassination as strengthening the colony's relationship with the Pokanokets. In this way, the unraveling of the conspiracy becomes an unlikely cause of peace.

In their transatlantic correspondence, the Pilgrims presented an image of powerful conquerors subjecting territory through diplomacy and just war. However, as their writings reveal, they relied heavily on Native allies, such as Squanto, the Indian guide who had explained the meaning of the Narragansetts' snakeskin bundle. For centuries, Squanto has been celebrated as a selfless mediator who showed the Pilgrims how to plant corn and helped them survive their first winters. However, the details of Squanto's life and his role in English alliances are more complicated than admiring portraits reveal. Taken captive by traders in the early part of the seventeenth century, Squanto had traveled widely before meeting the Pilgrims, even living in London from 1616 to 1617.[21] When he returned home, he found that his tribe had been destroyed by plague. I will argue here that Squanto helped the Pilgrims, not out of altruism, but rather as part of an attempt to use the diplomatic power of European firearms to rebuild the Patuxet sachemship. While gunpowder diplomacy offered the Pilgrims a way to publicize their legitimacy, it offered Squanto a means to appear powerful in the eyes of other Natives through his association with the Pilgrims and their weapons.

The Guns of the Pilgrims

When William Bradford stuffed the Narragansetts' snakeskin bundle with gunpowder, he intended to communicate a message of defiance to their leader, Canonicus. Bradford wanted to show Canonicus that the Pilgrims were not afraid to fight. He also wanted to show the colony's Pokanoket allies that the Pilgrims would join them in any war against common foes. As Winslow's later recounting of the incident shows, the Pilgrims were equally concerned about how such an aggressive gesture would appear to European onlookers. Winslow wanted to demonstrate that the action against the Narragansetts was justified and that the conflict with Canonicus had only strengthened the Pilgrims' alliances with other groups. When Winslow pointed to the colony's display of weaponry as a force for "the inlarging of his Majesties Dominions," he was also asserting, indirectly, that the Pilgrims themselves were good subjects of the crown. Winslow had reason to be defensive on this point. Unlike the Virginia colonists, who had clear permission from the king, the Pilgrims were on uncertain legal footing. Their relations with the crown were complicated by their embrace of dissenting religion and their long residence in exile in the Netherlands. The group that settled Plymouth Colony had its origins in a congregation led by Richard Clyfton at All Saints' Parish Church in Babworth, Nottinghamshire, from 1586 to 1605. Like other Independent, or Separatist, pastors, Clyfton preached that the Church of England had departed from biblical principles. He rejected the church and its bishops and sought to reconstitute a primitive church based around Old Testament law.[22] After Clyfton lost his position at Babworth, he relocated to Scrooby, where he began preaching to the group that became the Pilgrims. The group considered emigration abroad after royal ministers began to enforce acts of religious uniformity that made their beliefs illegal.[23] Eventually, they settled in Amsterdam on the advice of William Brewster, one of their leaders and a former secretary to a royal diplomat. After an internal dispute over church practice in 1609, most of the group that would eventually populate Plymouth Colony moved from Amsterdam to Leiden, where they established a church under the leadership of John Robinson.[24] As Bradford would later put it in *Of Plimmoth Plantation*, his history of the colony, the Leiden group "came to raise a competent and comfortable living" working in the city's thriving textile and printing industries.[25] By 1617, however, several factors, such as anxiety about being absorbed into Dutch society, and fear of a Spanish invasion of the United Provinces, led them to consider settlement in America.[26]

This decision plunged the Pilgrims into the world of colonial promotion and lobbying, recently infused with cash and excitement by the explosion of the tobacco crop in Virginia. The Pilgrims first considered settling in Guiana, which they knew about from Dutch reports as well as from Sir Walter Raleigh's *The Discoverie of the Large, Rich, and Beautiful Empire of Guiana* (1596). Guiana offered a supposedly temperate climate as well as the potential protection of the Dutch colony of Essequibo, located on an island in the Mazaruni River. However, settling in Guiana raised more concerns about group cohesion. Guiana was also a key battleground in the colonial theater of the Eighty Years' War, leaving some in the group to fear that they might find themselves threatened yet again by Spanish invasion.[27] The Virginia Colony, another possibility, seemed a better location. By 1617, the Virginia Company had supply ships going to the colony on a regular basis, making it relatively easy to find passage. Virginia was also more secure. In the event of an attack by Indians or other Europeans, the Pilgrims could seek the protection of the Jamestown fort. To pursue royal authorization to settle in Virginia, the Leiden group sent Robert Cushman and John Carver to London to negotiate the terms of a patent.[28]

Cushman and Carver had no problem persuading the Virginia Company to help the Pilgrims. Anxious to cultivate more tobacco, the company wanted to flood the region with settlers in order to bring more arable land under control and create a buffer between Jamestown and the Powhatans. Cushman and Carver had trouble, however, when it came to the crown. The king was angry with the group for printing religious materials in Amsterdam and smuggling them into England. It was also necessary to downplay the Pilgrims' differences with the Anglican Church in order to avoid provoking opposition from the bishops. Unable to carry out the suit on his own, Carver enlisted Sir Edward Sandys, one of the founders of the Virginia Company and a leading parliamentarian, to lobby the crown for approval. Though the crown declined to issue an official charter, Sandys claimed the king had promised not to interfere, and the group sailed with a patent from the Virginia Company and funding from a group of merchant adventurers organized by Thomas Weston.[29]

Unhappiness with financial and legal agreements may have contributed to the Pilgrims' abrupt decision to abandon their original plans and settle part of the coast claimed by the Plymouth Council for New England, a newly revived concern that was pursuing a patent for lands north of Virginia. The Pilgrims claimed to have been driven off course by fear of shipwreck, but they were aware of New England and the possibilities it offered. Intended or not, the change of course had advantages. It gave the colony some degree of autonomy from controlling investors. It also enabled them to replace some of the terms of their agreement with the Virginia Company and other investors with a set of laws drafted and signed aboard ship, now known as "The Mayflower Compact."[30] At the same time, the unauthorized departure complicated the colony's already uncertain rights in international space. While the land on which the group settled was part of the Plymouth Council's grant, the council had only recently received a charter from the king. The status of the land was also in dispute with the French, who claimed it on the basis of an earlier grant.[31] When the colony began to build houses and a fort, they were in a state of legal limbo, anxious to acquire clearer authorization and unsure of their rights.[32]

This legal uncertainty was part of what drove Winslow to describe the colonists' exchange with Canonicus as an extension of the king's dominions. Native treaties enabled the Pilgrims to portray themselves as royal subjects at a time when their status was far from certain. By negotiating with Indians on behalf of the crown, they showed their loyalty to it. But Bradford's decision to use gunpowder as a diplomatic tool (and Winslow's decision to publicize it) reflected an even more urgent legal imperative. As their venture lacked direct royal authorization, the Plymouth colonists had sailed without any clear instructions for possessing land. On the one hand, this was a concerning liability. Should French ambassadors claim the right to attack the group, for example, no English diplomats were certain to come to the Pilgrims' defense, and no English forces were nearby to defend them. Yet the lack of clear authorization also gave the Pilgrims freedom to demonstrate their possession of land in the way most suitable to their purposes. They were not weighed down by royal instructions or by scripts for carrying out tribal diplomacy, leaving them free to formulate their own models of diplomacy or to reach to coastal political systems for justification.

When the Narragansetts sent the bundle to Plymouth, they were following—and perhaps parodying—a routine of political communication created by commercial interactions among many different groups. The political situation in southern New England was vastly different from the one Christopher Newport and John Smith had encountered in the Chesapeake Bay. Since at least the early sixteenth century, French ships had traded furs on the coast of Newfoundland and around the Gulf of St. Lawrence, slowly introducing European goods such as beads, metals, and tools into coastal channels of trade and diplomacy. In the early seventeenth century, Dutch traders had begun to operate out of trading posts and drying stations around Long Island, and the French had begun to expand into New England, trading in the Massachusetts Bay from a fort at Port Royal.[33] These activities had slowly but irrevocably changed political communication among tribal groups, even in places where there was no direct contact with Europeans. As Neal Salisbury has shown, the fur trade ushered in "a striking degree of unity" among New England Native peoples, as economic specialization led to interdependency.[34] As the northern Abenakis increasingly organized their economy around fur trading, groups around Massachusetts Bay began to specialize in hunting and farming, trading food to the Abenakis in exchange for the lucrative European goods used as payment by Dutch and French traders. This interdependence led to the creation of new channels connecting Native groups and European traders. It also gave birth to seasonal diplomatic routines based around exchanges of skins, European goods, and wampum, a trade currency made of coastal shells.

Within this expansive trading network, guns had special meaning. Shortly before the Pilgrims' arrival, a number of Native groups had begun to purchase firearms from European traders. The first may have been the Innu people, a group living in the northeastern part of latter-day Quebec, who in 1620 acquired guns from French traders.[35] The Powhatans also acquired guns by stealing them or purchasing them illicitly from renegade English traders. European governments sought to put a stop to this trade, fearing that Indians with guns would present a formidable military foe. In 1622, James I issued a Royal Proclamation announcing punishment for those who "did not forbear to barter away to the Savages Swords, Pikes, Musquets, Fowling-peeces, Match, Powder, Shot, and other warlike Weapons, and teach them the Use thereof."[36] Other European crowns issued similar proclamations.[37] As Brian J. Given has pointed out, however, Indians did not buy guns only for fighting. Guns quickly came to assume political and religious meanings that went well beyond their utility as weapons. As Given argues, Native peoples may have wanted to acquire guns because of "the effect such ownership might have on the attitudes of tribes farther removed from contact with the newcomers." While guns themselves were extraordinary objects, "the intercourse and alliance [they] symbolized would likely inspire some measure of respect, or at least caution."[38] Guns took their place in existing channels of exchange that included goods like wampum and metalwork, and other weapons such as knives and arrows.

The exchange between Bradford and Canonicus thus followed an established coastal pattern. It was a display of weapons that was intended to communicate a political message, in this case, one of hostility. Yet as well as expressing longstanding routines, it also reflected a more recent event, one that had dramatically reshaped the tribal landscape to the north of the Virginia grant. In the years before the Pilgrims' arrival, a virgin soil epidemic, probably introduced by French traders, had severely depopulated many Native groups.

The area most affected was the Massachusetts Bay, where the village bands of the Massachussets, Pennacooks, and Pokanokets lost the majority of their population.[39] Other groups, such as the Narragansetts and Pequots, were less severely affected. This uneven depopulation led to sudden changes in political alliances, radically weakening the Pennacooks, Pokanokets, and other groups that had born the brunt of the losses while strengthening the groups that were relatively untouched. Surviving sachems from depopulated tribes moved to consolidate their remaining subjects into new groups and sought the protection of stronger neighbors.[40]

While the Pilgrims had little knowledge of these shifting relationships before their arrival, they were aware of the plague and its effect on the availability of land. Before disembarking from England, the Pilgrims had met John Smith, who had just returned from a voyage scouting the area north of Virginia.[41] Smith knew that the Pokanokets no longer occupied their land, and he believed it was open for possession.[42] He may have told the Pilgrims about the land in the hopes that they would bring him along. While the Pilgrims refused Smith's offer, they heeded his advice to seek out the emptied territory. Landing near the area Smith had described, the Pilgrims quickly found evidence to support his claims, discovering shallow graves as well as unburied bodies. As Thomas Morton, a trader frequently at odds with the Pilgrims, remarked in a survey of a similar scene, "the livinge being (as it seemes) not able to bury the dead, they were left for Crowes, Kites, and vermin to pray upon."[43] More to the Pilgrims' purposes, the land itself seemed a *vacuum domicilium*, a waste space that could be brought under control by the act of settling.

While the Pilgrims were attracted by the emptiness of the land around the bay—even attributing the plague to a miraculous providence of God—they were keenly aware of their own visibility.[44] Plymouth Bay was a site of intense commercial and political activity. A number of tribes and trading concerns were jockeying for control over access to trading routes, a competition made even more intense by the plague and the power vacuum it had created in now-empty places. To the north, French and English traders contended for the allegiance of surviving Pennacooks and Abenakis. To the south, where many Native groups had remained largely unscathed by the epidemic, ships under the auspices of the Dutch West India Company pursued trade with the Munsee. Plymouth Bay itself was firmly in the sights of the Narragansetts, the Pequots, and other Algonquian-speaking groups who saw the plague as an economic opportunity.[45] Even before the Pilgrims landed, they understood the

necessity of proving what Cushman called "the lawfulnesse of English plantations" in a region dotted with French and Dutch outposts and the camps of
expansion-minded sachems.[46]

The Plymouth settlers were hostile to the first Native people they met. Unlike
the Virginia settlers, the Pilgrims were not bound to "entreat" the Indians. They
initially believed their claims to depopulated lands could be justified by *vacuum
domicilium*, as John Smith had suggested. Another reason for the distance was
the wariness of surrounding groups. The Pilgrims were not the first English to
appear in the bay. Earlier, Sir Ferdinando Gorges and Thomas Hunt, two English
explorers, had made separate voyages to the bay and kidnapped Native people
as guides.[47] The Pokanokets recognized the Pilgrims as being from the same
nation and were afraid of coming close for fear they would be kidnapped. This
mutual wariness began to relax in March 1621, when the Pokanokets reached out
to the English. While initially averse to any diplomatic contact, the Pokanokets
had slowly changed their opinion of the newcomers. One reason is that they saw
how vulnerable these particular English were. Despite scavenging abandoned
stores of corn, the colonists had starved during the winter, losing about half
their number to illness and hunger.[48] The surviving Pokanokets, no strangers to
massive death themselves, had watched this unfold from afar with grim understanding. Another reason for their dawning interest is that the Pokanokets were
coming to understand the newcomers as a potential source of trade goods and
military power. While the Pilgrims seemed horrendously ill-equipped to survive
even one more winter, the Pokanokets had reason to believe there was more to
the newcomers than appeared. Living with the Pokanokets were two survivors
of the plague, Samoset, an Abenaki who had some experience with the English,
and Squanto, a Patuxet who had been kidnapped by the Spanish and had a wide
knowledge of Europeans.[49] Both men understood the political and economic
opportunities that might follow from an alliance with the English. Squanto, in
particular, had considerable expertise in Anglo-Native alliances. During his time
in London, he had learned something about English royal authority and its reach
across the ocean (ironically, many of the English Pilgrims, who had spent much
of their adult lives in exile in Leiden, had never been to London, while Squanto
was at least somewhat familiar with the city and its politics). Moreover, these
men, long schooled in European ways, could mediate between the Pokanokets
and the Pilgrims and protect Massasoit from kidnapping or any other stratagems
the English were known to use. Their presence gave the Pokanokets confidence to
approach the newcomers and sound out their intentions.

The Indians first sent Samoset to open negotiations.[50] Then, Squanto "brought word" of Massasoit's desire "to parley" with the English. The negotiations proceeded warily. At first, Massasoit and the English governor kept their distance, communicating through messengers and gifts. The English sent Winslow to deliver a pair of knives and a jeweled copper chain to Massasoit, along with some biscuit, butter, and a "Pot of strong water."[51] Speaking through Squanto, Winslow accepted an offer of alliance on behalf of King James. To confirm this treaty, Massasoit crossed the river and proceeded to an English house. There, the parties exchanged drinks of "strong water" and "treated of Peace." Some of the terms were reciprocal. They agreed to trade and protect one another and respect one another's property. Other conditions, at least as they were later reported by the English, decidedly favored the newcomers. The English acquired rights of extradition of Pokanokets who had violated English laws while declining to extend the same rights to Massasoit or his people. The treaty also compelled Massasoit to enforce the conditions on "neighbour Confederates," making the terms of the treaty effective far beyond Pokanoket territory.[52] While it is possible that Massasoit may have willingly given up some of his power in what he viewed as a strategic submission, it is not likely that he agreed to enforce the treaty on his neighbors, since this kind of absolute sovereignty was largely foreign to coastal notions of political authority.

The treaty negotiations also included a controversy over weapons. Each side was worried about the other's arms. Before the treaty "two or three Savages," unidentifiable to the Pilgrims, had "presented themselves" and "made semblance of daring" to the English, licking their fingers and wetting the strings of their bows as if preparing to fire.[53] Frightened by the incident, the English raised the question of weapons at the treaty negotiations. In the version of the treaty printed in 1621 in *Mourt's Relation*, the Indians agree that "when [the Indian] men came to us, they should leave their Bowes and Arrowes behind them," while the colonists agree that they would likewise leave behind their guns "when [they] came to [the Pokanokets]."[54] However, a later version of the treaty in Nathaniel Morton's *New-Englands Memoriall* (1669) includes the same clause but omits any mention of the colonists leaving behind their guns, restricting only the Indians' carriage of weapons.[55] The version in Morton's book may be closer to the way the Pilgrims recorded the treaty, since it is taken from Bradford's records. Another fact that supports the faithfulness of the Morton copy is that the Pilgrims did not leave their guns behind when they attended future diplomatic gatherings with the Pokanokets. The Pilgrims' promise to abandon their guns in the printed treaty reflected their desire to appear evenhanded to readers across the Atlantic.[56]

The treaty came under great strain in the months following the meeting. Despite its decidedly hierarchical nature, the Pokanokets understood the treaty as a friendship between peoples. They performed their compliance by extending hospitality and expecting it in return, as was the custom among friends. The English found this hospitality invasive and draining. Edward Winslow and Stephen Hopkins delicately broached the issue with Massasoit, telling him (truthfully) that the English were too impoverished to meet his demands.[57] The treaty was tested more profoundly when the Narragansetts attacked the Pokanokets. Observing the treaty from afar, Canonicus, the Narragansett sachem, had not liked the prospect of a revitalized Pokanoket sachemship. He wanted the land himself. Acting at the behest of Canonicus, Corbitant, a Pokanoket sachem, attacked Massasoit and kidnapped Squanto. Fearing that their friends were dead, the English launched a violent raid during which they used their guns to frighten Corbitant into fleeing.[58]

The successful rescue led to a further expansion of the terms of the treaty. A number of sachems made their way to Plymouth to add themselves to the alliance between Massasoit and the colony. While the Pilgrims may have overstated the extent of Indian submission in the first treaty, this agreement was unmistakably a consolidation of the newcomers' power. The group of supplicants included Quadequina, the brother of Massasoit, as well as leaders from Manomet and Martha's Vineyard. Surprisingly, it also included Corbitant, whom the Pilgrims apparently forgave (at least temporarily) for kidnapping Squanto. In a later account of the treaty, Winslow wrote that the gathered leaders "acknowledged themselves the subjects of our Soveraigne Lord the King."[59] Fitting this subjection to English power, the agreement was clinched in English fashion: the Indians "subscribed unto a Writing to that purpose with their own hands."[60] Speaking through Squanto, Winslow explained to visitors the power of James I and their obligations and rights as his subjects. The treaty had also given the newcomers an opportunity to discharge their firearms as a way of ceremonially marking the peace.

Throughout the tense negotiation of the treaty, the leaders of Plymouth Colony had been careful to conduct themselves according to widely accepted diplomatic norms. Winslow had made sure to explain, through Squanto, that the Pilgrims were acting on behalf of a higher authority, King James. And during the chaotic raid to free Squanto, the Pilgrims had behaved in a way consistent with the laws of war, making sure, for example, to avoid killing the innocent, and even bringing wounded Indians to Plymouth for medical treatment.[61] In pursuing this course, the Pilgrims were not particularly concerned about the rights of their Native neighbors. Certainly, their survival depended on good relationships with the groups who could supply corn, and they were willing to go to great lengths to protect the treaty. But the Indians' precise understanding of English legal justifications troubled the colonists little. Though performed before a Native audience, the invocation of the name of the king was not solely intended for the colonists' Native neighbors. It was also addressed to a distant audience, one that had to be courted just as carefully as Massasoit.

Quiet Guns in *Mourt's Relation*

The treaty and raid had done much to resolve the Pilgrims' doubt about their position in Plymouth Bay. While they knew there were strong and hostile groups living just miles away, they could count on the friendship of nearby leaders. Yet one issue remained unresolved—the colony's legality under European frameworks for claiming foreign territory. Lacking a direct royal charter, the Pilgrims lived in a state of legal uncertainty. Their repeated treaties with Natives were therefore a curious gesture from the point of view of international legal systems; they made treaties in the king's name while their own status as landholders was in doubt. This legal cloud was partly lifted in October 1621 when Robert Cushman arrived in Plymouth on the *Fortune* carrying a patent from the Council for New England.[62] In one sense, the patent represented progress for the fledgling settlement. It gave the Pilgrims formal permission to occupy territory. However, the document also made the colonists more visible in London and therefore susceptible to challenge. Before the issuance of the patent, few in London or anywhere else had even known that the Pilgrims had settled in the bay. Afterward, the existence of the settlement became common knowledge, and Plymouth began to attract interest from potential rivals. The patent was the subject of dispute even before the Pilgrims themselves learned of it. It was made out to John Pierce, a company investor. The Pilgrims had agreed to issue their patents to Pierce, a merchant with no connections to their church, to conceal the colony's affiliation with Separatist dissenters. The move was a necessary expedient, but it ended up exposing the Pilgrims to legal challenges. Angry about the Pilgrims' refusal to sign the articles of agreement issued by the Virginia Company, Pierce claimed the new lands for himself and drew up a compact that effectively made the Pilgrims indentured servants. Pierce's plans collapsed when he was unable to raise funds to mount an expedition across the Atlantic (he extracted some measure of revenge by selling the patent to the company at a great cost and leaving the colonists further in debt to their backers).[63] Yet while Pierce's own lack of funds ensured that his threat would fizzle out, it was imperative for the Pilgrims to find a strategy for establishing their claim more securely.

Treaties offered part of a solution. The Pilgrims had little access to the legal and financial resources needed to assert and defend land claims in London. When it came to lobbying metropolitan authorities, they were no match for Pierce or other adventurers who were well connected and close to those in power. However, the Pilgrims did have one advantage. While their opponents could only assert the future intention to settle land, the Pilgrims could establish control of territory directly, through treaties.

It was this strategy that Bradford and Winslow pursued when they gave Cushman several letters to deliver to the colony's backers when he returned to London. The letters documented the colony's building of houses and fences, their construction of forts, and their negotiations with surrounding Native "kingdome[s]," as they somewhat grandiosely referred to nearby tribes.[64] The handing off of papers to Cushman was an established routine; they had done the same thing when he left Leiden for London to negotiate with the Virginia Company. Yet, as it had then, such delegation involved misunderstanding and conflict. Bradford and Winslow intended the letters to circulate in manuscript. They hoped to dissuade challenges from within their own investment group. Cushman, perhaps better understanding the many threats to the Pilgrims, instead printed the letters in a book. In an open letter to John Pierce that essentially serves as the book's preface, and is intended as a warning to other potential challengers, Cushman writes that the colony has already "obtained the honour to receive allowance and approbation of [its] free possession" from the council.[65] Against Pierce's claim to own the land and the settlers that occupy it, Cushman describes the Pilgrims' official permissions and the acts of settlement that prove their possession, including their treaty with the Pokanokets. Crucially, however, it is not simply the treaty agreement itself, but rather the Pokanoket response to English weapons, that provides the surest evidence of Plymouth's control.

From the beginning, the book emphasizes the role of guns in creating and defending political friendship. After an initial run-in with some frightening Indians at Cape Cod, the Pilgrims travel across the bay, make their landing, and meet Massasoit and his people. In contrast to the Cape Cod Indians, who fire a volley of arrows at the newcomers, the Pokanokets lay down their bows and arrows "in signe of peace, and to parley."[66] In the absence of a shared language, this obviously diplomatic gesture gives Bradford a way of explaining the Indians' behavior to readers. While Bradford cannot credibly claim to understand what the Indians say, these rituals give him a way of grasping Massasoit's intentions. After the laying down of weapons, the English are approached by Samoset, an Indian whom Bradford describes as speaking "broken English."[67] Like Navirans in Archer's "Relatyon," Samoset brokers the meeting between peoples. However, Bradford does something more with Samoset than Archer does with Navirans. Instead of making the legal justification for settlement himself, Bradford gives the job to Samoset. Shortly before diplomacy commences, Samoset explains to the English why there are so many graves on their land, telling them that they live in a place called Patuxet where "about foure yeares agoe, all the Inhabitants dyed of an extraordinary plague."[68] Samoset himself draws out the legal implications of this fact for English claims. "[H]e told us," Bradford writes, that "there is neither man, woman, nor childe remaining, as indeed we have found none, so as there is none to hinder our possession, or to lay claime unto it."[69] The fact that Bradford goes to the trouble to put this language into Samoset's mouth suggests the usefulness of Native consent in transatlantic legal disputes. While Bradford could have explained the Pilgrims' claim himself, a unilateral statement of possession would have made readers wonder if the Indians agreed. By allowing Samoset to frame the legal argument for possession, Bradford demonstrates that nearby Indians acknowledge the Pilgrims' claim.

Though Samoset's explanation of legal principles seems to clear English title to Patuxet, it leaves unresolved the Pilgrims' relationships with their neighbors. Here weapons come into play again, as Bradford tells the story of the first diplomatic parley with the Pokanokets. The English initiate diplomacy with the kind of gift familiar to the Indians from fur trading. "Saturday in the morning we dismissed the Salvage [Samoset], and gave him a knife, a bracelet, and a ring; he promised within a night or two to come againe, and to bring with him some of the *Massasoyts* [Pokanokets] our neighbors, with such Bevers skins as they had to trucke with us."[70] The gift of a ceremonial knife was a common way of showing an intention to form a recurring trade alliance. Knives had practical usefulness in the trade, but elaborately decorated blades functioned as gifts of tribute, signs that one was willing to give up something valuable at the beginning in anticipation of later, mutual profit. After some back-and-forth with Samoset and Squanto, Massasoit himself appears. Bradford presents him as a stately figure, a "great Sagamore," with a "trayne [of] sixtie men" trailing him. English writers frequently used this kind of language when describing Native kings. By emphasizing Massasoit's grandeur, Bradford primes the reader to be impressed when the English later secure his voluntary agreement to a treaty. Fitting Massasoit's status as a great leader, the English treat him with all due respect, sending "a payre of Knives, and a Copper Chayne, with a Jewell at it." In recognition of these gifts, Massasoit makes an offer of friendship, which Winslow formally accepts on behalf of the Plymouth governors, who have cautiously stayed behind. Reporting the speech (which he did not hear), Bradford relies on a standard diplomatic formula: "our Messenger made a speech unto him, that King JAMES saluted him with words of love and Peace, and did accept of him as his Friend and Alie, and that our Governour desired to see him and to trucke with him, and to confirme a Peace with him, as his next neighbor."[71] Massasoit "seem[s] to like well" the terms of the treaty, and embraces English friendship.[72]

While Bradford describes a peaceful treaty, however, he also shows his awareness of the increasing skepticism about Anglo-Native friendship. This is where guns enter the narrative. Though Massasoit appears to be an Indian friend—talking of peace and professing loyalty—his subtle reactions in the presence of the English betray his real motivation: fear of their guns. From the beginning, Bradford notes that something is wrong with his Indian counterpart. Though Massasoit has a powerful build and "lustie" countenance, strangely, "he tremble[s] for feare" while sitting beside his English counterpart.[73] Quadequina, Massasoit's brother, reveals to Bradford the reason for the great sachem's apparent nervousness: "[Massasoit] was very fearefull of our peeces," Bradford writes.[74] On the face of it, this seems like an extreme reaction on Massasoit's part. To this point in the negotiations, guns have scarcely appeared. Indeed, the only weapons present at the scene are hanging unused on the Pilgrims' shoulders, and when Quadequina informs the English of the reason for Massasoit's trembling, they obligingly put their guns away. But the firearms are crucial symbols nonetheless. While it was necessary for the Pilgrims to show the Indians' consent to agreements, in the years after the outbreak of wars between colonists and coastal peoples, peaceful accounts would only inspire skepticism. Guns provide a motivation for the Indians to negotiate beyond a simple desire to befriend the newcomers. Massasoit's trembling, more than his friendly agreement, supplies the truest evidence that the English are in control. The act of carrying guns on their shoulders enables the Pilgrims to inspire Massasoit's fearful compliance while maintaining a friendly bearing. There is no real violence, only subtle, even unintended, intimidation, and consent is thereby preserved.

Later in the narrative, however, things turn violent, as Corbitant launches his attack against Massasoit and Squanto. In this part of the book (penned by Winslow), the Pilgrims again wield their guns in the course of negotiations with their neighbors. However, the meaning of guns is different in Winslow's letter. While the Pilgrims have previously used guns to intimidate their allies into a queasy kind of consent, they now use them to frighten enemies while saving Massasoit and his people. After hearing intelligence that the Narragansetts, jealous of the alliance between Plymouth and the Pokanokets, have driven Massasoit from his territory and murdered Squanto, the colonists assemble into a military company and embark on a quest to exact revenge and reassert control. Actual violence, however, is not needed. Fear of guns is enough to subdue the Indians. After having "beset the house" of the malefactors, the colonists demand to know the whereabouts of Corbitant, the Pokanoket lieutenant who has betrayed Massasoit and kidnapped Squanto. No answer is forthcoming, but not because the Indians are rebelling. "[F]eare," Winslow writes, "had bereft the Savages of speech." Facing the gawking Indians, now rendered compliant by terror, Bradford, covering his legal bases, offers a justification for violence consistent with the laws of war. "We charged them not to stirre," he continues, "for if *Coubatant* [Corbitant] were not there, we would not meddle with them, if he were, we came principally for him, to be avenged on him for the supposed death of *Tisquantum*, and other matters: but howsoever wee would not at all hurt their women, or children."[75] Though justified, this speech turns out to be unnecessary. Guns, it turns out, are all the Pilgrims need to resolve the conflict. "In this hurley burley," Winslow writes, "we discharged two Peeces at randome, which much terrified all the Inhabitants," leading the villagers to flee and enabling the English to solicit confessions from the terrified parties responsible for the kidnapping.[76] Winslow uses ambiguous language to describe the firing of the guns. The word "random" could mean that the pieces are fired accidentally, which was always a possibility with matchlock weapons.[77] It could also mean that the Pilgrims merely discharge their guns in the air. Whatever the case, the effect is the same: by firing their weapons without targeting the Indians, the Pilgrims assert control without spilling blood.

While the bad Indians shrink from the sound of gunfire, the report of the Pilgrims' weapons has an uplifting effect on their allies, alerting them to the presence of their rescuers. As the chaotic scene unfolds, there are two Indians who show themselves undaunted by the guns, Squanto and Tokamahamon, another ally, who are hiding nearby. After the dust clears, Hobomok, another friend of the Pilgrims, "gat on the top of [a] house," Winslow writes, "and called *Tisquantum* and *Tokamahamon*, which came unto us." The captives come without fear and "assur[e]" the other Indians that the Pilgrims "would not hurt them."[78] While the sound of gunfire inspires stark terror in the hearts of the Pilgrims' enemies, to allies, it acts as a homing beacon, alerting them to the Pilgrims' presence and signaling that it is safe to come out.

Like Argall's kidnapping of Pocahontas, which inspires the Chickahominies to treaty, the Pilgrims' gunpowder diplomacy becomes the basis for the creation of new alliances. The last letter in the book, also authored by Winslow, describes English travels to the Massachusetts, a group that, according to Squanto, "had often threatned" the Pilgrims in the hearing of other Indians.[79] The rescue of Squanto has given the Pilgrims a reputation, but not one they are eager to exploit. "With much feare [the Massachusetts] entertained us at first," Winslow writes, "but seeing our gentle carriage towards them, they tooke heart and entertained us in the best manner they could, boyling Cod and such other things as they had for us." The Pilgrims' "gentle carriage" vanquishes any fear, but it is important, as in Bradford's letters, that the fear is displayed before it dissipates. In *Mourt's Relation*, it is fear that guarantees friendship. This same pattern plays out when a Massachusett man arrives on the scene, "At length with much sending for came one of their men, shaking and trembling for feare," Winslow writes. "But when he saw we intended them no hurt, but came to trucke, he promised us his skins also." Here, the fear is no longer inspired by the presence of guns. It has instead become ambient, an atmosphere that follows the Pilgrims everywhere they go. Mindful that fear could void any treaty, the Pilgrims are careful to show they have done nothing unlawful to inspire it. When Squanto suggests that they rob some Native women, the Pilgrims give him a lecture on what constitutes a "just occasion" for violence. Despite the Pilgrims' professed respect for justice, however, the fear remains. The women are so eager to embrace the Pilgrims' offer to trade that they "[sell] their coats from their backes, and ty[e] boughes about them, but with great shamefastnesse."[80] With weapons like guns, the Pilgrims have no need for threats.

Mourt's Relation concludes with a great feast between the Pilgrims and their allies. In describing this feast, today identified as the First Thanksgiving, Winslow emphasizes the friendship between the Pilgrims and Pokanokets.

His purpose, however, is not to praise his allies for their loyalty, but to show that the Pokanokets have been brought under control by an outwardly friendly treaty that is backed by fear: "it hath pleased God so to possesse the *Indians* with a feare of us, and love unto us, that not onely the greatest King amongst them called *Massasoyt*, but also all the Princes and peoples round about us, have either made sute unto us, or beene glad of any occasion to make peace with us."[81] The feast represents a celebration between friends, but fear and trepidation have brought the guests to the table. While Winslow insists that the treaty is voluntary, emphasizing the Pokanokets' love for the Pilgrims, the Indians' fear of guns gives added assurance that the treaty will hold, should love turn to hate.

Guns are a powerful diplomatic tool, enabling the Pilgrims to inspire terror in the Indians while winning their consent to treaties. Though it produced convincing evidence of the Pilgrims' control, however, this model of diplomacy inspired some of the same questions that had dogged John Smith and Samuel Argall. How, for example, can an agreement made under duress satisfy *consensus ad idem*? And if violence is the way to create peace, how can a small group pacify a large body of powerful people? Will fear not inspire rebellion, as it had among Indians under the Spanish? In a legal treatise appended to the end of the book, Cushman attempts to answers such questions. While Winslow and Bradford emphasize guns, Cushman adopts a different strategy, arguing that the Pokanokets have agreed to the treaty "more out of love then out of feare."[82]

Cushman begins his essay by proving that the Pilgrims can occupy territory without an owner. After strategically raising and setting aside the question of ancient English claims in the region ("lest I be thought to meddle further then it concerns me," he notes), Cushman reports that the Indians' land is "spatious and void." Citing the book of Genesis, he invokes the familiar notion that it is "lawfull now to take a land which none useth," provided the colony "make use of it." Yet Cushman also recognizes that this argument has little applicability because nearby land is inhabited even if Patuxet is empty. Though technically legal, it meant little to occupy a waste space if the land around it was in firm control of indigenous leaders. In order to account for the Pilgrims' control of the territory that surrounds Patuxet, Cushman employs a shifty legal syllogism that likens the openness of the Indians' land to the openness of their kings to treaties. "And as it is a common land or unused, & undressed countrey," he writes, "so we have it by common consent, composition and agreement."[83] Just as the land is open to common cultivation, Cushman reasons, so are the kings open to joint or common rule.[84] This "agreement is double," he notes. First, "the Imperial Governor *Massasoyt*, whose circuits in likelihood are larger then *England* and *Scotland*, hath acknowledged the Kings Majestie of *England* to be his Master and Commander, and that once in my hearing, yea and in writing, under his hand."[85] Cushman describes Massasoit as the same kind of expansionist, imperialistic monarch as Queen Elizabeth or James I. Yet he also reports that Massasoit has become a willing subject of the English crown, ceding his "circuits" to the English king, as evidenced by both his verbal agreement and a signed document, a double ratification that will satisfy those who do not recognize Indian rituals of consent. Second, Massasoit "hath promised and appointed [the Pilgrims] to live at peace, where we will in all his dominions, taking what place we will, and as much land as we will. . . . First, because we are the servants of *James* King of *England*, whose the land (as [Massasoit] confesseth) is, 2. because he hath found us just, honest, kinde and peacable, and so loves our company."[86] Massasoit's commitment establishes the Pilgrims' rights to the land, and demonstrates their secure possession of territory, but it also sends a subtle message to the English crown. Cushman suggests that Massasoit's acceptance of the Pilgrims is a good reason for James to support the colony, not because the Indian king possesses sovereignty on the order of a Christian prince, but because Massasoit's embrace of the Pilgrims means they have brought land under control. If Massasoit seeks an alliance with the English crown, Cushman implies, the Pilgrims are the brokers of that alliance, and are therefore deserving of the king's support. By settling the question of possession under the law of nations, the Pilgrims make a subtle appeal to the crown to support their venture.

Recognizing that the colonists' numerical inferiority might inspire skepticism about any claims to have cowed the Indians into submission, Cushman describes a form of colonization based around civil behavior and missionary outreach. This is not violent conquest, he insists, but a bloodless takeover: "our warring with them is after another manner," he writes, "namely by friendly usage, love, peace, honest and just cariages, good counsell, &c." Here, Cushman describes an approach to diplomacy that sharply contradicts the stories about guns and fear. However, though Cushman emphasizes love and gentleness, he is not simply trying to contradict Bradford and Winslow. The Pilgrims needed to appear both powerful and peaceful. Cushman needed the letters about guns to show the colony's strength, but he also recognized a potential limitation of the colonists' gunpowder diplomacy and sought to modulate their claims. His essay joins with the earlier letters to form a hybrid legal argument, one that takes advantage of the diplomatic possibilities of both fear and love. To the story of

Massasoit's trembling in the face of guns, Cushman adds an account of the sachem's "peaceable composition" with the English.[87]

As Cushman well knew, this was an unstable mix. Soon after he left, his claims were put to the test of events. Cushman, Winslow would later write, "was not long departed our Coast, ere the great people of *Nanohigganset* [Narragansett], which are reported to be many thousands strong, began to breath forth many threats against us."[88] These threats were compounded by rumors of a Massachusett conspiracy against Plymouth. Belligerence from Indian quarters was accompanied by encroachments from other English as well. Around the same time Cushman was sailing to London, a group of settlers organized by Thomas Weston, one of the colony's agents, was headed to the coast to claim a parcel of land under a grant of their own from the Plymouth Council. Their arrival made the colony's relations with surrounding groups even more tense. The Pilgrims tried to maintain control by taking decisive action, assassinating the Massachusett sachems and dissolving Weston's group. This action greatly strengthened the colony's standing in the region, but it also led to questions about their diplomatic strategy and, ultimately, the lawfulness of their settlement. The questions came from Indians, who wondered how the colony could mix threats with love. They came from English travelers, such as Thomas Morton, who resisted the Pilgrims' attempts to control the gun trade. Finally, they came from the leader of the congregation in Leiden, John Robinson, who openly questioned how a policy of preemptive killing could be reconciled with the colony's orderly and religious image. In 1624, the colony sent Winslow to London to explain their actions. He published *Good Newes from New-England*, a printed narrative of the events of 1623. The narrative hearkens back to the 1621 treaty, celebrating the strength of the colony's bond with Massasoit. However, Winslow also sets about a grimmer and more complicated task: reconciling the bloody attack against the Massachusetts with the colony's claims about peaceful treaties.

Knives Kissing: Preemptive Strikes in *Good Newes from New-England*

"*Witawamat* bragged of the excellency of his knife, on the end of the handle there was pictured a womens face, but sayd hee, I have another at home wherewith I have killed both *French* and *English*, and that hath a mans face on it, and by and by these two must marry." This is how Winslow reports the words of Wituwamat, a Massachusett sachem, to Hobomok, a Native ally of the Pilgrims, during a confrontation between the two in *Good Newes from New-England*. Hobomok goes to Massachusetts country with Captain Miles Standish, the leader of the Pilgrims' militia, to assassinate the Massachusett sachems, believing they are planning to attack the English. The Massachusetts refuse to declare their intentions to Standish directly, but Hobomok is greeted with "many . . . insulting gestures and speeches," including Wituwamat's boastful display of the womanly knife.[89] Though the threat is couched as an elaborate metaphor, its meaning is obvious. His clean knife, he hints, will soon join his bloody one in a matrimony of violence against Europeans. Seizing on this final proof, Standish springs into action, killing the sachems in a surprise attack.

Good Newes from New-England is the story of a conspiracy. It tells how the Massachusett sachems have plotted against the English and how the English have defended themselves in a bloody preemptive raid that claims the lives of the scheming sachems. However, the book is also a legal justification. It presents, piece by piece, the evidence of a Massachusett plot against the English, and describes "just and necessarie occasions of warre" between the colonists and the Indians.[90] The signs of conspiracy come in many forms: whispers, overheard conversations, intercepted messages. The most dramatic, however, are English observations of the Massachusetts' handling of weapons. The Indians squirrel away arms. They brandish knives at fateful moments. Accumulating over the course of the narrative, these actions present a threat that, according to Winslow's understanding of the laws of war, demands a preemptive attack by the Pilgrims. If *Mourt's Relation* points to Plymouth governors' judicious handling of guns as the source of their legal legitimacy and control, *Good Newes* arraigns the Massachusett sachems on the basis of a different use of weapons: threatening displays of knives that evince a clear danger to the colony's safety. However, while the book describes preparations for war and the brutal assassination of Massachusett leaders, it does not leave political relations in a state of chaos and violence. Winslow also describes how the killings strengthen the earlier treaty with the Pokanokets, ensuring continued peace. In this way, weapons again offer a way of explaining treaties and possession.

Winslow had good reason to try and defend the attack. In the fall of 1624, the Pilgrims were again in a battle for transatlantic legitimacy. They believed that the action against the Massachusetts had saved their plantation from violent overthrow, but the assassination of the sachems had also left them in the embarrassing position of aggressing against a Native polity that, unlike the Narragansetts, had made no obvious move to attack them. Indeed, in the aftermath of the assassination, a number of onlookers questioned the Pilgrims' actions. In a letter to Bradford, John Robinson, a pastor who had remained in Leiden, wrote bitterly of the colony's lost opportunity to evangelize the Indians: "Oh, how happy a thing had it been," he wrote, "if you had converted some before you had killed any!"[91] To Bradford, Robinson's lamentation must have seemed woefully out of touch with the reality of the American coast. Robinson seemed to believe that the New England Indians were like the savages of Elizabethan propaganda, pliant and open to evangelism. Bradford had learned that coastal peoples were politically savvy and staunchly committed to Native power. Nevertheless, Robinson's words, which echoed the arguments about Indian conversion put forward by Las Casas, were a sharp reminder of the contradiction between the colony's religious goals and its military policy.[92] According to Robinson, the Pilgrims stood in danger of appearing to the world as land-hungry conquistadors rather than conversion-minded saints.

Plymouth governors faced protests from nearer quarters as well. Their Native allies offered pointed criticisms of the seeming contradiction in the Pilgrims' diplomacy. In *Good Newes*, Winslow recorded one of these criticisms, voiced by Corbitant, who questioned whether the Pilgrims' casual display of guns at diplomatic events was truly consistent with their expressed interest in diplomacy and peace: "if your love be such, and it bring forth such fruits," Corbitant complained, "how commeth it to pass, that when wee come to *Patuxet*, you stand upon your guard, with the mouths of your Peeces presented towards us?" Winslow had tried to respond by arguing that carrying their weapons had always been a sign of the Pilgrims' political recognition of "best respected friends," an explanation Corbitant did not find satisfying.[93] Yet the fact that Winslow would publish the complaint (and Corbitant's answer to it) suggests that the Pilgrims were aware of the circulation of such accusations in Europe, and felt the need to respond in print.

Good Newes from New-England represents the colony's attempt to frame the assassination of the Massachusett sachems as a lawful act. In the book, Winslow defends the assassination by citing justifications for preemptive attack under the laws of war. While the authors of the *Relation*, including Winslow himself, had publicized the Pilgrims' use of guns as a tool of diplomacy, Winslow now frames the Massachusetts' traffic in weapons as a threat requiring preemptive attack. In making this argument, Winslow strode onto contested terrain. Legal authorities were equivocal about the question of preemptive strikes. In the *De Jure Belli*, for example, Vitoria wrote, "It is quite unacceptable that a person should be killed for a sin he has yet to commit. . . . It is not lawful to execute one of our fellow members of the commonwealth for future sins, and therefore it cannot be lawful with foreign subjects either."[94] Seeming to follow Vitoria, Grotius wrote in *De Jure Belli* that it is "abhorrent to every principle of equity" to hold that "the possibility of being attacked confers the right to attack."[95] Yet Grotius also claimed that preemptive attack is permissible if the danger is "immediate and imminent in point of time." One issue for exponents of natural law was how to assess immediate danger. Weapons were an important form of evidence. As Grotius wrote, "if the assailant seizes weapons in such a way that his intent to kill is manifest the crime can be forestalled" by preemptive action.[96]

Winslow's *Good Newes* is an attempt to establish the "immediate and imminent" danger of attack. It describes how the Massachusett sachems have brandished or exhibited their weapons in a threatening manner, giving the English a clear justification for assassinating them. However, it is also an attempt to salvage the colony's other alliances by showing that the exercise of just war has brought Plymouth closer to the Pokanokets, their long-time allies. In this way, Winslow tries to make an act of war the basis for a renewal of the 1621 treaty.

Winslow's book proceeds like a legal argument, accumulating intelligence about the sinister intentions of the Massachusetts and fitting it into a conspiracy. The first glimpse of evil designs comes in a form the Pilgrims at first do not understand—an exchange of knives that Standish unexpectedly witnesses while trading among the Massachusetts. Standish travels to Manomet to pick up some corn Bradford had purchased the previous spring from the sachem Canacum. He meets a surprisingly cold reception among a group he had thought were allies. While he is at the house of Canacum, other Massachusetts arrive, including Wituwamat, known to the English as "a notable insulting villaine." In Standish's company, the sachems engage in a sinister ritual and dialogue that, though unintelligible to the English, fills Standish with a sense of foreboding. "This villaine took a dagger from about his necke (which hee had gotten of Master *Westons* people)," Winslow writes, "and presented it to the *Sachim*, and after made a long speech in an audacious manner, framing it in such sort, as the Captaine (though he be the best Linguist amongst us) could not gather any thing from it." Later, after subsequent events have made the meaning of the exchange clear, Winslow retroactively glosses it. "The end of it was afterward discovered to be as followeth," he wrote. "The *Massacheuseucks* had formerly concluded to ruinate Master *Westons* Colonie . . . yet they durst not attempt it, till such time as they had gathered more strength to themselves to make their party good against us at *Plimoth*, concluding . . . we would never leave the death of our Countrymen unrevenged, and therefore their safety could not be without the overthrow of both Plantations." This interpretation of the exchange requires some awkward explanation on Winslow's part. Even given the language barrier, why would Wituwamat foment a conspiracy against the English in the presence of Standish, performing his dark ritual before the captain's very eyes? Winslow claims it is because Wituwamat wants to interrupt any possible rekindling of friendship between Canacum and Plymouth. He explains that "since there was so faire an opportunitie offered by the Captaines presence, they thought best to make sure [Canacum] and his company."[97] Given the good terms Standish is offering to Canacum, Wituwamat sees it as urgent to interrupt the trading ne-gotiations and "make sure," or secure, Canacum's allegiance. Wituwamat thinks the English, being ignorant of his words, will simply interpret the knife as a sign of friendship between two peoples, as knives and blades had been in prior exchanges between the Pilgrims and Pokanokets. Instead, the English begin to awaken to the sinister implications of Massachusett diplomacy in the region. The identification of the knife as being from Weston's people is important as well. Weston is not implicated as a confederate; he is one of the victims of the conspiracy, a target of Massachusett aggression. Yet the exchange shows that Weston and his men are unwittingly trading weapons with conspiring Indians, who will use them to overthrow the English.

After this alarming encounter, Winslow travels to Pokanoket territory, hearing that Massasoit, the colony's great ally, has fallen ill. This shift in venue is important for Winslow's purposes in the book. Though Corbitant and other Natives have accused the English of using guns to menace Native people, Winslow wants to show that the colony's real allies know the difference be-tween a threatening use of weapons and the Pilgrims' diplomatic carriage of firearms. Winslow describes the Pokanokets' reaction to English weapons in a way that stands in stark contrast to Corbitant's unhappy questioning. Winslow uses his guns, not to threaten Indians—as Corbitant has alleged—but rather to communicate with them. "The next day about one of the clocke," he writes, "we came to a ferrie in *Corbatants* Countrey, where upon discharge of my peece, divers Indians came to us from a house not farre off."[98] This is a very different reaction from the one portrayed in *Mourt's Relation*. The Indians are no longer afraid of guns, but instead view their discharge as a form of friendly hailing. Rallying around Winslow's firearm, the group makes its way to Massasoit's house, where they find Indian priests "making such a hellish noise" that even the English fall ill. Winslow quickly begins to minister to the sickly leader after English fashion. Knives, in the previous scene a sign of fear, are here a tool for cultivating political friendship. "I called *Hobbamock* and desired him to tell *Massassowat*, that the Governour hearing of his sicknesse was sorry for the same," Winslow writes, "and whereof if he pleased to take, I would presently give him; which he desired, and having a confection of many comfortable conserves, &c. on the point of my knife, I gave him some, which I could scarce get thorow his teeth; when it was dissolved in his mouth, he swallowed the juice of it."[99] Here, it appears as if Corbitant and other angry Indians have merely misinterpreted the Pilgrims' armed diplomacy. Though some Indians are afraid of the Pilgrims, Massasoit trusts them completely, letting Winslow bring the knife to his lips. Winslow's gun is likewise domesticated in the scene. Awakening to an appetite, Massasoit, Winslow writes, "requested me that the day following, I would take my Peece, and kill him some Fowle, and make him some English pottage, such as he had eaten at *Plimoth*."[100] To be sure, the Indians are still amazed at the power of English technology. "I tooke a man with me," Winslow writes, "and made a shot at a couple of Ducks, some six score paces off, and killed one, at which he wondered."[101] Yet while the Indians are rapt with wonder, there is no longer any trembling. The Pilgrims' guns now serve only to strengthen their friendship with the Pokanokets.

Massasoit's ease around Winslow's knife—and the Pokanokets' response to Winslow's guns—suggest that the Pilgrims' habit of going armed in no way impedes political friendship. In effect, the story of Winslow's embassy to Massasoit answers Corbitant's objections, showing that weapons are tools of peace. Yet the healing knife also has another effect, one even more significant for the narrative—it inspires Massasoit to divulge what he knows of the conspiracy to Hobomok, an Indian friendly to the English, who duly conveys the information to Winslow. "At our coming away, he called *Hobbamock* to him," Winslow writes, "& privately (none hearing save two or three other of his *Pneeses* [priests], who are of his Councell) revealed the plot of the *Massacheuseucks* before spoken of, against Master *Westons* Colony, and so against us." All of a sudden, the meaning of Wituwamat's conspiratorial whispering becomes horribly clear. Massasoit's intelligence gives sinister meaning to the signs the Pilgrims have previously observed. Yet the revelation also places them in a difficult legal position. How does one respond to an attack that has not yet happened? In making the colony's case, Winslow employs a rhetorical strategy similar to the one Bradford had used in justifying the possession of empty land in the 1621 *Relation*. He has an Indian make the argument for him. "Therefore as we respected the lives of our Countrymen, and our owne after-safety," Winslow writes, "[Massasoit] advised us to kill the men of *Massachuset*, who were the authors of this intended mischiefe. And whereas wee were wont to say, we would not strike a stroke till they first begun; if said he upon this intelligence, they make that answer, tell them, when their Countrymen at *Wichaguscusset* [Wessasauget] are killed, they being not able to defend themselves, that then it will be too late to recover their lives, nay through the multitude of adversaries they shall with great difficulty preserve their owne, and therefore he counselled without delay to take away the principals, and then the plot would cease."[102] Massasoit, not Winslow, makes the argument for immediate assassination. The English try to hold him off, insisting on a more conservative understanding of just war. Massasoit convinces them of the threat, however, arguing that if they wait for an attack it will be "too late."

Having established that Massasoit not only supports the assassination of the Massachusett sachems, but understands its justice in European terms, Winslow turns to the colony's relations with another set of neighbors, Weston's men at Wessasauget. The correspondence with Weston's men is meant to further demonstrate that the Pilgrims are pursuing judicious means, even as they plan a bloody raid. John Sanders, the governor of Wessasauget, writes to Bradford that he is "resolved to take [corn] by violence" from the withholding Massachusetts, potentially provoking an all-out war.[103] Bradford, however, rebuffs Sanders for violating the law of nations, and insists that all English follow widely recognized norms of engagement, even in war. "[T]he Governour answered his Letter," Winslow writes, "and caused many of us to set our handes thereto, the contents whereof were to this purpose; Wee altogether disliked their intendment, as being against the law of God and Nature, shewing how it would crosse the worthy ends and proceedings of the Kings Majestie, and his honorable Councell for this place, both in respect of the peaceable enlarging of His Majesties Dominions, and also of the propagation of the knowledge and Law of God."[104] Sanders's proposal shows the threat Weston's men pose to the international standing of the English. However, it also leaves the Pilgrims looking moderate. In contrast to the lawless violence proposed by Sanders, the Pilgrims' strategy of selective assassination appears to be a carefully justified middle path.

Winslow's account of the assassination itself is consistent with the Pilgrims' need to appear both measured and lawful in their violence. Winslow omits any description of the precise way the Pilgrims lure the sachems to their deaths. Instead, he tells a story that is vague on specifics but thick with legal justification. "On the next day," he writes, "seeing hee could not get many of them together at once, and this *Pecksuot* and *Wituwamat* both together, with another man, and a youth of some eighteene yeeres of age, which was brother to *Wituwamat* . . . and having about as many of his owne Company in a roome with them, gave the word to his men, and the doore being fast shut began himself with *Pecksuot*, and snatching his owne knife from his neck though with much struggling killed him therewith, the point whereof hee had made as sharpe as a needle, and ground the backe also to an edge: *Wituwamat* and the other man, the rest killed, and tooke the youth, whom the Cap. caused to be hanged."[105] Weapons are again important here, not only as an instrument of violence, but as a legal symbol. The Pilgrims kill Pecksuot with his own knife, one presumably sharpened for use against the Pilgrims themselves, thereby making him the symbolic author of his own death. The English also place Hobomok at the scene as a kind of impartial observer: "*Hobbamocke* stood by all this time as a spectator and meddled not, observing how our men demeaned themselves in this action."[106] Hobomok's presence shows that the attack is not an assault against all Indians, but rather has the support of allied Native groups. Winslow concludes by noting that Standish preserved the lives and property of the women, following the laws of just war applying to noncombatants.[107]

News of the killing travels with remarkable speed. Like the story of Pocahontas's marriage, it brings about a profound change in political relations. While Winslow had previously emphasized the use of weapons as friendly implements of healing and husbandry, at this moment, their capacity to frighten suddenly comes back. "Concerning those other people that intended to joyne with the *Massachuseucks* against us," Winslow writes, "though we never went against any of them, yet this suddaine and unexpected execution, together with the just judgment of God upon their guiltie consciences, hath so terrified and amazed them, as in like manner they forsooke their houses, running to and fro like men distracted, living in swamps and other desert places, and so brought manifold diseases amongst themselves, whereof very many are dead."[108] With the help of God, the Pilgrims' justified "execution" triggers a bloodless conquest. Terrified, the other conspirators unwittingly do themselves in by fleeing for safety to inhospitable climates, where they experience a recurrence of the plague that had killed so many Indians before. According to Winslow's providential understanding of the laws of war, these Indians are the agents of their own undoing, and the Pilgrims are merely the medium through which their unlawful aggression returns to them.

Good Newes ends with a cautionary note entitled "a brief Relation of a credible intelligence of the present estate of *Virginia*." Winslow appends this relation without describing its immediate significance for Plymouth, merely writing that the "earnest intreatie" of "much respected friends" has compelled him to report on Plymouth's English neighbor. Yet the report is unmistakably included to corroborate the legal justifications of the assassination of the Massachusetts. In it, Winslow describes the Powhatan Uprising and "the bloudy slaughter committed by the *Indians* upon our friends and Country-men."[109] While the Massachusetts never launched any attack against Plymouth, Winslow implies that the colonists might have met the same fate as the Virginia colonists had they followed a more diplomatic course in response to the threats of Wituwamat and the intelligence from Massasoit. Winslow also reports that in response to the Powhatan attack "*Opachancano*, the chief Emperour, was supposed to be slaine [by the English], [and] his sonne also was killed at the same time."[110] News of Opechancanough's demise was premature (though it may have reflected what Winslow was told by Governor George Yeardley or another correspondent in Virginia). Yet in including this information, Winslow suggests that targeted assassination has been employed by English colonists up and down the coast. If any metropolitan administrators wish to criticize the Pilgrims, Winslow implies, they must also criticize the Virginia colonists.

In *Good Newes*, Winslow depicts the Pilgrims and their allies deploying weapons in a way that is consistent with just war, while the Massachusetts use them in a way that invites preemptive attack. And though Winslow frames these behaviors according to natural law, his argument depends upon Native acts and behaviors. Massasoit's trembling shows he is in awe of the English and will do their bidding. The Narragansetts' rejection of the acrid-smelling bundle of gunpowder reveals the tribe's lack of resolve in the face of English power. Hobomok's and Massasoit's vocal support of the assassination is the key to its legality. Even the uprising of the Powhatans provides a precedent for the Pilgrims' attack, showing the consequences of ignoring a threat. Winslow is interested in these behaviors only to the extent that they support the legality of the Plymouth governors' actions and provide evidence of the colony's lawful control of territory. Yet as Winslow sometimes acknowledges, the Indians had reasons, beyond simple friendship or malevolence, to respond to the Pilgrims' guns in the ways that they did. What can Plymouth writings tell us about the people who befriended and fought with the Pilgrims, and trembled in the face of their firearms?

Squanto's Plague and the Patuxet Sachemship

In Winslow's eyes, the exchange of the snakeskin bundle was a confrontation between the English and the Narragansetts. Canonicus, the Narragansett sachem, backs down from the challenge because he fears the superiority of English weapons. This story perpetuates a colonial stereotype that was old even in 1621: the primitive savage shrinking from the superior technology of the colonizer.[111] But Winslow's text contains a stray detail that opens out onto another interpretation of gunpowder diplomacy in Plymouth: the bundle was originally delivered to Squanto, not to Bradford. Writing up the story, Winslow is careful to add that it was quickly whisked to Standish's house. This fact enables Winslow to depict all later threats as passing between Narragansett and English principals. But Squanto was clearly the intended recipient, as Winslow notes. What are we to make of this fact—that the bundle was delivered first to Squanto and that the response was inspired by his advice? Did the Narragansetts intend Squanto as the target of the threat? Is it possible to read Bradford himself, or Winslow's text, as a record of intertribal communication that Winslow either did not comprehend or chose to suppress because he found it irrelevant, or perhaps threatening?

Viewing Squanto as the intended recipient of the snakeskin bundle would go against centuries of American historiography that has prized the Patuxet interpreter for his role as a mediator. This tradition goes back to Bradford himself, who memorialized Squanto in *Of Plimmoth Plantation* as "a special instrument sent of God for [the Pilgrims'] good beyond their expectation."[112] However, contrary to Bradford's (and subsequent history's) depiction of Squanto as a selfless helper, there are many reasons to believe that the Narragansetts and other groups viewed him as a figure on the rise. There are also reasons to believe that in sending back the gunpowder—and in otherwise brandishing their firearms—the Pilgrims were unwittingly engaged in a diplomatic performance orchestrated by Squanto himself. In *Good Newes from New-England*, Winslow points to "one notable (though wicked) practice of this *Tisquantum*" that provides some evidence as to why he might have advised the Pilgrims on an aggressive response.[113] So that he "might possesse his Countrymen with the greater feare of us, and so consequently of himselfe," Squanto, Winslow writes, told [other Indians] wee had the plague buried in our store-house, which at our pleasure wee could send forth to what place or people wee would, and destroy them therewith, though wee stirred not from home. Being upon the fore-named brabbles sent for by the Governour to this place, where *Hobbamock* was and some other of us, the ground being broke in the middest of the house, (whereunder certaine barrels of powder were buried, though unknowne to him) *Hobbamock* asked him what it meant? To whom he readily answered; That was the place wherein the plague was buried, whereof hee formerly told him and others. After this *Hobbamock* asked one of our people, whether such a thing were, and whether wee had such command of it? Who answered no; But the God of the English had it in store, and could send it at his pleasure to the destruction of his and our enemies.[114]

Invoking a magical connection between gunpowder and plague, Squanto's story frightens other Indians into submission. While the Pilgrims are using their guns to intimidate Indians, Squanto channels the fearsome reputation of English weapons for his own ends.

What were those ends, and how did Squanto use matchlocks and powder to accomplish them? In linking gunpowder to plague, Squanto was repeating a story he had heard before, that much is certain. Up and down the northern seaboard during the colonial period, priests looked to settlers' weapons as an explanation for the virgin soil epidemics that had shaken the foundations of coastal chiefdoms. The English traveler Thomas Hariot recorded some of the theories of Chesapeake Bay groups in his *A brief and true report of the new found land of Virginia* (1588). "Some woulde likewise seeme to prophesie," he reports, "that there were more of our generation yet to come. . . . Those that were immediately to come after us they imagined to be in the aire, yet invisible & without bodies, & that they by our intreaty & for the love of us did make the people to die in that sort as they did by shooting invisible bullets into them. . . . Some also thought that we shot them ourselves out of our pieces from the place where we dwelt, and killed the people in any such towne that had offended us as we listed, how farre distant from us soever it were."[115]

It is unlikely that Squanto got his story from an English source. He probably heard it from Indians at some point in his travels. But whatever its winding course, its appearance in Plymouth tells us something about diplomacy and power on the coast. As recounted in Hariot's text, the story has received an enormous amount of attention from scholars.[116] As Ed White has shown, it shaped power struggles among Native people just as much as it influenced their view of the English.[117] Priests told it in order to hold on to their power as explainers of the world during a time of great upheaval and unpredictable events. The story gave them a way of fitting new technology into a familiar cosmology. Squanto's retelling of the story is different, though. He was no priest, and he had no ceremonial role to uphold. Indeed, when the Pilgrims arrived, he had only a weak tribal affiliation. He lived with the Pokanokets only because his people were dead. His actions therefore suggest a political rather than a religious agenda. No source records his reaction upon returning to Patuxet and finding that his entire community had disappeared, but his actions show that throughout his remarkable travels Patuxet identity remained a central concern. After being kidnapped, he attempted to go back despite the enormous obstacles that stood in his way. The fact that he successfully overcame such obstacles shows how important it was to him to rejoin his family and tribe. After his discovery that there was no one to return to, his plans changed, but there is evidence that he exploited the newcomers' own diplomatic tactics to try to revive the Patuxet sachemship around himself. Winslow says that Squanto spread the story about gunpowder and the plague in order to "possesse his Countrymen with the greater feare of us, and so consequently of himselfe." Throughout the period of his residence among the English, Squanto worked behind the scenes to leverage his association with the English and their fear-inducing diplomatic implements into political authority over families and kin groups loosely affiliated with Massasoit. Winslow writes of the colony's loss of faith in Squanto upon discovering that he has manipulated diplomacy and treaties to his advantage:

> Thus by degrees wee began to discover *Tisquantum*, whose ends were onely to make himselfe great in the eyes of [h]is Countrymen, by means of his neerenesse and favour with us, not caring who fell so hee stood. In the generall, his course was to perswade them hee could lead us to peace or warre at his pleasure, and would oft threaten the *Indians*, sending them word in a private manner, wee were intended shortly to kill them, that thereby hee might get gifts to himselfe to worke their peace, insomuch as they had him in greater esteeme than many of their *Sachims*; yea they them-

selves sought to him, who promised them peace in respect of us; yea and protection also, so as they would resort to him. So that whereas divers were wont to relie on *Massassowat* for protection, and resort to his abode, now they began to leave him, and seeke after *Tisquantum*.[118]

Though lengthy, this description of Squanto's motives seems incomplete, especially given Winslow's interest in the legal implications of Native rituals. Squanto plays the parties against each other merely so that "hee might get gifts to himselfe." But material acquisition did not exist as an end in itself for Algonquian-speaking peoples, at least not in the same way as for English investors. In issuing threats and gathering gifts, Squanto was behaving like a sachem, acquiring tribute, making treaties, and extending military protection. His activities show that he was attempting to rebuild his tribe, install himself as its sachem, and again make Patuxet a power.

If the 1621 *Relation* presents Squanto as a selfless guide, Winslow's *Good Newes* portrays him as an increasing threat. But the story of Squanto's hidden political brokering can also be read against the backdrop of the story of the snakeskin in order to draw a different conclusion about what the bundle meant. In light of the connection between gunpowder and plague that Squanto exploited elsewhere, Squanto's advice to Bradford to stuff the skin with powder looks like an act of attempted intertribal intimidation. It is unlikely Squanto believed he could frighten the powerful Narragansetts into submission with a gunpowder bundle alleged to contain plague. The group had survived the plague the first time and, despite colonial stereotypes, Indians were not any more superstitious than the English. But Squanto also knew the bundle would pass through many hands on its way to Canonicus. He knew the story of the exchange would be told far and wide, among Massasoit's subjects as well as among the Narragansetts. Squanto intended the bundle as a talisman of his power, one that would make known his connection to the English and his ability to manipulate their behavior. Winslow cites the snakeskin bundle as evidence of the legality of English possession, telling a story in order to assert control; in his account, Squanto is a mediator. But Squanto also used the English as a medium. In following the interpreter's advice, Bradford himself becomes, if only fleetingly, a channel of Patuxet power, an instrument of Squanto's attempt to revive his tribe. Squanto and Bradford depended on one another's political signs. Squanto's attempts to inspire fear produced the Narragansett response the Pilgrims needed as evidence of their own possession. In turn, the Pilgrims' arms and shot furnished Squanto with the symbols he needed to transform the plague that had destroyed his people into the force that might lead to their revitalization.

Squanto died abruptly while prospecting with some English, ironically from an illness to which he had no immunity. As Bradford recorded it, "Squanto fell sick of an Indian fever, bleeding much at the nose (which the Indians take for a symptom of death) and within a few days died there; desiring the Governor to pray for him that he might go to the Englishman's God in Heaven; and bequeathed sundry of his things to sundry of his English friends as remembrances of his love; of whom they had a great loss."[119] Through their gunpowder diplomacy, the Pilgrims dominated their neighbors and drove Weston's men from the area, securing the claim and establishing a relationship with the crown that would last until 1691.[120] The Patuxets were not part of their plans.

The suppression of the Powhatan Uprising and the assassination of the Massachusett sachems were turning points in the relationship between English settlers and coastal peoples. The notion that Indians would spontaneously agree to treaties with English settlers had died long ago. But with the victory over the Powhatans and the creation of a treaty between the Pilgrims and their neighbors, the English had established a firm foothold over the Chesapeake Bay and northern latitudes. In 1629, Charles I granted a charter to the Massachusetts Bay Company, a settlement venture led by Puritans. This decision was a sign of the crown's increasing confidence in the profitability and legality of its overseas ventures. However, power brought a new set of problems relating to the law of nations and its application to Native peoples. One problem was water. For many decades, the crown had argued for *mare liberum*, or the right to travel the seas. This had been a useful argument for challenging Spanish dominance. Now that the English crown possessed territory, however, it was expedient to argue instead for *mare clausum*, or the extension of princely sovereignty over coastal waters. Otherwise, English settlements and trading routes could be traveled by French, Dutch, and Swedish ships. Another problem was the increased travel of English people themselves. The financing and endorsement of the Massachusetts Bay Colony had sparked a wave of emigration to New England. Fur traders from many nations traveled the New English seas, and English emigrants increasingly moved beyond the bounds of Plymouth Colony and Massachusetts Bay. While the threat from the Spanish had died down, the movements of people across water and land, and the increasing contact between settlers and

Native people, raised a novel problem for English colonial proprietors and their metropolitan supporters. For decades, the crown and its councils had encouraged its colonists to publicize treaties as support for their claims. How would metropolitan authorities respond if fur traders came forward, treaties in hand, seeking support for claims of their own?

Chapter 4

—ᴍᴍ—

Trading Sovereignty: The Fur Trade and the Freedom of the Seas

In early summer 1632, the Dutch commercial trader *Eendracht* sailed cautiously into the harbor at Plymouth Sound after being blown off course in the English Channel. The ship, whose name, meaning "harmony," would later prove ironic, was not the first vessel to seek refuge in the harbor. Ships under many flags had retreated there for protection from the chaotic weather of the narrow passage. But the atmosphere aboard the *Eendracht* was even tenser than might be expected. Drenched and beleaguered—and perhaps doubtful of their survival—the crew had taken advantage of the Plymouth landing to demand immediate payment of their wages. More ominously still, there were rumors that the ship's provost, angry with the captain, had begun to whisper to Plymouth authorities about the possibility that contraband goods were aboard. Soon, English port controllers swooped in, seizing the *Eendracht* on the accusation that the ship had traded beaver pelts with Delaware groups along part of the North American coast claimed by the English. As Dutch diplomats voiced their indignation in a flurry of written protests, a dispute about wages quickly escalated into an international controversy over clashing Dutch, English, and Native concepts of sovereignty.[1]

Three years later, another trader sparked an international controversy by running afoul of English authorities. This time it was an English ship, the *Longtail*, owned by William Claiborne, a fur trader who operated a post at Kent Island. Near the waters disputed in the *Eendracht* case, authorities from the colony of Maryland seized the *Longtail* and confiscated the cargo, which Claiborne had intended to use as currency in trade with the Susquehan-nocks, an economically powerful tribe that controlled the fur market north of the Chesapeake Bay. Unlike the *Eendracht*, the *Longtail* was ready for the authorities. Commandeered at cannon point by Henry Fleet, a captain in the employ of Maryland, the ship's crew produced a sheaf of documents that included trading licenses stating that they "in no sort be interrupted in their Trade."[2] Despite their legal diligence, though, they met the same fate as the owners of the *Eendracht*. Fleet seized the ship's cargo and claimed it for Maryland.[3]

Though powerless to protect their goods, the captains of the impounded vessels were not without recourse. After the seizure of the *Eendracht*, Dutch ambassadors quickly submitted appeals to the English crown, demanding the release of the ship and its cargo. The *Longtail*, too, was the subject of heated correspondence. For years its owners had been engaged in a running war with the proprietors of Maryland over trading rights, and Fleet's act sparked a fresh round of pleas and remonstrances that reached Charles I about the same time as the *Eendracht* appeals.[4] Yet the two groups of aggrieved petitioners had something more in common than a shared means of redress. In their petitions to the king, both grounded their trading rights in commercial exchanges with the Native polities that controlled the coast. The Dutch shippers claimed rights on the basis of their trade with the Delawares, while Claiborne pointed to his friendship and long history of commerce with the Susquehannocks. Denied redress under European law, both cited their participation in Native politics as a source of rights to trade and travel.

In the previous chapters, I have examined how colonial governors (and their rivals and enemies) negotiated the possession of territory by publishing Native treaties. While the governments of chartered colonies derived their rights from the crown, treaties with Native peoples demonstrated control of territory. These treaties usually took the form of diplomatic relations or reports, though they often found their way into print. In this chapter, I consider how the documentary genres of the fur trade, such as trading licenses and receipts, served as a means of publicizing Native treaties. The legal needs of fur traders differed from those of settlers. Settlers were primarily interested in demonstrating control of territory. They used treaties to show that they were secure from challenges or attacks by Indians. Fur traders, however, rarely cared about owning the land beyond their trading posts. Instead, they sought trading rights, or the right to travel particular areas of the coast and engage in commerce with Native groups. Both the English crown and the United Provinces controlled trading rights through the granting of monopolies to companies. However, the ownership of

Atlantic waters was often subject to international dispute, as princes and their companies competed for access to the coast.

In this chapter, I show how fur traders publicized agreements with Native peoples in order to assert rights to travel and trade. Fur concerns operated in murky legal waters, articulating and defending their rights in response to the shifting policies and maritime claims of European crowns. As late as the early seventeenth century, the Spanish crown claimed Atlantic trading rights on the basis of the papal bulls that had awarded most of the Americas to the Spanish crown in 1493. The Spanish crown articulated these rights in terms of the legal principle of *mare clausum*, or the enclosure of the sea under the sovereignty of a princely power.[5] As they had in negotiations over territorial sovereignty, northern princes challenged Spain's claims by asserting alternative legal frameworks deriving from natural law and Roman legal traditions. Starting in the late sixteenth century, English monarchs cited the notion of *mare liberum*, or the freedom of the seas, to defend the activities of traders and adventurers.[6] Derived from the Roman notion of open seas, *mare liberum* held that all the peoples of the world possessed a universal right to travel and trade. The concept received its definitive early modern codification in the *Mare liberum* (1619) of Hugo Grotius, who argued that "Every nation is free to travel to every other nation, and to trade with it."[7] While Grotius published *Mare liberum* largely to support the tradings rights of the United Provinces, English diplomats found it useful to employ his arguments in the course of their disputes with Spain, Portugal, and Baltic powers, as well as in contests over trading rights in Africa and the New World.[8] However, as the English began to acquire territory in North America and maritime dominance in the Atlantic, the English crown increasingly set aside *mare liberum* in favor of a restricted notion of maritime rights that gave English traders exclusive access to waters off the North Atlantic coast.[9] In 1635, at the behest of Charles I, the jurist John Selden published *Mare clausum*, which drew upon natural law and the law of nations to argue for the sovereignty of the crown over Atlantic latitudes.[10] Selden's argument for closed seas reflected the consolidation of English power over the coastal territories stretching from the Chesapeake Bay to New England. It forced both English traders and those under rival flags to explain their rights in ways that accorded with the crown's assertion of power over the seas.

Here I will argue that documenting Native treaty performances was a way for trading concerns to assert rights to travel and trade when other kinds of arguments had failed. From the beginning, disputes over *mare clausum* and *mare liberum* were bound up with debates over the recognition of Native polities. In the negotiations with the Spanish crown over the Treaty of London, English diplomats had argued that Spanish claims of *mare clausum* violated the natural right of commerce possessed by both the English and the Indians.[11] As the English shifted to defenses of *mare clausum*, the status of Native polities in diplomatic arguments changed as well. While English diplomats no longer evoked Native rights as a way of establishing the ownership of the seas—asserting instead the unilateral power of the crown to claim jurisdiction over coastal waters—a number of Dutch and English trading concerns resurrected the crown's earlier arguments, depicting *mare clausum* as a violation of their own freedoms as well as those of Indians. As a version of an argument the English crown had itself once employed, the articulation of trading rights by way of Native treaties seemed to many traders like a potentially successful strategy. Yet this diplomatic back-and-forth did not involve only competing interpretations of the law of the seas. It also involved questions about how to understand the meaning of Native trading rituals under the law of nations.

This chapter compares two sets of texts from the North Atlantic coast, the *Eendracht* writings (1632–1636), a collection of appeals to Charles I authored by Dutch company agents, and the Claiborne papers (1622–1677), a series of petitions and other documents put forward by an English trading concern led by William Claiborne and William Cloberry. While both sets of papers include deeds, trading licenses, and other commercial genres, they also draw upon indigenous forms of political arbitration in order to make claims to free trade and free waters. In the *Eendracht* writings, Dutch company agents challenge the English crown's seizure of their ship by arguing that they have established trading rights through participation in the networks of tribute and exchange that link Unami- and Munsee-speaking Delaware peoples.[12] The papers document the traders' participation in the riverside rituals where Delaware peoples exchange goods and form alliances. Their authors argue that Dutch participation in these rituals amounts to a political treaty, one that has given them rights well beyond the power of the English crown. Claiborne's appeals advance a parallel claim, arguing that his purchase of Kent Island from the Susquehannocks gives him a right that supersedes the patent of Maryland. In advancing his case, Claiborne combines trading licenses, permissions from the king, and accounts of Susquehannock gifting ceremonies to assert his rights to trade particular waters. As I will show in a concluding section, Native groups such as the Susquehannocks were not given as much access to metropolitan officials as important political

Figure 10. Matthäus Merian's engraving of an exchange between an English merchant and Beothuk people in Trinity Bay, Newfoundland, from Matthäus Merian, *Dreyzehender Theil Americae* (1628). Courtesy of The Newberry Library.

figures like Pocahontas had been, and, because their primary contacts were with traders rather than prolific writers such as John Smith, they make few appearances in colonial records. Nevertheless, the Susquehannocks used trade agreements and treaties to gain an upper hand in conflicts with Maryland colonists and surrounding Iroquois groups.

The Fight over Harmony

The English had their reasons for seizing the *Eendracht*. While the English and Dutch had maintained a relationship of amity since the signing of the Treaty of Nonsuch in 1585, several incidents leading up to the seizure had heightened tensions between the English crown and the United Provinces. A few years before the incident, the Dutch East India Company had assaulted some English traders at Ambon Island in Indonesia.[13] Dutch and English traders had also made competing claims to the island of Saint Martin in the northeast Caribbean, leading to a dispute over land rights.[14] In the flurry of letters and petitions penned in response to the seizure of the *Eendracht*, Dutch diplomats anxiously debated the underlying cause for the action, speculating about the existence of a Spanish conspiracy operating through unwitting English agents.[15] In their correspondence, however, both the Dutch and the English ambassadors limited themselves to a discussion of the legality of the ship's travels. After seizing the *Eendracht*, the crown claimed that the ship had violated English jurisdiction by trading on inland routes that cut through a claim between the thirty-ninth and forty-first lines of latitude. In pressing this accusation, the English resorted to the familiar argument for possession by settlement they had employed against the Spanish a few years earlier, claiming the coastal area traveled by the *Eendracht* for the English crown on the basis of "first discovery, occupation and the possession which they have taken thereof." At the same time, they asserted that the Dutch, as a solely commercial enterprise, "had not of themselves and did not assume, such pretension."[16] Though a number of issues were concealed between the lines of such terse, legalistic statements, the dispute essentially revolved around whether Dutch trading posts could claim the same kind of rights to American territory as English settler colonies. According to the crown, the English had asserted *corpus*, or control, while the Dutch had not.

In framing the case in this way, royal advisors were construing English practices of colonization as acts of possession while classifying those of the Dutch as mere travel. It was true, as the crown pointed out, that the Dutch did not plant colonies after the fashion of the English at Virginia or Plymouth. Netherlanders traveled to the coast primarily under the auspices of trading companies. As Patricia Seed has detailed, Dutch traders employed protocols for establishing possession that often conflicted with those of other Europeans. For the Dutch, Seed writes, "Possession was not sustained by landing or settling but by sailing and trading."[17] The States General in Amsterdam carefully controlled trading rights, at first extending monopoly status to the West India Company. Later on, rights were extended to *vrije burghers*, or private traders, who were authorized to enter into separate agreements with tribal groups.[18] The scope of these ships' travels and landings was governed by treaties signed by the English and Dutch during negotiations in 1613 and 1615.[19] By the 1630s, Dutch ships were traveling circular routes from the Hudson River Valley to destinations in London and the Netherlands, returning to Amsterdam with monies and provisions to sustain the network of trading posts that dotted the coast.

While the Dutch and English had different understandings of how to establish ownership of American territory, in the Dutch view, the practice of staking claims through trade seemed to find an equivalent in the customs of coastal Native groups. In his account of Hudson River Valley Native peoples during the early colonial period, anthropologist Paul Otto has described how the Munsee-speaking Delawares who traded with the Dutch used exchanges of goods such as wampum and fur to maintain political order among the villages and larger groups that came together during times of crisis or change. As Otto details, the Munsees marked political affiliation through ceremonial transfers of goods, acts which could both renew relations with friends and create alliances with outsiders. Tribal leaders drew analogies between Dutch company officers and Munsee political leaders who were in charge of formally exchanging goods. "The Munsees welcomed Dutch supercargoes [company agents] as representatives of new groups and sought to establish new relationships based upon the exchange of goods," Otto writes. Trade served as both "an exchange which established . . . alliance" and "the object of . . . alliance."[20] Supercargoes often embraced the political meanings of trade in coastal economies. Many entered into ceremonial roles in indigenous rituals, while others offered Dutch ships and sloops as venues for ceremonies of tribute and gift giving.[21] These riverside exchanges functioned as both acts of trade and rituals of alliance, and dramatically embodied the many political, commercial, and legal frameworks along the Connecticut and Delaware Rivers.

In transatlantic correspondence, the Dutch frequently emphasized indigenous understandings of trade. In an appeal to the States General in 1634, for example, several Dutch traders sought to assert their independence from imperial restrictions by claiming that, when acquiring the land for their trading post, they had "bought and paid for not only the grounds belonging to the chiefs and natives of the lands in New Netherland, but also their [the natives'] rights of sovereignty [jura Majestatis] and such others as they exercised."[22] Such descriptions creatively construed the purchase of land from Indians as an acquisition of sovereign power. Throughout the 1630s, many Dutch traders adopted this strategy, publicizing their exchanges with Natives in order to position themselves as powerful, landholding entities. As Otto points out, such assertions were a calculated misrepresentation of the meaning of exchange in indigenous contexts.[23] In the *Eendracht* writings, as in other Dutch texts, colonial agents largely described indigenous political systems in order to advance their own agendas rather than to make any claims for the recognition of tribal polities. Yet as I will argue here, the Dutch recorded riverside ceremonies not simply to acquire access to tribal resources but also to generate novel conceptions of sovereignty that could support claims in European diplomatic venues. In their written defenses of the *Eendracht*, Dutch company agents cite the political meanings attached to trade by the Indians in order to depict New Netherland as part of a Dutch-Native colonial order where possession is established by the construction of trading posts and the exchange of goods.

The Dutch ambassadors begin their defense of the *Eendracht* by recounting a familiar saga from Dutch colonial history. In a letter to the States General that is the first written narrative of the seizure, Dutch ambassadors defend their claims—and by extension, the legality of the *Eendracht*—by telling the well-known story of the purchase of Manhattan. However, instead of limiting their derivation of sovereignty to European sources, they argue that Indian trading has long been a legitimate channel for establishing rights to land and waters. Accused by the English of being a company rather than a colony, the diplomats testify to "hav[ing] long peaceably traded, and, moreover, many years ago planted a colony on a certain island named Manathans, situate on the river also of the same name, which they purchased from the native inhabitants and paid for."[24] The description of Dutch-Munsee relations as "peaceabl[e]" draws on terminology that had recently been employed by Grotius, who suggested in *Mare liberum* that rights to enter the ports of foreign nations should extend to all vessels with peaceful intentions.[25] Yet the Dutch authors import this line of reasoning to land, strategically blurring the difference between trading post and colony. Even though the Dutch have not settled or "improved" the land in any sense recognized by the English, they assert possession instead through peaceful trading activities and the purchase of part of the coast from the Indians. Through trade and land transactions, commercial ventures are transformed into the kind of landholding colonies the English crown might recognize.

Along with the repeated appeals to the king, the Dutch cite their exchanges with the Munsee and other Delaware groups.[26] In a plea on behalf of the *Eendracht*, the company refers to these exchanges as marking out a separate jurisdiction independent from English control. "[I]t is directly contrary to all right and reason," they irritably assert, "for one potentate. . . . to lay claim to countries of which [Dutch] subjects have acquired the property, partly by confederation with the owners of the lands, and partly by purchase."[27] Taken together, the commercial purchases from the Munsee amount to a record of political alliance, voiding any claim by the English. Dutch-Delaware order is conjured as a dense political network already operating in channels well beyond the king's control.

In contrast to the English assertion of monarchical right, the Dutch see their exchanges with Indians as modeling a political "confederation." The idea of a confederation was an important concept in Dutch political discourse throughout the late sixteenth and early seventeenth centuries, as Dutch nationals negotiated the terms of their independence from Spain. In the wake of the successful rebellion against Spanish occupation, Dutch jurists formulated new concepts of political sovereignty deriving from multiple confederated states rather than from a sovereign prince.[28] In a colonial context, the insistence on an exchange-based confederation between Dutch and coastal groups resonated with attempts to elaborate the differences between Dutch and Iberian colonial regimes. In a brief to English governors, for example, Dutch director-general Wouter van Twiller outlined the differences between Dutch and Spanish colonialism, saying that the Dutch companies will never "take the land from the poor Natives, as the Kinge of Spaine hath done by the Pope's Donation."[29] Van Twiller's weepy rhetoric echoed the Black Legend of Spanish conquest, which colonial writers frequently invoked in order to conceive of Protestant colonization as a redemptive mission to save Indians from Spanish terror. But Dutch depictions of alliances with Indians could also serve as a model for what Dutch republican order might look like in both America and the Netherlands. As the Dutch ambassadors pled for the ship's release, they were also engaged in lobbying for continued English support of the Dutch rebellion against Spain. In a brief to Charles I on behalf of the *Eendracht*, Dutch government officials describe the relations between New Netherland and the Munsees using the vocabulary of republicanism. "Thus it is," they write, "that the subjects of their Lordships, the States [General], have, for a long time, traded in the river Manathans, now called Maurice, in the West Indies, having purchased from the native inhabitants and paid for a certain island called also Manathans, where they remain surrounded on all sides by the Natives of the country, and have, from all time, in coming and going, freely enjoyed your Majesty's [Charles I's] ports and harbors without any objection."[30] In contrast to the Spanish or English colonial system, where possession derives from a sovereign head, the

Dutch imagine sovereignty as coming from a relationship of mutual recognition with surrounding Native polities. Much like the United Provinces themselves, New Netherland is conceived as a republican order where numerous groups share space and derive sovereignty from peaceful relations with each other rather than from a distant prince.

In the context of the seizure of Dutch ships, such binary oppositions between Dutch and Spanish colonialism had the effect of subtly casting the English in the role of Spanish conquistadors greedily seizing territory on the basis of unilateral grants from imperial sovereigns. In response to the Dutch appeals, Charles and his representatives moved swiftly to reassert the prerogatives of the English crown and to clarify their views on the freedom of the seas. In a document entitled "Answer to the Remonstrance of the Dutch Ambassadors," English authorities offer a point-by-point rebuttal of the Dutch case, performing a complex triangulation of English, Dutch, and Spanish positions. On the one hand, the English refuse the notion that the Munsees are like European powers, writing, "it is denied that the Indians were *possessores bonae fidei* of those countries, so as to be able to dispose of them either by sale or donation, their residences being unsettled and uncertain, and only being in common." Repeating well-worn rationales for seizing Indian lands, the crown claims that Indians can never truly possess territory because they construct temporary, seasonal settlements rather than permanent forms of dwelling. On the verge of denying Native sovereignty, however, the English authors pull back, theoretically admitting the existence of indigenous rights while denying their import for the case at hand. "[I]n the second place," they assert, "it cannot be proved, *de facto*, that all the Natives of said country had contracted with them at the said pretended sale." While recognizing Native dominion in the abstract, the English assert that the exchanges between the traders and the Indians do not fulfill the criterion of *consensus ad idem* because the Dutch have not proved that all the Indians agreed to the sale. While the English crown had elsewhere encouraged English colonists to cite treaties as a way of establishing land claims, it here rejects similar claims from Dutch ambassadors. As a medium of sovereign authority, the exchanges cited by the Dutch as records of "confederation" are trumped by English patents—an assertion of the primacy of documents over exchange: "the right his Majesty's subjects have in that country," they write, "is justified by first discovery, occupation and the possession which they have taken thereof, and by the concessions and letters patents they have had from our Sovereigns . . . the true and legitimate proprietors thereof in those parts."[31] In asserting that patents are the only guarantee of sovereignty, the English sever land and water rights from commercial exchanges, recognizing indigenous sovereignty while asserting that Dutch deeds are an unreliable medium of its expression.

The story of the *Eendracht* came to an uncertain end. While eventually deciding to release the ship itself, the crown insisted on its right to detain Dutch vessels if they traded along areas of the coast claimed by the English.[32] The appeals were thus a mixed success, restarting Dutch trade but failing to win recognition for Munsee concepts of political mediation. In rejecting the Dutch case, the English insisted on the status of documentary patents as the sole medium for expressing sovereignty in international space, denying the validity of indigenous political rituals. This represented a tactical reversal of the crown's previous policy of viewing Native treaty rituals as a channel for acquiring rights in the New World. When it came to colonial disputes, the English crown and its agents preferred exigent means to principled stands. As the *Eendracht* sped out of Plymouth harbor toward the safe ports of Holland, English authorities moved just as quickly to exclude Native exchanges from future negotiations with Dutch trading concerns.

Spanish English on Kent Island

Unlike the owners of the *Eendracht*, William Claiborne was an English subject, trading colonial waters at the pleasure of the crown. He was also a rising figure in Virginia politics, and had played a key role in suppressing Powhatan resistance and expanding the crown's dominions through conquest and trade. Yet the story of the *Longtail* had much in common with that of the *Eendracht*. Claiborne, too, was the victim of an attack by English interests when colonists affiliated with Maryland took one of his ships. And, when other channels were closed to him, he also sought redress by circulating accounts of his alliances with Native peoples.

The conflict over the *Longtail* had its roots in a larger boundary dispute between Virginia and Maryland. As I described at the end of Chapter 2, after the Powhatan Uprising, the Virginia Colony abandoned the strategy of publicizing control of territory through voluntary treaties, asserting instead its rights to conquer the Powhatans in a just war. However, this policy of "expulsion," as Governor Francis Wyatt called it, applied only to the Powhatans and their allies.[33] After the quelling of the uprising, the colony continued to pursue the lucrative fur trade of the northern Chesapeake. The appearance of the English along this part of the coast was not unwelcome to the Native peoples living there. The Iroquois-speaking Susquehannocks who controlled the trade were eager to find European markets for their furs. Situated between French, Dutch, and English settlements, they had a long history with Europeans and a well-developed network for procuring furs and delivering them to the coast. In 1608, they had initiated trade relations with the Virginia colonists, but these efforts had largely been abandoned when John Smith, their chief contact in Virginia, had returned to England.[34] In 1626, they sought out an alliance with Isaack de Rasière, secretary of New Netherland, but abandoned it because the Dutch were shorthanded and unable to staff trading visits. The reappearance of the Virginia colonists offered a lucrative economic opportunity of the kind the Susquehannocks had been seeking after the collapse of their relationship with the Dutch.[35]

The Virginia Colony's entrance into the northern trade represented an opportunity for colonists as well. When the colony's government directed its attention to the north, many important political and military leaders began to forge relationships with Native traders. William Claiborne was one of the most active of these commercially minded planters.[36] From the time of his arrival in the Chesapeake Bay, Claiborne's career had been shaped by Native diplomacy. Claiborne migrated to Virginia after the crown appointed him surveyor. During running battles with Powhatan-affiliated groups during the Second Anglo-Powhatan War (1622–1630), Claiborne assumed a role as a military commander and enjoyed several successes, including a victory in a highly publicized raid against Opechancanough's forces at Pamunkey in 1629. From 1626 to 1632, the Virginia Colony granted Claiborne a series of licenses to trade the northern Chesapeake and Potomac River Valley, including a seasonal license to trade with the Susquehannocks, issued in 1630. Under this license, Claiborne purchased Palmer's Island from the Susquehannocks and set up a trading post.[37]

Claiborne's relationship with the Susquehannocks was lucrative, as evidenced by the willingness of colonial authorities to back his ventures. Yet Claiborne's activities also involved him in the burgeoning territorial disputes that would lead to the seizure of the *Longtail* and, ultimately, the loss of his trade. While Claiborne was establishing a rapport with the Susquehannocks from his base at Palmer's Island, other English were setting their sights on the same territory. The most powerful was George Calvert, Lord Baltimore, a former Secretary of State of James I and a recently confessed Catholic. Calvert had prior experience with colonial adventuring. In 1624, he had received a royal patent for an English colony in Newfoundland, but had abandoned the claim because of the harsh weather in the region. In 1630, he arrived in the Chesapeake Bay to scout the location for a new colony. His appearance alarmed the group at Palmer's Island. As they well knew, Calvert was a formidable foe. While he had been forced into resignation after failing to procure a marriage alliance between Charles and a Spanish princess, and his public embrace of Catholicism had caused a stir in London, Calvert still enjoyed the support of the English crown.[38] His arrival posed a serious threat to Claiborne's continuation of the Susquehannock trade, and, after Calvert's departure, Virginia traders dispatched Claiborne to London to seek royal recognition of their trading rights around the Potomac.[39]

Claiborne appeared in London at a good time. After the end of the Anglo-French War (1627–1629), Charles I agreed to cede Canada to the French in return for the payment of Henrietta Maria's dowry, over the furious objections of English merchants with investments in the northern trade.[40] Claiborne's venture represented an opportunity for those looking to invest elsewhere after the loss of Canada. Claiborne partnered with the merchant William Cloberry, and they organized the venture into a joint-stock company.[41] On May 16, 1631, Claiborne acquired a trading license under the signet of the Scottish crown that granted his concern rights to trade "these parts of America for which ther is not alreadie a patent grantit."[42]

After returning to America, Claiborne's first move was to expand his operations to Kent Island. In order to consolidate the Susquehannock trade and preempt any forthcoming claims from the proprietors of Maryland, it was imperative to establish a base of operations that could connect Susquehannock territory and Jamestown. Kent Island represented just such a territory. Though the island was partly occupied by the Matapeake tribe, the Susquehannocks claimed control of it, and they were eager for new trading partners. Thomas Savage, the former English interpreter of Powhatan, acted as a translator in a ceremonial purchase of the land. Claiborne paid them with trade goods, and they in turn offered him support, protection, and a promise to trade in the future. After the ceremony, Claiborne constructed an armed outpost and began collecting pelts from the Susquehannocks.[43]

The trade brought in startling revenues. In forming an alliance with the Susquehannocks, Claiborne tapped into a source of furs that had lain dormant after the collapse of the Dutch-Susquehannock alliance.[44] However, the purchase of the island in a Susquehannock ceremony did not protect Claiborne's trade from Maryland. After George Calvert died in 1632, the charter intended for him was instead issued to his son Cecil Calvert, who appointed his brother Leonard Calvert governor of Maryland and dispatched him to America. While Claiborne possessed a semi-official document under the Scottish signet, Calvert's charter represented a far more secure form of permission. Moreover, it was based on legal arguments for possession that were more familiar to the English crown than Claiborne's unusual amalgamation of Scottish and Susquehannock permissions. In his petition to the king, George Calvert had reported that the Potomac was "not yet cultivated and planted," and was therefore open to the possession of any Christian prince under the law of nations.[45] In making this argument, Calvert was partly taking advantage of the effect of Susquehannock trading policy on English settlement patterns around the Susquehanna River. Out of concerns over security, the Susquehannocks tried to prevent European traders from settling near their habitations. Claiborne's traders consequently sailed from Kent Island and an outpost at Accomack to collect the Susquehannocks' pelts.[46] While this arrangement made little difference to the profitability of their trade, the lack of English settlements near the points of exchange enabled Calvert to argue that the land was "inhabited and possessed of the Barbarous Heathen or Savages" and therefore available for the king to grant.[47] On this basis, Calvert sought the power of "debarring" other English from "Trade with the Natives." In the discussion of this petition, a member of the Privy Council had worried about granting the proprietor of Maryland such power. He cited natural law and the inherent right of nations and peoples to adventure and trade as a reason the crown should not interfere with Claiborne. To grant Calvert the right of barring the trade of others, he argued, "will disable all Planters and discourage all Adventurers which right of Trade doth de mere Jure as to an Adventurer or Planter in his proper nature essentially beelonge."[48] Despite these objections, the crown ultimately granted Calvert the patent, and his group sailed to the newly won grant with the intention of planting a colony.

The arrival of Maryland colonists, many of them Catholic, troubled Claiborne and Virginia councilors with a political and financial stake in Kent Island. Claiborne immediately began to plot the overthrow of Maryland. Seeking to quell unrest and to uphold what he understood to be the crown's commands, John Harvey, governor of Virginia, arrested Claiborne for conspiring with the Susquehannocks to attack the newcomers. Other Virginia colonists, perhaps inspired by Claiborne, attempted to convince the Susquehannocks that the

Maryland colonists were in fact Spaniards, or "Waspaines," whom the Susquehannocks hated because of rumors of Spanish atrocities they had heard second-
hand from English and Dutch traders.[49] In June 1634, the governors of Virginia
and Maryland, along with many of the most important *werowances* in the fur
trade, met to negotiate an end to hostilities. The conference had little effect. In
the spring of 1635, the Virginia Colony, under pressure from Cecil Calvert's
lobbying, began to enforce Maryland's jurisdiction over Kent Island, and Henry
Fleet captured Claiborne's *Longtail* and confiscated its cargo. After Claiborne
revolted against Governor Harvey of Virginia, Charles I officially sided with
Maryland, restored the governor, and granted Calvert the right to Kent Island
and adjacent waters.[50]

Violence played a significant role in deciding the ownership of Kent Island.
Indeed, the clash over the *Longtail* was the first military confrontation between
English vessels in North American history. But the battle for legal rights was
also conducted through competing transatlantic public relations campaigns
on the part of Claiborne and the Calverts. In their respective documents,
each group draws on a number of legal frameworks. The Calverts claim that
the land is unoccupied by Christians and therefore available for possession. In
countering this argument, Claiborne does not directly challenge its logic. While
English colonists in Virginia and Plymouth had recognized—and even argued
for—Native ownership of territory, proving that the Susquehannocks were
landowners was difficult for Claiborne to do, given that they simply ran trading
routes across the land, and, unlike the Powhatans in Virginia, did not control
it in any sense recognized by Europeans. Claiborne instead adopts a different
legal strategy. He defends his title by asserting that his purchase of land from
the Susquehannocks, combined with his construction of a trading post, gives
him rights to the land as well as lawful access to the waters.

The most direct statement of Claiborne's argument is a brief describing
his purchase of Kent Island, probably composed around April 1635. Since
Claiborne did not travel to London to lobby in person, he probably sent the
document or copies of it to his investment partner William Cloberry and his
ally Sir John Wolstenhome, who presented it to the crown along with a timeline
of events. In the brief, Claiborne combines two legal protocols for establishing
title: possession by improvement, and the purchase of land from Indians:

> William Claiborne enters upon the Isle of Kent unplanted by any
> man. But possessed by the Natives of that Country with about 100

men and there contracted with the natives and bought their right
to hould of the Crowne of England to him and his Company and
their heires and by force or virtue thereof William Claiborne and
his Company stood seized of the said Island about 3 yeares after his
Majesty's Graunts a Patent to the lord Baltamore from 38 degrees
to 40 of lands unplanted.

That Claiborne having planted and stocked the Island the lord
Baltamore claimeth the Island to be within his Degreese and soe
enters by force and seized upon the Island and keepeth the same
and all the stock and Cattle there upon the value of £7.000 and the
same deteyneth by force.[51]

The brief is framed by the claim that Claiborne owns the land because he has
improved it. Claiborne finds Kent Island a wasteland "unplanted by any man,"
and describes his own efforts to "plan[t] and stoc[k]" it. Alongside this familiar
legal rationale, Claiborne also tells a story about purchasing the island from the
Susquehannocks. He "contract[s] with the natives and [buys] their right to hould
of the Crowne of England to him." Though slightly awkward, the phrasing is conventional enough. Common law land sales usually recognized the ultimate derivation of title from the king; Claiborne, therefore, purchased title "of the Crowne."
However, Claiborne makes the unusual assumption that the Indians are also
holding title "of the Crowne" even before they sell it to him. Because the crown
has asserted dominion in the New World, Claiborne assumes that the Indians
own land in the king's name just as any Englishmen would, and are therefore
capable of selling it the same way one Englishman would sell it to another. By
assimilating this transaction to the common law, Claiborne transforms his ceremony with the Susquehannocks into a regular transfer of title, in effect rendering
moot Calvert's argument for possession, which had described the land as *terra
nullius*, or land without an owner.

Making the case for ownership was important if Claiborne wanted to keep
Kent Island. However, the dispute with Maryland revolved more centrally
around the question of trading rights. Claiborne's central goal was to acquire
the right to travel particular areas of the coast for the purposes of commerce
with the Susquehannocks. To this end, Cloberry presented to the Privy Council a petition supporting Claiborne's right to trade on the basis of the previously described common law purchase. Uncharacteristically for records of the
council's proceedings, the petition takes the form of a timeline, suggesting that

Cloberry supported Claiborne's case with a narrative of events. There is a good reason why Cloberry made this choice. Chronology was crucial to debates about possession. While the English crown had long disputed the centuries-old argument that discovery by itself entitled a prince to possession, it was still an important criterion in determining who owned land, especially in cases of competing claims. Like Claiborne's brief, Cloberry's timeline locates the origin of Claiborne's right in a combination of plantation and purchase. Yet the timeline extends these territorial rights into an ambiguously defined right to travel and trade the surrounding waters:

16 May, 1631.	His Majestie's Commission was granted to Captaine Clayborne and Partners.
17 Aug., 1631.	The Ile of Kent was planted and soone after purchased of the Indyans as may appeare.
20 June, 1632.	The Lord Baltimore obteyned a patent of land not cultivated nor planted.
June, 1633.	Upon reference from the Kinge to the Lords. It was ordered that the Ile of Kent should not be included in Maryland Patent and that there should be free Trade.
27 Mar., 1634.	Maryland was planted.
8 April, 1634.	By proclamation they interdicted trade, surprised boates, some out of their lymitts....[52]

Though presented as support for the brief, the petition makes a slightly different argument. While insisting that Kent Island is firmly the property of Claiborne, Cloberry grudgingly acknowledges that the Marylanders have occupied land "not cultivated or planted" by anyone else, in essence ceding Calvert's claims. However, Cloberry further asserts that this land patent, however secure it may be, gives Lord Baltimore no proprietary *mare clausum* to restrict the trade of other English subjects in adjacent waters. Cloberry cites a letter from Charles I expressing the exemption of Kent Island from the Maryland charter, and presents this document as the basis of the more general right of England's subjects to "free Trade" in coastal waters. While Maryland possesses proprietary rights to particular latitudes, Claiborne enjoys a broad right to travel elsewhere.

Throughout the appeals, Claiborne and his party frequently repeat the accusation that the Calverts are seeking to assert power "out of their lymitts." Though this phrase was conventional in land and maritime disputes, in the case of the Calverts, it evoked suspicions that English Catholics were working as agents for Rome.[53] George Calvert had faced frequent accusations that he was surreptitiously advancing the interests of the papacy. These accusations had first appeared during his tenure as Secretary of State, when anti-Catholics such as Sir Edward Coke attacked him for working with the Spanish ambassador to advance the match between Prince Charles and the Spanish *infanta*. Calvert was also criticized for defending the right of English Catholics to attend Mass at the chapel of the Spanish ambassador. Allegations of covert disloyalty intensified when Calvert openly declared his Catholicism and refused to take the oath of allegiance in early 1625.[54]

Even before the seizure of the *Longtail*, Claiborne and his allies had repeated these allegations in order to cast doubt on the legality of the Calverts' Chesapeake ventures. On November 30, 1629, Claiborne and other Virginia colonists had written a letter to the Virginia Council describing their first meeting with George Calvert, who had just arrived from Newfoundland. In the letter, they claim to have greeted Calvert by demanding he take oaths of loyalty: "wee tendered the oathes of Supremacie and Aleidgance to his Lordshipp and some of his followers, who making profession of the Romishe Religion, utterly refused to take the same, a thing which wee could not have doubted in him, whose former employments under his late Majestie might have indeared to us a persuasion, he would not have made denyall of that, in poynt whereof consisteth the loyaltie and fidelitie, which every true subjecte oweth unto his Soveraigne."[55] This letter, however, was omitted from Claiborne's transatlantic appeals over the *Longtail*. Despite the rumors that followed prominent English Catholics like the Calverts, Claiborne and his party understood that open accusations of treason against a former secretary of state were not a winning rhetorical tactic. Rather than voicing such suspicions himself, Claiborne instead uses accounts of Indian negotiations to reinforce the notion that the Calverts represent Spanish rather than English interests. In 1635, the governors of Maryland and Virginia summoned Claiborne and nearby sachems to answer questions about a potential conspiracy against Maryland. Claiborne or one of his secretaries took minutes of the meeting in order to create a documentary record that would reveal Claiborne's supposed innocence in the matter. Claiborne retained his copy of the proceedings and submitted it as part of his appeal.[56] While the document purports to be an exact transcription of the words and gestures of the sachems, it is in reality an exculpatory account of Claiborne's own actions. Over the course of the proceedings, Claiborne depicts the Calverts as Spanish agents who will bring about the overthrow of the king's holdings in America.

In the minutes, the governors ask Macquacomen, a *werowance* of Patuxent, a series of questions about Claiborne's alleged activities, in particular the accusation that Claiborne had portrayed the Maryland colonists as "Waspaines," or Spanish invaders. In a series of careful responses, Macquacomen clears Claiborne's name and, in a dramatic reversal, places blame for the rumor on the Marylanders themselves:

> The third question [the governors put to Macquacomen]
> · Wee demanded the reason why [the Indians] conceived the inhabitants of Maryland to bee Waspaines.
> The answere [from Macquacomen]
> That at their first comeing, some of the Indians who were none of the greate men nor of the Councell did thinke the Marylanders to bee Waspaines, But afterward this my Cosen Maichicuttah (pointing to him) comeing from Yawocomico [Maryland] did bring the newes to us that Capt: Fleete should tell him, that neither Captaine Clayborne nor Captaine Fleete himselfe nor Mr Harman should trade with them but only the English of Yawocomico and therefore they thought them to bee Waspaines.[57]

Here it is not the whisperings of Claiborne, but rather those of Henry Fleet, Maryland's agent for hire, that are the source of the rumor about the English colonists' Spanish origins. Maryland's barring of trade and assertion of *mare clausum* leads the Indians to believe that the newcomers are not English at all, but rather Spanish interlopers, set to attack English interests. The suggestion, unstated but everywhere implied, is that Indians believe the Catholic colonists are Spanish because Fleet is employing the tactics of Catholic Spain. Indeed, under further questioning, Errammahonda, a lower sachem, implicates not Claiborne, but rather Fleet, as a conspirator and source of treasonous rumors about Claiborne. "Then Errammahonda said that Captaine Fleete bad him tell Captaine Clayborne that the greate men of Pasbehayes would kill him and that it would bee in vaine for him to runne away any where, for that if hee goe to the Isle of Kent the greate men can fetch him there, And if he runne away any where among the Indians I will have six Indians for tenne armes length of

Roanoake [wampum] a peice to fetch him to mee."[58] The exchange turns the Marylanders' accusations on their own heads. Captain Fleet is revealed to be working through indigenous channels to intimidate Claiborne and drive him from the island. While the Calverts accuse Claiborne of slandering the Maryland colonists, Errammahonda's words are cited to confirm broader suspicions that English Catholic colonists are more Spanish than English.

In response to Cloberry's petition, the crown decided to act to protect the rights of adventurers and planters, affirming Claiborne's freedom to trade the waters. Claiborne's relationship with the Susquehannocks figures prominently in Charles's protective order to the Governor and Council of Virginia. The order acknowledges that Claiborne's concern has "traded, planted and inhabited an Iland neare to Virginia which they have nominated the Kentish Iland." In particular, Claiborne has "sent over a good number of people and Cattle but bought the Interest of the Natives in that Iland." The affirmation echoes Claiborne's own argument for Native purchase as a mode of improvement that deserves recognition. The Susquehannocks are not granted powers; rather, Claiborne's purchase of land and construction of a trading post is classed with the importation of people and cattle as a form of improvement that establishes his rights to the land. From this, the crown extrapolates a right to trade, stating that Claiborne's group "be in noe sort interrupted in trade or plantation by [Calvert] or any other in his right."[59]

The king's order represented a clear victory for Claiborne and opened the way for his trade. However, Claiborne's victory was short-lived. News of Claiborne's mutiny against Governor Harvey radically changed the crown's view of Claiborne's earlier appeals, giving the Calverts powerful political ammunition. Vastly better connected than his colonial adversary, Cecil Calvert used this window of opportunity to petition for exclusive rights to the waters. If Claiborne bases his rights on exchanges with the Susquehannocks, Calvert attacks him by classifying these indigenous alliances as part of a hidden plot against lawful English interests. In addition to recklessly disregarding the Privy Council's royal order affirming the Maryland patent, Claiborne, Calvert writes, "did conspire with the Indians to destroy two of your petitioners Brothers, with divers Gentlemen, and others of your Majesties subjects, and by many other unlawfull wayes to overthrow his plantations, whereof he fayling, (but continuing his malice to your petitioner) whilst he is a prisoner at the Boord upon a complaint of the Governor of Virginia for his contemptuous and mutinous carriage towards the government there."[60] While Claiborne points to his relationship with the Susquehannocks as a legal basis for territorial ownership and derivative rights to the seas, Cecil Calvert describes the alliance as part of Claiborne's broader pattern of mutinous behavior against the crown. In a sense, this argument is similar to the one Zúñiga made against the Virginia Colony. What Claiborne claims are Indian alliances, or at the very least economic relationships, Calvert portrays as conspiracies. In Calvert's assessment, these schemes are evidence that Claiborne should be stripped of his rights.

On April 4, 1638, the Commissioners for Foreign Plantations officially decided against Claiborne, ordering that "the said Isle of Kent is within the Bownds & Lymitts of the Lord Baltimores Pattent." This decision was heavily influenced by Claiborne's mutinous conduct in the affair of Governor Harvey. However, just as Claiborne and Calvert had disputed the claim by making arguments about the rights of Native peoples, so does the commission, in revoking Claiborne's rights, dismiss the validity of Claiborne's alliances with the Susequehannocks. The logic of the dismissal is twofold. First, the commission decides that Claiborne's earlier documentary support from the king is "only a Lycense under the Signett of Scotland, to trade with the Indians of America," not a "right or tytle thereby, to the said Island of Kent, or to plant, or trade there, or in any other parts or places, with the Indians or Savages within the precincts of the Lord Baltemores Pattent."[61] This statement refutes Claiborne's claims that the letter from Charles, combined with the Susquehannock ceremony, gives him a title under any law. Second, the commission gives Lord Baltimore the right to restrict travel and control trade with Indians, ruling that "noe Plantation or Trade with the Indians ought to be within the precincts of his Pattent without Lycence from him."[62] The report bears comparison with the *Eendracht* ruling in the way it reasserts the prerogatives of the crown by denying legal status to exchanges with Native groups. The report insists first on the crown's prerogative to redraw the map regardless of existing arrangements with Natives, and second, on its power to invest colonial proprietors with rights of *mare clausum* and delegated power to control Indian trade. While Claiborne had attempted to attach meaning to Susquehannock friendship in his appeals, the order effectively closes off Native alliances as a channel for fur traders to assert either title or trading rights, reaffirming the supremacy of royal charters and trading licenses issued by colonial proprietors.

The owners of the *Longtail* never recovered their property. Fleet, believing that the Susquehannocks would desire it, sold it to Lord Baltimore's concern.[63] Fleet was right that the Susquehannocks preferred Claiborne's goods. However, he misunderstood the reason. This became clear when Marylanders occupied Kent Island and reached out to Claiborne's former allies. The Susquehannocks rebuffed their offer, moving away at a great financial cost and instead pursuing alliances with the Swedish. Apparently the Susquehannocks were not indifferent to which English they traded with.

Marks and Signatures in the 1652 Anglo-Susquehannock Treaty

Historian Francis Jennings has noted the lack of a documentary record of the Susquehannocks' activities during the crucial period of their trading relationship with Claiborne.[64] Unlike the Powhatans and Pokanokets, whose histories and prominent personalities find dramatic expression in colonial texts, the Susquehannocks rarely appear as anything other than a tribal collective. One reason for this is that the Susquehannocks were located on the periphery of the Native peoples Europeans first encountered. This fact is registered in European names for them, which all come second-hand by way of other Native groups. Following the usage of the Delaware, the Susquehannocks' enemies, the Dutch called them *Minquas*, which meant "traitors." The English name for the tribe derives from *Sasquesahanough*, the name given them by the Powhatans.[65] Another reason for the dearth of information about the Susquehannocks is the commercial nature of their relations with Europeans. The Virginia and Plymouth colonists set their sights on territory. They detailed Native languages, rituals, and political calculations because such information supported their own claims to have solicited the voluntary consent of Native peoples to their possession of land. Fur traders, however, were interested in profits, and they set down the information that was relevant to commercial ends. Unless challenged, they had little need of formalizing agreements with Native peoples or gathering evidence of their validity under the law of nations. Claiborne, for example, only began circulating his agreements with the Susquehannocks after Calvert arrived. Unlike Archer or Winslow, who offer detailed portrayals of the workings of Native polities and of the personalities of their principals, Claiborne notes little beyond their sale of land to him and their consent to his seasonal presence.

The Susquehannocks therefore present a different kind of challenge to historical understanding. The tribe's own view of alliances seems a casualty of European disinterest. Even cryptic remarks, such as those left behind by Pocahontas, are nowhere to be found. The most direct material evidence of their political intentions is a 1652 treaty document between the tribe and

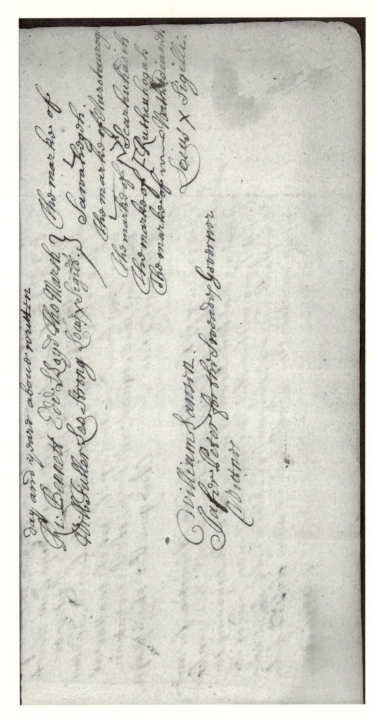

Figure 11. "Articles of Peace and freindshipp" between the Susquehannocks and Maryland Colony. The secretary has written the names of the Native signatories over their marks, which are visible just above each of his transcriptions. Courtesy of the Maryland State Archives.

the Maryland Colony, which is signed by their marks. This treaty was a first for both Claiborne and the Susquehannocks. Prior to this moment, neither had possessed any reason for forming an alliance conceived purely in political terms. Their relationship had been motivated primarily by trade and profit, and any arguments about the political meanings of such trade only surfaced later, during Claiborne's attempts to retroactively depict his exchanges with the Susquehannocks as a source of trading rights. But during the English Revolution, events brought Claiborne and the Susquehannocks together again under vastly changed circumstances. In 1652, Claiborne received authorization from Parliament to take control of Maryland.[66] The Susquehannocks, fighting a war on two fronts against Maryland and their Iroquois enemies, seized the opportunity to propose a treaty with the English that would free them to fight the Iroquois.[67] Any direct material traces of the tribe in the treaty itself are quite sparse, consisting only of their marks (see Figure 11). The marks are highly irregular, suggesting that the Susquehannock leaders had little or no experience holding pens or signing agreements. They are also crowded by the annotations of the English secretary, Richard Bennett, who wrote the name of each Susquehannock across the marks, perhaps out of an anxiety that their irregular signatures would not persuade readers that they had consented to the terms. Quite literally overwritten by alphabetic names, the marks resemble the notorious, uncomprehending x's through which many Native leaders gave away land and marked agreement to treaties they did not understand. And truthfully, the 1652 treaty is remarkably one-sided. In it, the Susquehannocks cede land around the Chesapeake to the English in Maryland. The treaty seems to anticipate the future land grabs by expansionist European states that continued well into the twentieth century, and it poses a challenge to my contention here that colonial documents often reflected Native as well as European agendas. Given the asymmetrical nature of the agreement, the marks seem little more than alibis for dispossession. Yet I want to argue now that a good deal of information about Susquehannock views of European alliances can be glimpsed in the series of ragged marks at the bottom of the document. If the turbulent nature of European maritime law during the early period of North American colonization led fur traders to seek out Native alliances, the Susquehannocks also sought to capitalize on transatlantic legal squabbles in order to protect their trade and territory from encroachment.

After Claiborne lost his appeal, the Susquehannocks lost their greatest English ally and most reliable source of European goods. Their connection to him was more than economic opportunism. While Claiborne does not refer anywhere to his personal interactions with Susquehannock sachems, his alliance with them was based, at least in part, on personal regard. Their decision to seek out Swedish markets surprised Cecil Calvert, who had sought to seize Claiborne's property largely because he thought it would give him easy entry into the lucrative Susquehanna River trade. Calvert failed to consider that Claiborne's relationship with the Susquehannocks might have involved something other than commercial considerations.[68] In 1642, Maryland declared war on the tribe, but the Susquehannocks, with secret aid from the Swedish, overwhelmed Maryland's forces and brutally tortured a number of English captives, sending a strong message that they were independent of European control.[69]

Hostile relations between tribe and colony continued until a series of developments among both the Iroquois and the English led the Susquehannocks to seek peace with Maryland. In 1652, the Mohawks, having successfully defeated or subjugated western rivals for the beaver trade, turned their attention toward the Susquehannocks, launching a sudden raid that netted hundreds of captives. Facing the prospect of war with the Iroquois, several Susquehannock leaders sought a treaty with their English neighbors. Their timing was lucky, coinciding with the change in Claiborne's fortunes that had temporarily restored his authority.[70] Claiborne's resumption of control reflected his deft negotiation of the English Revolution. Though Claiborne had lost his petition for Kent Island, he had maintained a network of transatlantic connections. In 1650, one of his allies, George Thomson, had assumed a position on the Committee for Foreign Plantations. Thomson's ascension gave Claiborne the influence he had been lacking during his struggle with the Calverts in the 1630s. While Claiborne had previously condemned the Calverts as disloyal papists, he now argued that they were Royalists in an open state of rebellion against Parliament. The Committee immediately granted Claiborne and his ally Richard Bennett permission to impose parliamentary authority on the governments of Virginia and Maryland and supplied them with a military force. Claiborne and his allies toppled the governments of Virginia and Maryland and assumed power. While Claiborne had little authority over the traders on Kent Island, he promptly claimed it as his territory on the basis of his Susquehannock trading decades before.[71]

After subjugating Virginia and Maryland, Claiborne and his allies turned their attention to the Susquehannocks' offer. The treaty itself marks the first political recognition of the Susquehannocks by a European crown. Bennett titles the treaty "Articles of Peace and freindshipp, treated and agreed upon the

5th day of July 1652 Between the English Nation in the Province of Maryland on the one party, And the Indian Nation of Sasquesahanogh on the other partie."[72] The portrayal of the English party as "the English Nation in the Province of Maryland" certainly supports Claiborne's agenda. The Susquehannocks are a bargaining agent, a "nation," but Maryland is not; Claiborne depicts himself as a representative of Parliament, while the Marylanders, whose territory Claiborne has conquered, are provincial figures. Moreover, the treaty offers a resolution to the ongoing quarrel between Claiborne and Maryland, one decidedly in Claiborne's favor. The Susquehannocks give up their land to Maryland, "Excepting the Ile of kent, and Palmers Ilands which belongs to Captaine Clayborne."[73] This exception is strategic. The Susquehannocks transfer to the crown everything but Kent Island and Palmer's Island, which are portrayed as having always been Claiborne's. By exempting his islands from the transfer (and writing Charles's grant of Kent Island to Maryland out of the historical record), Claiborne sneaks his own property rights into an exchange that is ostensibly between the Susquehannocks and the crown.

The treaty is ratified by the signatures of Bennett and other English authorities, Swedish witnesses, and finally the marks of the Susquehannock sachems Sawahegeh, Aurotaurogh, Scarhuhadih, Ruthcuhogah, Wathetdianeh, and Sigilli. Looked at one way, the marks seem to represent a profound capitulation on the part of the tribe. Facing war with the Iroquois, they concede defeat in their contest with Maryland, losing their land in the process. Putting pen to paper in a European political context, the Susquehannocks submit to the English documentary systems that have come to replace Native practices of arbitration. In some sense, the signatures are an image of domination. Claiborne clearly intends to portray the Susquehannock leaders as kings agreeing to conditions that will bind both them and their people. To this end, the treaty offers a series of analogies—between European and Native nations, between European kings and Native leaders, and most of all between European signatures and Native marks. As Heidi Bohaker has shown, however, the analogy between signatures and marks was always a limited one.[74] Native marks could possess many different meanings. They may have represented the will of sachems or kinship groups, or have expressed only the intentions of individuals. One way of reading the document is to see it as an imposition of European systems on Native people. Claiborne, like many English before him, frames an analogy between two different political systems in order to bring territory under his control. But it is worth keeping in mind that signatory marks were not a traditional or longstanding way of marking assent among the Susquehannocks. As is clear from the unsteady movement of the pens, the marks represented a recent adoption of a new way of doing things.

In a study of the significance of treaty marks to Native understandings of political history, Scott Richard Lyons has argued that the x-mark was always an expression of Native political will, even in contexts where it seems to represent a capitulation or an incomplete understanding of treaty terms. While pointing out that treaty marks were a "coerced sign of consent," Lyons argues that they also embodied claims on the future.[75] "[I]t is always possible . . . that an x-mark could result in something good," he writes. "Why else, we must ask, would someone bother to make it?"[76] Lyons's notion of x-marks as representing an optimistic Native modernity may not be particularly useful in understanding the Susquehannocks. The treaty with Maryland was above all a military maneuver, designed to pacify their eastern frontier. But Lyons's argument that x-marks represent Native visions of the future offers a way of understanding the marks as something other than a defeat. In reading treaty concessions, made by marks or in other ways, it is always important to consider not only what Natives lost but also what they might have hoped to gain, even if those hopes were never realized. The Susquehannocks had a complicated claim to the land they relinquished to Maryland. While they considered it their territory, several other Native groups that were already informal allies of Maryland inhabited the land at the time. The treaty refers to these groups twice, in elliptical terms. In the second article, it states that "if any Damage or Injury be done on either Side at any tyme hereafter, either by the English or Indians aforesaid, or by any other Allyes, Confederats Tributaries or Servants, that Reparation be made and satisfaction given from each to other from tyme to tyme as the Case requires, and as in Reason should be done betweene those that are freinds, and that desire soe to Continue."[77] And in the fifth article, it mentions them again, stating "that these Articles and every particular of them shalbe really and inviolably observed kept and performed by the two Nations before named, and by all the people belonging to them, or that are in amity with them for Ever, to the End of the World."[78] There is certainly English strategy in these lines. By giving the Susquehannocks authority over the "Allyes, Confederats Tributaries or Servants" that occupy the territory, the treaty implies that Claiborne and his allies have done more than simply acquire land. They have conquered subjects. The document gives the Susquehannocks power over peoples already living under the informal subjection of Maryland so that the tribe can relinquish that power to the English crown. The unusual nature of this agreement may be one reason the document is so vague about who these people are—it specifies only that "people belonging" to either party are subjected by the agreement. But the fact that the Susquehannocks did not possess authority over these unnamed peoples—and apparently did not want it—suggests another way of interpreting the treaty. Francis Jennings has suggested that the treaty might be understood as a Native version of a quitclaim.[79] Given that the Susquehannocks did not occupy the land, and did not attempt to rule the people who lived there, the signatures may represent the relinquishing of any future claim to the land rather than the transfer of territory from Susquehannock to English control. In other words, the Susquehannocks may have given up very little, and hoped at least to gain peace on one frontier.

The complications surrounding the treaty suggest the many agendas that could stand behind Native marks and find expression in them. In 1652, Claiborne and his Susquehannock partners were less interested in trading than in defeating their enemies in other places. The treaty settled the border between tribe and colony and enabled them to direct their military resources elsewhere. Neither Claiborne's nor the Susquehannocks' plans were successful. Claiborne's designs on Kent Island, embodied by the 1652 treaty, collapsed yet again. In 1655, Oliver Cromwell reinstalled Calvert as the governor of Maryland, sparking a civil war between Puritans and Catholics in the colony. Facing defeat, Claiborne signed a capitulation in 1657, formally acknowledging Calvert's power in exchange for amnesty.[80] The Susquehannocks faced an even bleaker future. The 1652 treaty was followed by a series of long-running wars with the Iroquois and with colonists that eventually culminated in the tribe's destruction.[81] Yet even in the face of this genocidal conclusion, it is a mistake to read later events into earlier x-marks, or to make treaties into an allegory of colonization. Settlement produced many alliances, running in many different directions. Though the treaty is an episode in a history of dispossession, it meant something different to the people who signed it, or marked it with their x's.

In this chapter, I have examined how fur traders used Native alliances to defend trading rights on the coast. Traders were constantly worried about their legal permissions. European crowns frequently (and strategically) changed positions on what constituted rightful authorization, necessitating reactive lobbying by traders. In this climate of uncertainty, Native political systems paradoxically offered a source of legal stability that European law did not. By rooting rights in exchanges with Native peoples, fur traders tried to make their claims valid under many legal systems. The Dutch ambassadors who authored the *Eendracht* papers used trading agreements with Native peoples to depict their own maritime rights as deriving from a republican order that included Delawares. William Claiborne, in contrast, construed his trading with the Susquehannocks as an improvement of land that formed the basis of rights to trade the seas. Ultimately, English monarchs and parliamentary leaders were hesitant to admit Native alliances as evidence of trading or maritime rights. Though the *Eendracht* was released, and though Claiborne was granted rights for a short window of time, both concerns ultimately failed in their suits. While the English crown had cited Native alliances in order to support its own rights in conflicts with Spain, it was not willing to recognize Native alliances as a source of rights for traders within its own waters. However, in the uncertain climate of the English Revolution, Parliament did find some outsiders worth supporting. While many fur traders lost their bid to derive freedom of the seas from Native alliances, another group, religious dissenters from Narragansett Bay, met with a different kind of welcome when they arrived in London, Native treaties in hand. The crown's recognition of Native treaties was always strategic, and sometimes it still proved useful to reward them.

Chapter 5

———ധ———

Gift of an Empire: The Land Market and the Law of Nations in Narragansett Bay

In early 1638, John Winthrop, governor of the Massachusetts Bay Colony, wrote to Roger Williams to ask about some recent news from Narragansett Bay. The letter had to be carefully worded. Winthrop had heard that Narragansett Indians were selling land to religious dissenters who had been banished from Massachusetts. The irony, not lost on either man, was that a few years prior Williams himself had been exiled for preaching "dyvers newe & dangerous opinions," and had afterward brokered sales between dissenters and Indians.[1] With a keen sense of the delicacy of his position, Winthrop now turned to his banished adversary for information about the latest English to flee to Narragansett country.

The letter was not a complete surprise to Williams. Proficient in several languages and deeply immersed in the colonial land market, Williams had for years advised colonial governors on title disputes between English, Dutch, and Native claimants. It made sense that Winthrop would turn to him. Still, Williams could only be amused by the letter. He was apparently the lesser of two evils now that whispers of a Narragansett conspiracy against Massachusetts Bay had gotten louder. Obliging his former adversary, Williams wrote back to confirm the sales, reporting that a party led by William Coddington had claimed land on the north shore of the Isle of Aquidneck. Not wasting an opportunity to tease the governor, though, Williams highlighted Winthrop's misunderstanding of how such sales were conducted. They were not, in fact, sales at all, he wrote, but a different kind of transaction, one Winthrop would be hard pressed to comprehend. "[B]e pleased to understand your great mistake," Williams replied: "neither of [the islands] were sold properly, for a thousand fathom would not have bought either, by strangers. The truth is, not a penny was demanded [by the sachems] for either, and what was paid was only gratuity, though I chose, for better assurance and form, to call it sale."[2] While Winthrop assumes that the sales have taken the form of an exchange of money for land—as they would under the common law in England—Williams informs him that Coddington has acquired the land through an act of tribute to Narragansett sachems, what Williams, reaching for an English analogy, describes as a "gratuity." The sale was based on personal regard, generosity, and reciprocity, Williams insists. It was not a mere exchange.

The problem of regulating the land market was much on the mind of Boston leaders as the population of the Massachusetts Bay Colony swelled from successive waves of emigration in the 1630s.[3] As the Antinomian controversy and other theological disputes flared, groups of religious dissenters and squatters fanned out across the Narragansett Bay, making treaties with Native peoples, staking land claims, and entering markets in cattle, pelts, and wampum.[4] In describing the exchange as a "gratuity," Williams hit on the anxiety, often noted in Winthrop's journal, that settlers would acquire land and power through indigenous channels. To Winthrop, English deeds emphasizing Native politics were evidence that dissenters might have "turned Indian," as Williams tauntingly put it in his reply to Winthrop.[5] Yet the sales raised another problem as well, one having little to do with racial anxieties. Williams and other dissenters moved to Narragansett territory at a time of crisis for Massachusetts Bay. The colony's royal patent, which authorized it to occupy land and negotiate with foreign powers, was under attack in England.[6] The colony had also just concluded a brutal war against the Pequot Indians, with the Narragansetts as its allies. But now that alliance was beginning to fray, and the governors of Massachusetts Bay found themselves competing for Narragansett allegiance with the English colony of Connecticut, which along with the Bay Colony had signed a treaty with Narragansett and Mohegan sachems at Hartford in 1638. Given this uncertainty, Winthrop was glad he could turn to Williams, who had been instrumental in making the Narragansett alliance, yet Winthrop was also worried to find Williams and other dissenters traveling so freely among the Narragansetts. Developments in Narragansett Bay were being closely watched in London and Connecticut, as well as in New Netherland, New France, and New Sweden, and Williams, though an erstwhile ally, had always been controversial. Indeed, his radical arguments about the law of nations and its application to Indians were part of what had gotten him exiled in the first place. The fact that he was now so important and so visible in international negotiations troubled the governor of Massachusetts Bay.

Winthrop's fears were soon realized. Just a few years later, Williams and other religious dissenters began to travel to London to voice their opinions about Native diplomacy and appeal to royal authorities for charters that would give them independence from Massachusetts Bay.[7] In bringing their cases before the newly seated English Parliament, these dissenters cited their acquisition of land from Narragansett sachems in voluntary treaties that combined purchase and political agreement. These transatlantic travels sparked a public relations struggle between the Bay Colony and exiled dissenters.[8] While the Massachusetts Bay Colony asserted sole authority to govern land transactions, Williams and others claimed that Narragansett exchanges were a valid channel for acquiring land and political power. These exchanges involved the sales of land for wampum, but also involved a range of acts that Williams calls "gratuity"—gifts, shows of hospitality, the transmission of military intelligence, and other exchanges that elevated the act of purchase into a form of tribute. Few Narragansetts drew the distinction between land purchase and political treaty that operated in European law. They saw land sales as part of broader agreements that involved tribute, friendship, and pledges of military or diplomatic support. During their campaigns in London, religious dissenters often adopted the same perspective as their Native allies, claiming that exchanges with the Narragansetts were a legal way to establish settlements.

In what follows, I focus on the transatlantic publications of Williams, as well as those of another dissenter, Samuel Gorton, who made his own agreements with the Narragansetts a few years later. While Williams and Gorton had different theological orientations, their lives had parallel trajectories. Williams was banished from the Massachusetts Bay Colony in 1635, and in 1643 traveled to London to appeal to the recently convened parliamentary Committee for Foreign Plantations for a charter for Providence Plantations, an independent settlement colony. Gorton, too, was banished from several colonies and settlements and followed Williams's maritime path to London in 1646, petitioning the same committee that had heard Williams's case. This chapter will consider how Williams and Gorton used printed accounts of Narragansett land sales and treaties to support their transatlantic appeals. While both their campaigns involved disputes about religious doctrine, they also claimed that their way of negotiating treaties with the Narragansetts has brought land under English control, making them deserving of parliamentary support. Williams first attacked the colonial land system in sermons and in manuscript. The colony tried to censor his arguments about the law of nations and its application to Native peoples, but they also found his writings useful in conflicts with New Netherland and employed him as an agent in negotiations with Natives and other Europeans. In the course of his transatlantic campaign to establish Providence Plantations, Williams worked through many channels, including letters and face-to-face appeals to the Committee for Foreign Plantations, which had assumed authority over England's overseas holdings after the beginning of the English Revolution. The most remarkable product of Williams's appeal to the Committee was *A Key into the Language of America* (1643), a phrasebook of the Narragansett dialect printed by Gregory Dexter in London. Many of the phrases translated and glossed in *A Key* focus on land and its relationship to the law of nations. Through the genre of the phrasebook, Williams shows that the Narragansetts, far from being benighted savages, have intricate legal systems regulating the transfer of land. By demonstrating that the Narragansetts have a working political system and legally valid practices for the transfer of property and rights, Williams tries to prove the validity of his own purchases from the tribe. Along with establishing his own landholdings, Williams also exposes what he believes are the treaty violations of the Massachusetts Bay governors, who he claims are endangering the international image of the English crown through their unscrupulous treatment of Native allies.

Williams's journey from Narragansett Bay to the world of metropolitan print established a route that others soon followed. In 1646, Gorton traveled to London and published *Simplicities Defence Against Seven-Headed Policy* (1646), an account of his own running disputes with colonial authorities. In the book, Gorton likewise makes a land claim by describing his treaty with Narragansett sachems. The centerpiece of *Simplicities Defence* is an "Act of Submission" from the Narragansetts to the English crown. The document, which was signed by Narragansett sachems, narrates Gorton's subjection of a people who had resisted English domination for much of the colonial period. Even before Williams and Gorton had embarked upon their transatlantic embassies, English leaders were well aware of the Narragansetts from the reports of Plymouth leaders and accounts of the Pequot War. The possibility that the tribe might submit to the English crown was of great interest to the Committee for Foreign Plantations. Bringing the tribe under English control would represent a definitive political victory, and, as always, treaties were a cheaper and easier way of conquering territory than war. Yet the document also expresses the political will of the Narragansetts during a time when the tribe was rapidly losing ground to the English colonies, which in 1643 had united in a political confederation, in part in order to face Native resistance. If Williams and Gorton used the Narragansetts to carry out their agendas, the sachems also used mobile religious dissenters to seek an independent alliance with Parliament that would protect the territory they had won during the upheaval of the Pequot War.

As these campaigns unfolded, the Massachusetts Bay Colony moved quickly to respond, both through Native diplomatic channels and in print. In 1643, the United Colonies assassinated Miantonomi for his alleged violations of the terms of the Treaty of Hartford. While Gorton traveled to London to expose the assassination as a war crime, Winthrop went into print himself on the colonial press at Cambridge, publishing an account of Anglo-Native treaty negotiations that singled out Miantonomi as a peace breaker. In this book, entitled *A Declaration of Former Passages and Proceedings Betwixt the English and the Narrowgansets* (1645), the Bay Colony sought to answer the legal arguments made by Williams and Gorton and to preempt any future criticisms from dissenting quarters. While Massachusetts Bay's move against Miantonomi and their intervention in print made it much more difficult for dissenters to work through Native political channels (and effectively brought about the end of the transatlantic treaty traffic under discussion in this book), the Narragansetts continued to work through English channels to secure their control of territory and political autonomy. Their efforts to negotiate English treaties had significant consequences for the power balance in New England long after Williams, Gorton, and others had disappeared from the scene.

Ancient Apostles and Pequot Conquerors: Roger Williams and the Land Market

Williams's writings have often struck readers as unusually sympathetic to Native Americans. Indeed, the historian Joyce E. Chaplin has described Williams's running conflicts with Massachusetts Bay governors as "counterparts to the Las Casas-Sepulveda debates" over Native rights in New Spain a century earlier.[9] Like the Spanish debates, Williams's disputes with New England magistrates were driven by conflicting understandings of the nature of the law. Williams had many kinds of legal expertise. He had studied at Cambridge under Sir Edward Coke in the early 1630s, learning common law and natural law texts. Williams's understanding of the law was also shaped by reformist theology. Williams moved to the Massachusetts Bay Colony in 1630, most likely at the invitation of colonial leaders, who anticipated that he would bring with him much-needed legal expertise. Around the time of his emigration, however, Williams had begun to pursue a more extreme form of Separatism from the Anglican Church than any practiced in Boston, and, upon arriving in New England, began to publicize manifold disagreements with Bay Colony governors. Williams's criticisms revolved around a basic dispute about typology. An interpretive method commonly employed by Puritans, typology enabled Christian readers to smooth over discontinuities in biblical history by viewing the Old Testament as an allegory of events in the New Testament. Puritan interpretive practices held that the events recounted in the Bible were the "type" and the subsequent history of the church the "antitype" or fulfillment of the Bible. This way of reading scripture enabled readers to posit links between the early church and the institutions Puritans hoped to realize on earth. For Williams, however, the rise of the Catholic Church, with its consolidation of ecclesiastical and state powers, had disrupted any continuity between ancient times and the present. Williams leveled the brunt of his criticisms at the mixing of religious and civil power, a sin he identified both in the Church of England and in Boston churches. In a pamphlet attacking the Anglican ministry written in 1652, Williams explained, "I do absolutely deny it (against all *commers*) to be the *Burthen* of the *Civil State* to take *cognisance* of any *Spiritual cause*; and I do positively assert it, to be the proper and alone work of the holy *Son* and *Spirit* of *God* in the hands of his *Saints* and *Prophets*, to manage *Heavenly* and *Spiritual causes*."[10] According to Williams, the use of civil power to police religious experience was an Antichristian usurpation of the work of the Son and the Holy Spirit. As Williams wrote, clarifying his views on how to discern the workings of grace, "I prejudice not an External *Test* and *Call*, which was at first and shall be againe in force at the *Resurrection* of the *Churches*. . . . But in the present *State* of things, I cannot but be humbly bold to say, that I know no other *True Sender*, but the most *Holy Spirit*."[11] In a world where state power has corrupted the ministry, only an internal experience of the Holy Spirit has any validity as a sign of salvation.

Williams's beliefs led him to criticize the intrusion of the state into spiritual matters, but he also attacked the undue influence of religion over civil power.[12] In his preaching in Boston, Williams spoke out against many forms of state authority, including the rules governing the colonial land market and the application of the law of nations to Native peoples.[13] In the colony's 1629 charter,

Charles I had given the colony's governors the right to control the land market.[14] In the colony's early years, Winthrop had met many times with tribal represen-tatives to exchange gifts and discuss diplomatic business, and, for the sake of good form, the colony had documented most land purchases from neighboring Indians.[15] However, the Bay Colony ultimately derived its authority to occupy land from the king's grant, and Williams viewed this royal dispensation as no different from the pope's donation of land to the Spanish and Portuguese crowns. In Williams's view, English colonial land policies were merely an out-growth of the crown's broader, idolatrous use of religion to justify the exercise of state power. Sometime in the early 1630s, Williams began to preach against the Bay Colony's patent. No text of these sermons survives, but John Cotton, a Massachusetts Bay minister and opponent of Williams, recorded the thrust of Williams's criticisms. "This Patent," Cotton wrote, "Mr. *Williams* publickly, and vehemently preached against, as containing matter of falshood, and injustice: Falshood in making the King the first Christian Prince who had discovered these parts: and injustice, in giving the Countrey to his *English* Subjects, which belonged to the Native *Indians*."[16] In 1634, Williams wrote down his criticisms in a treatise, which he circulated among English colonial leaders. Its contents received scornful attention from John Winthrop, who noted in his journal that Williams "disputes [the magistrates'] right to the landes they possessed heere: & concluded that claiminge by the kinges grant they could have no title: nor otherwise except they componded with the natives."[17] Williams attempted to send a version of his arguments to Charles I by letter, an act that would have left the impression that the Massachusetts Bay Colony was breeding treasonous opinion.[18]

In addition to threatening the colony's relationship with the king, Wil-liams's vocal criticism of the Massachusetts Bay Colony's land grant imperiled the colony's standing in international space. The royal charter gave the colony's governors the right to make treaties with other European colonies. By attack-ing it, Williams also attacked the colony's international legitimacy. As John Cotton wrote, describing why Williams's argument against the patent system so alarmed Boston authorities, "To this Authority established by this Patent, *English-men* doe readily submit themselves: and foraine Plantations (the *French*, the *Dutch*, and *Swedish*) doe willingly transact their Negotiations with us, as with a Colony established by the Royall Authority of the State of *England*."[19] Though Williams was never a serious threat to the colony's legitimacy under the law of nations, as Cotton's response shows, even the appearance of controversy over the colony's rights was enough to weaken its hand in negotiations with French, Dutch, and Swedish neighbors.

While Williams advanced worrisome legal arguments, his knowledge of the law of nations and its application to Native title could also be an asset. Neal Salisbury has argued that in composing the treatise Williams was at least partly serving the interests of Plymouth Colony.[20] In 1633, Plymouth had purchased a tract of land in the Connecticut River Valley from the sachem Natawanute, who sold the title to the English after having been expelled from the land by some Pequots, who intended to transfer it to the Dutch West India Company. The Dutch had challenged the claims of the Plymouth governors, asserting that the title was rightly theirs on the basis of their purchase of land from the Pequots. While Plymouth had rights according to the English land grant system, this way of establishing title was not persuasive to the Dutch, who did not recognize English law as binding. Plymouth instead cited Williams's natural law arguments, rejecting Dutch claims by asserting that the Pequot sellers had obtained the land through an unjust conquest of another tribe that violated the law of nations. In selling Natawanute's claim, the reasoning went, the Pequots were no better than the Spanish conquistadors, seizing land through violent conquest. While Williams's public preaching has often been viewed as an expression of his religious conscience, the use of his land law treatise to support the Plymouth claim suggests some of the tactical significance of his ideas in English disputes with other Europeans. Though Plymouth governors derived their power to hold and purchase land from the English crown, when it suited their purposes, they were happy to invoke Williams's expansive idea of the law of nations, and Williams himself was perfectly willing for his ideas to be cited in support of English claims. Williams's friendship with Native people and insight on questions of international law made him an undeniable resource in border conflicts with Native and European neighbors.

The circumstances surrounding the land law treatise suggest the complicated relationship between theology, the law of nations, and Native diplomacy in southern New England. While religion and politics were intertwined, when it came to protecting English interests against Native threats, theological opponents could find themselves working together for a common diplomatic purpose. While Williams made arguments that jeopardized the legal standing of the Massachusetts Bay Colony, his goal was always to gain leverage in his disputes with colonial governors, not to bring about the overthrow of their settlements. That his opponents in Boston understood this fact can be seen in their handling of his exile. While Williams eventually backed away from the land treatise, consenting to have it burned, he continued to proclaim against the patent system and to voice other disagreements with the Massachusetts Bay Colony to listeners at his house in Boston. This agitation led the governors to attempt to deport him to England, prompting Williams to move to Narragansett Bay.[21] As John Winthrop explained, the decision to banish Williams was primarily an attempt to maintain church order. In a journal entry, Winthrop recorded that "it was agreed, to sende [Williams] into England by a shippe then readye to departe: the reason was because he had drawne above 20: persons to his opinion & they were intended to erecte a plantation about the Naragansett Baye, from whence the infection would easyly spread into these Churches."[22] However, there are reasons to believe that Winthrop wanted to keep Williams in New England so he could continue to advise Boston governors on Native diplomacy. Williams would later claim that Winthrop had intervened at the last minute to warn him of the deportation and direct him to Narragansett Bay "for many high and heavenly and publike Ends."[23] The governors needed to put a stop to Williams's preaching, but they also recognized the usefulness of his diplomatic and legal acumen, especially when it came to disputes over contested territory. However, while it seemed undesirable to deport Williams—and unthinkable to allow him to remain in Boston—letting him settle in Narragansett Bay would soon create its own set of problems.

Vanishing Deeds: The Politics of Narragansett Land Sales

There was another reason the English governors needed Williams, aside from his legal expertise. Williams traveled to Narragansett Bay in the early stages of the conflict with the Pequots that would later erupt into a vicious war. The causes of the war were complicated. During the early 1630s, the Pequots had been involved in running conflicts with several of their neighbors over supremacy in the fur trade and control of wampum production. The Pequots had sought alliances with the Dutch, while their enemies, the Mohegans, had pursued friendship with the English. In a case of mistaken identity, the Pequots had killed the English trader John Stone in retaliation for the Dutch execution of the Pequot sachem Tatobem.[24] The English had also blamed the Pequots for the killing of another trader, John Oldham. After several running battles, the English, along with Narragansett and Mohegan allies, had launched a violent raid on the Pequot fort at Mystic River, killing hundreds of women and children.

Later they sold dozens of Pequots into slavery in the West Indies.[25] After his emigration to Narragansett Bay, Williams played a key role in brokering the 1636 treaty that secured Narragansett support. Throughout the war, Williams and Winthrop exchanged dozens of letters about strategy, intelligence, and Indian diplomacy. Williams also advised Winthrop on the disposal of Pequot captives and the justice of enslaving defeated enemies under the law of nations.[26]

Like his involvement in the land market, Williams's diplomatic activity was enormously useful to New England governors but also a cause for concern. At the same time that Williams was helping Massachusetts Bay against the Pequots, he was consolidating his own power in Narragansett Bay by buying land from the Narragansetts and making treaties with their sachems. Of the many tribes and groups of Natives who operated in the coastal region at this time, the Narragansetts were the most open to alliances with dissenters.[27] Like other Native groups after the war, the Narragansetts were adapting to a waning influence in fur markets by taking on brokerage roles between European traders and inland tribes.[28] However, unlike the Mohegans and Pokanokets, who had befriended Plymouth, the Narragansetts had few English contacts.[29] Though the Narragansetts had been English allies during the Pequot War, the experience had left them wary of English power (they had reacted with horror to the violence of the English assault during the massacre of Pequot women and children at Mystic Fort).[30] This diplomatic isolation had an effect on the political dynamics within the tribe. After the war, many Narragansetts began to defer to Canonicus and Miantonomi on questions of land ownership, and Native people from other groups began to look to them for direction.[31]

Williams purchased land from the Narragansetts by offering tribute to Canonicus and Miantonomi, as well as to lesser sachems. Defending his participation in these ceremonies required some careful explanation, especially as relations between Massachusetts Bay and the Narragansetts turned hostile after the massacre of the Pequots and the Treaty of Hartford. Williams sometimes ridiculed what he supposed to be the pretentious gestures associated with Narragansett tributary politics, largely in an attempt to defend himself from anyone who questioned his English loyalty.[32] Another way Williams explained his participation in Narragansett tributary rituals was by citing his own religious prohibitions against acts of civil recognition. In a letter to Winthrop, Williams compared Narragansett acts of tribute to the act of hat doffing and donning. I have already discussed hat etiquette in English courtly culture in Chapter 1, where I described how Virginia Company officials coached the

Powhatan Indian Namontack to leave his hat on in the presence of the king so that he would appear to be a foreign dignitary. Among Puritans, such practices had even greater significance. In the early seventeenth century, many Puritan churchgoers had adopted hat doffing as a way of showing piety.[33] Williams predictably rejected the use of such gestures as a sign of church membership. According to him, not even royal pronouncements could embody God's truth, much less the doffing of a hat.[34] Writing to Winthrop in June of 1638, Williams drew a comparison between hat etiquette and Narragansett tribute as a way of reassuring the governor of his true allegiances. As he explained, "I have long held it will-worship to doff and don to the Most High in worship; and I wish also that, in civil worship, others were as far from such a vanity, though I hold it not utterly unlawful in some places. Yet surely, amongst the barbarians, (the highest in the world,) I would rather lose my head than so practise, because I judge it my duty to set them better copies, and should [rather] sin against mine own persuasions and resolutions."[35] If Williams will not doff his hat in church, or among his fellow Englishmen, he will certainly not do it before Indians. While Williams describes his participation in tributary ceremonies throughout his letters, here he makes it clear that these acts have not left him in the employ of "barbarians."

In his own deeds, Williams most often describes the land claims at Providence Plantations as a purchase obtained through acts of friendship rather than conquest or subjection. According to Williams, the Narragansetts understand his ongoing work as a trader and go-between as a gift to them, and, in return, have paid him a reciprocal offering of land and permission to settle. In the deed for his first purchase of land near the Mooshassick and Wanasquatucket rivers, Williams describes an economy that involves gifts and debts of many kinds. "[B]y Gods merciful Assistance," he writes, "I was the procurer of the purchasse [of the land], not by monies nor payment the Natives being so shy & jellowes [jealous] that monies Could not doe it, but by that language aquaintance & ffavour with the natives & other advantages which it pleased God to give me; and also bore the charges & venture of all the gratuetyes which I gave to the great Sachims, & other Sachims & Natives round about us, & lay ingaged for a loving & pecable Neighbour hood with them to my great charge & Travill."[36] Here Williams conceives of the land market as an intercultural economy that includes both the workings of the Holy Spirit and Narragansett understandings of tribute. Williams cannot buy the land; only God's gift of "language aquaintance & ffavour with the natives" is enough to secure it. The whole ordeal involves "charges & venture" on Williams's part, leaving no doubt that he has invested effort in improving the territory.[37] Though he employs esoteric theological language, Williams demonstrates the validity of his claim in several ways that were widely accepted by other Europeans.

Williams's familiarity with the sachems and his willingness to learn their language and legal protocols certainly helped him accomplish great feats of diplomacy. Williams consolidated and extended his holdings without the benefit of the financial, military, or legal resources available to other planters. However, as Winthrop's letter of 1638 shows, the speedy expansion of Providence Plantations was the source of much anxiety in Boston. Though Winthrop and Bradford were eager to use Williams for their own ends, they were not comfortable with a growing colony of religious dissenters at their border, and they objected to the idea that exchanges with Native people could be transacted independently of a charter from the crown. One way the governors of the Massachusetts Bay Colony attacked Williams was by assisting other English people who had rival claims in the bay. While purchase from Native sellers offered a ready means of acquiring land, the validity of such exchanges was open to challenge, especially since there was no universally accepted way of translating Native signs of consent into English law. A common European method of recognizing Native permission in land sales was to secure a Native signatory mark below European signatures at the bottom of deeds. The adoption of this practice among New England Natives was largely the result of the attempts of the Massachusetts Bay Colony to document land sales and other political transactions. While Native people did not inscribe their names on paper before the arrival of the Puritans, they quickly learned to sign legal documents with pictographs. Developing a signature of some sort enabled them to participate in the land market that had sprung up at the borders of English settlements. Pictographic signatures portrayed animals or objects that may have been meaningful to the signers in some political or religious sense, or may have represented identities or marks developed in the course of negotiations with the English. A 1637 deed from Canonicus and Miantonomi to Williams, for example, included a bow and arrow graphic as Canonicus's mark and an arrow for Miantonomi (see Figure 12).[38] Native marks may have conferred privileges ranging from usufruct rights to occupancy in perpetuity, and they often represented the intentions of individual Indian sellers rather than the will of a sachem. The possibility of radically different interpretations of pictographs made the system inherently unstable. Rival claims often led to conflicts between English and Native people

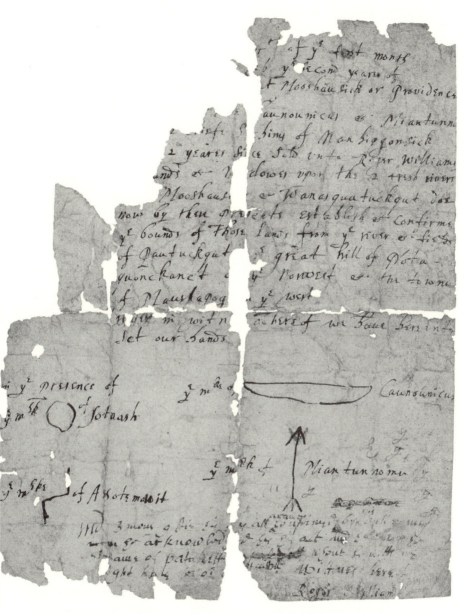

Figure 12. 1637 deed of land purchase from Canonicus and Miantonomi. Canonicus signed the deed with a pictograph of a bow; Miantonomi signed with an arrow. Courtesy of the Providence City Archives.

(as well as surprising alliances that pitted particular Anglo-Native groups against others). They also inspired questions about the legality of exchanges, as well as controversies over the media on which they were recorded.

One of the most significant challenges to Williams's deeds came from William Arnold, a former ally. In 1642, Arnold purchased land from a lesser sachem and submitted to Massachusetts Bay Colony authorities along with several allies.[39] According to later, controversial testimony by William Field, Arnold also cut out of the Providence Town Evidence any mention of Williams's purchase from the sachems.[40] Accepting the subjection of Arnold was an indirect way of attacking Williams, but there was a reason the colony's governors employed it. To deny the validity of Native consent outright would have deprived them of a legal instrument they also found useful. Moreover, it would have contravened decades of English colonial policy and centuries of common-law tradition. It was easier to try and undermine Williams's purchases by accepting the submission of nearby English people, or of Narragansett Indians who did not want to remain allied with Canonicus and Miantonomi.[41]

Such challenges were endemic to the unstable land market of Narragansett Bay, and left Williams and other settlers at Providence Plantations in search of a more secure form of ownership. In response to the fear that challenges like Arnold's would chip away at their territory and autonomy, the settlers at Providence voted to send Williams to London to lobby directly for a royal charter. Williams's embassy would culminate in the publication of his book *A Key into the Language of America*. Though titled in the manner of a philological treatise, *A Key* was much more than an account of the Narragansett language. If Arnold had subjected himself to the Massachusetts Bay Colony as a way of strengthening his claim, Williams would now seek to outdo him by going directly to the crown.

A Key to the Colonial Land Market

Williams set sail for London in early 1643 on a Dutch trading ship bound for Amsterdam. Upon arriving, he brought into print a series of books, publishing four items and leaving a fifth with the printer John Humphrey for later publication. Williams's works addressed a diverse set of theological and political questions. His most urgent task, however, was to counter the Massachusetts Bay Colony and to support the validity of his own purchase from the Narragansett sachems.[42] To this end, he argued that Indians controlled land according to international law and could therefore transfer it to other parties.

Williams addressed his specific request for a charter to the Committee for Foreign Plantations, which at this time was headed by the earl of Warwick and Sir Henry Vane.[43] Williams was not the first New England traveler to use print lobbying to support an appeal to this body. He was preceded by Hugh Peter and Thomas Weld, agents of Massachusetts Bay sent to London to publish information about the colony's evangelical progress in a book entitled *New Englands First Fruits* (1643).[44] Along with publicizing New World missionary efforts, Peter and Weld were engaged in a campaign to preempt Williams's claim to land around Narragansett Bay, one which would culminate in Weld's forgery of a rival title to the land, the so-called "Narragansett patent."[45] As J. Patrick Cesarini has shown, Williams saw the publication of *New Englands First Fruits* as an important target for his own lobbying efforts.[46] Like Peters's and Weld's book, *A Key into the Language of America* is tailored to the Committee for Foreign Plantations, which, during the English Revolution, had taken over the role of the crown as the ultimate authority on colonial affairs.[47] There is a good reason Peter, Weld, and Williams printed books even though they were primarily concerned with influencing a government body. Printing documents gave transatlantic lobbying efforts an air of broader importance. Moreover, when parliamentarians read printed accounts of Indian diplomacy, they could be sure that other Europeans were reading them as well. Print was thus a way to leverage international pressure. Printing *A Key* was a difficult job and required considerable labor on Williams's part. Given the nature of the typesetting, which involved hundreds of Narragansett words, Williams probably oversaw the process closely. After the book was printed, he submitted copies to the Committee in support of his appeal for a charter for Providence Plantations.

While Williams's differences with the Massachusetts Bay Colony were rooted in theology, in *A Key* he launches his criticisms from the position of a chronicler of the human world. The book is a mix of different genres. Organized as a guide to the New World for the purposes of "Travell, Discourse, Trading &c," it offers phrases in the Narragansett dialect of Algonquian under chapter headings that concern topics such as marriage, hunting, government, and debt, with the Algonquian and italicized English equivalents arranged in facing vertical columns.[48] To these lists are added ethnographic observations on Indian life ostensibly drawn from Williams's own experiences among the Narragansetts. Each chapter culminates in a lyric poem comparing English and Indian culture from a millennial perspective.

A Key implicitly targets the Massachusetts Bay Colony and its political lobby. The layout of the title page has the effect of suggesting that travelers to the colonies may quickly find themselves beyond the political reach of Boston and Plymouth. The subtitle advertises the book as "An help to the *Language* of the *Natives* in that part of America called *New-England*," emphasizing the "America" of the title over a "New-England" which is dwarfed by the vastness of the newly discovered continent (see Figure 13).[49] This portrayal of the diminished place of English colonial endeavors in America contradicted that of *New Englands First Fruits*, which depicted the English as a dominant political presence in America poised to convert Indian souls. Williams also associates his book with the evangelical issues raised by Weld and Peter, announcing in the preface that the book will address the "hopes of the *Indians*" for "receiving the Knowledge of Christ!"[50] Williams is subtle in his approach to his rivals, mentioning them only indirectly. "I Present you with *a Key*," he writes, "I have not heard of the like, yet framed, since it pleased God to bring that mighty *Continent* of *America* to light: Others of my *Countrey-men* have often, and excellently, and lately written of the *Countrey* (and none that I know beyond the goodnesse and worth of it)."[51] On the face of it, this statement sounds like praise of Weld and Peter. But in depicting America as a continent whose immense size and worth surpass English attempts to describe it, Williams reduces the Massachusetts Bay Colony to an outpost in a vast and incomprehensible continent, undercutting their claims to have made any great progress converting Indians.

Williams's portrayal of Indian languages supports the argument that America is a sprawling land peopled by many different nations.[52] While Weld and Peter had made an optimistic report about the Bay Colony's evangelical prospects, Williams suggests that the linguistic reality of America is far more complex than any existing account has admitted:

> With this [language] I have entred into the secrets of those *Countries*, where ever *English* dwel about two hundred miles; betweene the *French* and *Dutch* Plantations; for want of this, I know what grosse *mis-stakes* my selfe and others have run into.
>
> There is a mixture of this *Language North* and *South*, from the place of my abode, about six hundred miles; yet within the two hundred miles (aforementioned) their *Dialects* doe exceedingly differ; yet not so, but (within that compasse) a man may, by this *helpe*, converse with *thousands* of *Natives* all over the *Countrey*: and by such converse it may please the *Father* of *Mercies* to spread

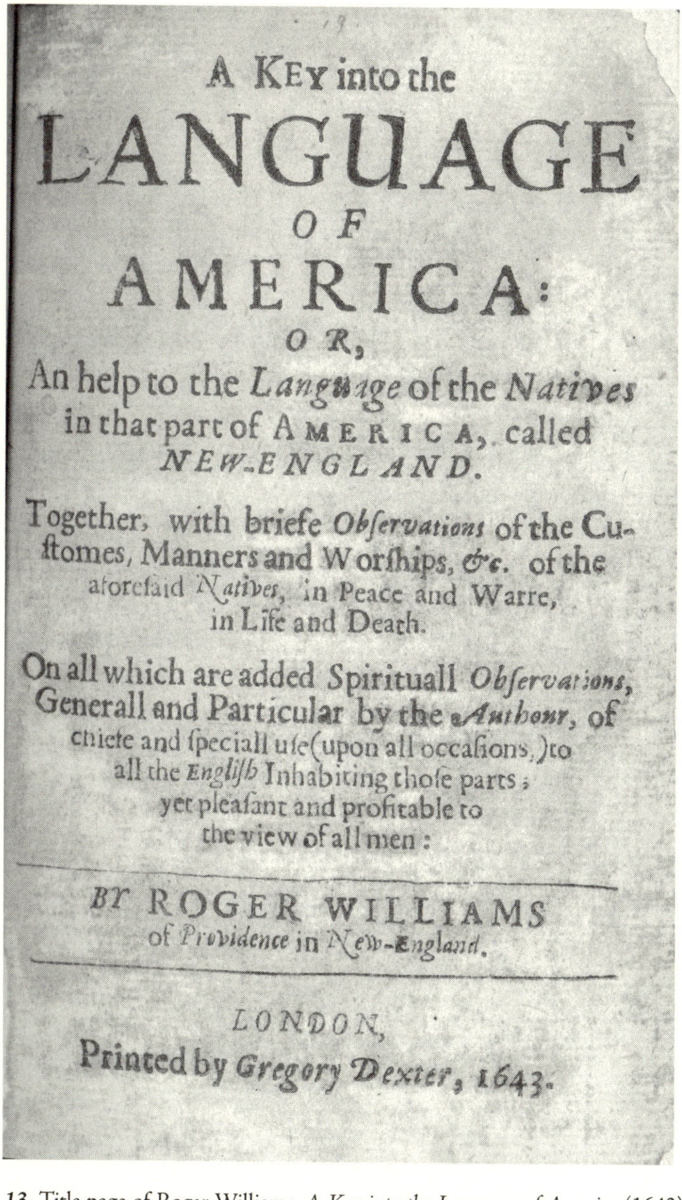

A KEY into the

LANGUAGE

OF

AMERICA:

OR,

An help to the *Language* of the *Natives*
in that part of AMERICA, called
NEW-ENGLAND.

Together, with briefe *Observations* of the Customes, Manners and Worships, &c. of the
aforesaid *Natives,* in Peace and Warre,
in Life and Death.

On all which are added Spirituall *Observations,*
Generall and Particular by the *Authour,* of
chiefe and speciall use (upon all occasions,) to
all the *English* Inhabiting those parts;
yet pleasant and profitable to
the view of all men:

BY ROGER WILLIAMS
of *Providence* in *New-England.*

LONDON,
Printed by *Gregory Dexter,* 1643.

Figure 13. Title page of Roger Williams, *A Key into the Language of America* (1643). RHi
X5 255. Courtesy of the Rhode Island Historical Society.

civilitie, (and in his owne most holy season) *Christianitie*; for *one* Candle will light *ten thousand*, and it may please *God* to blesse a *little Leaven* to season the *mightie Lump* of those *Peoples* and *Territories*.[53]

In *Plain Dealing: or, Newes from New-England* (1642), a book critical of the Massachusetts Bay Colony, the repatriated Anglican Thomas Lechford had asserted that Massachusetts Bay colonists had made no discernible effort "to learne the Natives language, or to instruct them in the Religion."[54] In emphasizing his own lack of facility in Native languages, Williams reprises Lechford's critique, but does so in order to suggest the political diversity of the New World. The many language barriers in America suggest that strategies for converting Indians to the state church will quickly falter in the New World, where the dialects of European and Indian nations proliferate. Williams portrays a New World sprawling with peoples, kingdoms, and territorial markers. Far from being the only landholder on the coast, the Massachusetts Bay Colony is one of many.

In order to support his claim to land ownership in Narragansett Bay, however, Williams had to do more than simply undercut rival accounts. With the knowledge that the Massachusetts Bay Colony was challenging his purchases before the Committee, Williams also carried the burden of proving the legality of his transactions with the Narragansetts. In particular, he had to prove that the Narragansetts had a valid title to the land and could transfer it to him through some normalized protocol. While his adversaries in Boston largely respected Native title, and documented their own purchases in regular English deeds, Williams knew that many in London believed that the Massachusetts Bay Colony had settled in a *vacuum domicilium*, an empty or waste space open for settlement. To counter this idea, Williams had to translate his interactions with the Narragansetts into the language of the law of nations, and prove that Indians owned land.

Houses That Fly

In a fantastical moment in a chapter entitled "Of the Family and businesse of the House," Williams describes the land occupancy practices of coastal Indian tribes. "They are quicke; in halfe a day, yea, sometimes at few houres warning to be gone and the house up elsewhere; especially, if they have stakes readie pitcht for their *Mats*. I once in travel lodged at a house, at which in my returne I hoped to have lodged againe there the nex[t] night, but the house was gone in that interim, and I was glad to lodge under a tree."[55] Like many images of cross-cultural accord in *A Key*, this one works as a call for separating church and state. While the Indians' practice of moving dwellings by the hour may seem strange from the English point of view, the social cooperation required for the awesome task of lifting entire towns makes the Indians a model for England and its colonies, which, according to Williams, have been driven to civil war by the use of state power to enforce religious conformity. At the close of the chapter, Williams provides a lyric theological gloss on his observations of the domestic economies of both English and Indian life:

> *English* and *Indians* busie are,
> In parts of their abode:
> Yet both stand idle, till God's call
> Set them to worke for God.   Mat. 20.7[56]

Though the portability of Native homes may appear radically alien to English notions of domesticity, Williams cautions against confusing local customs with signs of grace. English civility is no proof of salvation.

From the point of view of the land controversy on Narragansett Bay, equally important in the passage is Williams's engagement with the international legal doctrine of *vacuum domicilium*. John Cotton provided a succinct summary of this principle in a sermon published in London in 1630, arguing that "in a vacant soyle, hee that taketh possession of it, and bestoweth culture and husbandry upon it, his Right it is."[57] While this argument was a powerful way to establish land rights under international legal systems, and had been frequently repeated by the promoters and governors of the Massachusetts Bay Colony for several years, it also carried a certain risk, admitting the existence of prior Native economy as a possible basis for Native title—and independent English purchase—directly from sachems.[58] If the Natives were found to have used a parcel of land, their ownership was secure, and they possessed the right to sell it. *Vacuum domicilium* also required Boston leaders to defend their possession of unused lands under English control. In a debate with John Cotton over international law and its application to vacant territory, Williams had argued that by the logic of *vacuum domicilium* Indians might themselves appropriate the "great Parkes" and "great Forrests in *England*," which were only occasionally used by English nobility for hunting.[59]

The argument had irked Cotton, and Massachusetts Bay authorities had banished Williams. In *A Key*, however, Williams reprises the same argument, only this time from London, where he can do much more damage to the colony's relationship with metropolitan authorities. In a chapter entitled "Of the Earth, and the Fruits thereof," Williams details indigenous uses of fruits, berries, and corn to produce food staples, and points out that Indians have a form of agriculture based on rapid turnover rather than fixed improvement.[60] "When a field is to be broken up, they have a very loving sociable speedy way to dispatch it: All the neighbours men and Women forty, fifty, a hundred &c, joyne, and come in to help freely."[61] Not only do Indians own land, but they do so in a spirit of social cooperation not evident in the Massachusetts Bay Colony's treatment of religious dissenters. More importantly, Williams reveals the existence of Native territorial boundaries, which have gone unrecognized by the English but are equivalent to those found in European kingdoms. "The *Natives* are very exact and punctuall in the bounds of their Lands, belonging to this or that Prince or People, (even to a River, Brooke) &c," he observes. "And I have knowne them make bargaine and sale amongst themselves for a small piece, or quantity of Ground: notwithstanding a sinfull opinion amongst ma[n]y that Christians have right to *Heathens* Lands."[62] Williams again criticizes the use of Christianity as an argument for the territorial expansion of European crowns. However, this observation also demonstrates the validity of the whole range of purchases that made up Providence Plantations, from the large tracts Williams acquired to the "small piece[s]" of ground many settlers had negotiated for independently. This portrayal of American political order reflected Williams's legal needs in London in 1643. While Williams had negotiated with powerful sachems such as Canonicus and Miantonomi, he had also purchased land from many lesser sachems, whose authority to sell to him might be disputed even if more powerful sachems were recognized. By portraying America in terms of many "Lands, belonging to this or that Prince or People," Williams suggests that the New World is ruled by countless sovereign powers, all of whom have dominion and the right to sell their land without consulting any higher authority. Though couched in ethnographic terms, this observation supports Williams's claim to have acquired land and permission to settle through channels beyond the jurisdiction of the Massachusetts Bay Colony. It is important to point out that in describing Native modes of occupancy, Williams was not primarily driven by a moral obligation to Indians. His motives were strategic, even if his theology was not. The purchases that made up Providence Plantations would be valid only if the Narragansetts had the right to sell. Though *A Key* has struck many readers as a unique book, in this regard, it represented a familiar strategy.

In addition to this abstract argument about land rights, there are also a number of other observations in the book that deal with concrete persons and events that are relevant to the Pequot War. While Williams's description of Narragansett landholding undermines the basis for the Massachusetts Bay Colony's patent, his account of political treaties calls into question another source of the Bay Colony's power—their claim to have brought Indian groups under control through an Anglo-Narragansett alliance against the Pequots. Under the heading of the Narragansett word *wunnaumwáyean*, which Williams translates as "If he say true," the book reports a bracing first-hand observation of how the Narragansetts, and in particular their chief Canonicus, view treaties with the English:

> Wunnaumwáyean. | *If he say true.*
> *Obs. Canounicus*, the old high *Sachim* of the *Nariganset Bay* (a wise and peacable Prince) once in a solemne Oration to my self, in a solemne assembly, using this word, said, I have never suffered any wrong to be offered to the *English* since they landed; nor never will: he often repeated this word, *Wunnaumwáyean, Englishmen;* if the *Englishman* speake true, if hee meane truly, then shall I goe to my grave in peace, and hope that the *English* and my posteritie shall live in love and peace together. I replied, that he had no cause (as I hoped) to question *Englishmans, Wunnaumwaúonck*, that is, faithfulnesse he having had long experienced their friendlinesse and trustinesse. He tooke a sticke and broke it into ten pieces, and related ten instances (laying downe a sticke to every instance) which gave him cause thus to feare and say; I satisfied him in some presently, and presented the rest to the Governours of the *English*, who, I hope, will be far from giving just cause to have *Barbarians* to question their *Wunnaumwâuonck*, or faithfulnesse.[63]

While presented without context in *A Key*, this story describes a famous moment of diplomacy in the Pequot War. By his own account, Williams played a decisive role in the war, convincing the Narragansetts to help the English governors destroy the Pequots (Williams may have left out this context because he did not want to be associated in London with the massacre). The breaking of the stick was Canonicus's answer to accusations that the tribe had broken a prior agreement. In a letter to Winthrop, Williams described this dispute. "I produced the copy of the league [with the English]," he wrote, "and with breaking of a straw in two or three places, I showed them what they had done [by breaking a treaty with the English]. In sum their answer was, that they thought they should prove themselves honest and faithful, when Mr. Governour understood their answers; and that (although they would not contend with their friends) yet they could relate many particulars, wherein the English had broken (since these wars) their promises, etc."[64] Rather than demanding that the Narragansetts recognize the written copy of the league, Williams uses Narragansett technology to persuade them of their wrongs and secure their friendship. Retelling the incident in *A Key*, however, he focuses on Canonicus's use of the same technology to accuse the English, and emphasizes his own ability to create a cross-cultural forum where the air can be cleared through a recognition of mutual breaches of trust. Equally important for parliamentary readers is Williams's description of how Canonicus's stick transmits information about the English and their actions to an international audience. While the English can only explain the violations by pointing to a written treaty that Native people cannot read, Canonicus has at his disposal a much more dramatic way of representing a broken treaty. Though the stick appears to be a crude form of communication in comparison to writing, in his portrayal of the broken pieces falling to the ground, Williams shows just how quickly stories of English wrongdoing can be multiplied. Williams offers the story as a kind of geopolitical alarm, a warning of the potential effects of English treaty breaking in international space. Moreover, Canonicus's indictment of the "English" shows that, in the sachem's eyes, Massachusetts Bay authorities have become synonymous with the English nation in general. With their bullying tactics, Boston governors are giving the English a bad name. Williams clears the English name by presenting the broken pieces of the stick to English governors for satisfaction, yet he also implies that potentially damaging records of future breaches may not be so safely collected and contained. The description suggests that no written treaty text can ever be the final word on Anglo-Narragansett relations, and that indigenous records may be telling a different story about American politics, one the English would do well to heed. Williams's description of his ability to pacify the Narragansetts dramatizes the importance of learning to interpret Native political media and exert control over their function and circulation.

The "love and peace" described by Canonicus was of great interest to the Committee for Foreign Plantations. In the language of the charter granted to Williams in recognition of his "printed Indian labors," the Committee makes significant reference to Williams's diplomacy among the Narragansetts.[65] Enumerating the warrants for the charter, they describe granting Williams's request because "divers well affected and industrious English inhabitants of the towns of Providence, Portsmouth and Newport . . . have adventured to make a nearer neighborhood to, and society with, that great body of the Narragansetts, which may in time, by the blessing of GOD upon their endeavor, lay a surer foundation of happiness to all America."[66] The language of happiness has replaced the language of peace common in other colonial writings, yet the formula is familiar. Williams has brought the land under control, extending English dominion beyond the frontiers of the Massachusetts Bay Colony through his agreements with the Narragansetts, and for this he is rewarded with a charter. For all of his radical criticisms of the English state and church, Williams succeeded in publishing a vision of English territorial possession that was consistent with decades-old policies.

Sovereignty and Subjection: Gorton's *Simplicities Defence*

Samuel Gorton also tells a story of captivity at the hands of colonial authorities. The details of his ordeal can be hard to extract from his verbose and impassioned narration in *Simplicities Defence*, a book that has more in common with a diatribe than a legal document. As he tells it, in the "extremity of winter" in 1642, Gorton, a heterodox Puritan and preacher, was driven from his settlement near Providence by Massachusetts Bay forces persecuting him for his religious beliefs and brandishing a fraudulent claim to his land.[67] Overwhelmed, Gorton fled "into the vast wilderness" accompanied only by a straggling group of followers, surviving by melting snow for water and "buying severall parcels of Land of the Indians there inhabiting."[68] Before long, however, Gorton was again arrested for squatting on the land of Indians loyal to the Massachusetts Bay Colony, and this time was banished on pain of death. Like other dissenters, Gorton set sail for London in order to appeal to royal authorities. Yet before Gorton's departure, the Narragansett sachem Canonicus dramatically intervened to direct him to deliver an act of submission to the English Parliament, with the hopes of gaining royal protection for the tribe.[69] Armed with this treaty, which was ratified by the pictographic signatures of Narragansett sachems, Gorton traveled to London to air his own grievances as well as those of his Indian neighbors.

Simplicities Defence was published as part of a multi-pronged appeal Gorton made to the Committee for Foreign Plantations for a charter to protect his settlement at Shawomet (later Warwick) from attacks by Massachusetts Bay.[70] It was printed by John Macock, who had previously published the works of William Prynne and other dissenters.[71] *Simplicities Defence* is largely a collection of governmental documents, including affidavits, warrants, and appeals produced during Gorton's trial and banishment. It also includes a Narragansett treaty of submission to the English king signed with the pictographs of Narragansett sachems. Throughout the book, the Narragansetts are portrayed as Gorton's fellow victims. Gorton stakes his case for a charter on a joint Anglo-Narragansett appeal, inviting Parliament to intervene to protect both him and his Native allies.

In its narrative trajectory, *Simplicities Defence* is loosely organized around the story of Gorton's banishment into the wilderness. At each twist and turn, Gorton and his company are pursued by a Massachusetts Bay government that has lost all regard for royal authority. They are chased from "*Boston* in the *Massachusets* Bay" to "*Plymouth*," from "*Mooshawset*" (Providence) to "*Shawomet*," and finally "scattered" by exile to a "little Island, called *Road Island*, situate in the *Nanhyganset* Bay."[72] Everywhere, Bay Colony authorities aggressively pursue Gorton, "stretching their line," "insinuat[ing] themselves" into his group, and finally attempting "to take in all the *Nanhyganset* Bay under their Government and Jurisdiction"[73] As encroachments pile up, the overwhelming impression is of a rebellious Massachusetts Bay Colony that has cast off royal direction and is pursuing its own expansionist course.

Gorton's response to this "assault" is to turn to the Narragansetts as a potential channel for acquiring land.[74] While the Narragansetts had a reputation as power brokers in much English colonial writing, Gorton moved to Narragansett Bay during a time of precipitous decline in their power. Even though the Narragansetts had sided with the English in wars against the Pequots and other tribes, the United Colonies turned on the tribe in early 1643 after the Narragansetts invaded the Mohegans, arresting the sachem Miantonomi and turning him over to the Mohegans for execution.[75] The outcome of the war motivated Narragansett sachems, including Miantonomi's uncle Canonicus, to seek out alliances with other tribes as well as with English dissenters unaffiliated with Williams.

The Narragansetts primarily appear in *Simplicities Defence* by way of their political ties to the English. At first, Gorton emphasizes settlement and agriculture as evidence of possession. After multiple offenses against their persons at the hands of colonial magistrates, Gorton writes, "we were constrained with the hazard of our lives to betake our selves into a part of the Country called the *Nanhyganset* Bay, buying severall parcels of Land of the Indians there Inhabiting; and sat down in, and neer the place where Master *Roger Williams* was where we built houses, and bestowed our labors to raise up means."[76] Citing the successful settlement at Providence Plantations, Gorton carefully demonstrates that Shawomet settlers have improved their territory. He and his party purchase land, build houses, and plant crops, recapitulating in miniature the settlement history of a legally chartered colony. By this account, Shawomet is not simply a community of squatters, but a colony in its own right with valid and defensible possession of its lands.

As his narrative progresses, however, Gorton reinforces this settlement history with the story of his treaties with the Narragansetts. The tribe welcomes Gorton as a political neighbor, in part because of their common cause as victims of Massachusetts Bay. Gorton draws on the Black Legend of Spanish colonialism, placing his Puritan persecutors in the role of Spanish conquistadors who acquire territory through a campaign of blood and fire. The Massachusetts Bay Colony forces act like conquerors, exiling "wives and children" and "depriving women and children of things necessary" during the violence of their sieges.[77] This language resonated with that of anti-Spanish propaganda published in England and the Netherlands, such as *The Spanish Colonie* (1583), a translation of some of the writings of Bartolomé de Las Casas, which described the conquering Spanish as "sparing neyther children, nor old men, neyther women with child."[78] The violence of the Massachusetts Bay Colony also extends to their treatment of Native Americans, particularly the Narragansetts, whose sachem dies at the hands of Boston authorities even after the tribe pays his ransom. In his retelling of the killing of Miantonomi, Gorton emphasizes the unscrupulous tactics of Bay Colony authorities, who "[take] away *the life of* [the Narragansetts'] *Prince, after so great a ransome given, and received for his rescue.*"[79] Echoing the kind of language used by Las Casas, who described the "great weeping and crying" of Indians persecuted by conquistadors, Gorton describes "*the mourning women*" of the Narragansetts "*morning and evening upon their knees, with lamentations, and many tears along time together.*"[80]

Due to their shared lot as victims of Boston's aggression, Gorton and the Narragansetts find common cause. At first, interacting with the sachems is a delicate enterprise for Gorton, given the recent murder of Miantonomi and

Narragansett suspicions about the English. Soon, however, the Indians welcome Gorton and his party as friends. "[W]hen wee were come to the old *Sachims* house," Gorton writes, "we were courteously entertained," in telling contrast to their treatment in Boston.[81] Canonicus, Gorton reports, "told us that [the] condition [of the Narragansetts], might (in great measure) be paraleld with ours . . . they told us, they had not only lost their *Sachim*, so beloved amongst them, and such an instrument of their publick good; but had also utterly impoverished themselves, by paying such a ransome for his life."[82] While the Massachusetts Bay Colony considers Gorton a squatter, the Narragansetts extend him formal hospitality. They entertain him at their house, and draw a comparison between the Shawomet settlers and their own group, casting Gorton's company as allies.[83]

In answer to Canonicus's offer of alliance, Gorton suggests that both groups might find redress through the channels of communication that tie Gorton and his party to the English crown. "[W]e made answer unto them," he writes, "that for our parts, we were not discouraged, in any thing that had befalne us, for we were subjects to such a noble State in *Old-England*, that however we were farre off from our King and State, yet we doubted not but in due time, we should have redresse." Gorton's use of the phrase "King and State" is strategic. Uncertain about who will be in power, the king or Parliament, he describes English authority in a way that could encompass both.[84] Awed by the power of English authority to rectify wrongs across great distances, the sachems suggest to Gorton that they, too, might also find protection from the king who promises to shelter him from civil persecution. "[T]hey called a generall Assembly," Gorton writes, "to make known their minds, and to see the minds of their people, and with joynt and unanimous consent, concluded to become subjects to the State and Government of *Old-England* . . . whereupon they chose four of us, as Commissioners in trust for the safe custody, and conveyance of their Act and Deed unto the State of *Old-England*."[85] Gorton's description of the assembly satisfies the criterion for Native consent set out by Charles I in documents such as his "Answer" to the *Eendracht*, in which he expressed skepticism that Native sachems could express the true intentions of tribal members.[86] In reporting how the sachems "see the minds of their people," Gorton produces eyewitness verification of the integrity of Narragansett government, demonstrating that the decision represents the consent of every member of the tribe.

In the book, Gorton prints the deed the sachems have supposedly given him, describing it as "The Act and Deed of the voluntary and free submission of the chiefe *Sachim*, and the rest of the Princes, with the whole people of the *Nanhygansets*, unto the government and protection of that Honourable State of Old-England."[87] As Jonathan Beecher Field has pointed out in his comprehensive account of Gorton's transatlantic publishing ventures, the deed largely conforms to the standards of English legal documentation, making its composition by the Narragansetts (or even by most English settlers) next to impossible.[88] And indeed, the act reflects the agenda of Gorton and his party. The sachems' appeal to the English government buttresses Gorton's own request for a charter, making it appear to colonial administrators that Gorton has captured the loyalty of a vast Native American kingdom, what he calls "a great people and Country of the *Indians*."[89] In printing the deed in a book addressed to the English Parliament, Gorton shows that he is capable of colonizing the Americas by integrating tribal polities rather than enslaving or exterminating them. Tying his own persecution to that of the Indians, Gorton suggests that Narragansett modes of political organization are fully compatible with English subjecthood.

At the same time, however, Narragansett political intentions are not entirely effaced from the document.[90] While the Narragansetts submit to the crown, they do so as "chiefe *Sachims*, or Princes successively, of the countrey, time out of mind."[91] Gorton's rhetoric conveys a sense of the ancientness of the Narragansett presence in the region. The Narragansetts occupy their own distinct homeland and share a form of timeless ownership over it that parallels Gorton's professed attachment to Old England. Moreover, the Narragansetts' acceptance of this new arrangement with the English crown is ratified by their signing of a written copy of the act of submission (see Figure 14). Pessicus marks his name with a bow and arrow, Canonicus a peace pipe, Mixan a hammer, Anwashoesse a hammer or hatchet, and Tomanick a dog or wolf. The pictographic signatures were transferred into print through the use of woodcut engravings. While the signatures of English witnesses are produced in italic lettering, the pictographic signatures of the Narragansett sachems dominate the page, visually suggesting the importance of their voluntary consent to the submission.

In some ways, then, the "Act" represents a convergence of the hopes of English and Native peoples. Indeed, after Gorton accepted the Narragansett submission, the sachems Pessicus and Canonicus were able to resist commands from the Massachusetts Bay Colony. In one letter to Boston governors, for example, they asserted their status as "*subjects now, (and that with joynt and voluntary consent) unto the same King and State*" as the Bay Colony itself.[92] While such autonomy was largely rhetorical, it does suggest significant Narragansett design

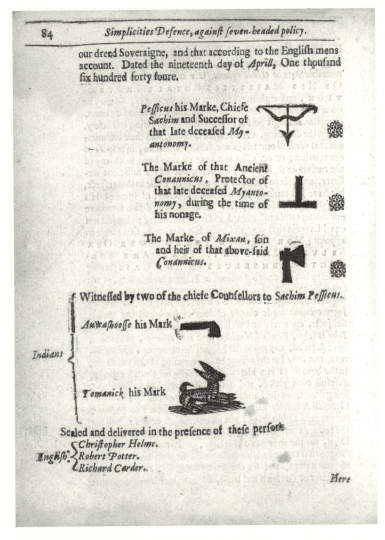

our dread Soveraigne, and that according to the English mens account. Dated the nineteenth day of *Aprill*, One thousand six hundred forty foure.

Pessicus his Marke, Chiefe *Sachim* and Successor of that late deceased *My-antonomy.*

The Marke of that Ancient *Conaunicus*, Protector of that late deceased *Myanto-nomy*, during the time of his nonage.

The Marke of *Mixan*, son and heir of that above-said *Conannicus.*

Witnessed by two of the chiefe Counsellors to *Sachim Pessicus.*

Auwashoosse his Mark

Indians

Tomanick his Mark

Sealed and delivered in the presence of these persons

⎧ *Christopher Helme.*
English ⎨ *Robert Potter.*
⎩ *Richard Carder.*

Here

Figure 14. Printed copy of the second page of the Narragansett Act of Submission, which shows the pictographic signatures of the sachems, from Samuel Gorton, *Simplicities Defence* (1646). US 10867.1 Courtesy of Houghton Library, Harvard University.

in sending the deed of submission to London by way of Gorton. In subjecting themselves to the king, the Narragansetts traded the belligerent local authority of the Massachusetts Bay Colony for a distant and less invasive subjection to the English crown. While Gorton's book embodied the political goals of the religious dissenters at Shawomet, it was also a medium of the hopes of the

Narragansetts, who put their pictographs on Gorton's paper in order to gain some measure of autonomy from Boston governors. Their survival was directly linked to his, and the story of their suffering buttressed Gorton's own case, just as his did theirs.

In the closing pages of the book, Gorton reinforces this mutual appeal by printing a story the Narragansetts have circulated about English settlement. From Gorton's point of view, this story exposes much about how Boston governors maintain their grip on power. Like Williams's account of the broken stick, it shows that the Massachusetts Bay Colony is giving the English a bad name among Natives and Europeans alike. It also shows how the Narragansetts explain colonization and the power struggles they see among the newcomers. As the story reveals, the Narragansetts were not simply local victims of colonization, but possessed an acute understanding of transatlantic communication and colonial politics.

First-Contact Stories

The story Gorton passes on is an ancient one, an account of the beginnings of settlement. It is similar to stories that anthropologists have found elsewhere along the Eastern Seaboard. In their recent work recording Native storytellers, Jennifer S.H. Brown and Roger Roulette have traced a centuries-old tradition of "first-contact stories" that describe the onset of colonization.[93] Brown and Roulette argue that Native stories of contact were attempts to identify the dynamics behind European colonization and to explain their disruptive effects on political order. As they show, a common device in such stories is the attribution of magical powers to trickster figures who restore tribal order after the upheaval of contact. "Such stories may have historical elements," they write, "but with the passing of the generations, they shade into what Anglophones call myth, and their personages may assume remarkable spiritual or magical powers."[94] Such powers include the ability to accomplish miraculous escapes, as well the capacity to cross great distances to be reunited with family or tribe after displacement or captivity. These mobile figures, who possessed *manitou* or spiritual power, mapped the spatial trajectories of colonization, tracing the pathways of power that tied colonies to European homelands.

In *Simplicities Defence*, Gorton calls attention to how such stories have shaped tribal perceptions of the English. "Now our country men [the Bay Colony] having given out formerly, amongst the *Indians*, that we were not English men, to encourage them against us . . . they [the Bay Colony] then called us *Gortoneans*, and told the *Indians* we were such kind of men, not English." In response, Gorton writes, "now the *Indians* calling the English in their language *Wattaconoges*, they now called us *Gortonoges*."[95] Having "heard a rumour of great war to be in *Old-England* . . . they presently framed unto themselves a cause of our deliverance, imagining that there were two kinds of people in *Old-England*, the one called by the name of English men, and the other *Gortonoges*; and concluded that the *Gortonoges* were a mightier people then the English, whom they call *Wattaconoges*; and therefore the *Massachusets* thought it not safe to take away our lives, because . . . that great people, that were in *Old-England* would come over, and put them to death, that should take away our lives from us, without a just cause."[96] The story represents a complex engagement with both English and Indian understandings of geopolitical relations. The Bay Colony governors attempt to distance Gorton and his group from their home country by calling them "Gortoneans"—in Native terms, consigning them to a different tribe. Yet the Narragansetts respond to this information by declaring Gorton a member of a powerful and faraway tribe that will come to his rescue. Gorton will be saved by the Gortonoges, magically mobile figures who transcend the spatial constraints of the mundane world and travel across the seas to restore order. Gorton implies that the Indians might be right in believing that he has more in common with leaders in London than he has with his countrymen in Massachusetts Bay. Through the story, Gorton presses London authorities to reclaim the name of the English from the Wattaconoges in Boston and restore the empire's pride of place in the Narragansett imagination. Yet the story also reflects the tribe's hopes of holding onto land by submitting to the faraway leader of the Gortonoges, whom they endow with mythical powers.

Gorton uses the Narragansett story to influence parliamentary debates about colonial order. The story suggests that Gorton is more English than the governors of the Massachusetts Bay Colony, despite his religious radicalism. However, it is equally important to consider the book from the Narragansett point of view. Gorton's appeal would have failed without the tribe's participation. While *Simplicities Defence* inspired the Committee to issue Gorton a charter and extend English dominion into the bay, it also played a role in the Narragansetts' attempts to reestablish tribal order and invent new forms of alliance. Gorton's book was a channel through which the Narragansetts sought to capitalize on the political realignments that had followed in the wake of Miantonomi's death. As the geographic reach of the story of the Gortonoges shows, the tribe's aim was more then mere survival. They wanted to expand, and they saw the arrival of the English as an opportunity for creating new forms of political order that would stretch across the seas. As it turned out, the powerful and faraway Gortonoges were indeed paying attention to the Narragansetts, and they would eventually arrive to restore order. But not before a long delay.

Miantonomi the Treaty Breaker

Stephen Daye, the printer of the Massachusetts Bay Colony, squinted at the manuscript in front of him. Entitled *A Declaration of Former Passages and Proceedings Betwixt the English and the Narrowgansets*, it had arrived from the Commissioners of the United Colonies with an official printing order. The text was simple enough; it would work out to about seven or so typeset pages, and it was written in the neat hand of John Winthrop, the governor of the Massachusetts Bay Colony. Yet Daye quickly gathered that the subject was serious. The narrative promised to explain "the grounds and justice" of a looming war between the Narragansetts and the colonies.[97]

A Declaration has received little attention in histories of the first printing presses in North America. The only book to appear on the Boston press that deals specifically with the law of nations and its application to Native America, it has been overlooked by scholars concerned with the psalms, bibles, and other devotional materials that made up most of the press's output. Compared to the complicated printed works published by Williams and Gorton, which included typeset Narragansett words and engraved pictographs, *A Declaration* offers little in the way of Native political expression. It is instead a terse narrative of Miantonomi's alleged treaty violations and his later execution by English-allied Mohegans. The only political agreement that appears in the book—a short excerpt from the Treaty of Hartford—is typeset in the legalistic English used by the colony's governors in written treaty agreements. The document thus appears remarkably biased, favoring English ways of recording treaties at the expense of Native practices. Yet I will suggest here that the book represents a defining moment in the early history of Anglo-Native treaty relations. Against Williams's and Gorton's vision of a league between the Narragansetts and the crown, Winthrop puts forward a Massachusetts Bay-Mohegan alliance, reiterating the strength of the Treaty of Hartford and suggesting that it has the consent of English-allied tribes.

A Declaration opens by linking the colony's evangelical imperatives to the law of nations. Affirming that the Massachusetts Bay colonists have planted a colony "to injoye [Christ's] precious Ordinances with peace," Winthrop asserts that Christ is "King of righteousnes and peace" and "gives answerable lawes" governing English interactions "not only with the nations of Europe, but with the barbarous natives." By emphasizing Christ's role as the "King of righteousnes and peace," Winthrop ties the colony's sense of evangelical mission to the broader injunction of the law of nations to travel and communicate peacefully. The colony has embraced a model of diplomacy based on divine and natural law. "[B]oth in their treaties & converse," Winthrop claims, the Puritans "have had an awfull respect to divine rules, endeavouring to walk uprightly and inoffensively." Winthrop likewise emphasizes the capacity of Native peoples to make treaties within this divinely guided international order, pointing in particular to the Treaty of Hartford and other agreements as evidence that Indians are subjects of the law of nations. After the conquest of the Pequots, who were "subdued," Winthrop writes, for "turn[ing] aside from all wayes of justice & peace," the English have been "carefull to continue and establish peace with the rest of the Indians, both for the present & for posterity, as by several treaties with the Narrowganset & Mohiggin Sagamores may appeare."[98]

The impending collapse of this peace, Winthrop claims, is the result, not of any English aggression, or even of any inherent Indian savagery, but rather of the lawlessness of Miantonomi, and his refusal to abide by the Treaty of Hartford. Like the designing Powhatan in the narratives of John Smith and Argall, Miantonomi is the villain of *A Declaration*. He appears as a treaty breaker who triggers a just war with the English. While the Treaty of Hartford and other agreements "for a while were in some good measure duly observed by all the Indians. . . . of late the Narrowgansets & especialy the Nianticks their confederates have many wayes injuriously broken & violated the same."[99] What follows is a laundry list of Narragansett violations, enumerated in legalistic detail. The Narragansetts are guilty of "entertaining and keeping amongst them, not only many of the Pequot nation, but such of them as have had their hands in the blood & murder of the English"; "seizing and possessing at least a part of the Pequots Country, which by right of conquest justly appertaines to the English"; "alluring, or harboring and withholding several Pequot captives"; and "making proud & insolent returnes, when [the captives] were redemanded."[100] Standing behind all of this is Miantonomi, whose "ambitious designes" and "treacherous plots" are "confirmed" by "many strong & concurrent Indian testimonies, from Long-Island, Uncoway, Hartford, Kinnibeck, and other parts."[101]

According to Winthrop, even with this overwhelming evidence of Miantonomi's treaty violations, the colonists await "more legal and convincing proof." They find it when their ally, Uncas, sachem of the Mohegans, brings Miantonimi to Hartford, charging the Narragansett sachem with an attempt on his life in violation of the terms of the Treaty of Hartford. Unlike Williams's *Key* or Gorton's *Simplicities Defence*, *A Declaration* offers no reproduction of any specifically indigenous way of arbitrating agreement or marking consent. Winthrop supplies only "one of the Articles" of the Treaty of Hartford, which states, "*Though either of the said Indian Sagamores shold receive injurie from the other; yet neither of them shall make or begin warr, untill they had appealed to the English.*"[102] The language of the article clearly convicts Miantonomi as a violator of the peace for his attempt on Uncas's life. It offers legal justification for the English decision to hand over Miantonomi to the Mohegans for execution. Yet Winthrop's presentation of the article also makes a claim about the language and form of the law of nations in North America. While Winthrop relies on Mohegan testimony in order to convict Miantonomi, the treaty itself is an English instrument. Rather than citing Native political practices in support of an English claim, as Williams and Gorton had done, Winthrop describes instead the Mohegan reliance upon English conventions for recording agreements and arbitrating violations.

Documents, then, seem to have replaced Native practices, at least according to Winthrop. Not only do the Commissioners of the United Colonies arbitrate the dispute between Miantonomi and Uncas by referring to a written document, they also publish the definitive account of that dispute on their own press. There was a pragmatic reason for printing the book in the Bay Colony itself. William Weld and Hugh Peter, the two agents the colony had sent to London to publish *New Englands First Fruits*, had never returned, finding themselves caught up in the events of the English Revolution, and Roger Williams had adroitly manipulated the London press, leading to the Bay Colony's loss of all claims to Providence Plantations.[103] Printing the book in Cambridge and sending it to London gave Winthrop and other governors much more control. It was also symbolically important. By his choice of publication venue, Winthrop asserts that the colonies, and not London, are the appropriate site for airing disputes about Native treaties. This is evident in the way Winthrop depicts Miantonomi's alleged violations of the Treaty of Hartford. Though Winthrop describes the treaty as "a tripartit agrement" between the Mohegans, Narragansetts, and United Colonies over the course of *A Declaration*, the commissioners alone reserve the authority to interpret it and apply it to unfolding events.[104]

When Miantonomi fails in his assassination attempt on Uncas, for example, Uncas brings him to Hartford rather than killing him right away, so that the English can assure Uncas that the terms of the treaty are being followed. The English conduct a trial, and then turn Miantonomi over to Uncas, instructing him to execute the Narragansett sachem "in his owne Jurisdiction, without torture or crueltie." When the Narragansetts claim that "they had payd a ransome for their Sachems life, and gave in particulars to the value of about 40 li," and an "imputation of foule & unjust dealing" settles on Uncas, the commissioners likewise hold a hearing, finding that "no such parcels were brought," and that the execution can proceed.[105] The Narragansetts' claim to have paid a ransom for Miantonomi's life was one of the allegations that Gorton had taken to Parliament, but here Winthrop locates the authority to settle such disputes in the colonial commissioners. In place of a transatlantic relay of Native consent, Winthrop offers a vision of treaty authority consolidated in Boston and Hartford.

In the closing pages of A Declaration, the colonists' extreme measures are justified primarily as an exigency of war. Though the execution of Miantonomi is presented as a just action, one consistent with the Treaty of Hartford, it alienates the Narragansetts, leaving them bent on revenge. Winthrop proves that the tribe has turned against the colony by interleafing a letter from Roger Williams to the commissioners, which states "That the Country would sudainly be all on fyre" as a result of the Narragansetts' planned uprising.[106] One purpose of including the letter is to disprove Williams's statements about the Narragansetts. If the tribe is so belligerent toward the English, then Williams's own claims to have purchased their land in a treaty of friendship can hardly stand up to scrutiny. Williams's letter witnesses against him, contradicting the claims about Narragansett friendship he had made to Parliament only a few years earlier. More importantly, the letter offers a pretext for a preemptive attack against the Narragansetts. On the basis of Williams's intelligence, the colony is authorized to wage a just war. Even as Winthrop presents a vision of a landscape overrun by fire, he does not abandon the idea that the English will continue to stand with Native allies. The war against the Narragansetts will be waged both in the name of the Massachusetts Bay Colony and for the benefit of "other Indians under the protection of Massachusets, and not at all ingaged in this quarrel."[107] In the midst of war, the English are still the Indians' friends, at least in print.

Breaking Treaties and Putting Them Back Together

The war predicted by Winthrop in *A Declaration* never happened. On August 27, 1645, the Narragansetts signed a treaty of capitulation with the United Colonies.[108] The treaty was the first of a series that the tribe signed with the colonies over the next decade. Each demanded humbling concessions from the Narragansetts; each recognized the sovereign authority of the Massachusetts Bay Colony; and each left the tribe, on paper, increasingly subject to colonial power. More significant for my argument, colonial governors declined to publish these treaties in London. The English colonies' consolidation of power over southern New England coincided with broader shifts in European diplomacy that had made such treaties largely irrelevant to territorial dominion. In the Treaty of Münster (1648), one of the series of agreements that culminated in the Peace of Westphalia and brought an end to the Thirty Years' War (1618–1648), Spain conceded the claims of other Europeans to North American territories, rendering moot supplementary forms of legal justification such as Native treaties.[109] The Treaty of Westminster (1654), in which Portugal recognized England's holdings, and the Treaty of Madrid (1667), in which Spain belatedly followed suit, further confirmed the dominion of the English crown in the New World.[110] Each of these agreements lessened the international threat to England's overseas holdings, and in doing so, made it less important to publicize accounts of treaty relationships with Native Americans. Rather than broadcasting their agreements with the Narragansetts far and wide, the English colonists instead archived them for consultation during Native appeals, a political strategy that reflected the new understanding of treaties Winthrop had announced in *A Declaration*.

Surprisingly, however, this consolidation of power in the colonial state did not represent a diplomatic defeat for the tribe. In the years after signing the 1645 treaty, the Narragansetts constantly delayed the fulfillment of promises made during treaty negotiations. They refused to pay restitution to the Mohegans, and declined to release any captives; they continued to threaten Uncas and carry out raids against his friends; they accepted tribute from the Pequots—a group whose very name had been outlawed by the colonies; and they even arranged a marriage between a Narragansett woman and a former Pequot sachem, a move that seemed to imply a Narragansett claim to Pequot-held territory.[111] In 1654, ambassadors from the Massachusetts Bay Colony went to the tribe again, demanding that Ninigret, the sachem who had succeeded Canonicus, live up to the terms of the 1645 treaty or face execution. Ninigret quickly signed another treaty, this time formally disavowing the Pequots. Again, though, the Narragansetts dragged their feet on fulfilling the conditions.[112]

As I have attempted to show in this book, the transatlantic publication of treaties created opportunities for Native peoples as well. Sometimes, they used treaties to try and conquer the colonists, as Powhatan, and later his brother Opechancanough, had done. They also adopted the role of mediators, a strategy that could lead to the acquisition of considerable influence, as Pocahontas's and Squanto's stories show. Yet Canonicus and his successor Ninigret declined to take either of these paths. They pursued yet another strategy—formally agreeing to humiliating treaties but indefinitely delaying their performance. What enabled this evasive approach was, paradoxically, the Massachusetts Bay governors' attempt to consolidate treaty authority in their own hands. With their military actions against the Pequots, and with their diplomatic isolation of Miantonomi, the United Colonies had achieved dominance over southern New England. Their insistence that they had the right to judge questions of treaty violations went largely unchallenged because Parliament was too preoccupied with the events of the Revolution to supervise events in the colonies. Yet even after the United Colonies had abandoned the project of justifying themselves to the broader world, the Narragansetts still pursued transatlantic channels of redress. The Narragansetts knew that the Massachusetts Bay Colony did not want to fight another long and bloody war that would invite metropolitan intervention. And they also knew that merely delaying the performance of the conditions of a treaty—for however long—was not a strong enough pretext for a just war, at least as colonists understood such things. They knew the United Colonies had to explain themselves to a faraway power that looked upon the Narragansetts as loyal subjects. In this respect, *A Declaration* ended up working against the Massachusetts Bay Colony to some degree. Winthrop had claimed the tribe was under control; if the colonists now attacked, it would suggest that his *Declaration* had misrepresented the case. With each treaty they signed and ignored, the Narragansetts gave a greater appearance of regularity to their own proceedings, and made it more and more difficult for the Massachusetts Bay Colony to move against them as they had against the Pequots. The Puritan governors, a people of the book, found themselves outwitted in transatlantic correspondence by a nation whose leaders could not read or write alphabetic letters.[113]

The Narragansetts and the United Colonies remained locked in this stalemate for almost two decades. What eventually brought it to an end was a sequence of events that also bring this book to a close. In 1660, Charles II restored the English monarchy to power and undertook a review of the crown's colonial holdings, anxious to bring the colonies into a "nearer prospect and consultation."[114] To this end, he established a Council for Foreign Plantations, modeled on the now defunct parliamentary committee.[115] The seating of the Council opened up new channels of communication between the colonies and their metropolitan governors. Aggrieved petitioners bombarded councilors with stories of mismanagement in New England and the persecution of the king's subjects by the United Colonies. In response to these appeals, the Council sent a royal commission to subject the colonies to royal authority. The commission had wide-ranging powers. They reviewed the colonies' violation of the Navigation Acts, their printing of currency, and their involvement in sheltering Puritans who had participated in the execution of Charles I.[116] But the commission also reviewed the archive of the colonists' treaties with the Narragansetts and other groups, which, for the past twenty years, had resided in New England.[117] The Council knew that the colonies had political relationships with nearby tribal polities, but no treaties had been forthcoming, and the running conflicts between the Narragansetts and other groups suggested that the frontier was not under control. If the colonies would not send Indian treaties home, the king would go and get them.

The results of the commissioners' investigation drastically reconfigured the relations of authority between tribes, colonists, and the crown. While the signing of European treaties recognizing England's North American claims had made it less urgent for colonists to document interactions with Native peoples, the royal recognition of the Narragansetts in 1664 removed altogether the colonial middlemen that for so many decades had been tasked with sending home treaty documents. Prompting this direct assertion of authority was the New England colonies' disregard of the 1644 "Act of Subjection" and their negotiation of separate treaties with the Narragansetts. According to the commission's report, in defiance of the 1644 act, the colonies' governors had taken the Narragansetts' "whole country in mortgage."[118] The commission did not object to conquest as a way of expanding the crown's dominions, but they viewed the Narragansetts as English subjects who held land in the name of the king. Referencing Gorton's treaty with Canonicus, the governors affirm "that [the Narragansetts'] country was submitted to his Majestie, as well by witnesses, as by the said submission being eighteen years agoe Printed." This statement gives Gorton's book the status of an official treaty. In response to continued encroachments on the Indians, the commissioners reassert the will of the earlier Committee for Foreign Plantations, affirming direct royal control of the tribe and its land. The Council's order stands in stark contrast to the treaties from fifty years earlier. "[I]n his Majesties name," it reads "[the commissioners] order appoint and command that the said country be henceforward be called the Kings Province, and that no person of what colony soever presume to exercise any jurisdiction within this the Kings Province."[119] Absent in these lines is any mention of the kind of horizontal political order evoked by the English jurists and colonists who had used the law of nations to articulate Native and English rights. The commissioners do not work through Native rituals or protocols. On the contrary, they change the name of the Narragansetts' country to "King's Province," asserting direct royal control. The tribal members themselves seem almost absent. Indeed, the commissioners claim that the "country was submitted to his Majestie," making it seem as if the land itself has submitted to the king, without the need for any show of consent from its inhabitants. This language was reflective of a broader shift in Native treaty relations that occurred in the wake of the direct assertion of royal government of the colonies. The irony of the 1664 edict is that, from the Narragansetts' point of view, unilateral assertions of imperial control were preferable to the supposedly reciprocal treaty practices of the United Colonies. Indeed, it was the looming prospect of such top-down intervention that had enabled the Narragansetts to fight off colonial authorities for almost two decades.

After the commissioners' affirmation of the tribe's relationship with the crown, the Narragansetts enjoyed relative freedom from colonial incursions until King Philip's War in 1676, when Canochet, their sachem, was executed by Uncas on behalf of the victorious United Colonies. The war crippled the Native polities of southern New England and led to renewed justifications of violent conquest as a mode of subjugation.[120] I could very well end the story here, and in a sense I will; after King Philip's War, the New England colonies circled back to justifications of violent conquest that seemed to have more in common with the *Requerimiento* than with the reciprocity announced by Gabriel Archer or Roger Williams. But ending the story at this moment risks obscuring what the tribe accomplished before the war, as well as the meaning that prewar treaties had in the centuries after it.

Reappearing Acts: Narragansetts and Colonial Treaties

Understanding the Narragansetts' use of English treaties requires coming to grips with a series of ironies. The tribe viewed treaties with the colonists as a threat, despite the fact that such treaties conferred nominal recognition on them. They much preferred dealing directly with Parliament and with the royal commissioners, who did not recognize their independent standing but, by absorbing them as subjects, left their territorial boundaries intact. In pursuing this strategy of gaining power through submission, the Narragansetts (literally) left indelible marks on the archives of English colonial states.[121] They are by far the most visible tribe in the archives of the United Colonies and the parliamentary committees tasked with overseeing colonial endeavors. And while their near-destruction in King Philip's War made these treaties irrelevant from the point of view of the English crown, the Narragansetts themselves maintained both an oral and a written tradition of their treaty relationships with English colonists, and, in the decades and centuries after the death of Canonicus, Ninigret, and Canochet, continued to seek refuge in these agreements. In 1866, when Rhode Island government officials attempted to strip the tribe of its status in response to intermarriages between Narragansetts and African Americans, an unnamed Narragansett spokesperson quoted in the *Providence Journal* cited colonial treaties as evidence of the tribe's national purity dating to the colonial era: "We are not negroes," the spokesperson claimed, "we are the heirs of Ninagrit, and of the great chiefs and warriors of the Narragansetts. Because, when your ancestors stole the negro from Africa and brought him amongst us and made a slave of him, we extended him the hand of friendship, and permitted his blood to be mingled with ours, are we to be called negroes? And to be told that we may be made negro citizens? We claim that while one drop of Indian blood remains in our veins, we are entitled to the rights and privileges guaranteed by your ancestors to ours by solemn treaty, which without a breach of faith you cannot violate."[122] In response to the Jim Crow state's attempts to detribalize the Narragansetts, the spokesperson locates the tribe's purity in the political accomplishments of Ninigret and his treaties with the seventeenth-century colonial state. Here, intermarriage itself is a form of treaty making, an extension of friendship to another people that in no way dilutes the purity of the Narragansetts. In the wake of the U.S. Civil War, the tribe presses the state of Rhode Island to live up to its ancient agreements with Ninigret.

This argument was not successful, and the state of Rhode Island dissolved the tribe in 1880 and sold off its land.[123] In 1979, however, surviving Narragansetts drew upon their treaty history yet again, submitting a fifteen-volume petition for federal recognition to the Bureau of Indian Affairs.[124] Along with accounts of Narragansett languages and tribal customs, the successful petition also included references to the Narragansetts in colonial treaties as evidence of the tribe's cultural continuity in the region. Such petitions, which have been submitted by numerous tribes with varying degrees of success, offer a dramatic counter-narrative of colonial treaty history, one that views early Atlantic political correspondence as a bearer of contemporary tribal identity. Indeed, in legal contexts, tribal groups have been willing to grant a measure of credibility and authenticity to colonial treaties that many literary scholars, suspicious of colonizers' motives, have not.

Colonial treaties with the Narragansetts and other tribes were drafted in response to conflicts that happened far away from the North American coast. They reflected debates about rights and political order that stretched back to the Holy Roman Empire. Yet the English exploitation of Native treaties also created channels through which indigenous groups could attempt to remake their political worlds after the upheaval of European arrival. We should not romanticize what Native peoples did with any power they gained from treaties with the English. The Narragansetts, for example, used their freedom from the Massachusetts Bay Colony to wage a long and eventually unsuccessful war against the Mohegans. It is hard to suggest that there was anything noble or redemptive about this war. But the political successes of the Narragansetts and other groups—even if they did not endure for long—suggest that we should tell a different kind of story about colonialism, one not based around the inevitable defeat of Natives by Europeans. Treaties never had only one meaning, and their outcome was always in doubt.

Notes

—∿∿—

Introduction: A Great Shout

1. Archer, "A relatyon of the Discovery of our River," 1:86.

2. Ibid., 1:89.

3. Ibid., 1:84.

4. For a discussion of early modern analogies between European and indigenous polities, see Kupperman, *Indians and English*, 77–109.

5. For an account of how colonial states used treaties to conquer Native peoples, see Jones, *License for Empire*. For an account that focuses on colonial New England, see Jennings, *The Invasion of America*, 177–312. For the early national period, see Prucha, *American Indian Treaties*. For accounts that focus on multifaceted forms of diplomacy and treaty expression, see Merrell, *Into the American Woods*; Merrell, "'I desire all that I have said . . . may be taken down aright'"; and Calloway, *Pen and Ink Witchcraft*. Native American intellectuals and activists have powerfully influenced the scholarly criticism of colonial treaties. See for example Deloria, *Behind the Trail of Broken Treaties*. For an account of Native critiques of treaties in the nineteenth century, see Konkle, *Writing Indian Nations*.

6. For the role of oaths, documents, and signatures in early modern European treaties, see Lesaffer, "Peace Treaties from Lodi to Westphalia."

7. The English-language copy appeared as *Articles of Peace, Entercourse, and Commerce Concluded in the names of the most high and mighty Kings, and Princes James by the grace of God . . . And Philip the third, King of Spaine*. An account of the reception afforded English ambassadors in Spain can be found in *The Royal Entertainement of the Right Honourable the Earle of Nottingham*. See Dillon, *The Language of Space in Court Performance*, 83–90, for an account of early modern portrayals of the treaty negotiations. Earlier treaties, such as the Treaty of Nonsuch (1585), which cemented an Anglo-Dutch alliance against the Spanish,

and the Treaty of Berwick (1586), which cleared the way for James I to succeed Elizabeth, were also in the living memory of English colonists. On the negotiation of the Treaty of Nonsuch, see Wernham, *The Making of Elizabethan Foreign Policy*, 12. Elizabeth's defense of the treaty was printed as *A Declaration of the Causes Mooving the Queene of England to give aide to the Defence of the People afflicted and oppressed in the lowe Countries* (1585). The book was also published in France, Italy, and the Low Countries. See McDermott, *England and the Spanish Armada*, 157, for an account of its publication. On the Treaty of Berwick, see Doran, "James VI and the English Succession."

8. The debate about whether Indians could make treaties was part of broader debates about whether they could convert to Christianity, exercise reason, or own property. See Hanke, *All Mankind Is One*; Pagden, *The Fall of Natural Man*, 10–56, 109–19; and Castro, *Another Face of Empire*. English colonists, investors, and councilors grappled with the same questions over the course of disputes over American territory, and often cited Spanish authorities. For an account of how English colonial promoters acquired and read Spanish legal texts, see Fitzmaurice, "Moral Uncertainty in the Dispossession of Native Americans."

9. See Prucha, *American Indian Treaties*; Calloway, *Pen and Ink Witchcraft*; Fixico, ed., *Treaties with American Indians*.

10. Alden T. Vaughan has written that "a vast array of documents" were involved in the publication of treaties. Vaughan, "Preface," xiii.

11. For accounts of Anglo-Native alliances along the eastern seaboard, see Fausz, "Merging and Emerging Worlds"; Hatfield, *Atlantic Virginia*; Pulsipher, *Subjects unto the Same King*; and Van Zandt, *Brothers Among Nations*.

12. See Vaughan, *Transatlantic Encounters*.

13. For an account of these donations, see Weckmann-Muñoz, "The Alexandrine Bulls of 1493." The bulls and the many subsequent treaties are printed in Davenport, ed., *European Treaties Bearing on the History of the United States and Its Dependencies*, 1:56–198.

14. *Requerimiento*, in Grewe, ed., *Fontes Historiae Iuris Gentium*, 2:70. For a more detailed account of these performances, see Seed, *Ceremonies of Possession in Europe's Conquest of the New World*, 69–99.

15. For an account of debates about the *Requerimiento* in Spain, see Muldoon, *The Americas in the Spanish World Order*, 136–39.

16. For the later history of the *Requerimiento*, see Williams, *The American Indian in Western Legal Thought*, 93. For Spain's response to English colonization, see Quinn, "Some Spanish Reactions to Elizabethan Colonial Enterprises," 1–23. For the role of Roman law in European diplomatic negotiations over America, see MacMillan, *Sovereignty and Possession in the English New World*, 178–207.

17. For a discussion of Anglo-Spanish negotiations over piracy, see Carter, "The New World as a Factor in International Relations," 251–56.

18. For an overview of the legal justifications for settlement offered by Europeans, see Pagden, *Lords of All the World*. Important for my purposes is Benton, *A Search for Sovereignty*, which emphasizes the importance of delegation and adaptation in colonial legal justification. For accounts of English justifications in treatises, maps, and diplomatic correspondence, see MacMillan, *Sovereignty and Possession*. For English protocols for taking possession, see Seed, *Ceremonies of Possession*, 16–41; Slattery, "Paper Empires," 50–78; and Tomlins, "The Legal Cartography of Colonization, The Legal Polyphony of Settlement." Benton and Straumann, "Acquiring Empire by Law," argue that English colonists strategically combined many different kinds of ceremonies and protocols deriving from Roman law and European traditions. Benton's and Straumann's emphasis on how colonists combined multiple ways of showing possession will be important to my argument. For a broader historical perspective, see Jennings, *The Acquisition of Territory in International Law*.

19. MacMillan, *Sovereignty and Possession*. See also the essays in Kingsbury and Straumann, eds., *The Roman Foundations of the Law of Nations*. Relevant as well are Higgins, "International Law and the Outer World, 1450–1648"; and Grisel, "The Beginnings of International Law."

20. See Stein, *Roman Law in European History*, 38–103.

21. For the early development of Roman law in England, see Zulueta and Stein, *The Teaching of Roman Law in England Around 1200*.

22. See. Cheyney, "International Law Under Queen Elizabeth"; Juricek, "English Territorial Claims in North America Under Elizabeth and the Early Stuarts"; Green and Dickason, *The Law of Nations and the New World*; Armitage, *The Ideological Origins of the British Empire*; and MacMillan, *Sovereignty and Possession*. See also the essays in Kingsbury and Straumann, eds., *The Roman Foundations of the Law of Nations*.

23. On natural law, see Tuck, *Natural Rights Theories*; and Tierney, *The Idea of Natural Rights*. Also relevant are White, *Natural Law in English Renaissance Literature*; and Lockey, *Law and Empire in English Renaissance Literature*.

24. Justinian, *Institutes*, 1.2.1, in *The Civil Law*. All subsequent citations to Justinian's works are to this edition.

25. For the history of the law of nations and its relationship to the development of what is today called international law, see among many others Brierly, *The Law of Nations*; Nussbaum, *A Concise History of the Law of Nations*; Grewe, *The Epochs of International Law*, 137–424; Tuck, *The Rights of War and Peace*; and Nijman, *The Concept of International Legal Personality*. For a broader bibliography, see Macalister-Smith and Schwietzke, "Literature and Documentary Sources Relating to the History of Public International Law," 136–212.

26. There is much debate about the influence of Roman law in England. See Stein, *The Character and Influence of the Roman Civil Law*, 151–230. For English lawyers' reception of Roman legal texts in the seventeenth century, see Levack, *The Civil Lawyers in England*. For an example of how Roman law influenced the legal curriculum, see Knafla, "The Law Studies of an Elizabethan Student," 231–32.

27. See Hulsebosch, "The Ancient Constitution and the Expanding Empire."

28. Justinian, *Digest*, 41.2.3.3. For Elizabethans, demonstration of *corpus* required a "strong, fortified, physical presence in the territory." MacMillan, *Sovereignty and Possession*, 187. Indian treaties could support such a demonstration because they showed that nearby people recognized the rights of the English crown and did not intended to challenge its colonists' control of territory. For more on Roman criteria of possession and their application by early modern English jurists, see Juricek, "English Territorial Claims."

29. The concept of *terra nullius*, or land without an owner, derived from the concept of *res nullius*, or things without owners. For the history of *res nullius* and its manifold uses in legal debates about lands and seas beyond Europe, see Benton and Straumann, "Acquiring Empire by Law." The related term *vacuum domicilium* described empty land subject to possession. See Allen, "*Vacuum Domicilium*"; and Cronon, *Changes in the Land*, 54–58. As I will show in Chapter 5, *vacuum domicilium* was most often employed in New England, where many lands were empty because their original Native owners had died in a plague introduced by Europeans.

30. For the broader history of conquest as a legal doctrine, see Korman, *The Right of Conquest*.

31. See Seed, *Ceremonies of Possession*, 16–41. For an account that emphasizes the ecological transformations brought about by English settler colonization, see Cronon, *Changes in the Land*, 54–81, 127–56. On the shared Spanish and English rhetoric of the New World as a garden, see Cañizares-Esguerra, *Puritan Conquistadors*, 178–214.

32. For the enslavement of Indians, see Fickes, "'They Could Not Endure That Yoke'"; Newell, "Indian Slavery in Colonial New England"; and Everett, "'They shalbe slaves for their lives.'"

33. Ken MacMillan has traced how the English developed a discourse of "benevolent conquest" in order to justify their seizure of territory under the law of nations while distinguishing their regime from that of the Spanish. See MacMillan, "Benign and Benevolent Conquest?" For more on the the Black Legend of Spanish colonialism, see Hart, *Representing the New World*; and Greer, Mignolo, and Quilligan, eds., *Rereading the Black Legend*. On the humanism of English colonial texts, see Fitzmaurice, *Humanism and America*.

34. For the treatment of *foedera vel inaequalia* by medieval authorities, see Ziegler, "The

Influence of Medieval Roman Law on Peace Treaties," 155. Hugo Grotius argued that such treaties could be proposed by either the higher or lower ranking party. While they usually involved the "impairment of sovereignty," they could occasionally occur "without such impairment," such as when one party imposed temporary obligations on the other, or simply asked for a formal recognition of its "majesty." Grotius, *De Jure Belli ac Pacis Libri Tres*, 396. Grotius viewed the victory of one party over another in war as the most common occasion for unequal treaties, but he also argued that they could occur between "more powerful and less powerful peoples that have not even engaged in war with each other." Grotius, *De Jure Belli*, 397.

35. For references to America in early modern European diplomacy, see Hussey, "America in European Diplomacy"; and Carter, "The New World as a Factor in International Relations." For America in European treaties, see Davenport, ed., *European Treaties*, vols. 1–2.

36. For more on this argument, see Castro, *Another Face of Empire*. Las Casas engaged in a famous debate with Juan Ginés de Sepúlveda over the issue of Indian rights. See Hanke, *All Mankind Is One*.

37. Bartolomé de Las Casas, *Historia de las Indias*, 3:1998; trans. in Koschorke et al., eds., *A History of Christianity in Asia, Africa, and Latin America*, 290.

38. See Scott, *The Spanish Origin of International Law*, 96–194.

39. Francisco de Vitoria, "On the American Indians," in *Political Writings*, 233. On Vitoria's use of Aquinas, see Pagden, "Dispossessing the Barbarian."

40. Vitoria, "On the American Indians," in *Political Writings*, 288.

41. Ibid., 276. Vitoria claimed that the violent nature of Spanish colonization had rendered unlawful any of the Spanish crown's current claims about Indian submission.

42. Las Casas partly inspired the creation of new laws governing the treatment of Native slaves. For the history of these laws, see Simpson, *The Encomienda in New Spain*, 132–33.

43. See Kingsbury and Straumann, eds., *The Roman Foundations of the Law of Nations*.

44. Gentili, *De Jure Belli Libri Tres*, 81. By "equal laws," Gentili presumably meant European natural law. See MacMillan, "Benign and Benevolent Conquest?" 68–69, for a discussion of this passage.

45. Grotius, *De Jure Belli*, 397.

46. English commanders led the *cimarrónes* in plundering Spanish supply lines and ships around Panama and along the Pacific coast. See Morgan, *American Slavery, American Freedom*.

47. Hakluyt, *The Principal Navigations*, 3:45.

48. Drake, *The World Encompassed*, 76. This account, which was not authored by Drake, was printed much later by his nephew and others. See Keller et al., *Creation of Rights of Sov-*

ereignty Through Symbolic Acts, 59. See also Benton and Straumann, "Acquiring Empire by Law," 33.

49. Drake, *The World Encompassed*, 80.

50. Raleigh, *The Discoverie of the Large, Rich, and Beautiful Empire of Guiana*, 30.

51. Elizabeth I, "The Queen's Answer to the Portuguese Ambassador," in *Calendar of State Papers . . . Elizabeth*, VII, 820, trans. in 821. For a discussion of Anglo-Portuguese disputes in Africa, see Hair and Law, "The English in Western Africa to 1700," 1:246–47. See also Seed, *Ceremonies of Possession*, 9–10.

52. For representations of exchange and trade in English colonial texts, see Sacks, "The True Temper of Empire," 531–58.

53. James I, "Instructions to English Commissioners," 1:247n4.

54. Justinian law held that "nothing more accords with natural justice than to confirm the desire of an owner to transfer his property to another." Justinian, *Institutes* 2.1.40. This statement was cited approvingly by Vitoria, "On the American Indians," in *Political Writings*, 275. On the use of purchase as a way of acquiring territory from Natives, see Banner, *How the Indians Lost Their Land*. Jennings, *The Invasion of America*, 128–45, argues that colonists purchased land with mostly fraudulent intent.

55. Oberg, *Dominion and Civility*, describes how metropolitan ambitions to peacefully subjugate the colonial frontier quickly gave way to the recognition that Native people would defend their land from newcomers.

56. Williams, *The American Indian in Western Legal Thought*, 187. For the broader European history of just war, see Tuck, *The Rights of War and Peace*.

57. Vitoria, "On the American Indians," in *Political Writings*, 283.

58. Strachey identified that right as "[the] establishment of Christian religion . . . [and] the possession of such lands as are voide of Christian inhabitants." Strachey, *The Historie of Travaile into Virginia Britannia*, 20. Strachey adapted this language from Peckham, *A True Reporte*.

59. For more on this, see Korman, *The Right of Conquest*. For an account of the history of legal consent in colonial North America, see Pole, *Contract and Consent*.

60. The divide-and-ally strategy had its origins in the Elizabethan notion that England could rescue good Indians from cannibals or marauders. See Morgan, *American Slavery, American Freedom*, 18–19. For portrayals of cannibals in both English and Spanish texts, see Cañizares-Esguerra, *Puritan Conquistadors*, 88–94. For the First Anglo-Powhatan War, see Fausz, "An 'Abundance of Blood Shed on Both Sides.'"

61. With the exception of Winthrop's *A Declaration of Former Passages and Proceedings Betwixt the English and the Narrowgansets*, early colonial treaties were published only in manuscript in the colonies themselves. For the history of scribal publication in England, see Love,

Scribal Publication in Seventeenth-Century England. For New England manuscript culture, see Hall, *Ways of Writing*. The most important instructional manual for English legal secretaries was Day, *The English Secretary*. For more on English legal training, see Bland, "Rhetoric and the Law Student in Sixteenth-Century England"; and Schoeck, "Lawyers and Rhetoric in Sixteenth-Century England."

62. See the critiques offered in Fisch, "Law as a Means and as an End"; Keal, *European Conquest and the Rights of Indigenous Peoples*; Anghie, *Imperialism, Sovereignty and the Making of International Law*; and the essays in Ivison, Patton, and Sanders, eds., *Political Theory and the Rights of Indigenous Peoples*. For an overview of indigenous peoples and their historical relationship to international law, see Anaya, *Indigenous Peoples in International Law*. For a general account of Native Americans and law, see Hermes, "The Law of Native Americans."

63. The scholarly literature concerning coastal political cultures before and during colonization is vast. For the peoples of the Chesapeake Bay, see Potter, *Commoners, Tribute, and Chiefs*; Rountree, ed., *Powhatan Foreign Relations*; Gleach, *Powhatan's World and Colonial Virginia*; Axtell, *Natives and Newcomers*, 233–58; Gallivan, *James River Chiefdoms*; Williamson, *Powhatan Lords of Life and Death*; and Rice, *Nature and History in the Potomac Country*. For New England, see Salisbury, *Manitou and Providence*; and Bragdon, *Native People of Southern New England*. For accounts that are broader in scope, see Richter, *Facing East from Indian Country*; Richter, *Before the Revolution*; and Witgen, *An Infinity of Nations*.

64. My account relies on Bragdon, *Native People*, 184–216; Gleach, *Powhatan's World*, 22–60; Rice, *Nature and History*, 56–61; and Rountree, *The Powhatan Indians of Virginia*, 133–39.

65. Williams, *A Key into the Language of America*, 118.

66. Keary, "Retelling the History of the Settlement of Providence," 255.

67. See Cook, "The Significance of Disease in the Extinction of the New England Indians"; and Crosby, "Virgin Soil Epidemics as a Factor in the Aboriginal Depopulation of America." For the effect of disease on political relations, see Salisbury, *Manitou and Providence*, 101–9. For the cultural history of Native illness, see Jones, *Rationalizing Epidemics*. Silva, *Miraculous Plagues*, considers the effects of the New England plague on the production and reception of colonial writing.

68. The concept was not foreign to the English, who exchanged gifts in both formal and informal contexts. See Ben-Amos, *The Culture of Giving*.

69. As legal scholar Bernard J. Hibbitts has shown, many cultures, including those of early modern Europe, performed law. In cultures of legal performance, Hibbitts writes, "law and legal understandings are conveyed not only orally, but also in gesture, touch,

scent, and flavor. They are not only heard, but seen, felt, smelled, and tasted. . . . Frequently used in combination, these forms serve the same functions, and thus deserve the same respect, as the lengthy documents that often replace them in our society." Hibbitts, "Coming to Our Senses," 883–84. See also Peters, "Legal Performance Good and Bad," which examines how legal performances have both legitimated and challenged state power and other forms of authority. For a broader discussion of the diverse legal cultures of the Atlantic world, see Tomlins and Mann, eds., *The Many Legalities of Early America.* Goodman, "The Deer Indian Islands and Common Law Performance," considers the application of English common law to Native participation in King Philip's War. Though it does not explicitly employ the concept of performance, also relevant is Hermes, "'Justice Will Be Done Us.'"

70. These audiences included both company councils and royal bodies. See Egerton, "The Seventeenth and Eighteenth Century Privy Council in Its Relations with the Colonies." For an account of how colonists emphasized civility and good order in their writings, see Round, *By Nature and By Custom Cursed.* Scanlan, *Colonial Writing and the New World,* shows how English colonial writings engaged national political issues.

71. See, for example, Robert Treswell, *A Relation of Such Things As were observed to happen in the Journey of the right Honourable Charles Earle of Nottingham.* The nearest precedent for the English relation was the Italian diplomatic genre of the *relazioni. Relazioni* consisted of official summaries of the military and ambassadorial service of Venetians in the Ottoman Empire. While *relazioni* served immediate diplomatic needs for Italian city-states, they also circulated internationally as primers on political negotiation. Most were disseminated through copies made by scribes or civil servants or sold to collectors with investments in foreign affairs. However, others reached print as objects of general interest, such as the Italian diplomat Giovanni Botero's collected *relazioni* from foreign courts, printed in London in multiple editions (1601–1630). See Queller, "The Development of Ambassadorial Relazioni." Many aristocrats printed their own diplomatic correspondence in the format of the *relation* in order to influence policy. Catholic writer Robert Parsons, for example, documented Spanish courtly life in *A Relation of the King of Spaines Receiving in Valliodolid.* For more on the history of diplomatic writing, see Hampton, *Fictions of Embassy.* For another meaning of *relation,* see Dolan, *True Relations.*

72. Mattingly, *Renaissance Diplomacy.* See also Black, *A History of Diplomacy.* For the late seventeenth century, see Cross, *The European Diplomatic Corps,* 35–67.

73. "The Complaint of Certain Adventurers and Inhabitants of the Plantation in New England," 507.

74. The London Council of the Virginia Company, "A circular Letter of his Majestie's Counsil for Virginia," 1:463.

75. McKenzie, *Oral Culture, Literacy and Print in Early New Zealand*.

76. For the broader history of indigenous legal resistance against European empires, see Byrd, *The Transit of Empire*; and the essays in Belmessous, ed., *Native Claims*.

77. Many literary scholars have granted little credence to colonial representations of Native words and deeds, viewing colonial texts as distortions of reality that only reflected European interests and biases. For important studies that make this point, see Cheyfitz, *The Poetics of Imperialism*; Greenblatt, "Invisible Bullets"; and Hulme, *Colonial Encounters*. As Myra Jehlen and Ed White have pointed out in separate contexts, blanket skepticism about colonial representations can also have the effect of putting the intentions of indigenous people beyond our interpretive reach. See Jehlen, "Response to Peter Hulme"; and White, "Invisible Tagkanysough."

78. Adorno, *Guaman Poma*, documents how the Incan intellectual Guaman Poma adapted European genres to promote an indigenous critique of colonial rule intended to sway the policies of the Spanish crown. Boone and Mignolo, *Writing Without Words*, aims to recover Native ways of using European alphabetic systems to resist colonial power. Other studies, such as Brotherston, *Book of the Fourth World*; Rabasa, *Writing Violence on the Northern Frontier*; and Cañizares-Esguerra, *How to Write the History of the New World*, have shown how indigenous people used print and other kinds of written media to make claims for political recognition. For an account of Native American literature and media across the Americas, see the essays in Krupat and Swann, eds., *Recovering the Word*.

79. See, among many other works, Wyss, *Writing Indians*; O'Brien, *Dispossession by Degrees*; Brooks, *The Common Pot*; Cohen, *The Networked Wilderness*; Rasmussen, *Queequeg's Coffin*; and Newman, *On Records*.

80. Much of this work has considered communication or literary expression in terms of performance. Roach, *Cities of the Dead*, uses the concept of orature to consider Atlantic performance cultures and English literary traditions. Castillo, *Colonial Encounters in New World Writing*, considers how various voices and modes of performance converged in early American texts. For an account of pulpit oratory and performance in early America, see Gustafson, *Eloquence Is Power*. Taylor, *The Archive and the Repertoire*, considers performance as an embodiment of history and memory in Atlantic cultures. Fichtelberg, "The Colonial Stage," views John Smith's writings as an episode in the history of the performance of risk. Also relevant are Fliegelman, *Declaring Independence*; and Brown, *The Pilgrim and the Bee*, which consider various ways of reading as a performance. Gustafson and Sloat, eds., *Cultural Narratives*, considers a broad range of expressive practices as performances. Important works have used the concept of performance to understand Native American expression. Bross, *Dry Bones and Indian Sermons*, traces how New England colonists promoted their own ventures by documenting Native performances of the Puritan conversion narrative. Bellin, *Med-*

icine Bundle, considers Native religious performances and the literature of the United States. Also see the essays collected in Bellin and Mielke, eds., *Native Acts*.

81. Smith, *The Proceedings of the English Colonie in Virginia*, 42.

Chapter 1. Heavy Heads: Crowning Kings in Early Virginia

1. Edward Muir has described the role of gestures and props in these ceremonies. Confirming gestures such as bowing and stooping were crucial to the creation of vassals. Ceremonies were often repeated if a gesture seemed incompletely performed. For the details of these ceremonies, see Muir, *Ritual in Early Modern Europe*, 29–31. The English had attempted to create similar legal arrangements with the Irish. See Canny, *The Elizabethan Conquest of Ireland*, 32–34.

2. In England, lesser authorities frequently wore copper crowns in public processions. The copper distinguished their crowns from those made of gold, which were worn by princes. For example, a stage direction in Shakespeare's *Henry VIII* describes the Garter King-at-Arms "[wearing] a gilt copper crown" (4.1.36). In the years before Newport's attempt to crown Powhatan, Virginia colonists had observed lesser sachems wearing what appeared to be copper on their heads, leading them to believe that copper crowns marked out subordinate powers among the Powhatans as well. See Archer, "Relatyon," 92.

3. The Virginia Company had two branches, one based in London and one in Plymouth. The London branch had rights to the Chesapeake Bay, while the Plymouth branch had rights to what would later be called New England. The Plymouth division did not settle its grant and was reorganized as the Plymouth Council for New England in 1620. The Virginia Company exercised authority over Jamestown through the London Council, a royally appointed board. See Craven, *Dissolution of the Virginia Company*.

4. *A True Declaration of the estate of the Colonie in Virginia*, 14, 11, 14. Smith, *Proceedings*, 46, claims that Powhatan "gave his old shoes and his mantle to Captain *Newport*" in exchange for the gifts. This mantle has been identified by many historians as the one in the Tradescant Collection in the Ashmolean Museum at Oxford University. This mantle is 2.35 by 1.6 meters (7 feet 8.5 inches by 5 feet 3 inches), made of deer hides, and decorated with shells. However, Smith elsewhere describes Powhatan as wearing "a faire Robe of skins as large as an Irish mantle." Smith, *Proceedings*, 18. Irish mantles were made of textiles or furs, were draped around the neck, and served as blankets. On account of its size, weight, decoration, and cut, it is unlikely that the mantle in the Tradescant Collection is the one referred to in the *Proceedings*. For a discussion of the deer hide mantle, see Feest, "Powhatan's Mantle"; and Rountree, *Powhatan Indians*, 103. For early modern English representation of Irish clothing, including mantles, see Derricke, *The Image of Irelande*.

5. Magnel, "Francis Magnel's Relation of the First Voyage." Jamestown leaders never discovered the subterfuge.

6. Don Pedro de Zúñiga to Philip III, June 26, 1608, in Barbour, ed., *The Jamestown Voyages Under the First Charter*, 1:163.

7. For Anglo-Indian interactions in Virginia, see Morgan, *American Slavery, American Freedom*; Sheehan, *Savagism and Civility*; and Horn, *A Land as God Made It*. For accounts that place the Virginia Colony in international contexts, see Hatfield, *Atlantic Virginia*; Kupperman, *The Jamestown Project*; Van Zandt, *Brothers Among Nations*; the essays in Mancall, ed., *The Atlantic World and Virginia*; and the essays in Appelbaum and Sweet, eds., *Envisioning an English Empire*.

8. James I, "Instructions for Government," 1:43.

9. For accounts of the peoples of the Chesapeake Bay during the colonial period, see Rountree, *Powhatan Indians*; Gleach, *Powhatan's World*; and Williamson, *Powhatan Lords*. For accounts that consider the Powhatans in the context of the broader Potomac River Valley culture, see Potter, *Commoners, Tribute, and Chiefs*; Gallivan, "Powhatan's Werowocomoco"; Rice, *Nature and History*; and the essays in Rountree, ed., *Powhatan Foreign Relations*.

10. For the details of this exchange, see Vaughan, *Transatlantic Encounters*, 45. Savage served as an interpreter for many years.

11. Archer, "Relatyon," 1:85–86.

12. Ibid., 1:84.

13. Ibid., 1:86.

14. For the history of this doctrine, see Muldoon, "Discovery, Grant, Charter, Conquest, or Purchase."

15. Archer, "Relatyon," 1:88.

16. For the grant, see James I, "Letters patent to Sir Thomas Gates and others."

17. For the history of this massacre, which was notorious throughout Europe, see McGrath, *The French in Early Florida*, 96–115. The English were equally worried about Spanish assaults on their ships. In 1606, for example, the Spanish captured a ship financed by Sir Ferdinando Gorges after it went off course in the Caribbean. Gorges, *A Briefe Narration of the Originall Undertakings of the Advancement of Plantations*, 4–6. The English were also aware of competing French claims and the possibility of Dutch conspiracies in Jamestown. For the French claims to the area, see MacMillan, *Sovereignty and Possession*, 194–95. John Smith describes the Dutch conspiracy in *Proceedings*, 65–66, 73, 75, 80, 81, 91.

18. See Seed, *Ceremonies of Possession*, 69–99.

19. James I, "Instructions for Government," 1:43; "The London Council's 'Instructions given by way of Advice,'" 1:53.

20. See the brief account of Archer's life in Barbour, *The Three Worlds of Captain John Smith*, 122–23. Legal and secretarial expertise was highly valued by joint-stock colonial ventures.

21. See Rice, *Nature and History*, 59–60.

22. Archer, "Relatyon," 1:88.

23. Given the relatively intact state of the manuscript, it is unlikely that Archer composed on board Newport's barge itself. The report's specificity regarding the shape of the land, the names and political affiliations of the riverside polities, and the precise distance traveled by the party make it probable that he made notes and then digested them into reports for transatlantic readers.

24. Archer, "Relatyon," 1:82.

25. Ibid., 1:84.

26. See, for example, Geuffroy, *The order of the greate Turckes courte* (1542), which offers a suggestive point of comparison to Archer's "Relatyon."

27. Archer, "Relatyon," 1:84.

28. See Rountree, *Powhatan Indians*, 106–9 for a discussion of Powhatan practices of diplomacy and hospitality.

29. See Rountree, *Pocahontas, Powhatan, Opechancanough*, 58. Some readers of Archer's narrative have assumed that the English were simply mistaken about the king's identity and status. Yet there was a strategic advantage in calling Parahunt "Pawatah" or "Powatah," at least in transatlantic correspondence. By conflating him with his powerful father, the English could claim that their negotiations with him had brought the area under control.

30. Archer, "Relatyon," 1:84.

31. Ibid., 1:88.

32. For these ceremonies, which were performed by explorers under many flags, see Benton and Straumann, "Acquiring Empire by Law," 32. Sir Francis Drake performed a similar ritual in California in 1579, erecting a wooden post with a brass plate engraved with both the queen's name and his own. See Drake, *The World Encompassed*, 80. For a discussion of this ceremony, see Keller, Lissitzyn, and Mann, *Creation of Rights of Sovereignty Through Symbolic Acts*, 59. Newport may have read or heard about the planting of crosses during the discovery of the Kennebec River in 1605. In a report on that voyage, James Rosier, a cape merchant and secretary, described the planting of crosses on newly explored territory as "a thing never omitted by any Christian travellers." Rosier, *A True Relation of the most prosperous voyage*, n.p. See Strachey, *Historie of Travaile*, 160–61, for another account of the planting of a cross during the discovery of the Kennebec.

33. Archer, "Relatyon," 1:88.

34. Ibid.

35. See Greenblatt, *Marvelous Possessions*, for an account of literary portrayals of Native awe in response to European ceremonies.

36. Archer, "Relatyon," 1:89.

37. Ibid., 1:97–98.

38. Smith, *Proceedings*, 42.

39. Ibid., 32, 33.

40. For a reading of Smith's work that emphasizes Smith's engagement with Machiavelli, see Fitzmaurice, *Humanism and America*, 177–86.

41. Smith, *Proceedings*, 34.

42. Ibid., 42.

43. Abbay, "To the Reader," in Smith, *Proceedings*, n.p.

44. See Morgan, *American Slavery, American Freedom*, 25–70.

45. For the details of this conflict, see Fausz, "An 'Abundance of Blood Shed on Both Sides.'"

46. On the transatlantic management of the colony at this time, see Games, *The Web of Empire*, 117–46.

47. *True Declaration*, 10–11. The reference is to 2 Samuel 10. After the death of the king of the Ammonites, David sent servants to console the grieving prince. The prince accused them of being spies, prompting David to declare war on him.

48. For this strategy, see The London Council of the Virginia Company, "Instructions to Sir Thomas Gates," 2:266.

49. For internal company deliberations on this question, see "A Justification for planting in Virginia." Fitzmaurice, "Powhatan Legal Claims," argues that legal contests with Powhatans were an important factor in reversing the colony's decision to avoid public statements about title.

50. The most complete account of these voyages is in Rountree, Clark, and Mountford, *John Smith's Chesapeake Voyages*.

51. *Proceedings*, 12. For Smith's engagement with Spanish texts and models of Spanish colonization, see Griffin, "The Specter of Spain in John Smith's Colonial Writing."

52. The story is in Smith, *The Generall Historie of Virginia*, 48–49. Voigt, *Writing Captivity in the Early Modern Atlantic*, 306–9, describes how Smith likely adapted the story from Spanish writings about Juan Ortiz, who had reportedly undergone a similar ordeal in Florida. For the history of this controversial episode, see Lemay, *Did Pocahontas Save Captain John Smith?*

53. Smith, *Proceedings*, 16, 45, and 63–64, portrays Powhatan and Smith negotiating kinship alliances. See Gleach, *Powhatan's World*, 109–22; and Rice, *Nature and History*, 80–81, for a historical description of these alliances in the context of Anglo-Powhatan relations.

54. Smith, *Proceedings*, 68.

55. See Lemay, *Did Pocahontas Save Captain John Smith?* xvi.

56. "The London Council's 'Instructions given by way of Advice,'" 1:53–54.

57. See Barbour, "Introduction," in Smith, *The Complete Works of Captain John Smith*, 1:5.

58. See Fitzmaurice, *Humanism and America*, 58–61. See also Wright, *Religion and Empire*, 87–89. These promotional and fundraising efforts were a spectacular success. See Rabb, *Enterprise and Empire*, 38–39.

59. For a detailed account of the story retold below, see Barbour, "Introduction," in Smith, *Complete Works*, 1:121–26. Barbour's portrayal erroneously aims to vindicate Smith from the charge of being a fabricator. It is nevertheless the most carefully documented account of Smith's travels and writings.

60. Smith, *Map*, title page; Smith, *Proceedings*, title page.

61. Gaudio, *Engraving the Savage*, 92, describes how Hole adapted the image of Powhatan from other sources. See Blansett, "John Smith Maps Virginia," 81, for a discussion of the figure of the Susquehannock. Smith's map stands in stark contrast to many others, which replaced Native place-names with English ones.

62. Smith, *Map*.

63. Ibid., 34.

64. Ibid., 36.

65. Ibid., 25.

66. Ibid., 26.

67. Barrett, *The Theorike and Practike of Moderne Warres*, n.p.

68. Grotius held that "because of a certain kinship established among us by nature, it is sinful that man should lie in ambush for his fellow man." Grotius, *De Iure Praedae Commentarius*, 13. Vitoria refers in passing to ambush as a violation of civil law. Vitoria, "On Civil Power," in *Political Writings*, 41.

69. Knolles described how the Sultan Saladin launched "ambuscadoes" against Richard I at the Battle of Arsuf. Knolles, *The Generall Historie of the Turkes*, 72.

70. For a description of military tactics and ambushing in Ireland, see McGurk, "Terrain and Conquest."

71. Smith, *Map*, 19.

72. Ibid., 37.

73. Ibid.

74. Ibid., 26.

75. Ibid., 39.

76. Ibid.

77. For the publication of English governmental proceedings, see Kyle, *Theater of State*. For an account of printed news media in early modern England, see Raymond, *Pamphlets and Pamphleteering in Early Modern Britain*, 98–160.

78. See, for example, *A faithfull Report of proceedings anent the Assemblie of Ministers at Abirdeen*.

79. Digges, *A Breife and true report*, title page.

80. Abbay, "To the Reader," in Smith, *Proceedings*, n.p.

81. Smith, *Proceedings*, title page.

82. Ibid., 5.

83. Ibid., 4.

84. Ibid., 5.

85. Ibid., 6.

86. Ibid., 11.

87. The London Council of the Virginia Company, "Instructions to Sir Thomas Gates," 2:266.

88. Smith, *Proceedings*, 18.

89. Ibid., 19.

90. Mauss, *The Gift*. Some modern-day interpreters of Smith's texts sometimes view Powhatan's speeches as reflecting indigenous traditions. Such readings may inadvertantly deprive Native people of flexibility.

91. Smith, *Proceedings*, 19.

92. Ibid., 19–20.

93. See Vallance, "The Captivity of James II." See also Cormack and Mazzio, *Book Use, Book Theory*, 80–81.

94. Smith, *Proceedings*, 54.

95. Ibid., 57.

96. Ibid., 63.

97. Ibid., 64.

98. Ibid., 65.

99. Ibid., 67.

100. Ibid., 67–68.

101. Ibid., 69.

102. Ibid., 71.

103. See, for example, López de Gómara, *The Pleasant Historie of the Conquest of the Weast India*, 207–12; and Zárate, *The Discoverie and Conquest of the Provinces of Peru*, 29–31.

104. Smith, *Proceedings*, 78.

105. Ibid., 82.

106. Ibid., 83.

107. Pedro de Zúñiga to Philip III, June 26, 1608, in Barbour, ed., *Jamestown Voyages*, 1:163.

108. The English story about Savage involved two lies—that he was Newport's son, and that Newport was a sovereign of some kind. Smith, *Proceedings*, 19.

109. For an account of Namontack's visit, see Vaughan, *Transatlantic Encounters*, 45–50.

110. Pedro de Zúñiga to Philip III, June 26, 1608, in Barbour, ed., *Jamestown Voyages*, 1:163.

111. Zorzi Giustinian to the Doge and Senate, June 4, 1608, in *Calendar of State Papers . . . Venice*, XI, 261.

112. Pedro de Zúñiga to Philip III, September 22, 1607, in Barbour, ed., *Jamestown Voyages*, 1:115.

113. Pedro de Zúñiga to Philip III, January 24, 1607, in ibid., 1:69–70.

114. See Barbour, *Three Worlds*, for an account of Smith's travels in the Low Countries, 17–29.

115. Pedro de Zúñiga to Philip III, January 24, 1607, in Barbour, ed., *Jamestown Voyages*, 1:70.

116. See Mattingly, *Renaissance Diplomacy*, 198–208.

117. Pedro de Zúñiga to Philip III, March 15, 1609, in Barbour, ed., *Jamestown Voyages*, 2:257.

118. Zúñiga is misinformed on one detail. The Jamestown colonists did not claim that Thomas Savage was the son of James I. They claimed instead that he was the son of Newport.

119. Pedro de Zúñiga to Philip III, June 26, 1608, in Barbour, ed., *Jamestown Voyages*, 1:163.

120. See Jansson, "'The Hat Is No Expression of Honor,'" 26–34.

121. Qtd. and trans. in Jansson, "'The Hat Is No Expression of Honor,'" 27.

122. It should be noted that in making this claim the English were misrepresenting Powhatan succession, which was matrilineal. See Rountree, *Pocahontas, Powhatan, Opechancanough*, 23, 28, 77.

123. Pedro de Zúñiga to Philip III, March 15, 1609, in Barbour, ed., *Jamestown Voyages*, 2:257.

124. Zúñiga apparently acquired the map from an English source. See ibid., 1:257.

125. Pedro de Zúñiga to Philip III, March 15, 1609, in ibid., 2:258.

126. George Calvert to Sir Thomas Edmondes, August 1, 1612, in Brown, ed., *The

Genesis of the United States, 2:1067. See also the slightly different account by Chamberlain in Brown, ed., *Genesis*, 2:1067–68.

127. Spelman, "Relation of Virginea," cv.

128. Ibid., cxii.

129. Rice, *Nature and History*, 58.

130. See Richter, "Tsenacommacah and the Atlantic World," 58–59, for an account of this ceremony that has informed my own. Williamson, *Powhatan Lords*, 157, examines the sexual symbolism of this fertility ritual.

131. In his account of Virginia and the Powhatans, William Strachey recorded the lyrics of a Powhatan song, which suggest that Newport's gifts were viewed as a sign of weakness. Strachey translates the lyrics as reading, "[the Indians] killed us for all our poccasacks, that is our guns, and for all that Captain Newport brought them copper." Strachey, *Historie of Travaile*, 80.

Chapter 2. The Ransom of Pocahontas: Kidnapping and Dynastic Marriage in Jamestown and London

1. Hamor, *A True Discourse of the Present Estate of Virginia*, 6.

2. Ibid., title page.

3. On the print controversies over the direction of English colonial ventures in Virginia, see Fitzmaurice, "The Civic Solution to the Crisis of English Colonization."

4. For an account of the raid and the French diplomatic response, which explicitly challenged the boundaries of Virginia, see MacMillan, *Sovereignty and Possession*, 195–201; and Nicholls, *A Fleeting Empire*, 30. For the broader background, see Boucher, "Revisioning the 'French Atlantic.'"

5. See Diego de Molina to Alonso de Velasco [?], May 28, 1613, in Brown, ed., *Genesis*, 2:646–52, which indicts Virginia governors for what Molina believes to be their piratical intentions; and Diego de Molina to Diego Sarmiento de Acuña, June 14, 1614, in Brown, ed., *Genesis*, 2:743–45, written after Pocahontas's marriage. It is unlikely that Molina or any other Spanish or French prisoners attended the ceremony. However, they would undoubtedly have known about it, especially given that they were being held at the same fort as Pocahontas. Molina does not mention the ceremony in his letter, possibly because a marriage between an Englishman and a Powhatan queen would have undermined his argument that Jamestown was a piratical venture. For the negotiations to free them and a report on the state of the Virginia Colony, see Diego Sarmiento de Acuña to Philip III, October 5, 1613, in Brown, ed., *Genesis*, 2:659–62. An English captain, George Kendall, was also executed by Jamestown governors on suspicion of spying. See Magnel, "Francis Magnel's Relation of the First Voyage," 1:156.

6. Crowns publicized matches in lavish ceremonies, paintings and commemorative paraphernalia, and printed accounts of royal nuptials. See Warnicke, *The Marrying of Anne of Cleves.*

7. See Redworth, *The Prince and the Infanta.*

8. For the details of the abduction and marriage, see Rountree, *Pocahontas, Powhatan, Opechancanough,* 141–43, 156–57.

9. For an account of kidnapping and abduction throughout the British Atlantic world, see Colley, *Captives.* For an account of English and Native captivity in North America, see Kupperman, *The Jamestown Project,* 73–108. For accounts of the literature of captivity, see Greenblatt, *Marvelous Possessions,* 86–118; and Voigt, *Writing Captivity in the Early Modern Atlantic.*

10. Justinian codes generally distinguished between slave and freeborn captives. See Justinian, *Digest,* 49.11.15. The writings of Aquinas were another precedent for the taking and treatment of captives. For a discussion of Thomist justifications of captivity, see Russell, *The Just War in the Middle Ages,* 279.

11. In a commentary on Aquinas, Vitoria wrote, "A doubt arises as to whether or not it is permissible to seize men in war, taking them captive. I maintain, [in the first place,] that this is permissible. This fact is evident by the *jus gentium.* No [authority] censures this practice, nor does any condemn the captor to make restitution; on the contrary, such captors may retain these men until the latter are ransomed." Vitoria, "De Bello: On St. Thomas Aquinas," cxxiv. Alberico Gentili distinguished between captives and hostages, but endorsed the taking of both in just war. Gentili, *De Jure Belli Libri Tres,* 202–45.

12. See Richter, *Facing East from Indian Country,* 62–63, for a discussion of intertribal captivity. See also Rushforth, *Bonds of Alliance.*

13. For accounts of this visit see Rountree, *Pocahontas, Powhatan, Opechancanough,* 176–86; and Vaughan, *Transatlantic Encounters,* 77–112.

14. See Rountree, *Pocahontas, Powhatan, Opechancanough,* 76–82.

15. Fausz, "The 'Barbarous Massacre' Reconsidered."

16. Samuel Argall to Nicholas Hawes, June 1613, in Purchas, *Purchas His Pilgrimes,* 4:1765.

17. See Fausz, "Argall, Samuel," 1:197–99.

18. For these events, see Rice, "Escape from Tsenacommacah," 132.

19. Rountree, *Pocahontas, Powhatan, Opechancanough,* 160–61. The Jamestown colonists viewed Pocahontas as an important person, as Hamor's description of her "curteous usage" shows.

20. George Percy describes the murder of the Queen of the Paspaheghs and her children. "George Percy's Trewe Relacyon," 254.

21. See Rountree, *Pocahontas, Powhatan, Opechancanough*, 141–43, for the most complete account of Pocahontas's time in captivity.

22. See "International Convention Against the Taking of Hostages," in Lawson and Bertucci, eds., *Encyclopedia of Human Rights*, 696–98.

23. See Iwanisziw, "Hugh O'Neill and National Identity in Early Modern Ireland."

24. For New England Native peoples' collective memory of kidnapping (and desire for revenge), see Winslow, Bradford, and Cushman, *A Relation or Journall of the Beginning and Proceedings of the English Plantation*, 33.

25. See Kupperman, *The Jamestown Project*, 73–108; and Vaughan, *Transatlantic Encounters*. For a discussion of literary accounts of colonial captivity and hostaging, see Greenblatt, *Marvelous Possessions*, 86–152.

26. Purchas, *Pilgrimes*, 4:1764.

27. Ibid., 4:1764–65.

28. Ibid., 4:1765.

29. Ibid.

30. Vitoria had posited that "both masters and subjects" had to agree to treaties of subjection. Vitoria, "On the American Indians," in *Political Writings*, 288.

31. Iwanisziw, "Hugh O'Neill and National Identity in Early Modern Ireland," 33.

32. Purchas, *Pilgrimes*, 4:1765.

33. Ibid. In describing Powhatan's treatment of English captives, Argall referenced legal codes that provided for the protection of hostages during war. Vitoria, for example, argued that it was unjust to execute hostages because it did not help achieve victory. See Vitoria, "On the Law of War," in *Political Writings*, 319, 321–22.

34. Purchas, *Pilgrimes*, 4:1765.

35. Information from Argall's letter was widely discussed. See John Chamberlain to Sir Dudley Carleton, August 1, 1613, in *Letters of John Chamberlain*, 1:470–71. Foreign ambassadors viewed it as international news. For example, the Venetian ambassador Antonio Foscarini wrote to the Doge that "A ship has arrived here from Virginia which has caused universal rejoicing by the news of success. It appears that the soldiers of the colony have inflicted a great defeat upon the king of Poitan, and have taken prisoner one of his daughters, by reason of which he has offered friendship, peace and the knowledge of some rich gold mines." Foscarini to the Doge and Senate, August 9, 1613, in *Calender of State Papers . . . Venice*, XIII, 42. Other letters mentioned it as well. See Gregorio Barbarigo to the Venetian Cabinet, September 9, 1613, in *Calender of State Papers . . . Venice*, XIII, 82.

36. John Rolfe to Sir Thomas Dale, 1614, in Hamor, *True Discourse*, 67.

37. Hamor, *True Discourse*, n.p.

38. See Pagden, *Fall of Natural Man*, 10–56, for a discussion of Spanish debates about Indians' natural capacities.

39. Hamor, *True Discourse*, "To the Reader."

40. Ibid., 2.

41. Ibid., 3.

42. Ibid.

43. Ibid., 4.

44. Ibid.

45. Vitoria, among many other authorities, argued that "the law of nations (*jus gentium*) is clearly that travellers may carry on trade so long as they do no harm to the citizens; and second, in the same way it can be proved that this is lawful in divine law." Vitoria, "On the American Indians," in *Political Writings*, 279. In construing Argall's travel to the Patawomecks as a trade mission, Hamor seeks to give it legitimacy under this broadly accepted principle.

46. Hamor, *True Discourse*, 4.

47. Argall's portrait of reciprocal hostaging and military alliance was a more accurate description of both English and Patawomeck understandings of the trade alliance. After the kidnapping, the Patawomecks showed considerable autonomy in their dealings with the English. See Rice, *Nature and History*, 83–91.

48. Hamor, *True Discourse*, 4.

49. Ibid., 5.

50. Ibid., 5–6.

51. Rountree, *Pocahontas, Powhatan, Opechancanough*, 159.

52. Hamor, *True Discourse*, 4.

53. Ibid., 5.

54. Ibid., 6.

55. Ibid., 8.

56. Ibid., 10.

57. Ibid., 10–11.

58. Ibid., 11.

59. Ibid.

60. Ibid., 12.

61. Pulsipher, *Subjects unto the Same King*.

62. See Rice, "Escape from Tsenacommacah," 125–26, for the Anglo-Chickahominy alliance.

63. Hamor, *True Discourse*, 12.

64. Ibid., 12–13.

65. Ibid., 14.

66. Ibid., 13.

67. Ibid., 14.

68. Ibid., 2.

69. Ibid., 14.

70. Ibid., 15.

71. Ibid., 37.

72. Ibid., 38–39.

73. Ibid., 40.

74. Ibid., 42.

75. Ibid., 44.

76. Ibid., 46.

77. For historical debates about Pocahontas, see Tilton, *Pocahontas: The Evolution of an American Narrative*. See also Lemay, *Did Pocahontas Save Captain John Smith?*

78. For recent interpretations of the visit, see Vaughan, *Transatlantic Encounters*; and Rountree, *Pocahontas, Powhatan, Opechancanough*, 176–86. Robertson, "Pocahontas at the Masque," finds Pocahontas's voice in moments where a Native presence surfaces unexpectedly in European texts. Woodward, *Pocahontas*, reads the English archival record for evidence of Pocahontas's thoughts and intentions. Allen, *Pocahontas: Medicine Woman, Spy, Entrepreneur, Diplomat*, emphasizes Pocahontas's ability to navigate different roles.

79. See Vaughan, *Transatlantic Encounters*, 84, for the story of the negotiations before the visit. See Purchas, *Pilgrimes*, 4:1774, for an account of the company's financial investment in the visit. Chamberlain to Carleton, February 22, 1617, in *Letters of John Chamberlain*, 2:57, describes the cost.

80. For an account of what little is known about the couple's married life, see Rountree, *Pocahontas, Powhatan, Opechancanough*, 167.

81. Ibid., 178–79.

82. Smith, *Generall Historie*, 121.

83. See Rountree, *Pocahontas, Powhatan, Opechancanough*, 22, for an account of marriage in Tsenacomoco.

84. Ibid., 166. The fact that the English did not care about this previous marriage is characteristic of the English application of European legal systems to Native people. They recognized the marriage that benefited the Virginia Colony and quietly ignored complications arising from the first one.

85. See Vaughan, *Transatlantic Encounters*, 84, for an account of the Powhatan diplomatic retinue.

86. Chamberlain to Carleton, June 22, 1616, in *Letters of John Chamberlain*, 2:12.

87. For this story, see Vaughan, *Transatlantic Encounters*, 42.

88. De Passe later created portraits of notable diplomats such as Diego Sarmiento de Acuña, first Count of Gondomar, the ambassador from Spain, as well as important figures in English overseas endeavors, such as Sir Walter Raleigh. For more on Simon de Passe, see Wilks, "The Pike Charged," 200–201.

89. Purchas, *Pilgrimes*, 4:1774.

90. See Stevens, *The Poor Indians*, for an account of English evangelism to Native people.

91. Purchas, *Pilgrimes*, 4:1774.

92. Masques often supported James's foreign policy. See Holbrook, "Jacobean Masques and the Jacobean Peace."

93. This conflict is discussed in Antonio Foscarini to the Doge and Senate, January 23, 1615, in *Calender of State Papers . . . Venice*, XIII, 592. See also Mattingly, *Renaissance Diplomacy*, 264–68, for a discussion of Gondomar's relationship with other ambassadors.

94. See Giovanni Battista Lionello to the Doge and Senate, November 17, 1616, in *Calender of State Papers . . . Venice*, XIV, 512.

95. See Redworth, *The Prince and the Infanta*, 13–17.

96. A similar dispute led to an explosive diplomatic incident a year later, with the French ambassador asking to be recalled. See Sir Thomas Edmondes to Sir Dudley Carleton, March 13, 1618, in *Calender of State Papers . . . James*, IV, Addenda. Gondomar's triumph was temporary, as Charles married Henrietta Maria of France in 1625.

97. Chamberlain to Carleton, January 18, 1617, in *Letters of John Chamberlain*, 2:50. As a commoner, Rolfe was required to sit in the balcony. Uttamatomakkin stood in for her husband.

98. See Marcus, *The Politics of Mirth*, 64–76; Orrell, *The Theaters of Inigo Jones and John Webb*, 39; and Orgel, *The Jonsonian Masque*.

99. Barbour, *Pocahontas and Her World*, 177.

100. John Smith, who had witnessed one of these performances, even went so far as to describe it as "*A Virginia* Maske." "[T]hirtie young women came naked out of the woods," he wrote, "onely covered behind and before with a few greene leaves, their bodies all painted, some of one colour, some of another, but all differing, their leader had a fayre payre of Bucks hornes on her head, and an Otters skinne at her girdle, and another at her arme, a quiver of arrowes at her backe, a bow and arrowes in her hand; the next had in her hand a sword, another a club, another a pot-sticke; all horned alike: the rest every one with their severall devises. These fiends with most hellish shouts and cryes, rushing from among the trees, cast themselves in a ring about the fire, singing and dauncing with most excellent ill varietie, oft falling into their infernall passions, and solemnly againe to sing and daunce; having spent

neare an houre in this Mascarado, as they entred in like manner they departed." Smith, *Generall Historie*, 67. Powhatan girls labored behind the scenes of such festivities, preparing food. See Rountree, *Pocahontas, Powhatan, Opechancanough*, 76–77.

101. For a discussion of the function of these dances in the Jonsonian masque, see Johnson, *Ben Jonson*, 205.

102. Archer, "Relatyon," 92, reports that dancing was part of Powhatan diplomacy.

103. For speculation on this point, see Mossiker, *Pocahontas: The Life and the Legend*, 253.

104. Jonson, *The Irish Masque at Court*, ln. 140–41, in Jonson, *The Complete Masques*. For a discussion of this play that emphasizes imperial power and culture, see Howard, *The Politics of Courtly Dancing*, 126–28.

105. See Robertson, "Pocahontas at the Masque."

106. See Gleach, *Powhatan's World*, 109–22. See also Rice, "Escape from Tsenacommacah," 120.

107. Smith, *Generall Historie*, 122–23.

108. Ibid., 121.

109. Publishing a fabricated letter to the queen was potentially illegal. However, Queen Anne had died by the time *The Generall Historie* was published, and the details of her correspondence with colonial figures were beneath the notice of the councilors working under Charles I. Moreover, others who might have challenged Smith's account of his conversations with Pocahontas were either dead or in Virginia.

110. Smith, *Generall Historie*, 122.

111. Ibid.

112. It was common for early modern writers to invent conversations, though the practice was not as widespread by the seventeenth century. See Shapiro, *A Culture of Fact*, 41.

113. See Emerson, "Captain John Smith as Editor."

114. For letter writing in Tudor courts, see Lerer, *Courtly Letters in the Age of Henry VIII*. See also passing references in Smuts, *Court Culture and the Origins of a Royalist Tradition*.

115. In a process she terms "absurd transcription," Joyce E. Chaplin suggests that the English "may have accurately recorded true Indian statements because they believed them too ridiculous (absurd) to comment upon." Chaplin, *Subject Matter*, 28. While Smith did not view Pocahontas's statements as absurd, he also may have declined to edit them because the specifics were no longer important.

116. Smith, *Generall Historie*, 122. Some historians have viewed Smith's response as evidence of a genuine fear of appearing to have exceeded his authority in treaty negotiations with Powhatan. This interpretation makes a certain amount of sense, given Smith's prior

reputation as a usurper of authority. However, if Smith truly feared the impact of Pocahontas's words, he would have simply left them out of the book.

117. Smith, *Generall Historie*, 122–23.

118. For an account of Pocahontas's departure, see Vaughan, *Transatlantic Encounters*, 89.

119. Chamberlain to Carleton, January 18, 1617, in Letters of John Chamberlain, 2:50.

120. Vaughan, *Transatlantic Encounters*, 89.

121. See Fausz, "Opechancanough: Indian Resistance Leader," 21–37.

122. John Rolfe to Sir Edwin Sandys, June 8, 1617, in Kingsbury, ed., *The Records of the Virginia Company in London*, 3:71 (hereafter *VCR*). Rolfe reports these words as direct speech. However, he does not attribute them to any specific individual. Some scholars have believed that they are Pocahontas's deathbed words. This is not likely, however. After her death, Pocahontas's perspective on the future prospects of the alliance would have been irrelevant. More likely, Rolfe is reporting Powhatan's response to the news. This reading is corroborated by a report from Argall, which attributes similar phrasing to Powhatan around the same time. Hamor and Argall may have heard him say this when they told him the news, or a messenger reported it to them. However it reached them, the response confirms that the peace will hold even with the dissolution of the marriage.

123. "Governor Samuel Argall to the Virginia Company," March 10, 1617, 403.

124. Ibid., 404.

125. Samuel Argall to Council for Virginia, June 9, 1617, in *VCR*, 3:73–74.

1.26 Purchas, *Pilgrimes*, 4:1774.

127. See Vaughan, *Transatlantic Encounters*, 77.

128. See Rountree, *Pocahontas, Powhatan, Opechancanough*, 197, for an account of Uttamatomakkin's visit.

129. See The Governor and Council in Virginia, "The Putting Out of the Tenants that Came Over in the B.N. With Other Orders of the Councell," in *VCR*, 3:228.

130. The quotation is Sir Thomas Smith's paraphrase of a letter from Argall. Unnamed sources told Virginia Company officials that Argall was trying to exploit Pocahontas's child "to some espeaciall purpose," such as the acquisition of land or power for himself. Sir Thomas Smith et al., to Captain Samuel Argall, August 22, 1618, in *VCR*, 2:52–53.

131. Copland, *Virginia's God Be Thanked*, 9–10. The Virginia Company warned the colony "to have espetiall Care that no injurie or oppression bee wrought by the English against any of the Natives of that Countrie, wherby the present peace may bee disturbed and ancient quarrels (now buried) might bee revived." The Virginia Company, "Instructions to the Governor and Council of State in Virginia," in *VCR*, 3:469.

132. See Fausz, "The 'Barbarous Massacre' Reconsidered," for a discussion of the war and its causes.

133. Waterhouse, *A Declaration of the State of the Colony and Affaires in Virginia*, 22–23.

134. In 1623, Governor Francis Wyatt issued a proclamation "that no person whatsoever, (but only the chiefe Comander of any Plantation) shall hold any conference with any Indians (if at any time they shall in peacable maner resort unto them, and desire a parley) without first giuinge notice thereof to his Comander." Wyatt, "A Proclamation to bee carefull of the Savadges treacherie," in *VCR*, 4:167–68. In 1626, after continued skirmishes with the Powhatans, the Privy Council ordered Virginia Colony Governor George Yeardley to "strictly forbid all persons whatsoever to receive into their Houses any of the Indians, or to parly, converse or trade with them without especiall License and warrant given to that purpose." Privy Council, "Instructions to Yeardley, 1626," 395–96. In May 1623, Captain William Tucker poisoned and decapitated some Powhatans at a fraudulent treaty ceremony. Robert Bennett to Edward Bennett, June 9, 1623, *VCR*, 4:220–22.

Chapter 3. Gunpowder Diplomacy: Arms and Alliance in Plymouth and Patuxet

1. Winslow, *Good Newes from New-England*, 2. The following account is based on Winslow's.

2. For the kinds of arrows used by southern New England Native people, see Malone, *The Skulking Way of War*, 16.

3. Winslow, *Good Newes*, 3.

4. Ibid.

5. Ibid., 3, 3–4.

6. Ibid., 8.

7. Ibid., n.p.

8. For an account of early warfare between the English and coastal Native peoples, see Ferling, *A Wilderness of Miseries*; Steele, *Warpaths*; Chet, *Conquering the American Wilderness*; Grenier, *The First Way of War*; Chaplin, *Subject Matter*; and Lee, *Barbarians and Brothers*, 121–41. For an account of colonial weapons, including those used by the Pilgrims, see Peterson, *Arms and Armor in Colonial America*. For an overview of early modern weaponry, see Hall, *Weapons and Warfare in Renaissance Europe*.

9. See Given, *A Most Pernicious Thing*.

10. Modern international law generally draws a distinction between preemptive war, which is legitimate because it responds to an immediate threat, and preventive war, which is illegitimate because it is launched on the basis of a theoretical threat. On this distinction, see Doyle, *Striking First*. See also Flynn, *First Strike*; and Walzer, *Arguing About War*.

11. Bows and arrows "might be shown to the foe as a sign of imminent battle, placed in graves with fallen warriors, or offered to the gods." Chaplin, *Subject Matter*, 113.

12. See Peterson, *Arms and Armor*, 20, 44.

13. See Jennings, *The Invasion of America*, 131–34; and Salisbury, *Manitou and Providence*, 113–25. The Pilgrims did not carry the wide-flared blunderbusses often depicted in stereotypical images. Most of the guns they brought with them were matchlocks, in addition to a smaller number of flint weapons. Peterson, *Arms and Armor*, 44.

14. In viewing the Pilgrims as cosmopolitan figures, rather than religious dissenters on the edge of the wilderness, I am informed by recent work that has considered the transatlantic and international dimensions of the settlement of Plymouth. See Anderson, *William Bradford's Books*; Breen, *Transgressing the Bounds*; and Cohen, *The Networked Wilderness*, 65–91.

15. For an account of Anglo-Dutch conferences, see Clark and van Eysinga, *The Colonial Conferences Between England and The Netherlands in 1613 and 1615*.

16. See MacMillan, *Sovereignty and Possession*, 194–201. Bradford was cautious about any interactions with the French. See Bradford, *Of Plymouth Plantation*, 99.

17. Peterson, *Arms and Armor*, 44. Peterson suggests the Pilgrims may have also had flint weapons as well as wheel locks.

18. The English had not always been confident of their military superiority over Native peoples. In the sixteenth century, many English travelers believed that Native weapons were superior. As Chaplin, *Subject Matter*, shows, however, by the seventeenth century the English had begun to view themselves as the technological superiors of Indians and to assume that their weapons would intimidate Native peoples into acquiescence.

19. De Gheyn's book was only the most recent guide to arms and their use. Others less likely to have been available to the Pilgrims were Gates, *The Defence of Militarie profession* (1579); Barwick, *A Breefe Discourse, Concerning the force and effect of all manuall weapons of fire* (1592); and Johnson, *The nine Worthies of London Explaining the honourable exercise of Armes* (1592).

20. On the intelligence used to justify the attack, see Salisbury, *Manitou and Providence*, 130–31.

21. See Salisbury, "Squanto." The details of Squanto's early interactions with Europeans are not entirely clear. In 1614, he was kidnapped and sold into slavery in Spain by Captain Thomas Hunt. He was later smuggled out, brought to London, and eventually taken to Newfoundland, where he acted as a guide and navigator before making his way home. Another tradition, probably spurious, holds that he was earlier kidnapped in 1605 by Captain George Waymouth. For an account of the many stories of Squanto's origins (and the degree of their likelihood), see Ceci, "Squanto and the Pilgrims."

22. See Winship, *Godly Republicanism*, 85; and Wright, *The Early English Baptists*, 16–20.

23. See Marchant, *The Puritans and the Church Courts in the Diocese of York*, 149–59.

24. George, *John Robinson and the English Separatist Tradition*, 57–92.

25. Bradford, *Of Plymouth Plantation*, 17.

26. For anxieties about the Dutch and fear of Spanish invasion, see Bradford, *Of Plymouth Plantation*, 25, 23. According to Bradford, the Pilgrims reasoned that "the Spaniard might prove as cruel as the savages of America." Bradford, *Of Plymouth Plantation*, 27.

27. Ibid., 28. For the broader context, see Lorimer, "The Failure of the English Guiana Ventures 1595–1667 and James I's Foreign Policy."

28. Bradford, *Of Plymouth Plantation*, 31.

29. For this entire episode, see ibid., 29–34.

30. Ibid., 75–76.

31. See MacMillan, *Sovereignty and Possession*, 194–201, for an account of Anglo-French negotiations during this period.

32. Willison, *Saints and Strangers*, 102–20, 146–57.

33. On the French context, see Skinner, *The Upper Country*, and Podruchny, *Making the Voyageur World*. On the Dutch activities, see Merwick, *The Shame and the Sorrow*, 1–56.

34. Salisbury, *Manitou and Providence*, 76.

35. See Given, *A Most Pernicious Thing*, 53.

36. James I, "A Proclamation prohibiting interloping and disorderly Trading," 1:151.

37. Given, *A Most Pernicious Thing*, 53–54. This did not mean that European traders ceased trafficking weapons to Indian country, nor that colonial governments felt secure. Bradford lamented that the French had "made a common trade" of firearms and worried about the threat that the trade might pose to the survival of Plymouth. Bradford, *Of Plymouth Plantation*, 204.

38. Given, *A Most Pernicious Thing*, 53.

39. See Cook, "The Significance of Disease."

40. On these realignments, see Salisbury, *Manitou and Providence*, 104–6.

41. Willison, *Saints and Strangers*, 145.

42. Smith would write that "God had laid this country open for us, and slaine the most part of the inhabitants by cruell warres and a mortall disease; for where I had seene 100 or 200 people, there is scarce ten to be found." Smith, *New Englands Trials*, n.p. Such statements had clear implications for the right to occupy a territory under the law of nations.

43. Morton, *New English Canaan*, 23.

44. For the plague as an expression of God's providence, see Bradford, *Of Plymouth Plantation*, 270.

45. See Salisbury, *Manitou and Providence*, 50–140.

46. Winslow et al., *Relation*, title page. For more on Plymouth Colony alliances in the fur trade, see Van Zandt, *Brothers Among Nations*, 86–115.

47. For this incident and its fallout, see Van Zandt, *Brothers Among Nations*, 55–56.

48. Bradford, *Of Plymouth Plantation*, 447.

49. For the intertwined history of this pair, see Humins, "Squanto and Massasoit." On Squanto in particular, see Bradford, *Of Plymouth Plantation*, 81.

50. Bradford, *Of Plymouth Plantation*, 79–80.

51. Winslow et al., *Relation*, 36.

52. Ibid., 37.

53. Ibid., 35.

54. Ibid., 37.

55. See Salisbury, *Manitou and Providence*, 115.

56. In *A True Relation*, John Smith had described his refusal of Powhatan's demands that English visitors disarm in his presence: "he expected to have all these men lay their armes at his feet, as did his subjects. I tolde him that was a ceremonie our enemies desired, but never our Friends." *True Relation*, n.p.

57. Winslow et al., *Relation*, 40–41.

58. See Salisbury, *Manitou and Providence*, 119.

59. Winslow, *Good Newes*, 21.

60. Morton, *New-Englands Memoriall*, 29. Neal Salisbury has pointed out that Morton's list of signatories to the treaty includes two Massachusett sachems, Obbatinewat and Chicka-taubut. According to an account by Bradford, the colony did not make contact with them until September 18 at the earliest, meaning the sachems could not have been present for the September 13 negotiations. Salisbury concludes that Morton or some other party added the Massachusetts' names to the list of signatories so that their later alleged conspiracy against the English would appear to be a violation of the treaty. Salisbury, *Manitou and Providence*, 120.

61. Winslow et al., *Relation*, 55.

62. Bradford, *Of Plymouth Plantation*, 93n3.

63. See Willison, *Saints and Strangers*, 233.

64. Winslow et al., *Relation*, title page.

65. Ibid., n.p.

66. Ibid., 31.

67. Ibid., 32.

68. Ibid., 33.

69. Ibid., 32–33.

70. Ibid., 33.

71. Ibid., 36.

72. Ibid., 37.

73. Ibid.

74. Ibid., 38.

75. Ibid., 54. Here Bradford referenced the notion that women and children should be spared in war as innocent civilians. See Vitoria, "On the Law of War," in *Political Writings*, 314.

76. Winslow et al., *Relation*, 54–55.

77. On the frequent accidental firing of matchlocks, which required keeping a lit match near powder at all times, see Peterson, *Arms and Armor*, 19.

78. Winslow et al., *Relation*, 55.

79. Ibid., 57.

80. Ibid., 59.

81. Ibid., 61.

82. Ibid., 69.

83. Ibid., 68.

84. See Gentili, *De Jure Belli*, 81, for a theory of joint Christian-pagan rule of territory.

85. Winslow et al., *Relation*, 68.

86. Ibid., 69.

87. Ibid.

88. Winslow, *Good Newes*, 1.

89. Ibid., 42.

90. Ibid., 7.

91. John Robinson to Bradford, December 19, 1623, in Bradford, *Of Plymouth Plantation*, 374–75.

92. For a comparison between the two, see Jehlen, "The Literature of Colonization," in *The Cambridge History of American Literature*, 1:90.

93. Winslow, *Good Newes*, 33.

94. Vitoria, "On the Law of War," in *Political Writings*, 316.

95. Grotius, *De Jure Belli*, 184.

96. Ibid., 173.

97. Winslow, *Good Newes*, 24.

98. Ibid., 26.

99. Ibid., 28. See Cohen, *Networked Wilderness*, 72–82, for a reading of this scene that places it in the context of early modern understandings of the domestic arts.

100. Winslow, *Good Newes*, 29.

101. Ibid., 30.

102. Ibid., 32.

103. Ibid., 35.

104. Ibid., 35–36.

105. Ibid., 42.

106. Ibid., 43.

107. Ibid., 44.

108. Ibid., 46–47.

109. Winslow, "Brief Relation," in *Good Newes*, 1.

110. Ibid., 1–2.

111. For the history of this stereotype, see Greenblatt, "Invisible Bullets."

112. Bradford, *Of Plymouth Plantation*, 81.

113. Winslow, *Good Newes*, 10.

114. Ibid., 10–11.

115. Hariot, *A brief and true report of the new found land of Virginia*, n.p.

116. Stephen Greenblatt, "Invisible Bullets," argues that the passage is an allegory of the workings of power and language in the early modern period. White, "Invisible Tagkanysough," and Silva, *Miraculous Plagues*, 54–61, have offered powerful readings of the story that trace it across multiple Native sources and reveal how Native peoples used such narratives to comprehend the changes of the settlement period. White argues that in Hariot's lines we can see Native people performing a counter-ethnography that challenges Hariot's own colonialist reduction of Native culture. Silva makes an equal claim for the oppositional power of the story, viewing it as a form of indigenous resistance to the settlers' self-justifying accounts of open land emptied by plague.

117. White, "Invisible Tagkanysough."

118. Winslow, *Good Newes*, 8.

119. Bradford, *Of Plymouth Plantation*, 114.

120. The 1691 charter of the Massachusetts Bay Colony merged the two. See "The Charter of Massachusetts Bay," 1691.

Chapter 4. Trading Sovereignty: The Fur Trade and the Freedom of the Seas

1. Zee and Zee, *A Sweet and Alien Land*, 31, details the involvement of the Plymouth Council for New England in pressing English authorities to impound the ship. For a history of the *Eendracht* that emphasizes Dutch relationships with Native America, see Merwick, *The Shame and the Sorrow*, 78–85.

2. "The King to Lord Baltimore," 3:79. The quotation is the king's later summary of the licenses in a letter chastising Calvert for the action.

3. For accounts of this incident, see Fausz, "Merging and Emerging Worlds," 71; Rice, *Nature and History*, 100; and Russo and Russo, *Planting an Empire*, 1–2.

4. For an account of the genre of the appeal in English colonial contexts, see Bilder, "Salamanders and Sons of God."

5. Spanish diplomats portrayed the trading activities of French, Dutch, and English ships as a form of piratical incursion into Spanish waters. For Spanish and Portuguese debates about the laws of the seas, see Anand, *Origin and Development of the Law of the Sea*, 1–71. For the role of Spanish and Portuguese maritime claims in sparking pan-European debates about the laws of the seas, see Theutenberg, "Mare Clausum et Mare Liberum."

6. For the competing articulation of these principles by European crowns and their advisors, see Anand, *Origin and Development of the Law of the Sea*, 72–108.

7. Grotius, *The Freedom of the Seas*, 7. For an account of Grotius's role in developing the idea of free seas, see Roelofsen, "Grotius and the International Politics of the Seventeenth Century," 95.

8. For example, in 1599 Elizabeth challenged the seizure of several English ships by the Danish-Norwegian crown by citing the notion of *mare liberum*. See Theutenberg, "Mare Clausum et Mare Liberum," 484.

9. See Vieira, "*Mare Liberum* vs. *Mare Clausum*."

10. Selden, *Mare clausum*. For more on the intellectual context surrounding Selden and his engagement with Grotius, see Sommerville, "Selden, Grotius, and the Seventeenth-Century Intellectual Revolution in Moral and Political Theory."

11. James I, "Instructions to English commissioners."

12. This chapter follows anthropologist Ives Goddard in using the name "Delaware" to refer to groups with related language and customs around the Delaware and Hudson Rivers. Goddard, "Delaware." Delawares living around southeastern New York and speaking the Munsee dialect are referred to as "Munsee." "Delaware" is used in instances where Dutch sources were not specific about the tribal identity or geographic location of indigenous allies. For a discussion of the complexities (and anachronisms) of Delaware naming, see Otto, *The Dutch-Munsee Encounter in America*, 4–5.

13. As Merwick has observed in her account of the *Eendracht* seizure, the ship became "caught in a net of larger issues" that spanned the Atlantic world. Merwick, *The Shame and the Sorrow*, 80. For more on the massacre, see Chancey, "The Amboyna Massacre in English Politics." The attack at Ambon Island formed the basis for a Black Legend of Dutch colonialism that was propagated in ballads such as *Newes out of East India* (1624).

14. For the competing claims to Saint Martin, see Merwick, *The Shame and the Sorrow*, 4. See also Adams, "Spain or the Netherlands? The Dilemmas of Early Stuart Foreign Policy."

15. Gerrit van Arnhem, a deputy of the States General, believed that "this intrigue was

set on foot by the Spanish Ambassador in England." Gerrit van Arnhem to the States General, April 5, 1632, in O'Callaghan, ed., *Documents Relative to the Colonial History of the State of New York*, 1:45 (hereafter cited as *CHSNY*).

16. Charles I, "Answer to the Remonstrance of the Dutch Ambassadors," 1:58.

17. Seed, *Ceremonies of Possession*, 155.

18. For the early history of the Dutch West India Company and its monopoly, see Jacobs, *The Colony of New Netherland*, 20–31. For the broader context, see Schmidt, *Innocence Abroad*.

19. See Clark and Van Eysinga, *The Colonial Conferences Between England and The Netherlands*.

20. Otto, *Dutch-Munsee Encounter*, 54.

21. Ibid., 86.

22. Quoted and trans. in Merwick, *The Shame and the Sorrow*, 69.

23. Otto, *The Dutch-Munsee Encounter*, 61.

24. Albertus Joachimi and Govert Brasser to the States General, April 10, 1632, in *CHSNY*, 1:48.

25. For the history of this idea, see Roelofsen, "Grotius and the International Politics of the Seventeenth Century," 95.

26. The defenders of the *Eendracht* were not the last Dutch diplomats to try this strategy. In a 1634 plea to the States General concerning the expulsion of the trader Jacob Elkens, for example, Dutch officials cited the documentary trail left behind by their engagements with Native peoples, suggesting that Dutch colonial sovereignty derives from "divers deeds of conveyance and cession, executed in favor of the Patroons of the Colonies by the Sachems and Chief Lords of the Indians, and those who had any thing to say therein." "The Assembly of the XIX. to the States General," 1:94. In addition to acknowledging the rights of the sachems, the plea also recognizes all of those "who had any thing to say therein," suggesting that the exchanges have broad consent from all parties involved.

27. West India Company to the States General, May 5, 1632, 1:52.

28. See Wilson, *The Savage Republic*, 213, for an account of the meaning of confederation in the political theory of Grotius. For the broader history of the Dutch Republic, see Israel, *The Dutch Republic*; and Prak, *The Dutch Republic in the Seventeenth Century*.

29. Wouter van Twiller to Governor of Massachusetts Bay, October 4, 1633, quoted in Stokes, *The Iconography of Manhattan Island*, 4:79. See the discussion of this letter in Merwick, *The Shame and the Sorrow*, 82.

30. States General, "Remonstrance of the Ambassadors of the States General to King Charles I," 1:56.

31. Charles I, "Answer to the Remonstrance of the Dutch Ambassadors," 1:58.

32. Ibid., 1:60.

33. "Letter of Sir Francis Wyatt," 118.

34. Smith, *Proceedings*, 38–39.

35. For the above history, see Jennings, "Glory, Death, and Transfiguration." In 1615, they had also formed a short-lived alliance with Samuel de Champlain against the Onondagas.

36. J. Frederick Fausz has described how a group of oligarchy-minded Virginia leaders took control of the government of the colony in the aftermath of the war and sought to expand its political and economic influence into the Potomac. This new ruling elite benefited from the revocation of the company's charter and the assertion of direct royal control over the colony in 1624. The change gave colonial leaders broad latitude to pursue their own political and economic interests without supervision from the company. Fausz, "Merging and Emerging Worlds." For this period in Virginia history, see also Van Zandt, *Brothers Among Nations*, 116–36; and Rice, *Nature and History*, 92–107.

37. For an account of Claiborne's embattled life, see Hale, *Virginia Venturer*. For his commercial ventures (and those of other members of his class), see Olson, "The Virginia Merchants of London."

38. For an account of Calvert's life, see Krugler, *English and Catholic*, esp. 77–151, which describes the Calverts' colonial enterprises.

39. The Virginia Colony received Calvert with hostility. See John Pott et al., to the Council, November 30, 1629, in Browne, ed., *The Archives of Maryland*, 3:17 (hereafter cited as *Archives of Maryland*).

40. See Biggar, *The Early Trading Companies of New France*, 156–60. For a more recent account that emphasizes the role of the law of nations in Anglo-French negotiations, see MacMillan, *Sovereignty and Possession*, 198–201. Fausz, "Merging and Emerging Worlds," 61–62, describes the role of English fur traders in funding the English seizures of Port Royal, Tadoussac, and Quebec during the Anglo-French War.

41. Fausz, "Merging and Emerging Worlds," 62. For a broader discussion of Claiborne's relationships with Cloberry, see Brenner, *Merchants and Revolution*, 120–24. Sir William Alexander, the secretary of state for Scotland, and Maurice Thomson, a successful and well-connected colonial merchant, were also part of Claiborne's concern.

42. Charles I, "Articles of Exchequer," 2:527.

43. For these details, see Harrison, *History of Talbot County Maryland*, 1:497. For the broader history of the settlement, see Isaac, "Kent Island, Part I."

44. The operation was not without its problems. The Susquehannock demand for trade goods and the high cost of skilled labor threatened its profitability, yet Maryland was a far greater threat. See Fausz, "Merging and Emerging Worlds," 63–64.

45. "The Charter of Maryland," 3:1677.

46. See Fausz, "Merging and Emerging Worlds," 65.

47. Privy Council, "Considerations upon the Patent to the Lord Baltimore," 3:17.

48. Ibid., 3:19.

49. Claiborne, "Claiborne's Petition and Accompanying Papers," 5:165. Many of the records of Claiborne's dispute with the Calverts come from a petition he submitted to Charles II from 1676 to 1677.

50. For these events, see Thornton, "The Thrusting Out of Governor Harvey."

51. Claiborne, "Claiborne's Petition and Accompanying Papers," 5:162–63.

52. Claiborne, "A Breviate of Captain Claiborne's Petition to His Majesty," 3:32.

53. I draw my account of the following from Krugler, *English and Catholic*, 49–76.

54. The oath was administered to all members of the Privy Council and both houses of Parliament. Many Protestants viewed the oath as a means of identifying disloyal Catholics. In 1624, Calvert himself administered the oath to Cornelius O'Sullivan, an accused Papist. Krugler, *English and Catholic*, 73. Calvert's later refusal to take the oath inspired whispers about his loyalty. These grew louder after James's death and Charles's more energetic enforcement of uniformity. See Krugler, *English and Catholic*, 21–24, 85, for a discussion of these oaths.

55. Pott et al., to the Council, November 30, 1629, in *Archives of Maryland*, 3:17.

56. He continued to circulate it as late as 1677. See Van Zandt, *Brothers Among Nations*, 187–91.

57. Claiborne, "Claiborne's Petition and Accompanying Papers," 5:165.

58. Ibid., 5:167.

59. Charles I, "The King to the Governor and Council of Virginia," 3:29.

60. Calvert, "The humble Petition of Cecill Lord Baltimore," 3:69.

61. Lord Commissioners for Plantations., "Order Uppon Captain William Cleyborne & his Partners Petion against the Lord Baltemore," 3:72.

62. Ibid., 3:72–73.

63. See Fausz, "Merging and Emerging Worlds," 71.

64. See Jennings, "Glory, Death, Transfiguration," 15.

65. Jennings, *The Ambiguous Iroquois Empire*, 27. See also the discussion in Jennings, "Susquehannock," 15:367.

66. Fausz, "Merging and Emerging Worlds," 81–84, and Rice, *Nature and History*, 105, tell the story of this reversal.

67. See Jennings, *The Ambiguous Iroquois Empire*, 121–22, for the story of this treaty.

68. For an account of Calvert's failed attempts to enter into the Susquehannock trade, see Fausz, "Merging and Emerging Worlds," 73.

69. See Jennings, "Glory, Death, and Transfiguration," 20.

70. After the colony's successful suit against Claiborne, Maryland's fortunes had taken a turn for the worse as well. In 1648, the new governor, William Stone, repopulated the colony by letting in Protestant immigrants lured by rising tobacco prices. See Menard, "Population, Economy, and Society," 71, 81. Baltimore aided this repopulation effort by passing the 1649 Act Concerning Religion, which guaranteed Protestant rights while shielding Catholic settlers from persecution. For the text of the act, see Maryland General Assembly, "An Act Concerning Religion." See also Russo and Russo, *Planting an Empire*, 77.

71. See Rice, *Nature and History*, 92–107.

72. "Articles of Peace and freindshipp," 3:277.

73. Ibid.

74. Bohaker, "Nindoodemag: The Significance of Algonquian Kinship Networks."

75. Lyons, *X-marks*, 2.

76. Ibid., 3.

77. "Articles of Peace and freindshipp," 3:277.

78. Ibid., 3:278.

79. Jennings, *Ambiguous Iroquois Empire*, 122.

80. "Agreement between the Proprietary and Commissioners."

81. For this history, see Jennings, "Glory, Death, and Transfiguration."

Chapter 5. Gift of an Empire: The Land Market and the Law of Nations in Narragansett Bay

1. Shurtleff, ed., *Records of the Governor and Company of the Massachusetts Bay*, 1:160.

2. Roger Williams to John Winthrop, June 14, 1638, in Williams, *Correspondence*, 1:165.

3. See Anderson, *New England's Generation*.

4. For an account of the Antinomian controversy and related disputes, see Winship, *Making Heretics*. Gura, *A Glimpse of Sion's Glory*, considers New England dissenters in the context of Puritan radicalism in England. Salisbury, *Manitou and Providence*, 190–202, describes the emigration of religious dissenters to Narragansett Bay.

5. Williams to Winthrop, June 14, 1638, in *Correspondence*, 1:163.

6. Throughout the 1630s, Sir Ferdinando Gorges was lobbying to bring about the recall of the charter of the Massachusetts Bay Colony, and he was eager to assist renegades or dissenters. See Andrews, *The Colonial Period of American History*, 1:400–430.

7. For more on the genre of the appeal and its transatlantic history, see Bilder, "Salamanders and Sons of God."

8. See Field, *Errands into the Metropolis*, for an account of New England religious dis-

senters' transatlantic travels and lobbying campaigns. Cesarini, "The Ambivalent Uses of Roger Williams's *A Key into the Language of America*," describes the transatlantic public relations contest between Williams and agents of the Massachusetts Bay Colony.

9. Chaplin, "Enslavement of Indians in Early America," 64.

10. Williams, *The Hireling Ministry None of Christs*, n.p.

11. Ibid., 4.

12. Nussbaum, *Liberty of Conscience*, argues that Williams's work embodies a notion of political ethics and civic inclusiveness that is derived from religion. Goodman, "Banishment, Jurisdiction, and Identity in Seventeenth-Century New England," argues that Williams's tutelage under Sir Edward Coke and his experience with English common law was an important source of his insistence on the heterogeneous nature of individual experience before the law. Felker, "Roger Williams's Uses of Legal Discourse," considers Williams's arguments in the context of ideas of language embedded in English common-law traditions. I am emphasizing another source of Williams's position: the Roman-derived bodies of law regulating the transfer of land from one polity to another.

13. Immediately on arriving, Williams turned down a ministerial position in Boston and demanded that any practicing ministers make a declaration of separation from the Anglican Church. He also argued against the mixing of state and church in the use of oaths in civil contexts and the incorporation of the First Table (or first four commandments) into civil law. Gaustad, *Liberty of Conscience*, 31–38.

14. "The Charter of Massachusetts Bay," 1852. While the governors of the Massachusetts Bay Colony were vigilant about European threats, Spain and France were preoccupied by the outbreak of what would come to be known as the Thirty Years' War, and had largely abandoned diplomatic protests about English colonial holdings in North America. The English colonies' nearest European neighbor, New Netherland, was certainly a trade rival, but its governors possessed none of the territorial ambitions of their English neighbors. Because the land around the Massachusetts Bay Colony was sparsely populated, vacated by the plague introduced by Europeans years earlier, the Massachusetts Bay Colony claimed rights based on *vacuum domicilium*, or the idea that empty land became the possession of the Christians who settled it. As John White, an advocate of Massachusetts Bay settlement, put it in a promotional pamphlet, the plague had "swept away most of the Inhabitants all along the Sea-coast, and in some places utterly consumed man, woman & childe, so that there is no person left to lay claime to the soyle which they possessed." White, *The Planters Plea*, 25. Ultimately, the arguments of Williams and others would demand more sophisticated justifications from the governors of the Massachusetts Bay Colony.

15. The official policy of the Massachusetts Bay Colony was to purchase land from any Natives who might "pretend" to ownership, so that the colony could maintain its credibility as

an economic venture and "avoyde the least scruple of intrusion" from the crown or nearby Europeans. The Massachusetts Bay Company, "The Company's First General Letter of Instructions to Endicott and His Council," 90. The company was sure that "the Natives [would be] willing to treat & compound . . . upon very easie Conditions." The Massachusetts Bay Company, "The Company's Second General Letter of Instructions to Endicott and His Council," 98. For more on the Massachusetts Bay Colony's legal justifications for settlement, see Salisbury, *Manitou and Providence*, 172–82. For Winthrop's early meetings with Native leaders, see Winthrop, *Journal*, 35, 47, 51, 54. These meetings involved the extension of hospitality and the exchange of corn, beer, tobacco, cheese, and "other small thinges." Winthrop, *Journal*, 47.

16. Cotton, "Master John Cotton's Answer to Master Roger Williams," 2:46.

17. Winthrop, *Journal*, 107. According to Winthrop, Williams's vindication of Native sellers proceeded less from a specific concern with Native sovereignty than from Williams's belief that a charter issued in the name of the state church represented an invasion of secular power into religious matters. "There were 3: passages cheifly wherat [the magistrates] were muche offended," Winthrop wrote, "1: for that he Chargeth Kinge James to have tould a solemne publicke lye: because in his Patente he blessed God that he was the first Christian Prince that had discovered this land. 2: for that he chargethe him & others with blasphemy for callinge Europe Christendom or the Christian world: 3: for that he did personally apply to our present Kinge Charles . . . 3: places in the Revelation." *Journal*, 107. The three verses were Rev. 16:13–14, Rev. 17:12–14, and Rev. 18:9. Winthrop, *Journal*, 107n42.

18. The letter concerned "the *Evill* of that part of the *Pattent* which respects the *Donation of Land.*" Williams, *The Bloody Tenent Yet More Bloody*, 277.

19. Cotton, "Answer," 2:46.

20. Salisbury, *Manitou and Providence*, 195–96.

21. Winthrop, *Journal*, 163–64.

22. Ibid., 163. For an account of the events leading up to Williams's banishment, see LaFantasie, "The Road to Banishment," in Williams, *Correspondence*, 1:12–23.

23. Williams to John Mason and Thomas Prence, June 22, 1670, in *Correspondence*, 2:610.

24. The Dutch executed Tatobem because the Pequots had attacked a trading party cutting across their land to reach a Dutch trading post. For the broader history of Dutch-Native alliances in New Netherland, see Meuwese, *Brothers in Arms, Partners in Trade*, 228–85.

25. On the war, its context, and aftermath, see Cave, *The Pequot War*. See also Salisbury, *Manitou and Providence*, 222–25, on the justifications for the massacre of the Pequots.

26. See Williams to Winthrop, July 15, 1637, in *Correspondence*, 1:101–2; and Wil-

liams to Winthrop, July 31, 1637, in *Correspondence*, 108–9. For an account of Williams's shifting positions on this issue, see Newell, "Indian Slavery in Colonial New England."

27. For accounts of the tribe during the settlement era, see Salisbury, *Manitou and Providence*, 228–35; Robinson, "A Narragansett History from 1000 B.P. to the Present," 79–89; Robinson, "Lost Opportunities," 13–28; Rubertone, *Grave Undertakings*; and Simmons, "Narragansett."

28. As Paul A. Robinson has shown, the powerful position of the Narragansetts in Dutch trading networks involved the tribe in tensions between English settlers and other groups active in the wampum trade. Robinson, "A Narragansett History."

29. Salisbury, *Manitou and Providence*, 228–35.

30. See Underhill, *Newes from America*, 42–43.

31. Salisbury, *Manitou and Providence*, 228, 231.

32. Williams to Winthrop, June 14, 1638, in *Correspondence*, 1:163,165.

33. Ibid., 1:165n13.

34. Willian Coddington reported that John Cotton derisively referred to Williams as "a *Haberdasher* of *small Questions* against the *Power*." Coddington to George Fox, April 28, 1677, in Fox, *A New-England-Fire-Brand Quenched*, 2:246.

35. Williams to Winthrop, June 14, 1638, in *Correspondence*, 1:164–65.

36. Rogers, Carpenter, and Field, eds., *The Early Records of the Town of Providence*, 5:307.

37. In describing Canonicus and Miantonomi as "shy & jellowes," Williams employs the stereotype of the Indian giver. In a study of colonial writing about Indian giving, David Murray has pointed to the prevalence of this stereotype as evidence of a European "misrecognition" of Native gift-giving practices. Murray, *Indian Giving*, 19. "In European accounts of Indians," he writes, "we find on the one hand the enduring idea of generosity, cultures without market calculation, and on the other the idea of calculation, even coercion, that the phrase 'Indian gift' reflects." Murray, *Indian Giving*, 35.

38. "Deed from Cannaunicus and Miantonomi to Roger Williams," 1:18.

39. Winthrop, *Journal*, 413, describes the submission.

40. Field testified that "William Arnold, to obtain his own ends, to deprive us of our right of the said lands of Pawtuxet, that we might have nothing to show for it . . . cunningly cut out or otherwise got out of the said evidence all concerning the said our right of Pawtuxett and pasted the said writing together again so cunningly that it could hardly be discerned but by those who well knew by rote what was formerly in the Evidence." Providence Town Records, 01293; qtd. in Field, ed., *State of Rhode Island and Providence Plantations at the End of the Century*, 1:30n1.

41. See Salisbury, *Manitou and Providence*, 229–30. Cogley, *John Eliot's Mission to the*

Indians before King Philip's War, 23, discusses these political maneuvers in the context of colonial evangelism.

42. See Field, *Errands into the Metropolis*, 26–47, for an account of Williams's transatlantic campaign.

43. For an account of this committee in the context of the English Revolution, see Brenner, *Merchants and Revolution*, 521–22.

44. Stearns, "The Weld-Peter Mission to England."

45. For the patent, see "Charter of Narragansett to Massachusetts." According to Richard W. Cogley, Weld likely stressed issues of population growth, evangelism, and the importance of defusing Williams's theological radicalism as reasons that the Massachusetts Bay Colony's patent should be extended to include the Narragansett Bay. Cogley, *John Eliot's Mission*, 25–26. Weld's and Peter's embassy also involved dealing with any fallout from the Antinomian controversy. Dillon, *The Gender of Freedom*, 49–115, finds in Weld's and Peter's publications novel representations of gender that embody an emergent liberal political order.

46. Cesarini, "The Ambivalent Uses of Roger Williams's *A Key into the Language of America.*"

47. Field, *Errands into the Metropolis*, 33, 137n60.

48. Williams, *Key*, n.p.

49. Ibid., title page.

50. Ibid., n.p.

51. Ibid., n.p.

52. The Committee for Foreign Plantations also invited scholars and translators in the hopes of gathering information about potential colonial outposts. See Field, *Errands into the Metropolis*, 33.

53. Williams, *Key*, n.p.

54. Lechford, *Plain Dealing*, 21.

55. Williams, *Key*, 47.

56. Ibid., 48.

57. Cotton, *Gods Promise to His Plantation*, 5.

58. Such a purchase was theoretically provided for by Justinian and many other authorities on the law of nations. Justinian, *Institutes*, 2.1.40.

59. Cotton, "Reply to Mr. Williams," 2:47.

60. Williams, *Key*, 92.

61. Ibid., 101.

62. Ibid., 93.

63. Ibid., 57–58. In his account of Williams's writings and career, David Murray has pointed to the breaking of the sticks as an example of how Williams ironically juxtaposes

Indian words and English epithets in order to unsettle racial categories. Far from being "Barbarians" incapable of exchanging land or producing goods, the Narragansetts are revealed to have sophisticated record-keeping technologies. Murray, *Indian Giving*, 98–99.

64. Williams to Winthrop, August 20, 1637, in *Correspondence*, 1:112. Matt Cohen has argued that Williams's description of the stick would have summoned associations with the tally stick, a centuries-old English technology for keeping track of debts. Cohen, *The Networked Wilderness*, 110–11. The tally was a notched stick that, when split down the middle, produced duplicate copies of a transaction. On its function and history, see Clanchy, *From Memory to Written Record*, 95–96.

65. Committee for Foreign Plantations, "To the Right Worshipful the Governor and Assistants," 4:226.

66. Committee for Foreign Plantations, "Charter to Providence Plantations," in *Collections of the Rhode Island Historical Society*, 1:260.

67. Gorton, *Simplicities Defence*, 2.

68. Ibid., 2, 3.

69. A detailed account of this controversy and of Gorton's theology can be found in Gura, *A Glimpse of Sion's Glory*, 276-303. For the background of some of Gorton's ideas and their reception in New England, see Bozeman, *The Precisianist Strain*. For the details of Gorton's emigration to the bay area, see the admiring account found in Gadman, "'A strenuous beneficent force.'"

70. See Field, *Errands into the Metropolis*, 48–71.

71. See, for example, Prynne, *A Fresh Discovery of some Prodigious New Wandring-Blasing-Stars* (1645). Gorton may have been led to approach Macock after arriving in London and reading the works by Prynne and other theological radicals, which at that time were being published without fear of censorship or punishment.

72. Gorton, *Simplicities Defence*, 2, 4, 9, 76.

73. Ibid., 4, 8.

74. Ibid., 2.

75. For an account of the execution (or murder) of Miantonomi, see Salisbury, *Manitou and Providence*, 234–35. Also see Robinson, "Lost Opportunities."

76. Gorton, *Simplicities Defence*, 3–4.

77. Ibid., 6, 18.

78. Las Casas, *The Spanish Colonie* , n.p.

79. Gorton, *Simplicities Defence*, 92.

80. Las Casas, *The Spanish Colonie*, n.p.; Gorton, *Simplicities Defence*, 92.

81. Gorton, *Simplicities Defence*, 80.

82. Ibid., 81.

83. For an account of the ceremonial practices around Algonquian-speaking political leaders in southern New England, see Bragdon, *Native People*, 153–55.

84. Field points out that "the Committee for Foreign Plantations was pleased to receive" the Narragansetts' subjection because "control of the colonies was one of the many royal powers Parliament arrogated to itself in the early days of the revolution." Field, *Errands into the Metropolis*, 60.

85. Gorton, *Simplicities Defence*, 81.

86. Vitoria had also specified that in any agreement "one and all" Indians had to give their consent. Vitoria, "On the American Indians," in *Political Writings*, 288.

87. Gorton, *Simplicities Defence*, 82.

88. Field, *Errands into the Metropolis*, 58.

89. Gorton, *Simplicities Defence*, title page.

90. Pulsipher argues that over the course of early settlement history, New England settlers "shifted the basis of their relationship with the Indians . . . from expectations of reciprocal friendship to demands of subjection." Pulsipher, *Subjects unto the Same King*, 35.

91. Gorton, *Simplicities Defence*, 83.

92. Ibid., 85.

93. Brown and Roulette, "Waabitigweyaa," 160.

94. Ibid., 161.

95. Gorton, *Simplicities Defence*, 80.

96. Ibid., 79–80.

97. Winthrop, *Declaration*, title page.

98. Ibid., 1.

99. Ibid.

100. Ibid., 1, 1–2, 2.

101. Ibid., 2.

102. Ibid.

103. See Stearns, "The Weld-Peter Mission to England." See also Cressy, *Coming Over*, 200.

104. Winthrop, *Declaration*, 2.

105. Ibid., 4.

106. Ibid., 6.

107. Ibid., 7.

108. "Treaty between the New England Confederation and the Narragansetts, 27 August 1645."

109. "Treaty between Spain and the United Netherlands."

110. See "Treaty of peace and alliance between Denmark and Great Britain."; and

"Treaty of friendship and alliance between Sweden and the United Netherlands." For a discussion of concepts of Roman law in these treaties, see MacMillan, *Sovereignty and Possession*, 204. For the broader importance of the Treaty of Westphalia to American diplomacy, see Savelle, *The Origins of American Diplomacy*.

111. See Sehr, "Ninigret's Tactics of Accomodation."

112. For these events, see Oberg, *Dominion and Civility*, 128–34; and Pulsipher, *Subjects unto the Same King*, 30–59.

113. Though Pessicus, Canonicus, and Mixan were able to use a stylus or some other tool to inscribe signatory marks on paper. Gorton, *Simplicities Defence*, 84.

114. Charles II, "Patent of Charles II. constituting a Council for Trade," 3:31.

115. For the creation and constitution of this body, see Bremer, *The Puritan Experiment*, 126–27.

116. For an account of this review, see Bremer, *First Founders*, 219–22.

117. See Oberg, *Dominion and Civility*, 134–36, for an account of the place of the Narragansetts in this review.

118. King's Commissioners, "Extract from the Report of the King's Commissioners concerning the New England Colonies," 128.

119. King's Commissioners, "Order of the Commissioners about Narragansett," 180.

120. For an account of the war, its justifications, and its aftermath, see Lepore, *The Name of War*.

121. For more on the tribe's use of this strategy, see Pulsipher, *Subjects unto the Same King*, 20–21, 25–26.

122. *Providence Journal*, October 17, 1866, quoted in Gross, "'Of Portuguese Origin,'" 508. See also Gross, *What Blood Won't Tell*, 126–39; and O'Brien, *Firsting and Lasting*, 198. For the history of the tribe after King Philip's War, see Campbell and LaFantasie, "Scattered to the Winds of Heaven."

123. For more on the tribe's struggle against Rhode Island after the Civil War, see Gross, *What Blood Won't Tell*, 127–31.

124. For a discussion of this petition, see Miller, *Forgotten Tribes*, 278n13.

Bibliography

—〰—

Primary Sources

"Agreement between the Proprietary and Commissioners." February 27, 1657. In *Archives of Maryland*, 3:332-34.

Anghiera, Pietro Martire d'. *The Decades of the newe worlde....* Trans. Rycharde Eden. London, 1555.

Archer, Gabriel. "A relatyon of the Discovery of our River, from James Forte into the Maine...." In *The Jamestown Voyages Under the First Charter, 1606–1609*, ed. Philip L. Barbour, 1:80–98. 2 vols. Cambridge: Cambridge University Press, 1969.

Archives of Maryland. Ed. William Hand Browne et al. 72 vols. Baltimore, 1883–1972.

"Articles of Peace and freindshipp, treated and agreed upon the 5th day of July 1652 Betweene the English Nation in the Province of Maryland on the one party, And the Indian Nation of Sasquesahanogh, on the other partie as followeth." In *Archives of Maryland*, 3:277–78.

Articles of Peace, Entercourse, and Commerce Concluded in the names of the most high and mighty Kings, and Princes James by the grace of God ... And Philip the third, King of Spaine.... London, 1605.

"The Assembly of the XIX. to the States General." October 25, 1634. In *CHSNY*, 1:93–95.

Barbour, Philip L., ed. *The Jamestown Voyages Under the First Charter, 1606–1609*. 2 vols. Cambridge: Cambridge University Press, 1969.

Barrett, Robert. *The Theorike and Practike of Moderne Warres.* . . . London, 1598.

Barwick, Humfrey. *A Breefe Discourse, Concerning the force and effect of all man-uall weapons of fire.* . . . London, 1592.

Bradford, William. *Of Plymouth Plantation, 1620–1647: The Complete Text.* Ed. Samuel Eliot Morison. New York: Knopf, 1952.

Brown, Alexander, ed. *The Genesis of the United States.* . . . 2 vols. Boston: Houghton Mifflin, 1890.

Bry, Johann Theodor de. *Americae Pars Decima.* Oppenheim, 1619.

Bry, Theodor de. *Americae Pars Quarta.* Frankfurt, 1594.

Calendar of State Papers and Manuscripts Relating to English Affairs, Existing in the Archives and Collections of Venice, and in Other Libraries of Northern Italy. Ed. Horatio F. Brown et al., trans. Lubbock Brown et al. 38 vols. London, 1864–1947.

Calendar of State Papers, Domestic Series, of the reign of James I, 1623–1625. Preserved in the State Paper Department of Her Majesty's Public Record Office. Ed. Mary Anne Everett Green, Vol. 4, *1623–1625.* 4 vols. London, 1859.

Calendar of State Papers, Foreign Series, of the Reign of Elizabet. Preserved in the State Paper Department of Her Majesty's Public Record Office. Ed. Joseph Stevenson, Vol. 7, *1564–1565.* 23 vols. London, 1870.

Calvert, Cecil. "The humble Petition of Cecill Lord Baltimore." March 1638. In *Archives of Maryland*, 3:68–70.

Chamberlain, John. *The Letters of John Chamberlain.* Ed. Norman Egbert McClure. 2 vols. Philadelphia: American Philosophical Society, 1939.

Charles I. "Answer to the Remonstrance of the Dutch Ambassadors." April 1632. In *CHSNY*, 1:57–59.

———. "Articles of Exchequer." May 16, 1632. In *The Earl of Stirling's Register of Royal Letters, Relative to the Affairs of Scotland and Nova Scotia from 1615 to 1635*, 2:527. 2 vols. Edinburgh, 1885.

———. "The Charter of Maryland." June 20, 1632. In *The Federal and State Constitutions, Colonial Charters, and Other Organic Laws of the States, Territories, and Colonial Now or Heretofore Forming the United States of America*, ed. Francis Newton Thorpe, 3:1669–77, English trans. 3:1677–86. 7 vols. Washington, D.C.: Government Printing Office, 1909.

———. "The Charter of Massachusetts Bay." March 4, 1629. In *The Federal and State Constitutions, Colonial Charters, and Other Organic Laws of the States, Territories, and Colonial Now or Heretofore Forming the United States of*

America, ed. Francis Newton Thorpe, 3:1846–60. 7 vols. Washington, D.C.: Government Printing Office, 1909.

——. "The King to the Governor and Council of Virginia." October 8, 1634. In *Archives of Maryland*, 3:29.

Charles II. "Patent of Charles II. constituting a Council for Trade." November 7, 1660. In *CHSNY*, 3:31–32.

"Charter of Narragansett to Massachusetts." *New England Historical and Genealogical Register* 11, 1 (1857): 41–43.

Claiborne, William. "A Breviate of Captain Claiborne's Petition to his Majestie." April 1635. In *Archives of Maryland*, 3:32.

——. "Claiborne's Petition and Accompanying Papers." 1676–1677. In *Archives of Maryland*, 5:155–239.

Committee for Foreign Plantations. "Charter to Providence Plantations." November 2, 1643. In *Collections of the Rhode Island Historical Society*, ed. John Russell Bartlett, 1:259–62. 10 vols. Providence, R.I., 1827.

——. "To the Right Worshipful the Governor and Assistants, and the rest of our worthy friends in the plantation of Massachusetts Bay, in New-England." Before September 17, 1644. In *Collections of the Rhode Island Historical Society*, ed. John Russell Bartlett, 4:226–27. 10 vols. Providence, R.I., 1838.

"The Complaint of Certain Adventurers and Inhabitants of the Plantation in New England." In *The Story of the Pilgrim Fathers, 1606–1623 A.D.: As Told By Themselves, Their Friends, and Their Enemies*, ed. Edward Arber, 506–8. Boston, 1897.

Copland, Patrick. *Virginia's God be Thanked, or A Sermon of Thanksgiving for the Happie successe of the affayres in Virginia this last yeare. . . .* London, 1622.

Cotton, John. *Gods Promise to His Plantation*. London, 1620.

——. "Master John Cotton's Answer to Master Roger Williams." In *The Complete Writings of Roger Williams*, ed. J. Lewis Diman, 2:1–237. 7 vols. New York: Russell and Russell, 1963.

——. "Reply to Mr. Williams." 1647. In *The Complete Writings of Roger Williams*, ed. J. Lewis Diman, 2:46–47. 7 vols. New York: Russell and Russell, 1963.

Davenport, Frances Gardiner, ed. *European Treaties Bearing on the History of the United States and Its Dependencies*. Vols. 1–2. 4 vols. Washington, D.C.: Carnegie Institution, 1917–1937.

Day, Angel. *The English Secretary, or Methode of writing of Epistles and Letters.* . . . London, 1599.

"Deed from Cannaunicus and Miantonomi to Roger Williams." March 1637. In *Records of the Colony of Rhode Island and Providence Plantations, in New England*, ed. John Russell Bartlett, 1:18. 10 vols. Providence, R.I., 1856.

Derricke, John. *The Image of Irelande.* . . . London, 1581.

Digges, Thomas. *A Breife and true report of the Proceedings of the Earle of Leycester for the reliefe of the Towne of Sluce.* . . . London, 1590.

Drake, Sir Francis. *The World Encompassed.* . . . London, 1628.

Elizabeth I. *A Declaration of the Causes Mooving the Queene of England to give aide to the Defence of the People afflicted and oppressed in the lowe Countries.* London, 1585.

A faithfull Report of proceedings anent the Assemblie of Ministers at Abirdeen. . . . Middelburg, Netherlands, 1606.

Field, Edward, ed. *State of Rhode Island and Providence Plantations at the End of the Century: A History, Illustrated with Maps, Facsimiles of Old Plates and Paintings and Photographs of Ancient Landmarks.* Vol. 1. 3 vols. Boston: Mason, 1902.

Fox, George. *A New-England-Fire-Brand Quenched.* . . . 2 vols. London, 1679.

Gates, Geffrey. *The Defence of Militarie profession.* . . . London, 1579.

Gentili, Alberico. *De Jure Belli Libri Tres.* Trans. John C. Rolfe. Oxford: Clarendon, 1933.

Geuffroy, Antoine. *The order of the greate Turckes courte, of hys menne of warre, and of all hys conquestes, with the summe of Mahumetes doctryne.* Trans. Richard Grafton. London, 1542.

Gheyn, Jacob de. *The Exercise of Armes for Calivres, Muskettes, and Pikes.* . . . The Hague, 1608.

Gómara, Francisco López de. *The Pleasant Historie of the Conquest of the Weast India, now called new Spayne, Atchieved by the worthy Prince Hernando Cortes.* . . . Trans. Thomas Nicholas. London, 1578.

Gorges, Sir Ferdinando. *A Briefe Narration of the Originall Undertakings of the Advancement of Plantations into the parts of America.* . . . London, 1658.

Gorton, Samuel. *Simplicities Defence against Seven-Headed Policy.* . . . London, 1646.

Governor and Council in Virginia. "The Putting Out of the Tenants that Came Over in the B.N. With Other Orders of the Councell." November 11, 1619. In *VCR*, 3:226–29.

"Governor Samuel Argall to the Virginia Company." March 10, 1617. *Virginia Magazine of History and Biography* 15, 4 (1908): 403–4.

Grewe, Wilhelm G., ed. *Fontes Historiae Iuris Gentium: Quellen zur Geschichte des Völkerrechts. Sources Relating to the History of the Law of Nations.* Vol. 2, 1493–1815. 3 vols. Berlin: Walter de Gruyter, 1988.

Grotius, Hugo. *The Freedom of the Seas.* . . . Ed. James Brown Scott, trans. Ralph Van Deman Magoffin. New York: Oxford University Press, 1916.

——. *De Iure Praedae Commentarius: Commentary on the Law of Prize and Booty.* Trans. Gwladys L. Williams and W. H. Zeydel. 2 vols. Oxford: Clarendon, 1950.

——. *De Jure Belli ac Pacis Libri Tres.* . . . Ed. James Brown Scott, trans. Francis W. Kelsey et al. 2 vols. Oxford: Clarendon, 1913–1925.

Hakluyt, Richard. *The Principal Navigations, Voyages, Traffiques and Discoveries of the English Nation.* . . . 3 vols. London, 1599–1600.

Hamor, Ralph. *A True Discourse of the Present Estate of Virginia.* . . . London, 1615.

Hariot, Thomas. *A brief and true report of the new found land of Virginia.* . . . London, 1588.

"International Convention Against the Taking of Hostages." 1979. In *Encyclopedia of Human Rights*, ed. Edward Lawson and Mary Lou Bertucci, 696–98. New York: Taylor and Francis, 1996.

James I. "Instructions for Government." November 20, 1606. In *The Jamestown Voyages Under the First Charter, 1606–1609*, ed. Philip L. Barbour, 1:34–44. 2 vols. Cambridge: Cambridge University Press, 1969.

——. "Instructions to English commissioners." June 1, 1604. In *European Treaties Bearing on the History of the United States and Its Dependencies*, ed. Frances Gardiner Davenport, 1:247n4. 4 vols. Washington, D.C.: Carnegie Institution, 1917.

——. "Letters patent to Sir Thomas Gates and others." April 10, 1606. In *The Jamestown Voyages Under the First Charter, 1606–1609*, ed. Philip L. Barbour, 1:24–34. 2 vols. Cambridge: Cambridge University Press, 1969.

——. "A Proclamation prohibiting interloping and disorderly Trading to New-England in America." November 6, 1622. In *Historical Collections; Consisting of State papers, and Other Authentic Documents; Intended as Materials for an History of the United States of America*, ed. Ebenezer Hazard, 1:151–52. 2 vols. Philadelphia, 1792.

Joachimi, Albertus and Govert Brasser to the States General. April 10, 1632. In *CHSNY*, 1:47–50.

Johnson, Richard. *The nine Worthies of London Explaining the honourable exercise of Armes.* . . . London, 1592.

Jonson, Ben. *The Complete Masques.* Ed. Stephen Orgel. New Haven, Conn.: Yale University Press, 1969.

"A Justification for planting in Virginia." 1609 [?]. In *VCR*, 3:1–3.

Justinian. *The Civil Law Including the Twelve Tables, the Institutes of Gaius, the Rules of Ulpian, the Opinions of Paulus, the Enactments of Justinian, and the Constitutions of Leo.* Ed. and trans. S. P. Scott. 17 vols. Cincinnati: Central Trust Company, 1932.

King's Commissioners. "Extract from the Report of the King's Commissioners concerning the New England Colonies, made December 1665." In *Records of the Colony of Rhode Island and Providence Plantations in New England: 1664–1677,* ed. John Russell Bartlett, 2:127–29. 10 vols. Providence, R.I., 1857.

——. "Order of the Commissioners about Narragansett." March 20, 1664. In *Collections of the Rhode Island Historical Society,* ed. John Russell Bartlett, 3:179–81. 10 vols. Providence, R.I., 1835.

Kingsbury, Susan Myra. *The Records of the Virginia Company of London.* 4 vols. Washington, D.C.: Government Printing Office, 1906–1935.

Knolles, Richard. *The Generall Historie of the Turkes from The first beginning of that Nation to the Rising of the Othoman Familie.* . . . London, 1603.

Koschorke, Klaus et al., eds. *A History of Christianity in Asia, Africa, and Latin America, 1450–1990: A Documentary Sourcebook.* Grand Rapids, Mich.: Eerdmans, 2007.

Las Casas, Bartolomé de. *Obras Completas de Fray Bartolomé de Las Casas,* ed. Isacio Pérez Fernández et al., 15 vols. Vol. 3, *Historia de las Indias.* Madrid: Alianza, 1994.

——. *The Spanish Colonie* . . . . London, 1583.

Lechford, Thomas. *Plain Dealing: or, Newes from New-England.* . . . London, 1642.

The London Council of the Virginia Company. "A circular Letter of his Majestie's Counsil for Virginia." February 20, 1610. In *The Genesis of the United States* . . . , ed. Alexander Brown, 1:463–65. 2 vols. Boston, 1890.

——. "Instructions to Sir Thomas Gates." May 15, 1609. In *The Jamestown Voyages Under the First Charter, 1606–1609,* ed. Philip L. Barbour, 2:262–68. 2 vols. Cambridge: Cambridge University Press, 1969.

———. "The London Council's 'Instructions given by way of Advice,'" between November 20 and December 19, 1606. In *The Jamestown Voyages Under the First Charter, 1606–1609*, ed. Philip L. Barbour, 1:49–54. 2 vols. Cambridge: Cambridge University Press, 1969.

Lord Commissioners for Plantations. "The Lord Comissioners for plantations their Order Uppon Captain William Cleyborne & his Partners Petition against the Lord Baltemore." April 1638. In *Archives of Maryland*, 3:71–73.

Magnel, Francis. "Francis Magnel's Relation of the First Voyage and the Beginnings of the Jamestown Colony." July 1, 1610. In *The Jamestown Voyages Under the First Charter, 1606–1609*, ed. Philip L. Barbour, 1:151–57. 2 vols. Cambridge: Cambridge University Press, 1969.

Maryland General Assembly. "An Act Concerning Religion." April 21, 1649. In *Archives of Maryland*, 1:244–47.

The Massachusetts Bay Company. "The Company's First General Letter of Instructions to Endicott and His Council." April 17, 1629. In *Records of the Company of the Massachusetts Bay in New England: From 1628 to 1641*, ts. David Pulsifer and Joseph Barlow Felt, ed. S. F. Haven, 79–95. Cambridge, Mass., 1850.

———. "The Company's Second General Letter of Instructions to Endicott and His Council." In *Records of the Company of the Massachusetts Bay in New England: From 1628 to 1641*, ts. David Pulsifer and Joseph Barlow Felt, ed. S. F. Haven, 96–107. Cambridge, Mass., 1850.

Merian, Matthäus. *Dreyzehender Theil Americae*. Frankfurt, 1628.

Morton, Nathaniel. *New-Englands Memoriall: or, A brief Relation of the most Memorable and Remarkable Passages of the Providence of God. . . .* Cambridge, Mass., 1669.

Morton, Thomas. *New English Canaan. . . .* Amsterdam, 1637.

Newes out of East India: Of the cruell and bloody usage of Our English Merchants and others at Amboyna, by the Netherlandish Governour and Councell there. London, 1624.

O'Callaghan, E. B., ed. *Documents Relative to the Colonial History of the State of New York*. 15 vols. Albany, N.Y., 1853–1887.

Parsons, Robert. *A Relation of the King of Spaines Receiving in Valliodolid, and in the Inglish College of the same towne. . . .* Antwerp, 1592.

Peckham, Sir George. *A True Reporte, Of the late discoveries, and possession, taken in the right of the Crowne of Englande, of the New-found Landes. . . .* London, 1583.

Percy, George. "George Percy's 'Trewe Relacyon': A Primary Source for the Jamestown Settlement." Ed. Mark Nicholls. *Virginia Magazine of History and Biography* 113, 3 (2005): 212–75.

Peter, Hugh and Thomas Weld. *New Englands First Fruits*. . . . London, 1643.

Privy Council. "Considerations upon the Patent to the Lord Baltimore." June 20, 1632. In *Archives of Maryland*, 3:17–19.

——. "Instructions to Yeardley, 1626." *Virginia Magazine of History and Biography* 2, 4 (1895): 393–96.

Prynne, William. *A Fresh Discovery Of some Prodigious New Wandring-Blasing-Stars, & Firebrands*. . . . London, 1645.

Purchas, Samuel. *Purchas His Pilgrimes*. . . . London, 1625.

Raleigh, Sir Walter. *The Discoverie of the Large, Rich, and Beautiful Empire of Guiana*. . . . London, 1596.

Rogers, Horatio et al. *The Early Records of the Town of Providence*. Vol. 5, 21 vols. Providence, R.I., 1894.

Rosier, James. *A True Relation of the most prosperous voyage made this present yeere 1605, by Captaine George Waymouth*. . . . London, 1605.

The Royal Entertainment of the right Honourable the Earle of Nottinghame, sent Ambassador from his Majestie to the King of Spaine. London, 1605.

Selden, John. *Mare Clausum*. . . . London, 1635.

Shakespeare, William. *Henry VIII*. In *The Riverside Shakespeare*. Ed. G. Blakemore Evans and J. J. M. Tobin. Boston: Houghton Mifflin, 1997.

Shurtleff, Nathaniel B., ed. *Records of the Governor and Company of the Massachusetts Bay in New England*. Vol. 1, *1628–1641*. 5 vols. Boston, 1853.

Smith, John. *The Complete Works of Captain John Smith, 1580–1631*. Ed. Philip L. Barbour. 3 vols. Chapel Hill: University of North Carolina Press, 1986.

——. *The Generall Historie of Virginia, New-England, and the Summer Isles*. . . . London, 1624.

——. *A Map of Virginia. With a Description of the Countrey, the Commodities, People, Government and Religion*. . . . Oxford, 1612.

——. *New Englands Trials*. . . . London, 1620.

——. *The Proceedings of the English Colonie in Virginia*. . . . Oxford, 1612.

——. *A True Relation of such occurrences and accidents of noate as hath hapned in Virginia*. . . . London, 1608.

Spelman, Henry. "Relation of Virginea." 1613. In *Travels and Works of Captain John Smith: President of Virginia and Admiral of New England, 1580–1631*, ed. Edward Arber, ci–cxiv. Edinburgh: John Grant, 1910.

States General. "Remonstrance of the Ambassadors of the States General to King Charles I." 1632 [?]. In *CHSNY*, 1:55–56.

Strachey, William. *The Historie of Travaile into Virginia Britannia; Expressing the Cosmographie and Comodities of the Country, Togither with the Manners and Customes of the People* . . . [1612]. London, 1849.

"Treaty between the New England Confederation and the Narragansetts, 27 August 1645." In *Of Plymouth Plantation, 1620-1647: The Complete Text,* ed. Samuel Eliot Morison, 437-40. New York: Knopf, 1952.

"Treaty between Spain and the United Netherlands, concluded at Münster on January 30, 1648." In *European Treaties Bearing on the History of the United States and Its Dependencies,* ed. Frances Gardiner Davenport, 1:353–66. 4 vols. Washington, D.C.: Carnegie Institution, 1917.

"Treaty of friendship and alliance between Sweden and the United Netherlands, concluded at the Hague, July 18/28, 1667." In *European Treaties Bearing on the History of the United States and Its Dependencies,* ed. Frances Gardiner Davenport, 2:110–18. 4 vols. Washington, D.C.: Carnegie Institution, 1929.

"Treaty of peace and alliance between Denmark and Great Britain, concluded at Westminister September 15/25, 1654." In *European Treaties Bearing on the History of the United States and Its Dependencies,* ed. Frances Gardiner Davenport, 2:36–39. 4 vols. Washington, D.C.: Carnegie Institution, 1929.

Treswell, Robert. *A Relation of Such Things as were observed to happen in the Journey of the right Honourable Charles Earle of Nottingham, L. High Admirall of England, His Highnesse Ambassadour to the King of Spaine: Being sent thither to take the Oath of the sàyd King for the maintenance of Peace betweene the two famous Kings of Great Brittaine and Spaine.* . . . London, 1605.

A True Declaration of the estate of the Colonie in Virginia. . . . London, 1610.

Underhill, John. *Newes from America.* . . . London, 1638.

The Virginia Company. "Instructions to the Governor and Council of State in Virginia." July 24, 1621. In *VCR*, 3:468–82.

Vitoria, Francisco de. "De Bello: On St. Thomas Aquinas, *Summa Theologica,* Secunda Secundae, Question 40." Trans. Gwladys L. Williams. In James Brown Scott, *The Spanish Origin of International Law: Francisco de Vitoria and His Law of Nations,* cxiv–cxxxi. Oxford: Clarendon, 1934.

——. *Political Writings.* Ed. Anthony Pagden and Jeremy Lawrance. Cambridge: Cambridge University Press, 1991.

Waterhouse, Edward. *A Declaration of the State of the Colony and Affaires in Virginia. With a Relation of the Barbarous Massacre in the time of peace and League.* . . . London, 1622.

West India Company to the States General. May 5, 1632. In *CHSNY*, 1:50–52.

White, John. *The Planters Plea.* . . . London, 1630.

William and Mary. "The Charter of Massachusetts Bay." October 7, 1691. In *The Federal and State Constitutions, Colonial Charters, and Other Organic Laws of the States, Territories, and Colonial Now or Heretofore Forming the United States of America,* ed. Francis Newton Thorpe, 3:1870–86. 7 vols. Washington, D.C.: Government Printing Office, 1909.

Williams, Roger. *The Bloody Tenent Yet More Bloody.* London, 1652.

———. *Complete Writings.* 7 vols. New York: Russell & Russell, 1963.

———. *Correspondence of Roger Williams.* Ed. Glenn W. LaFantasie. 2 vols. Hanover, N.H.: University Press of New England, 1988.

———. *The Hireling Ministry None of Christs.* . . . London, 1652.

———. *A Key into the Language of America: or, An help to the Language of the Natives in that part of America, called New-England.* . . . London, 1643.

Winslow, Edward. *Good Newes from New-England.* . . . London, 1624.

Winslow, Edward, William Bradford, and Robert Cushman. *A Relation or Journall of the beginning and proceedings of the English plantation setled at Plimoth in New England.* . . . London, 1622.

Winthrop, John. *A Declaration of Former Passages and Proceedings Betwixt the English and the Narrowgansets, with their confederates, Wherein the grounds and justice of the ensuing warre are opened and cleared.* Cambridge, Mass., 1645.

———. *The Journal of John Winthrop, 1630–1649.* Ed. Richard S. Dunn, James Savage, and Leatitia Yeandle. Cambridge, Mass.: Harvard University Press, 1996.

Wyatt, Sir Francis. "Letter of Sir Francis Wyatt, Governor of Virginia, 1621–1626." *William and Mary Quarterly* 2nd ser. 6, 2 (1926): 114–21.

———. "A Proclamation to bee carefull of the Savadges treacherie." Before May 7, 1623. In *VCR*, 4:167–68.

Zárate, Agustin de. *The Discoverie and Conquest of the Provinces of Peru, and the Navigation in the South Sea, along that Coast.* . . . Trans. Thomas Nicholas. London, 1581.

Secondary Sources

Adams, Simon. "Spain or the Netherlands? The Dilemmas of Early Stuart Foreign Policy." In *Before the English Civil War: Essays on Early Stuart Politics and Government*, ed. Howard Tomlinson, 79–101. London: Macmillan, 1983.

Adorno, Rolena. *Guaman Poma: Writing and Resistance in Colonial Peru.* Austin: University of Texas Press, 1986.

Allen, David Grayson. "*Vacuum Domicilium*: The Social and Cultural Landscape of Seventeenth-Century New England." In *New England Begins: The Seventeenth Century*, ed. Jonathan L. Fairbanks and Robert F. Trent, 1:1–52. 3 vols. Boston: Museum of Fine Arts, 1982.

Allen, Paula Gunn. *Pocahontas: Medicine Woman, Spy, Entrepreneur, Diplomat.* New York: HarperCollins, 2003.

Anand, R. P. *Origin and Development of the Law of the Sea.* The Hague: Nijhoff, 1983.

Anaya, S. James. *Indigenous Peoples in International Law.* Oxford: Oxford University Press, 1996.

Anderson, Douglas. *William Bradford's Books: Of Plimmoth Plantation and the Printed Word.* Baltimore: Johns Hopkins University Press, 2003.

Anderson, Virginia DeJohn. *New England's Generation: The Great Migration and the Formation of Society and Culture in the Seventeenth Century.* Cambridge: Cambridge University Press, 1991.

Andrews, Charles M. *The Colonial Period of American History*, 4 vols. Vol. 1, *The Settlements, I.* New Haven, Conn.: Yale University Press, 1934.

Anghie, Antony. *Imperialism, Sovereignty and the Making of International Law.* Cambridge: Cambridge University Press, 2005.

Appelbaum, Robert and John Wood Sweet, eds. *Envisioning an English Empire: Jamestown and the Making of the North Atlantic World.* Philadelphia: University of Pennsylvania Press, 2005.

Armitage, David. *The Ideological Origins of the British Empire.* Cambridge: Cambridge University Press, 2000.

Axtell, James. *Natives and Newcomers: The Cultural Origins of North America.* New York: Oxford University Press, 2001.

Banner, Stuart. *How the Indians Lost Their Land: Law and Power on the Frontier.* Cambridge, Mass.: Belknap Press of Harvard University Press, 2005.

Barbour, Philip L. *Pocahontas and Her World.* . . . Boston: Houghton Mifflin, 1970.

———. *The Three Worlds of Captain John Smith*. Boston: Houghton Mifflin, 1964.

Bellin, Joshua David. *Medicine Bundle: Indian Sacred Performance and American Literature, 1824–1932*. Philadelphia: University of Pennsylvania Press, 2008.

Bellin, Joshua David and Laura L. Mielke, eds. *Native Acts: Indian Performance, 1603–1832*. Lincoln: University of Nebraska Press, 2011.

Belmessous, Saliha, ed. *Native Claims: Indigenous Law Against Empire, 1500–1920*. Oxford: Oxford University Press, 2012.

Ben-Amos, Ilana Krausman. *The Culture of Giving: Informal Support and Gift-Exchange in Early Modern England*. Cambridge: Cambridge University Press, 2008.

Benton, Lauren. *A Search for Sovereignty: Law and Geography in European Empires, 1400–1900*. Cambridge: Cambridge University Press, 2010.

Benton, Lauren and Benjamin Straumann. "Acquiring Empire by Law: From Roman Doctrine to Early Modern European Practice." *Law and History Review* 28, 1 (2010): 1–38.

Biggar, H. P. *The Early Trading Companies of New France: A Contribution to the History of Commerce and Discovery in North America*. Toronto: University of Toronto Library, 1901.

Bilder, Mary Sarah. "Salamanders and Sons of God: The Culture of Appeal in Early New England." In *The Many Legalities of Early America*, ed. Christopher L. Tomlins and Bruce H. Mann, 47–77. Chapel Hill: University of North Carolina Press, 2001.

Black, Jeremy. *A History of Diplomacy*. London: Reaktion Books, 2010.

Bland, D. S. "Rhetoric and the Law Student in Sixteenth-Century England." *Studies in Philology* 54, 4 (1957): 498–508.

Blansett, Lisa. "John Smith Maps Virginia: Knowledge, Rhetoric, and Politics." In *Envisioning an English Empire: Jamestown and the Making of the North Atlantic World*, ed. Robert Appelbaum and John Wood Sweet, 68–91. Philadelphia: University of Pennsylvania Press, 2005.

Bohaker, Heidi. "*Nindoodemag*: The Significance of Algonquian Kinship Networks in the Eastern Great Lakes Region, 1600–1701." *William and Mary Quarterly* 3rd ser. 63, 1 (2006): 23–52.

Boone, Elizabeth Hill, and Walter Mignolo. *Writing Without Words: Alternative Literacies in Mesoamerica and the Andes*. Durham, N.C.: Duke University Press, 1994.

Boucher, Philip B. "Revisioning the 'French Atlantic': or, How to Think About the French Presence in the Atlantic, 1550–1625." In *The Atlantic World and Virginia, 1550–1624*, ed. Peter C. Mancall, 274–306. Chapel Hill: University of North Carolina Press, 2007.

Bozeman, Theodore Dwight. *The Precisianist Strain: Disciplinary Religion and Antinomian Backlash in Puritanism to 1638*. Chapel Hill: University of North Carolina Press, 2004.

Bragdon, Kathleen. *Native People of Southern New England, 1500–1650*. Norman: University of Oklahoma Press, 1996.

Breen, Louise A. *Transgressing the Bounds: Subversive Enterprises Among the Puritan Elite in Massachusetts, 1630–1692*. Oxford: Oxford University Press, 2001.

Bremer, Francis J. *First Founders: American Puritans and Puritanism in an Atlantic World*. Durham: University of New Hampshire Press, 2012.

——. *The Puritan Experiment: New England Society from Bradford to Edwards*. New York: St. Martin's, 1976.

Brenner, Robert. *Merchants and Revolution: Commercial Change, Political Conflict, and London's Overseas Traders, 1550–1663*. Princeton, N.J.: Princeton University Press, 1993.

Brierly, J. L. *The Law of Nations: An Introduction to the International Law of Peace*. Oxford: Clarendon, 1930.

Brooks, Lisa. *The Common Pot: The Recovery of Native Space in the Northeast*. Minneapolis: University of Minnesota Press, 2008.

Bross, Kristina. *Dry Bones and Indian Sermons: Praying Indians in Colonial America*. Ithaca, N.Y.: Cornell University Press, 2004.

Brotherston, Gordon. *Book of the Fourth World: Reading the Native Americas Through Their Literature*. Cambridge: Cambridge University Press, 1992.

Brown, Jennifer S. H. and Roger Roulette. "Waabitigweyaa, the One Who Found the Anishinaabeg First," told by Charlie George Owen. In *Algonquian Spirit: Contemporary Translations of the Algonquian Literatures of North America*, ed. Brian Swann, 159–69. Lincoln: University of Nebraska Press, 2005.

Brown, Matthew P. *The Pilgrim and the Bee: Reading Rituals and Book Culture in Early New England*. Philadelphia: University of Pennsylvania Press, 2007.

Byrd, Jodi A. *The Transit of Empire: Indigenous Critiques of Colonialism*. Minneapolis: University of Minnesota Press, 2011.

Calloway, Colin G. *Pen and Ink Witchcraft: Treaties and Treaty Making in American Indian History*. Oxford: Oxford University Press, 2013.

Campbell, Paul R. and Glenn W. LaFantasie, "Scattered to the Winds of Heaven: Narragansett Indians, 1676–1880." *Rhode Island History* 37, 3 (1978): 66–83.

Cañizares-Esguerra, Jorge. *How to Write the History of the New World: Histories, Epistemologies, and Identities in the Eighteenth-Century Atlantic World.* Stanford, Calif.: Stanford University Press, 2001.

——. *Puritan Conquistadors: Iberianizing the Atlantic, 1550–1700.* Stanford, Calif.: Stanford University Press, 2006.

Canny, Nicholas P. *The Elizabethan Conquest of Ireland: A Pattern Established, 1565–76.* Hassocks: Harvester, 1976.

Carter, Charles H. "The New World as a Factor in International Relations, 1492–1739." In *First Images of America: The Impact of the New World on the Old,* ed. Fredi Chiappelli, Michael J. B. Allen, and Robert L. Benson, 1:231–63. 2 vols. Berkeley: University of California Press, 1976.

Castillo, Susan. *Colonial Encounters in New World Writing, 1500–1786: Performing America.* London: Routledge, 2006.

Castro, Daniel. *Another Face of Empire: Bartolomé de Las Casas, Indigenous Rights, and Ecclesiastical Imperialism.* Durham, N.C.: Duke University Press, 2007.

Cave, Alfred A. *The Pequot War.* Amherst: University of Massachusetts Press, 1996.

Ceci, Lynn. "Squanto and the Pilgrims: On Planting Corn 'in the manner of the Indians.'" In *The Invented Indian: Cultural Fictions and Government Policies,* ed. James A. Clifton, 71–89. New Brunswick, N.J.: Transaction, 1990.

Cesarini, J. Patrick. "The Ambivalent Uses of Roger Williams's *A Key into the Language of America.*" *Early American Literature* 38, 3 (2003): 469–94.

Chancey, Karen. "The Amboyna Massacre in English Politics, 1624–1632." *Albion: A Quarterly Journal Concerned with British Studies* 30, 4 (1998): 583–98.

Chaplin, Joyce E. "Enslavement of Indians in Early America: Captivity Without the Narrative." In *The Creation of the British Atlantic World,* ed. Elizabeth Mancke and Carol Shammas, 45–70. Baltimore: Johns Hopkins University Press, 2005.

——. *Subject Matter: Technology, the Body, and Science on the Anglo-American Frontier, 1500–1676.* Cambridge, Mass.: Harvard University Press, 2001.

Chet, Guy. *Conquering the American Wilderness: The Triumph of European Warfare in the Colonial Northeast.* Amherst: University of Massachusetts Press, 2003.

Cheyfitz, Eric. *The Poetics of Imperialism: Translation and Colonization from* The Tempest *to* Tarzan. New York: Oxford University Press, 1991.

Cheyney, Edward P. "International Law Under Queen Elizabeth." *English Historical Review* 20, 80 (1905): 659–72.

Clanchy, M. T. *From Memory to Written Record: England, 1066–1307.* Cambridge, Mass.: Harvard University Press, 1979.

Clark, G. N. and W. J. M. van Eysinga. *The Colonial Conferences Between England and The Netherlands in 1613 and 1615.* 2 vols. Leiden: Brill, 1940–1951.

Cogley, Richard W. *John Eliot's Mission to the Indians Before King Philip's War.* Cambridge, Mass.: Harvard University Press, 1999.

Cohen, Matt. *The Networked Wilderness: Communicating in Early New England.* Minneapolis: University of Minnesota Press, 2010.

Colley, Linda. *Captives: Britain, Empire and the World, 1600–1850.* London: Jonathan Cape, 2002.

Cook, Sherburne F. "The Significance of Disease in the Extinction of the New England Indians." *Human Biology* 45, 3 (1973): 485–508.

Cormack, Bradin and Carla Mazzio. *Book Use, Book Theory: 1500–1700.* Chicago: University of Chicago Library, 2005.

Craven, Wesley Frank. *Dissolution of the Virginia Company: The Failure of a Colonial Experiment.* New York: Oxford University Press, 1932.

Cressy, David. *Coming Over: Migration and Communication Between England and New England in the Seventeenth Century.* Cambridge: Cambridge University Press, 1987.

Cronon, William. *Changes in the Land: Indians, Colonists, and the Ecology of New England.* New York: Hill and Wang, 1983.

Crosby, Alfred W., Jr. "Virgin Soil Epidemics as a Factor in the Aboriginal Depopulation of America." *William and Mary Quarterly* 3rd ser. 33, 2 (1976): 289–99.

Cross, Maïa K. Davis. *The European Diplomatic Corps: Diplomats and International Cooperation from Westphalia to Maastricht.* Basingstoke: Palgrave Macmillan, 2007.

Deloria, Vine, Jr. *Behind the Trail of Broken Treaties: An Indian Declaration of Independence.* New York: Delacorte, 1974.

Dillon, Elizabeth Maddock. *The Gender of Freedom: Fictions of Liberalism and the Literary Public Sphere.* Stanford, Calif.: Stanford University Press, 2004.

Dillon, Janette. *The Language of Space in Court Performance, 1400–1625.* Cambridge: Cambridge University Press, 2010.

Dolan, Frances E. *True Relations: Reading, Literature, and Evidence in Seventeenth-Century England*. Philadelphia: University of Pennsylvania Press, 2013.

Doran, Susan. "James VI and the English Succession." In *James VI And I: Ideas, Authority, and Government*, ed. Ralph Houlbrooke, 25–42. Aldershot: Ashgate, 2006.

Doyle, Michael W. *Striking First: Preemption and Prevention in International Conflict*. Princeton, N.J.: Princeton University Press, 2008.

Egerton, H. E. "The Seventeenth and Eighteenth Century Privy Council in Its Relations with the Colonies." *Journal of Comparative Legislation and International Law* 3rd ser. 7, 1 (1925): 1–16.

Emerson, Everett H. "Captain John Smith as Editor: The Generall Historie." *Virginia Magazine of History and Biography* 75, 2 (1967): 143–56.

Everett, C. S. "'They shalbe slaves for their lives': Indian Slavery in Colonial Virginia." In *Indian Slavery in Colonial America*, ed. Alan Gallay, 67–108. Lincoln: University of Nebraska Press, 2009.

Fausz, J. Frederick. "An 'Abundance of Blood Shed on Both Sides': England's First Indian War, 1609–1614." *Virginia Magazine of History and Biography* 98, 1 (1990): 3–56.

——. "Argall, Samuel." In *The Dictionary of Virginia Biography*, ed. John T. Kneebone et al., 1:197–99. 3 vols. Richmond: Library of Virginia, 1998.

——. "The 'Barbarous Massacre' Reconsidered: The Powhatan Uprising of 1622 and the Historians." *Explorations in Ethnic Studies* 1 (1978): 16–36.

——. "Merging and Emerging Worlds: Anglo-Indian Interest Groups and the Development of the Seventeenth-Century Chesapeake." In *Colonial Chesapeake Society*, ed. Lois Green Carr, Philip D. Morgan, and Jean B. Russo, 47–98. Chapel Hill: University of North Carolina Press, 1988.

——. "Opechancanough: Indian Resistance Leader." In *Struggle and Survival in Colonial America*, ed. David G. Sweet and Gary B. Nash, 21–37. Berkeley: University of California Press, 1981.

Feest, Christian F. "Powhatan's Mantle." In *Tradescant's Rarities: Essays on the Foundation of the Ashmolean Museum, 1683, With a Catalogue of the Surviving Early Collections*, ed. Arthur MacGregor, 130–35. Oxford: Clarendon, 1983.

Felker, Christopher D. "Roger Williams's Uses of Legal Discourse: Testing Authority in Early New England." *New England Quarterly* 63, 4 (1990): 624–48.

Ferling, John E. *A Wilderness of Miseries: War and Warriors in Early America.* Westport, Conn.: Greenwood, 1980.

Fichtelberg, Joseph. "The Colonial Stage: Risk and Promise in John Smith's Virginia." *Early American Literature* 39, 1 (2004): 11–40.

Fickes, Michael L. "'They Could Not Endure That Yoke': The Captivity of Pequot Women and Children After the War of 1637." *New England Quarterly* 73, 1 (2000): 58–81.

Field, Jonathan Beecher. *Errands into the Metropolis: New England Dissidents in Revolutionary London.* Hanover, N.H.: University Press of New England, 2009.

Fisch, Jörg. "Law as a Means and as an End: Some Remarks on the Function of European and Non-European Law in the Process of European Expansion." In *European Expansion and Law: The Encounter of European and Indigenous Law in 19th- and 20th-Century Africa and Asia*, ed. W. J. Mommsen and J. A. de Moor, 15–38. Oxford: Berg, 1992.

Fitzmaurice, Andrew. "The Civic Solution to the Crisis of English Colonization, 1609–1625." *Historical Journal* 42, 1 (1999): 25–51.

———. *Humanism and America: An Intellectual History of English Colonisation, 1500–1625.* Cambridge: Cambridge University Press, 2003.

———. "Moral Uncertainty in the Dispossession of Native Americans." In *The Atlantic World and Virginia, 1550–1624*, ed. Peter C. Mancall, 383–409. Chapel Hill: University of North Carolina Press, 2007.

———. "Powhatan Legal Claims." In *Native Claims: Indigenous Law Against Empire, 1500–1920*, ed. Saliha Belmessous, 85–106. Oxford: Oxford University Press, 2011.

Fixico, Donald L., ed. *Treaties with American Indians: An Encyclopedia of Rights, Conflicts, and Sovereignty.* Santa Barbara, Calif.: ABC-CLIO, 2007.

Fliegelman, Jay. *Declaring Independence: Jefferson, Natural Language, and the Culture of Performance.* Stanford, Calif.: Stanford University Press, 1993.

Flynn, Matthew J. *First Strike: Preemptive War in Modern History.* New York: Routledge, 2008.

Gadman, G. J. "'A strenuous beneficent force': The Case for Revision of the Career of Samuel Gorton, Rhode Island Radical." M.A. Thesis, Manchester Metropolitan University, 2004.

Gallivan, Martin D. *James River Chiefdoms: The Rise of Social Inequality in the Chesapeake.* Lincoln: University of Nebraska Press, 2003.

———. "Powhatan's Werowocomoco: Constructing Place, Polity, and Personhood in the Chesapeake, C.E. 1200–C.E. 1609." *American Anthropologist* 109, 1 (2007): 85–100.

Games, Alison. *The Web of Empire: English Cosmopolitans in an Age of Expansion, 1560–1660*. Oxford: Oxford University Press, 2008.

Gaudio, Michael. *Engraving the Savage: The New World and Techniques of Civilization*. Minneapolis: University of Minnesota Press, 2008.

Gaustad, Edwin S. *Liberty of Conscience: Roger Williams in America*. Grand Rapids, Mich.: Eerdmans, 1991.

George, Timothy. *John Robinson and the English Separatist Tradition*. Macon, Ga.: Mercer University Press, 1982.

Given, Brian J. *A Most Pernicious Thing: Gun Trading and Native Warfare in the Early Contact Period*. Ottawa: Carleton University Press, 1994.

Gleach, Frederic W. *Powhatan's World and Colonial Virginia: A Conflict of Cultures*. Lincoln: University of Nebraska Press, 1997.

Goddard, Ives. "Delaware." In *Handbook of North American Indians*, ed. William C, Sturtevant, 17 vols. Vol. 15, *Northeast*, ed. Bruce G. Trigger, 213–39. Washington, D.C.: Smithsonian Institution, 1978.

Goodman, Nan. "Banishment, Jurisdiction, and Identity in Seventeenth-Century New England: The Case of Roger Williams." *Early American Studies* 7, 1 (2009): 109–39.

——. "The Deer Indian Islands and Common Law Performance." In *Native Acts: Indian Performance, 1603–1832*, ed. Joshua David Bellin and Laura L. Mielke, 53–79. Lincoln: University of Nebraska Press, 2011.

Green, L. C. and Olive P. Dickason, *The Law of Nations and the New World*. Edmonton: University of Alberta Press, 1989.

Greenblatt, Stephen. "Invisible Bullets." In *Shakespearean Negotiations: The Circulation of Social Energy in Renaissance England*, 21–65. Berkeley: University of California Press, 1988.

——. *Marvelous Possessions: The Wonder of the New World*. Chicago: University of Chicago Press, 1991.

Greene, Jack P. *Negotiated Authorities: Essays in Colonial Political and Constitutional History*. Charlottesville: University of Virginia Press, 1994.

Greer, Margaret R., Walter D. Mignolo, and Maureen Quilligan, eds. *Rereading the Black Legend: The Discourses of Religious and Racial Difference in the Renaissance Empires*. Chicago: University of Chicago Press, 2007.

Grenier, John. *The First Way of War: American War Making on the Frontier, 1607–1814*. Cambridge: Cambridge University Press, 2005.

Grewe, Wilhelm G. *The Epochs of International Law*. Trans. Michael Byers. Berlin: Walter de Gruyter, 2000.

Griffin, Eric. "The Specter of Spain in John Smith's Colonial Writing." In *Envisioning an English Empire: Jamestown and the Making of the North Atlantic World*, ed. Robert Appelbaum and John Wood Sweet, 111–34. Philadelphia: University of Pennsylvania Press, 2005.

Grisel, Etienne. "The Beginnings of International Law and General Public Law Doctrine: Francisco de Vitoria's *De Indiis prior*." In *First Images of America: The Impact of the New World on the Old*, ed. Fredi Chiappelli, Michael J. B. Allen, and Robert L. Benson, 1:305–34. 2 vols. Berkeley: University of California Press, 1976.

Gross, Ariela J. "'Of Portuguese Origin': Litigating Identity and Citizenship Among the 'Little Races' in Nineteenth-Century America." *Law and History Review* 25, 3 (2007): 467–512.

——. *What Blood Won't Tell: A History of Race on Trial in America*. Cambridge, Mass.: Harvard University Press, 2008.

Gura, Philip F. *A Glimpse of Sion's Glory: Puritan Radicalism in New England, 1620–1660*. Middletown, Conn.: Wesleyan University Press, 1984.

Gustafson, Sandra M. *Eloquence Is Power: Oratory and Performance in Early America*. Chapel Hill, N.C.: University of North Carolina Press, 2000.

Gustafson, Sandra M. and Caroline F. Sloat, eds. *Cultural Narratives: Textuality and Performance in American Culture Before 1900*. Notre Dame, Ind.: University of Notre Dame Press, 2010.

Hair, P. E. H. and Robin Law. "The English in Western Africa to 1700." In *The Oxford History of the British Empire*, ed. Wm. Roger Louis, 5 vols. Vol. 1, *The Origins of Empire: British Overseas Enterprise to the Close of the Seventeenth Century*, ed. Nicholas Canny, 241–63. Oxford: Oxford University Press, 1998.

Hale, Nathaniel C. *Virginia Venturer: A Historical Biography of William Claiborne, 1600–1677*. Richmond, Va.: Dietz Press, 1951.

Hall, Bert S. *Weapons and Warfare in Renaissance Europe: Gunpowder, Technology, and Tactics*. Baltimore: Johns Hopkins University Press, 1997.

Hall, David D. *Ways of Writing: The Practice and Politics of Text-Making in Seventeenth-Century New England*. Philadelphia: University of Pennsylvania Press, 2008.

Hampton, Timothy. *Fictions of Embassy: Literature and Diplomacy in Early Modern Europe*. Ithaca, N.Y.: Cornell University Press, 2009.

Hanke, Lewis. *All Mankind Is One: A Study of the Disputation Between Bartolomé de Las Casas and Juan Ginés de Sepúlveda in 1550 on the Intellectual and Religious Capacity of the American Indians.* DeKalb: Northern Illinois University Press, 1974.

Harrison, Samuel Alexander. *History of Talbot County Maryland.* Comp. Oswald Tilghman. Vol. 1, *1661–1861.* 2 vols. Baltimore: Williams and Wilkins, 1915.

Hart, Jonathan. *Representing the New World: The English and French Uses of the Example of Spain.* New York: Palgrave, 2001.

Hatfield, April Lee. *Atlantic Virginia: Intercolonial Relations in the Seventeenth Century.* Philadelphia: University of Pennsylvania Press, 2004.

Hermes, Katherine. "'Justice Will Be Done Us': Algonquian Demands for Reciprocity in the Courts of English Settlers." In *The Many Legalities of Early America,* ed. Christopher L. Tomlins and Bruce H. Mann, 123–49. Chapel Hill: University of North Carolina Press, 2001.

——. "The Law of Native Americans, to 1815." In *The Cambridge History of Law in America,* ed. Michael Grossberg and Christopher Tomlins, 3 vols. Vol. 1, *Early America (1580–1815),* 32–62. Cambridge: Cambridge University Press, 2008.

Hibbitts, Bernard J. "Coming to Our Senses: Communication and Legal Expression in Performance Cultures." *Emory Law Journal* 41, 4 (1992): 873–960.

Higgins, A. Pearce. "International Law and the Outer World, 1450–1648." In *The Cambridge History of the British Empire,* ed. J. Holland Rose, A. P. Newton, and E. A. Benians, 8 vols. Vol. 1, *The Old Empire from the Beginnings to 1783,* 183–206. Cambridge: Cambridge University Press, 1929.

Holbrook, Peter. "Jacobean Masques and the Jacobean Peace." In *The Politics of the Stuart Court Masque,* ed. David Bevington and Peter Holbrook, 67–87. Cambridge: Cambridge University Press, 1998.

Horn, James. *A Land as God Made It: Jamestown and the Birth of America.* New York: Basic Books, 2005.

Howard, Skiles. *The Politics of Courtly Dancing in Early Modern England.* Amherst: University of Massachusetts Press, 1998.

Hulme, Peter. *Colonial Encounters: Europe and the Native Caribbean, 1492–1797.* London: Methuen, 1986.

Hulsebosch, Daniel J. "The Ancient Constitution and the Expanding Empire:

Sir Edward Coke's British Jurisprudence." *Law and History Review* 21, 3 (2003): 439–82.

Humins, John H. "Squanto and Massasoit: A Struggle for Power." *New England Quarterly* 60, 1 (1987): 54–70.

Hussey, Roland Dennis. "America in European Diplomacy, 1597–1604." *Revista de Historia de América* 41 (1956): 1–30.

Isaac, Erich. "Kent Island, Part I: The Period of Settlement." *Maryland Historical Magazine* 52 (1957): 93–119.

Israel, Jonathan I. *The Dutch Republic: Its Rise, Greatness and Fall, 1477–1806.* Oxford: Clarendon, 1995.

Ivison, Duncan, Paul Patton, and Will Sanders, eds. *Political Theory and the Rights of Indigenous Peoples.* Cambridge: Cambridge University Press, 2000.

Iwanisziw, Susan B. "Hugh O'Neill and National Identity in Early Modern Ireland." In *Anglo-Irish Identities, 1571–1845*, ed. David A. Valone and Jill Marie Bradbury, 30–43. Lewisburg, Pa.: Bucknell University Press, 2008.

Jacobs, Jaap. *The Colony of New Netherland: A Dutch Settlement in Seventeenth-Century America.* Ithaca, N.Y.: Cornell University Press, 2009.

Jansson, Maija. "'The Hat Is No Expression of Honor.'" *Proceedings of the American Philosophical Society* 133, 1 (1989): 26–34.

Jehlen, Myra. "The Literature of Colonization." In *The Cambridge History of American Literature*, ed. Sacvan Bercovitch, 8 vols. Vol. 1, *1590–1820*, 11–168. Cambridge: Cambridge University Press, 1994.

——. "Response to Peter Hulme." *Critical Inquiry* 20, 1 (1993): 187–91.

Jennings, Francis. *The Ambiguous Iroquois Empire: The Covenant Chain Confederation of Indian Tribes with English Colonies from Its Beginnings to the Lancaster Treaty of 1744.* New York: Norton, 1984.

——. "Glory, Death, and Transfiguration: The Susquehannock Indians in the Seventeenth Century." *Proceedings of the American Philosophical Society* 112, 1 (1968): 15–53.

——. *The Invasion of America: Indians, Colonialism, and the Cant of Conquest.* New York: Norton, 1975.

——. "Susquehannock." In *Handbook of North American Indians*, ed. William C, Sturtevant, 17 vols. Vol. 15, *Northeast*, ed. Bruce G. Trigger, 362–67. Washington, D.C.: Smithsonian Institution, 1978.

Jennings, R. Y. *The Acquisition of Territory in International Law.* Manchester: Manchester University Press, 1963.

Johnson, A. W. *Ben Jonson: Poetry and Architecture*. Oxford: Clarendon, 1994.

Jones, David S. *Rationalizing Epidemics: Meanings and Uses of American Indian Mortality Since 1600*. Cambridge, Mass.: Harvard University Press, 2004.

Jones, Dorothy V. *License for Empire: Colonialism by Treaty in Early America*. Chicago: University of Chicago Press, 1982.

Juricek, John T. "English Territorial Claims in North America Under Elizabeth and the Early Stuarts." *Terrae Incognitae* 7 (1975): 7–22.

Keal, Paul. *European Conquest and the Rights of Indigenous Peoples: The Moral Backwardness of International Society*. Cambridge: Cambridge University Press, 2003.

Keary, Anne. "Retelling the History of the Settlement of Providence: Speech, Writing and Cultural Interaction on Narragansett Bay." *New England Quarterly* 69, 2 (1996): 250–86.

Keller, Arthur S., Oliver J. Lissitzyn, and Frederick J. Mann. *Creation of Rights of Sovereignty Through Symbolic Acts, 1400–1800*. New York: Columbia University Press, 1938.

Kingsbury, Benedict and Benjamin Straumann, eds. *The Roman Foundations of the Law of Nations: Alberico Gentili and the Justice of Empire*. Oxford: Oxford University Press, 2010.

Knafla, Louis A. "The Law Studies of an Elizabethan Student." *Huntington Library Quarterly* 32 (1969): 221–40.

Konkle, Maureen. *Writing Indian Nations: Native Intellectuals and the Politics of Historiography, 1827–1863*. Chapel Hill: University of North Carolina Press, 2004.

Korman, Sharon. *The Right of Conquest: The Acquisition of Territory by Force in International Law and Practice*. Oxford: Clarendon, 1996.

Krugler, John D. *English and Catholic: The Lords Baltimore in the Seventeenth Century*. Baltimore: Johns Hopkins University Press, 2004.

Krupat, Arnold and Brian Swann, eds. *Recovering the Word: Essays on Native American Literature*. Berkeley: University of California Press, 1987.

Kupperman, Karen Ordahl. *Indians and English: Facing Off in Early America*. Ithaca, N.Y.: Cornell University Press, 2000.

——. *The Jamestown Project*. Cambridge, Mass.: Belknap Press of Harvard University Press, 2007.

Kyle, Chris R. *Theater of State: Parliament and Political Culture in Early Stuart England*. Stanford, Calif.: Stanford University Press, 2012.

Lee, Wayne E. *Barbarians and Brothers: Anglo-American Warfare, 1500–1865.* Oxford: Oxford University Press, 2011.

Lemay, J. A. Leo. *Did Pocahontas Save Captain John Smith?* Athens: University of Georgia Press, 1992.

Lepore, Jill. *The Name of War: King Philip's War and the Origins of American Identity.* New York: Knopf, 1998.

Lerer, Seth. *Courtly Letters in the Age of Henry VIII: Literary Culture and the Arts of Deceit.* Cambridge: Cambridge University Press, 1997.

Lesaffer, Randall. "Peace Treaties from Lodi to Westphalia." In *Peace Treaties and International Law in European History: From the Late Middle Ages to World War I,* ed. Randall Lesaffer, 9–44. Cambridge: Cambridge University Press, 2004.

Levack, Brian P. *The Civil Lawyers in England, 1603–1641: A Political Study.* Oxford: Clarendon, 1973.

Lockey, Brian C. *Law and Empire in English Renaissance Literature.* Cambridge: Cambridge University Press, 2006.

Lorimer, Joyce. "The Failure of the English Guiana Ventures 1595–1667 and James I's Foreign Policy." *Journal of Imperial and Commonwealth History* 21, 1 (1993): 1–30.

Love, Harold. *Scribal Publication in Seventeenth-Century England.* Oxford: Clarendon, 1993.

Lyons, Scott Richard. *X-marks: Native Signatures of Assent.* Minneapolis: University of Minnesota Press, 2010.

Macalister-Smith, Peter and Joachim Schwietzke. "Literature and Documentary Sources Relating to the History of Public International Law: An Annotated Bibliographical Survey." *Journal of the History of International Law* 1 (1999): 136–212.

MacMillan, Ken. "Benign and Benevolent Conquest? The Ideology of Elizabethan Atlantic Expansion Revisited." *Early American Studies: An Interdisciplinary Journal* 9, 1 (2011): 32–72.

———. *Sovereignty and Possession in the English New World: The Legal Foundations of Empire, 1576–1640.* Cambridge: Cambridge University Press, 2006.

Malone, Patrick M. *The Skulking Way of War: Technology and Tactics Among the New England Indians.* Lanham, Md.: Madison Books, 1991.

Mancall, Peter C., ed. *The Atlantic World and Virginia, 1550–1624.* Chapel Hill: University of North Carolina Press, 2007.

Marchant, Ronald A. *The Puritans and the Church Courts in the Diocese of York, 1560–1642.* London: Longmans, 1960.

Marcus, Leah S. *The Politics of Mirth: Jonson, Herrick, Milton, Marvell, and the Defense of Old Holiday Pastimes.* Chicago: University of Chicago Press, 1986.

Mattingly, Garrett. *Renaissance Diplomacy.* London: Cape, 1955.

Mauss, Marcel. *The Gift: The Form and Reason for Exchange in Archaic Societies.* Trans. W. D. Halls. New York: Norton, 2000.

McDermott, James. *England and the Spanish Armada: The Necessary Quarrel.* New Haven, Conn.: Yale University Press, 2005.

McGrath, John T. *The French in Early Florida: In the Eye of the Hurricane.* Gainesville: University Press of Florida, 2000.

McGurk, John. "Terrain and Conquest, 1600–1603." In *Conquest and Resistance: War in Seventeenth Century Ireland,* ed. Pádraig Lenihan, 87–114. Leiden: Brill, 2001.

McKenzie, D. F. *Oral Culture, Literacy and Print in Early New Zealand: The Treaty of Waitangi.* Wellington: Victoria University Press, 1985.

Menard, Russell R. "Population, Economy, and Society in Seventeenth-Century Maryland." *Maryland Historical Magazine* 79 (1984): 71–92.

Merrell, James H. "'I desire all that I have said . . . may be taken down aright': Revisiting Teedyuscung's 1756 Treaty Council Speeches." *William and Mary Quarterly* 3rd ser. 63, 4 (2006): 777–826.

———. *Into the American Woods: Negotiatiors on the Pennsylvania Frontier.* New York: Norton, 1999.

Merwick, Donna. *The Shame and the Sorrow: Dutch-Amerindian Encounters in New Netherland.* Philadelphia: University of Pennsylvania Press, 2006.

Meuwese, Mark. *Brothers in Arms, Partners in Trade: Dutch Indigenous Alliances in the Atlantic World, 1595–1674.* Leiden: Brill, 2011.

Miller, Mark Edwin. *Forgotten Tribes: Unrecognized Indians and the Federal Acknowledgement Process.* Lincoln: University of Nebraska Press, 2004.

Morgan, Edmund. *American Slavery, American Freedom: The Ordeal of Colonial Virginia.* New York: Norton, 1975.

Mossiker, Frances. *Pocahontas: The Life and the Legend.* New York: Knopf, 1976.

Muir, Edward. *Ritual in Early Modern Europe.* Cambridge: Cambridge University Press, 1997.

Muldoon, James. *The Americas in the Spanish World Order: The Justification for Conquest in the Seventeenth Century.* Philadelphia: University of Pennsylvania Press, 1994.

———. "Discovery, Grant, Charter, Conquest, or Purchase: John Adams on the Legal Basis for English Possession of North America." In *The Many Legalities of Early America*, ed. Christopher L. Tomlins and Bruce H. Mann, 25–46. Chapel Hill: University of North Carolina Press, 2001.

Murray, David. *Indian Giving: Economies of Power in Indian-White Exchanges.* Amherst: University of Massachusetts Press, 2000.

Newell, Margaret Ellen. "Indian Slavery in Colonial New England." In *Indian Slavery in Colonial America*, ed. Alan Gallay, 33–66. Lincoln: University of Nebraska Press, 2009.

Newman, Andrew. *On Records: Delaware Indians, Colonists, and the Media of History and Memory.* Lincoln: University of Nebraska Press, 2012.

Nicholls, Andrew D. *A Fleeting Empire: Early Stuart Britain and the Merchant Adventurers to Canada.* Montreal: McGill-Queen's University Press, 2010.

Nijman, Janne Elisabeth. *The Concept of International Legal Personality: An Inquiry into the History and Theory of International Law.* The Hague: TMC Asser Press, 2004.

Nussbaum, Arthur. *A Concise History of the Law of Nations.* New York: Macmillan, 1947.

Nussbaum, Martha. *Liberty of Conscience: In Defense of America's Tradition of Religious Equality.* New York: Basic Books, 2008.

Oberg, Michael Leroy. *Dominion and Civility: English Imperialism and Native America, 1585–1685.* Ithaca, N.Y.: Cornell University Press, 1999.

O'Brien, Jean M. *Dispossession by Degrees: Indian Land and Identity in Natick, Massachusetts, 1650–1790.* Lincoln: University of Nebraska Press, 2003.

———. *Firsting and Lasting: Writing Indians Out of Existence in New England.* Minneapolis: University of Minnesota Press, 2010.

Olson, Alison G. "The Virginia Merchants of London: A Study in Eighteenth-Century Interest-Group Politics." *William and Mary Quarterly* 3rd ser. 40, 3 (1983): 363–88.

Orgel, Stephen. *The Jonsonian Masque.* Cambridge, Mass.: Harvard University Press, 1965.

Orrell, John. *The Theaters of Inigo Jones and John Webb.* Cambridge: Cambridge University Press, 1985.

Otto, Paul. *The Dutch-Munsee Encounter in America: The Struggle for Sovereignty in the Hudson Valley.* New York: Berghahn, 2006.

Pagden, Anthony. "Dispossessing the Barbarian: The Language of Spanish

Thomism and the Debate over the Property Rights of the American Indians." In *The Languages of Political Theory in Early Modern Europe*, ed. Anthony Pagden, 79–98. Cambridge: Cambridge University Press, 1987.

——. *The Fall of Natural Man: The American Indian and the Origins of Comparative Ethnology*. Cambridge: Cambridge University Press, 1982.

——. *Lords of All the World: Ideologies of Empire in Spain, Britain and France c. 1500–c. 1800*. New Haven, Conn.: Yale University Press, 1995.

Peters, Julie Stone. "Legal Performance Good and Bad." *Law, Culture and the Humanities* 4, 2 (2008): 179–200.

Peterson, Harold L. *Arms and Armor in Colonial America, 1526–1783*. Harrisburg, Pa.: Stackpole, 1956.

Podruchny, Carolyn. *Making the Voyageur World: Travelers and Traders in the North American Fur Trade*. Lincoln: University of Nebraska Press, 2006.

Pole, J. R. *Contract and Consent: Representation and the Jury in Anglo-American Legal History*. Charlottesville: University of Virginia Press, 2010.

Potter, Stephen R. *Commoners, Tribute, and Chiefs: The Development of Algonquian Culture in the Potomac Valley*. Charlottesville: University of Virginia Press, 1993.

Prak, Maarten. *The Dutch Republic in the Seventeenth Century: The Golden Age*. Trans. Diane Webb. Cambridge: Cambridge University Press, 2005.

Prucha, Francis Paul. *American Indian Treaties: The History of a Political Anomaly*. Berkeley: University of California Press, 1994.

Pulsipher, Jenny Hale. *Subjects unto the Same King: Indians, English, and the Contest for Authority in Colonial New England*. Philadelphia: University of Pennsylvania Press, 2005.

Queller, Donald E. "The Development of Ambassadorial Relazioni." In *Renaissance Venice*, ed. J. R. Hale, 174–96. London: Faber and Faber, 1973.

Quinn, D. B. "Some Spanish Reactions to Elizabethan Colonial Enterprises." *Transactions of the Royal Historical Society* 5th ser. 1 (1951): 1–23.

Rabasa, José. *Writing Violence on the Northern Frontier: The Historiography of Sixteenth-Century New Mexico and Florida and the Legacy of Conquest*. Durham, N.C.: Duke University Press, 2000.

Rabb, Theodore K. *Enterprise and Empire: Merchant and Gentry Investment in the Expansion of England, 1575–1630*. Cambridge, Mass.: Harvard University Press, 1967.

Rasmussen, Birgit Brander. *Queequeg's Coffin: Indigenous Literacies and Early American Literature*. Durham, N.C.: Duke University Press, 2012.

Raymond, Joad. *Pamphlets and Pamphleteering in Early Modern Britain*. Cambridge: Cambridge University Press, 2003.

Redworth, Glyn. *The Prince and the Infanta: The Cultural Politics of the Spanish Match*. New Haven, Conn.: Yale University Press, 2003.

Rice, James D. "Escape from Tsenacommacah: Chesapeake Algonquians and the Powhatan Menace." In *The Atlantic World and Virginia, 1550–1624*, ed. Peter C. Mancall, 97–142. Chapel Hill: University of North Carolina Press, 2007.

——. *Nature and History in the Potomac Country: From Hunter-Gatherers to the Age of Jefferson*. Baltimore: Johns Hopkins University Press, 2009.

Richter, Daniel K. *Before the Revolution: America's Ancient Pasts*. Cambridge, Mass.: Belknap Press of Harvard University Press, 2011.

——. *Facing East from Indian Country: A Native History of Early America*. Cambridge, Mass.: Harvard University Press, 2001.

——. "Tsenacommacah and the Atlantic World." In *The Atlantic World and Virginia, 1550–1624*, ed. Peter C. Mancall, 29–65. Chapel Hill: University of North Carolina Press, 2007.

Roach, Joseph. *Cities of the Dead: Circum-Atlantic Performance*. New York: Columbia University Press, 1996.

Robertson, Karen. "Pocahontas at the Masque." *Signs: Journal of Women in Culture and Society* 21, 3 (1996): 551–83.

Robinson, Paul A. "Lost Opportunities: Miantonomi and the English in Seventeenth-Century Narragansett Country." In *Northeastern Indian Lives, 1632–1816*, ed. Robert S. Grumet, 13–28. Amherst: University of Massachusetts Press, 1996.

——. "A Narragansett History from 1000 B.P. to the Present." In *Enduring Traditions: The Native Peoples of New England*, ed. Laurie Weinstein, 79–89. Westport, Conn.: Bergin and Garvey, 1994.

Roelofsen, C. G. "Grotius and the International Politics of the Seventeenth Century." In *Hugo Grotius and International Relations*, ed. Hedley Bull, Benedict Kingsbury, and Adam Roberts, 104–12. Oxford: Clarendon, 1990.

Round, Phillip H. *By Nature and By Custom Cursed: Transatlantic Civil Discourse and New England Cultural Production, 1620–1660*. Hanover, N.H.: University Press of New England, 1999.

Rountree, Helen C. *Pocahontas, Powhatan, Opechancanough: Three Indian Lives Changed by Jamestown*. Charlottesville: University of Virginia Press, 2005.

——, ed. *Powhatan Foreign Relations, 1500–1722.* Charlottesville: University of Virginia Press, 1993.

—— *The Powhatan Indians of Virginia: Their Traditional Culture.* Norman: University of Oklahoma Press, 1989.

Rountree, Helen C., Wayne E. Clark, and Kent Mountford. *John Smith's Chesapeake Voyages, 1607–1609.* Charlottesville: University of Virginia Press, 2007.

Rubertone, Patricia E. *Grave Undertakings: An Archeology of Roger Williams and the Narragansett Indians.* Washington, D.C.: Smithsonian Institution Press, 2001.

Rushforth, Brett. *Bonds of Alliance: Indigenous and Atlantic Slaveries in New France.* Chapel Hill: University of North Carolina Press, 2012.

Russell, Frederick H. *The Just War in the Middle Ages.* Cambridge: Cambridge University Press, 1977.

Russo, Jean B. and J. Elliott Russo. *Planting an Empire: The Early Chesapeake in British North America.* Baltimore: Johns Hopkins University Press, 2012.

Sacks, David Harris. "The True Temper of Empire: Dominion, Friendship and Exchange in the English Atlantic, c. 1575–1625." *Renaissance Studies* 26, 4 (2012): 531–58.

Salisbury, Neal. *Manitou and Providence: Indians, Europeans, and the Making of New England.* New York: Oxford University Press, 1982.

——. "Squanto: Last of the Patuxets." In *Struggle and Survival in Colonial America,* ed. David G. Sweet and Gary B. Nash, 228–46. Berkeley: University of California Press, 1981.

Savelle, Max. *The Origins of American Diplomacy: The International History of Angloamerica, 1492–1763.* New York: Macmillan, 1967.

Scanlan, Thomas. *Colonial Writing and the New World, 1583–1671: Allegories of Desire.* Cambridge: Cambridge University Press, 1999.

Schechner, Richard. *Between Theater and Anthropology.* Philadelphia: University of Pennsylvania Press, 1985.

Schmidt, Benjamin. *Innocence Abroad: The Dutch Imagination and the New World, 1570–1670.* Cambridge: Cambridge University Press, 2001.

Schoeck, R. J. "Lawyers and Rhetoric in Sixteenth-Century England." In *Renaissance Eloquence: Studies in the Theory and Practice of Renaissance Rhetoric,* ed. James J. Murphy, 274–91. Berkeley: University of California Press, 1983.

Scott, James Brown. *The Spanish Origin of International Law: Francisco de Vitoria and His Law of Nations.* Oxford: Clarendon, 1934.

Seed, Patricia. *Ceremonies of Possession in Europe's Conquest of the New World, 1492–1640.* Cambridge: Cambridge University Press, 1995.

Sehr, Timothy J. "Ninigret's Tactics of Accommodation: Indian Diplomacy in New England, 1637–1675." *Rhode Island History* 36, 2 (1977): 43–53.

Shapiro, Barbara J. *A Culture of Fact: England, 1550–1720.* Ithaca, N.Y.: Cornell University Press, 2000.

Sheehan, Bernard. *Savagism and Civility: Indians and Englishmen in Colonial Virginia.* Cambridge: Cambridge University Press, 1980.

Silva, Cristobal. *Miraculous Plagues: An Epidemiology of Early New England Narrative.* Oxford: Oxford University Press, 2011.

Simmons, William S. "Narragansett." In *Handbook of North American Indians,* ed. William C, Sturtevant, 17 vols. Vol. 15, *Northeast,* ed. Bruce G. Trigger, 190–97. Washington, D.C.: Smithsonian Institution, 1978.

Simpson, Lesley Byrd. *The Encomienda in New Spain: The Beginning of Spanish Mexico.* Berkeley: University of California Press, 1950.

Skinner, Claiborne A. *The Upper Country: French Enterprise in the Colonial Great Lakes.* Baltimore: Johns Hopkins University Press, 2008.

Slattery, Brian. "Paper Empires: The Legal Dimensions of French and English Ventures in North America." In *Despotic Dominion: Property Rights in British Settler Societies,* ed. John McLaren, A. R. Buck, and Nancy E. Wright, 50–78. Vancouver: University of British Columbia Press, 2005.

Smuts, R. Malcolm. *Court Culture and the Origins of a Royalist Tradition in Early Stuart England.* Philadelphia: University of Pennsylvania Press, 1987.

Sommerville, Johann P. "Selden, Grotius, and the Seventeenth-Century Intellectual Revolution in Moral and Political Theory." In *Rhetoric and Law in Early Modern Europe,* ed. Victoria Kahn and Lorna Hutson, 318–44. New Haven, Conn.: Yale University Press, 2001.

Stearns, Raymond P. "The Weld-Peter Mission to England." *Publications of the Colonial Society of Massachusetts* 32 (1934): 188–246.

Steele, Ian K. *Warpaths: Invasions of North America.* New York: Oxford University Press, 1994.

Stein, Peter. *The Character and Influence of the Roman Civil Law: Historical Essays.* London: Hambledon, 1988.

——. *Roman Law in European History.* Cambridge: Cambridge University Press, 1999.

Stevens, Laura M. *The Poor Indians: British Missionaries, Native Americans, and Colonial Sensibility.* Philadelphia: University of Pennsylvania Press, 2004.

Stokes, I. N. Phelps. *The Iconography of Manhattan Island, 1498–1909.* Vol. 4. 4 vols. New York: Robert H. Dodd, 1928.

Taylor, Diana. *The Archive and the Repertoire: Performing Cultural Memory in the Americas.* Durham, N.C.: Duke University Press, 2003.

Theutenberg, Bo Johnson. "Mare Clausum et Mare Liberum." *Arctic* 37, 4 (1984): 481–92.

Thornton, J. Mills, III. "The Thrusting Out of Governor Harvey: A Seventeenth-Century Rebellion." *Virginia Magazine of History and Biography* 76, 1 (1968): 11–26.

Tierney, Brian. *The Idea of Natural Rights: Studies on Natural Rights, Natural Law, and Church Law, 1150–1625.* Atlanta: Scholars Press, 1997.

Tilton, Robert S. *Pocahontas: The Evolution of an American Narrative.* Cambridge: Cambridge University Press, 1994.

Tomlins, Christopher L. "The Legal Cartography of Colonization, the Legal Polyphony of Settlement: English Intrusions on the American Mainland in the Seventeenth Century." *Law and Social Inquiry* 26, 2 (2001): 315–72.

Tomlins, Christopher L. and Bruce H. Mann, eds. *The Many Legalities of Early America.* Chapel Hill: University of North Carolina Press, 2001.

Tuck, Richard. *Natural Rights Theories: Their Origin and Development.* Cambridge: Cambridge University Press, 1979.

——. *The Rights of War and Peace: Political Thought and the International Order from Grotius to Kant.* Oxford: Oxford University Press, 1999.

Vallance, Ted. "The Captivity of James II: Gestures of Loyalty and Disloyalty in Seventeenth-Century England." *Journal of British Studies* 48, 4 (2009): 848–58.

Van Zandt, Cynthia J. *Brothers Among Nations: The Pursuit of Intercultural Alliances in Early America, 1580–1660.* Oxford: Oxford University Press, 2008.

Vaughan, Alden T. "Preface." In *Early American Indian Documents: Treaties and Laws, 1607–1789,* ed. Alden T. Vaughan, 20 vols. Vol. 1, *Virginia Treaties, 1607–1722,* ed. W. S. Robinson, xiii–xvi. Frederick, Md.: University Publications of America, 1979.

——. *Transatlantic Encounters: American Indians in Britain, 1500–1776.* Cambridge: Cambridge University Press, 2006.

Vieira, Monica Brito. "*Mare Liberum* vs. *Mare Clausum*: Grotius, Freitas, and Selden's Debate on Dominion over the Seas." *Journal of the History of Ideas* 64, 3 (2003): 361–77.

Voigt, Lisa. *Writing Captivity in the Early Modern Atlantic: Circulations of*

Knowledge and Authority in the Iberian and English Imperial Worlds. Chapel Hill: University of North Carolina Press, 2009.

Walzer, Michael. *Arguing About War.* New Haven, Conn.: Yale University Press, 2004.

Warnicke, Retha M. *The Marrying of Anne of Cleves: Royal Protocol in Early Modern England.* Cambridge: Cambridge University Press, 2000.

Weber, David J. *The Spanish Frontier in North America.* New Haven, Conn.: Yale University Press, 1992.

Weckmann-Muñoz, Luis. "The Alexandrine Bulls of 1493: Pseudo-Asiatic Documents." In *First Images of America: The Impact of the New World on the Old,* ed. Fredi Chiappelli, Michael J. B. Allen, and Robert L. Benson, 1:201–9. 2 vols. Berkeley: University of California Press, 1976.

Wernham, R. B. *The Making of Elizabethan Foreign Policy, 1558–1603.* Berkeley: University of California Press, 1980.

White, Ed. "Invisible Tagkanysough." *PMLA* 120, 3 (2005): 751–67.

White, R. S. *Natural Law in English Renaissance Literature.* Cambridge: Cambridge University Press, 1996.

Wilks, Timothy. "The Pike Charged: Henry as Militant Prince." In *Prince Henry Revived: Image and Exemplarity in Early Modern England,* ed. Timothy Wilks, 180–211. Southampton: Southampton Solent University, 2007.

Williams, Robert A., Jr. *The American Indian in Western Legal Thought: The Discourses of Conquest.* Oxford: Oxford University Press, 1990.

Williamson, Margaret Holmes. *Powhatan Lords of Life and Death: Command and Consent in Seventeenth-Century Virginia.* Lincoln: University of Nebraska Press, 2003.

Willison, George F. *Saints and Strangers.* . . . New York: Reynal and Hitchcock, 1945.

Wilson, Eric. *The Savage Republic: De Indis of Hugo Grotius, Republicanism, and Dutch Hegemony Within the Early Modern World-System (c. 1600–1619).* Leiden; Nijhoff, 2008.

Winship, Michael P. *Godly Republicanism: Puritans, Pilgrims, and a City on a Hill.* Cambridge, Mass.: Harvard University Press, 2012.

——. *Making Heretics: Militant Protestantism and Free Grace in Massachusetts, 1636–1641.* Princeton, N.J.: Princeton University Press, 2002.

Witgen, Michael. *An Infinity of Nations: How the Native New World Shaped Early North America.* Philadelphia: University of Pennsylvania Press, 2012.

Woodward, Grace Steele. *Pocahontas*. Norman: University of Oklahoma Press, 1969.

Wright, Louis B. *Religion and Empire: The Alliance Between Piety and Commerce in English Expansion, 1558–1625*. Chapel Hill: University of North Carolina Press, 1943.

Wright, Stephen. *The Early English Baptists, 1603–1649*. Woodbridge: Boydell, 2006.

Wyss, Hilary E. *Writing Indians: Literacy, Christianity, and Native Community in Early America*. Amherst: University of Massachusetts Press, 2000.

Zee, Henri van der, and Barbara van der Zee. *A Sweet and Alien Land: The Story of Dutch New York*. New York: Viking, 1978.

Ziegler, Karl-Heinz. "The Influence of Medieval Roman Law on Peace Treaties." In *Peace Treaties and International Law in European History: From the Late Middle Ages to World War One*, ed. Randall Lesaffer, 147–61. Cambridge: Cambridge University Press, 2004.

Zulueta, Francis de and Peter Stein. *The Teaching of Roman Law in England Around 1200*. London: Selden Society, 1990.

Index

Acknowledgments
—m—

Acknowledging my debts is the most enjoyable part of finishing this book. They start with my mentors. Wai Chee Dimock was there from the beginning, and she has been a steadfast supporter since. Elizabeth Dillon introduced me to the field of Early American literary studies. My work has benefited greatly from her many readings over the years, and she is my constant role model. Among colleagues, Matt Cohen deserves special mention. I cannot thank him enough for his unselfish help on matters large and small.

I am also grateful to the many people who read parts of this book along the way. Michael Warner, Hsuan Hsu, and Elliott Visconsi offered many excellent criticisms. Eric Wertheimer, Jennifer Baker, Ezra Greenspan, Ralph Bauer, Dana Nelson, and Carla Mulford read parts of the project and made many insightful suggestions. Donald Pease and Ivy Schweitzer commented on my presentations at the Futures of American Studies Institute. Finally, the two anonymous referees for the University of Pennsylvania Press read the entire manuscript and greatly influenced its final shape.

Colleagues from Early American literature and history have been wonderful sources of friendship and insight. Dennis Moore, Cristobal Silva, Sabine Klein, Joanne van der Woude, Sandra Gustafson, Kristina Bross, Kelly Wisecup, Drew Newman, Jordan Stein, Birgit Rasmussen, Karen Kupperman, Wayne E. Lee, Peter Charles Hoffer, and Hilary Wyss all commented on my work, facilitated its presentation at conferences, or supported it in other ways. Ken MacMillan, Ronald Lesaffer, James Horn, Glenn W. LaFantasie, and Craig Yirush answered questions about literature, law, and diplomacy. Ruben Roman, Erica Sayers, Nigel Alderman, Michael Denning, Lloyd Pratt, and Caleb Smith were supporters and friends. Thanks also go to Ariel Watson, Jinan Joudeh,

Anna Chen, Anthony Brooks, Ben Looker, Colin Gillis, Jordan Zweck, James Horowitz, KC Harrison, Gabriele Hayden, Maria Fackler, Sebastian LeCourt, Andrew Goldstone, Anne DeWitt, John Muse, Patrick Redding, Kathryn Reklis, Matthew Mutter, Sarah Mahurin, and Liz Twitchell. They made it possible for me to describe graduate school as the time of my life. Ian Baucom, Maureen Quilligan, Edna Andrews, and Buford Jones set me on the path to academia as an undergraduate.

I must thank John Michael, Genevieve Guenther, and Morris Eaves at the University of Rochester for making my time there formative and memorable. I have been lucky to have Joyce Wexler as chair at Loyola University Chicago. Also at Loyola, Jack Kerkering, Badia Ahad, Jack Cragwall, Peter Shillingsburg, Allen Frantzen, Edward Wheatley, Pamela Caughie, Steve Jones, Chris Kendrick, Tom Kaminski, Jim Knapp, Virginia Strain, Jim Biester, Suzanne Bost, David Chinitz, Mike Clarke, Verna Foster, Joe Janangelo, Paul Jay, and Harveen Mann have been supporters and friends. Frank Fennell, Samuel Attoh, and Reinhard Andress generously supported my work with timely funding. Bill Sellers at the Office of Research Services and Michael Schuck at the Center for Catholic Intellectual Heritage at Loyola administered grants to support my research, as did administrators at the Department of English at Yale University and the Department of English at the University of Rochester. My research assistant, David Macey, was superb.

I also want to thank the many librarians who made my work possible. Deserving particular mention are Niamh McGuigan at Loyola University Chicago, Maria Day at the Maryland State Archives, and Paul Campbell at the Providence City Archives. Their speedy responses to questions and requests for materials were crucial. I also owe debts of gratitude to the librarians and archivists at the Beinecke Rare Book and Manuscript Library, the Newberry Library, the Huntington Library, Lambeth Palace Library, Houghton Library, and the Rhode Island Historical Society.

At the University of Pennsylvania Press, I would like to thank Jerry Singerman, Caroline Winschel, Caroline Hayes, Alison Anderson, and the members of the marketing department.

Finally, I want to thank my family: my mother Jan Glover, for making me do my homework, my father, Carl Glover, for taking me to the library, and my brother Casey Glover, for being my first friend. Last, I must thank Ashlee Humphreys, an endless source of love, support, and friendship.